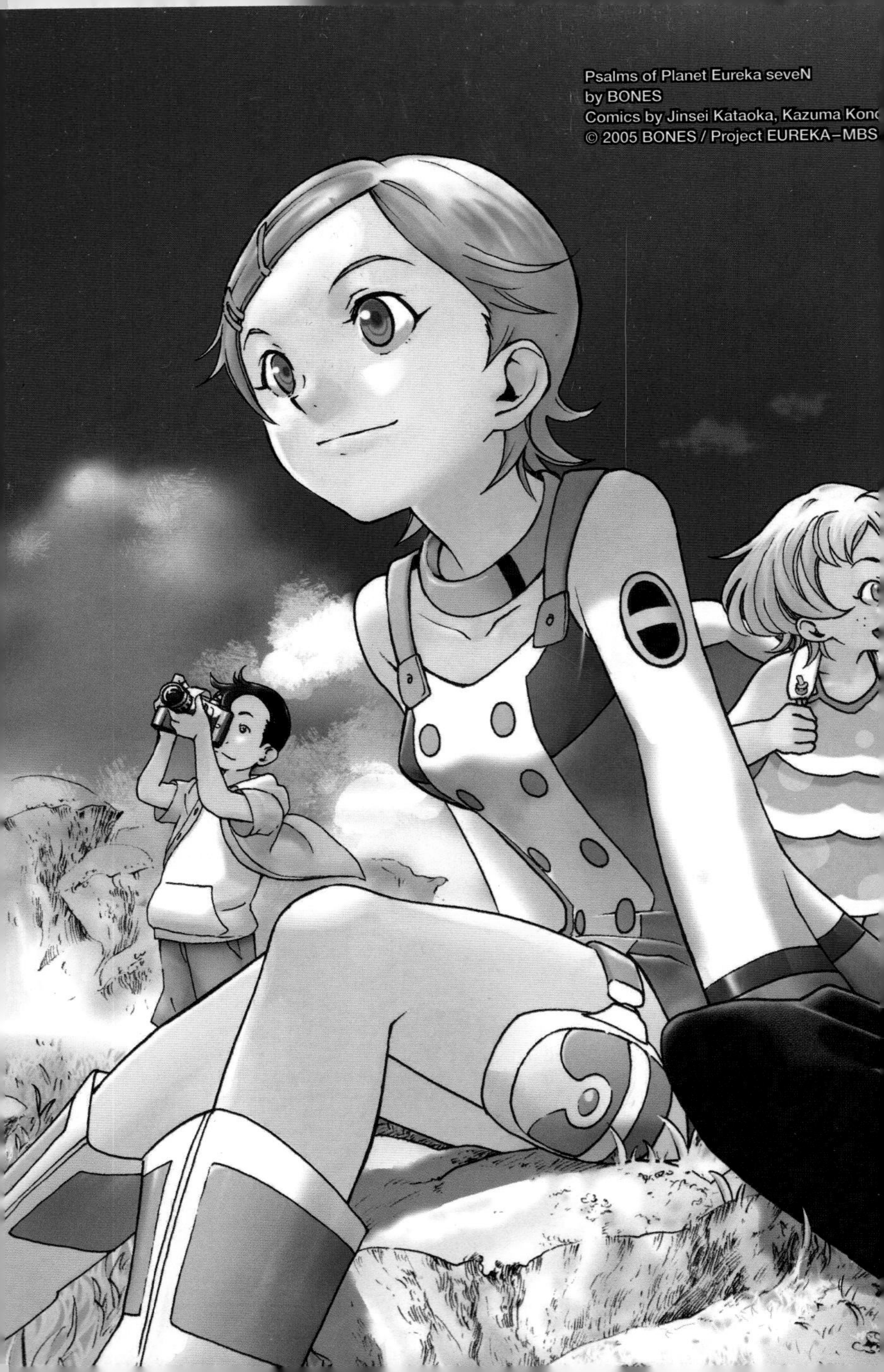

Psalms of Planets Eureka seveN
Volume 2

CONTENTS

ORIGINAL STORY
Bones
STORY AND ART
Jinsei Kataoka & Kazuma Kondou
ORIGINAL BOOK DESIGN
Tsuyoshi Kusano

ENGLISH PRODUCTION CREDITS

TRANSLATION	Toshifumi Yoshida
ADAPTOR	T. Ledoux
LETTERING	Fawn Lau
COVER DESIGN	Kit Loose
EDITOR	Robert Place Napton
COORDINATOR	Rika Davis
PUBLISHER	Ken Iyadomi

Published in the United States
by Bandai Entertainment, Inc.

© Jinsei KATAOKA 2005
© Kazuma KONDOU 2005
© 2005-2006 BONES/Project EUREKA-MBS
Originally published in Japan in 2005 by KADOKAWA SHOTEN PUBLISHING CO., LTD., Tokyo.
English translation rights arranged with KADOKAWA SHOTEN PUBLISHING CO., LTD., Tokyo.

ISBN-13: 978-1-59409-691-4
ISBN-10: 1-59409-691-0

Printed in Canada
First Bandai printing: July 2006

10 9 8 7 6 5 4 3 2 1

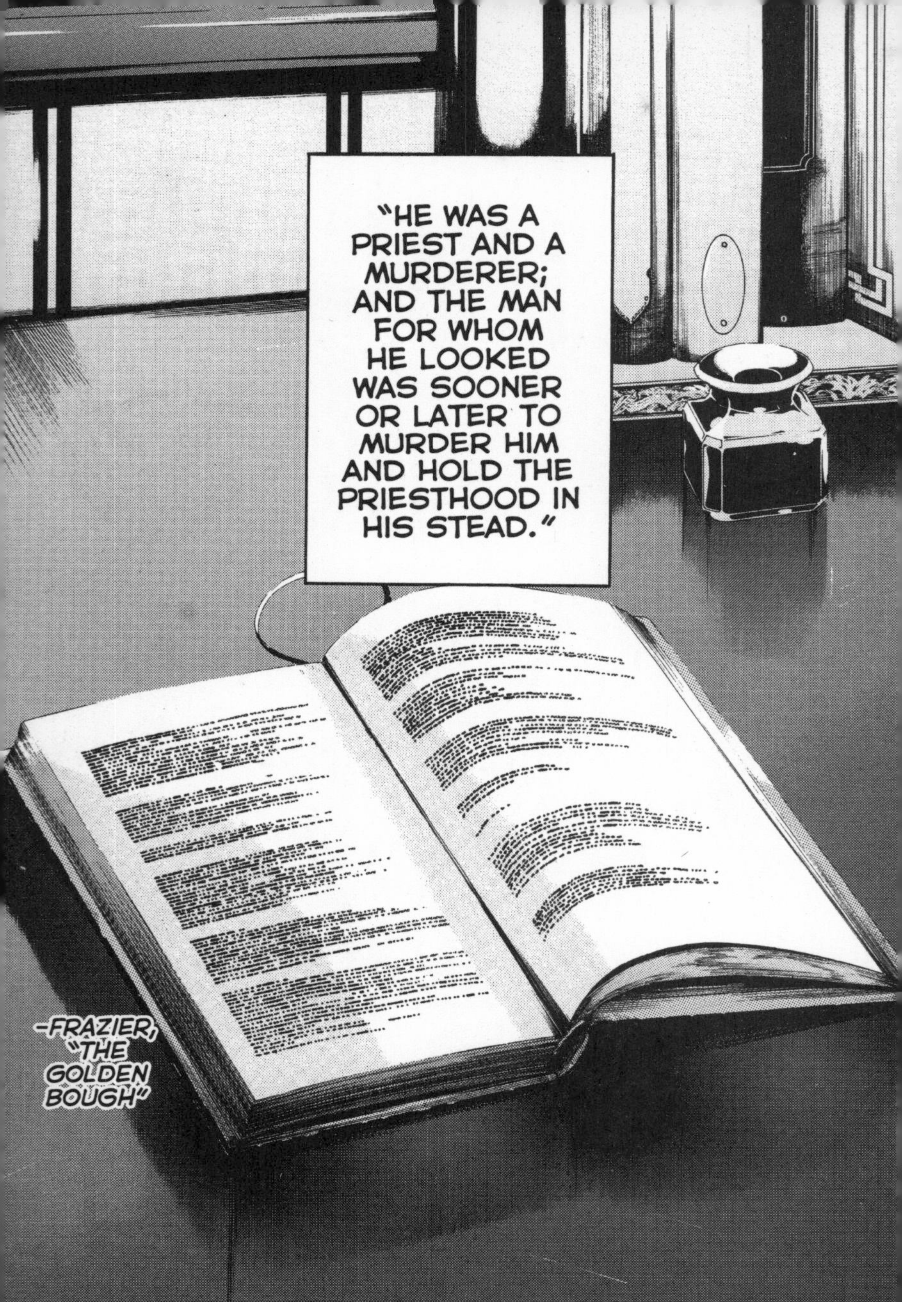
"HE WAS A PRIEST AND A MURDERER; AND THE MAN FOR WHOM HE LOOKED WAS SOONER OR LATER TO MURDER HIM AND HOLD THE PRIESTHOOD IN HIS STEAD."
-FRAZIER, "THE GOLDEN BOUGH"

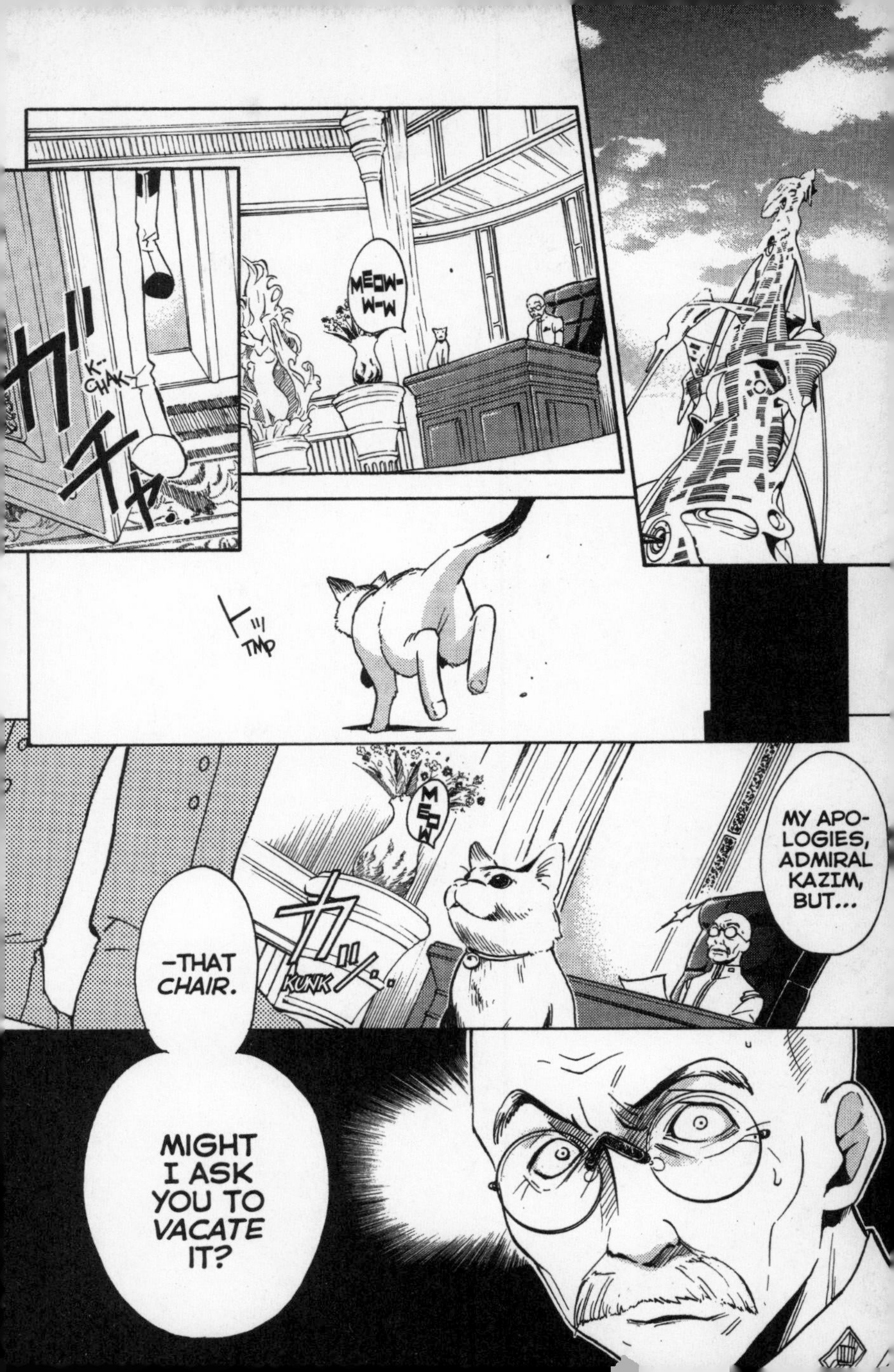
MEOW-W-W
ガチャ
K-CHAK
トッ
TMP
MY APOLOGIES, ADMIRAL KAZIM, BUT...
MEOW
カッ
KUNK
–THAT CHAIR.
MIGHT I ASK YOU TO VACATE IT?

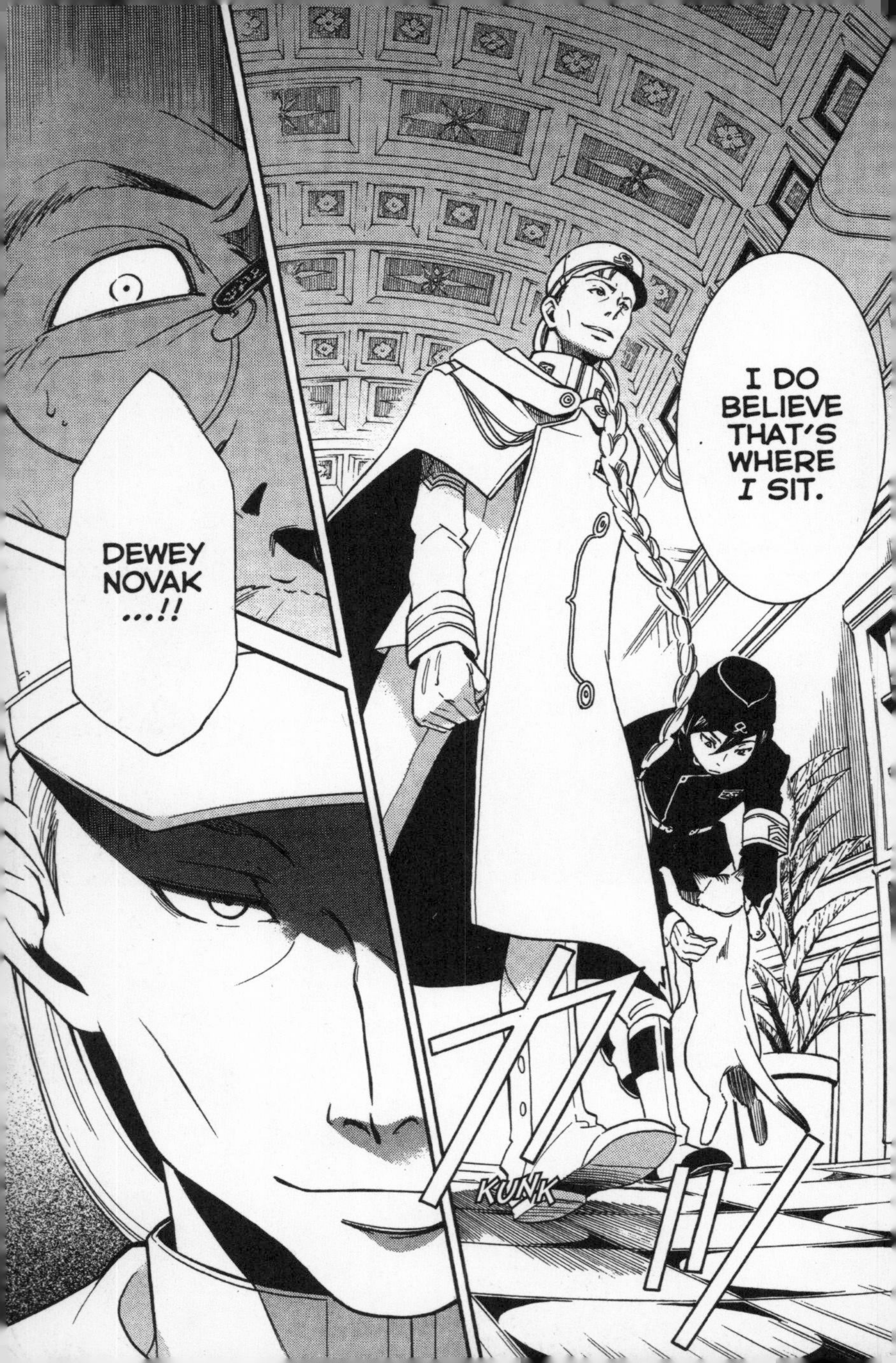
I DO BELIEVE THAT'S WHERE I SIT.
KUNK
DEWEY NOVAK ...!!

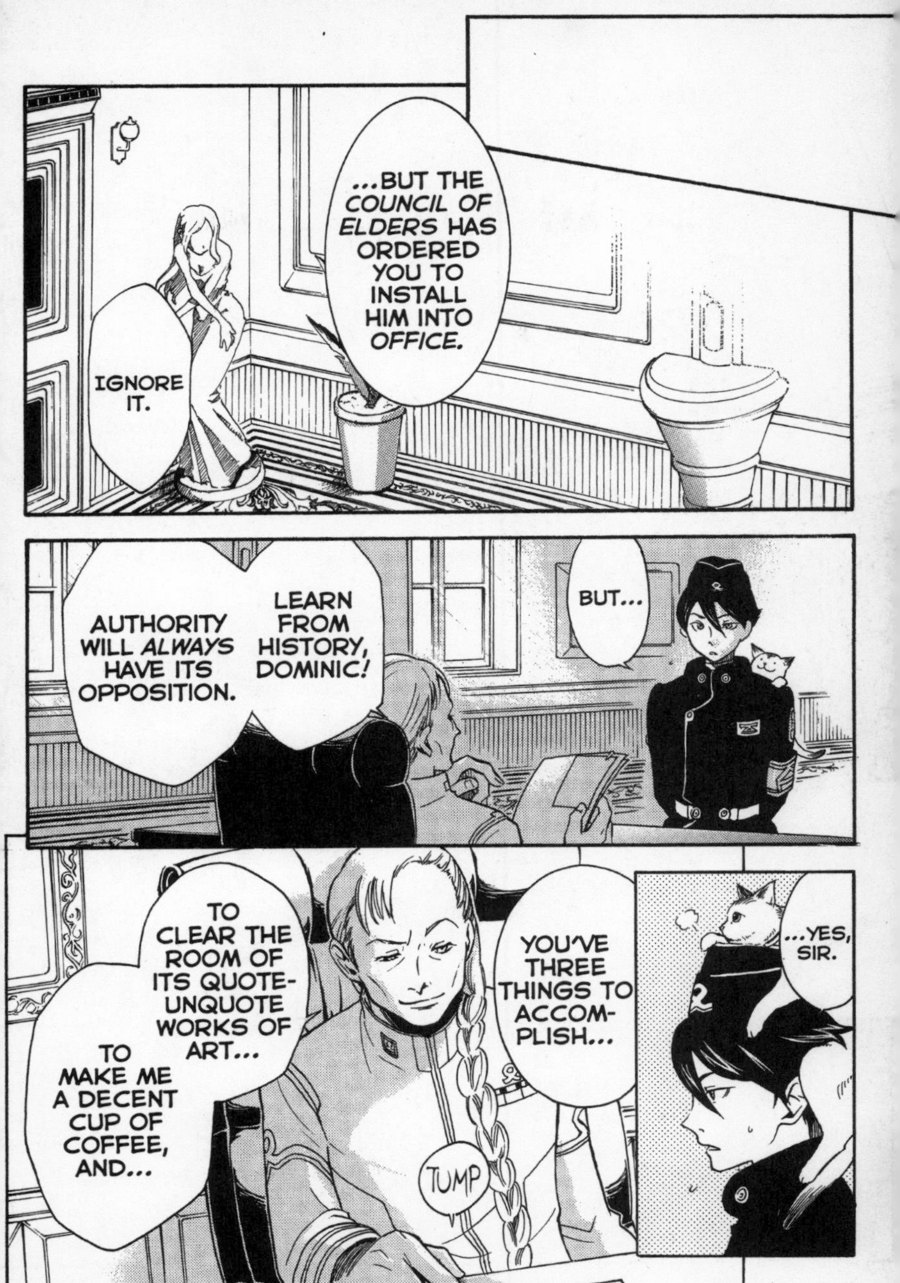
...BUT THE COUNCIL OF ELDERS HAS ORDERED YOU TO INSTALL HIM INTO OFFICE.
IGNORE IT.
BUT...
LEARN FROM HISTORY, DOMINIC!
AUTHORITY WILL ALWAYS HAVE ITS OPPOSITION.
...YES, SIR.
YOU'VE THREE THINGS TO ACCOMPLISH...
TO CLEAR THE ROOM OF ITS QUOTE-UNQUOTE WORKS OF ART...
TO MAKE ME A DECENT CUP OF COFFEE, AND...
TUMP

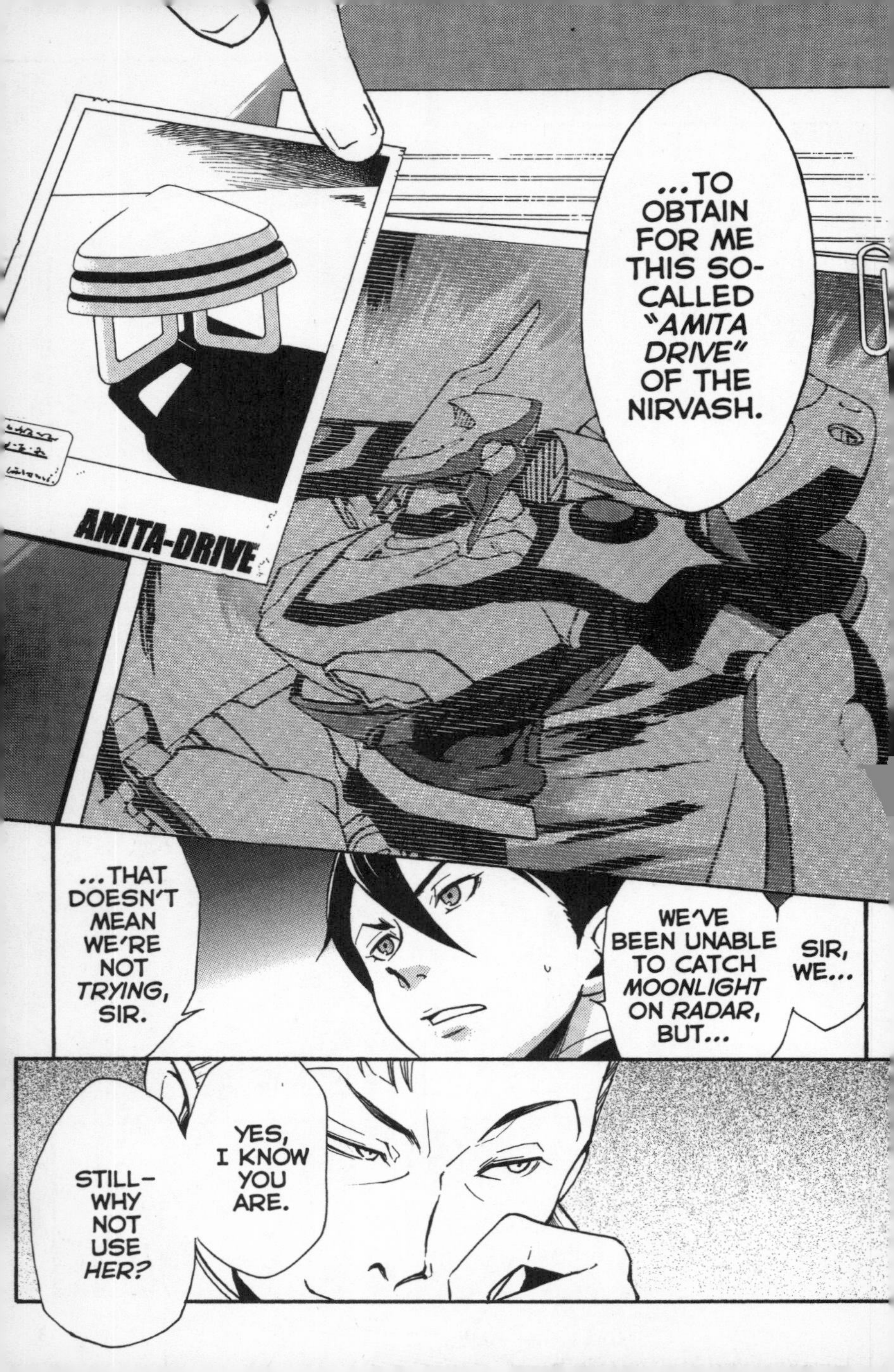
...TO OBTAIN FOR ME THIS SO-CALLED "AMITA DRIVE" OF THE NIRVASH.
AMITA-DRIVE
SIR, WE...
WE'VE BEEN UNABLE TO CATCH MOONLIGHT ON RADAR, BUT...
...THAT DOESN'T MEAN WE'RE NOT TRYING, SIR.
YES, I KNOW YOU ARE.
STILL—WHY NOT USE HER?

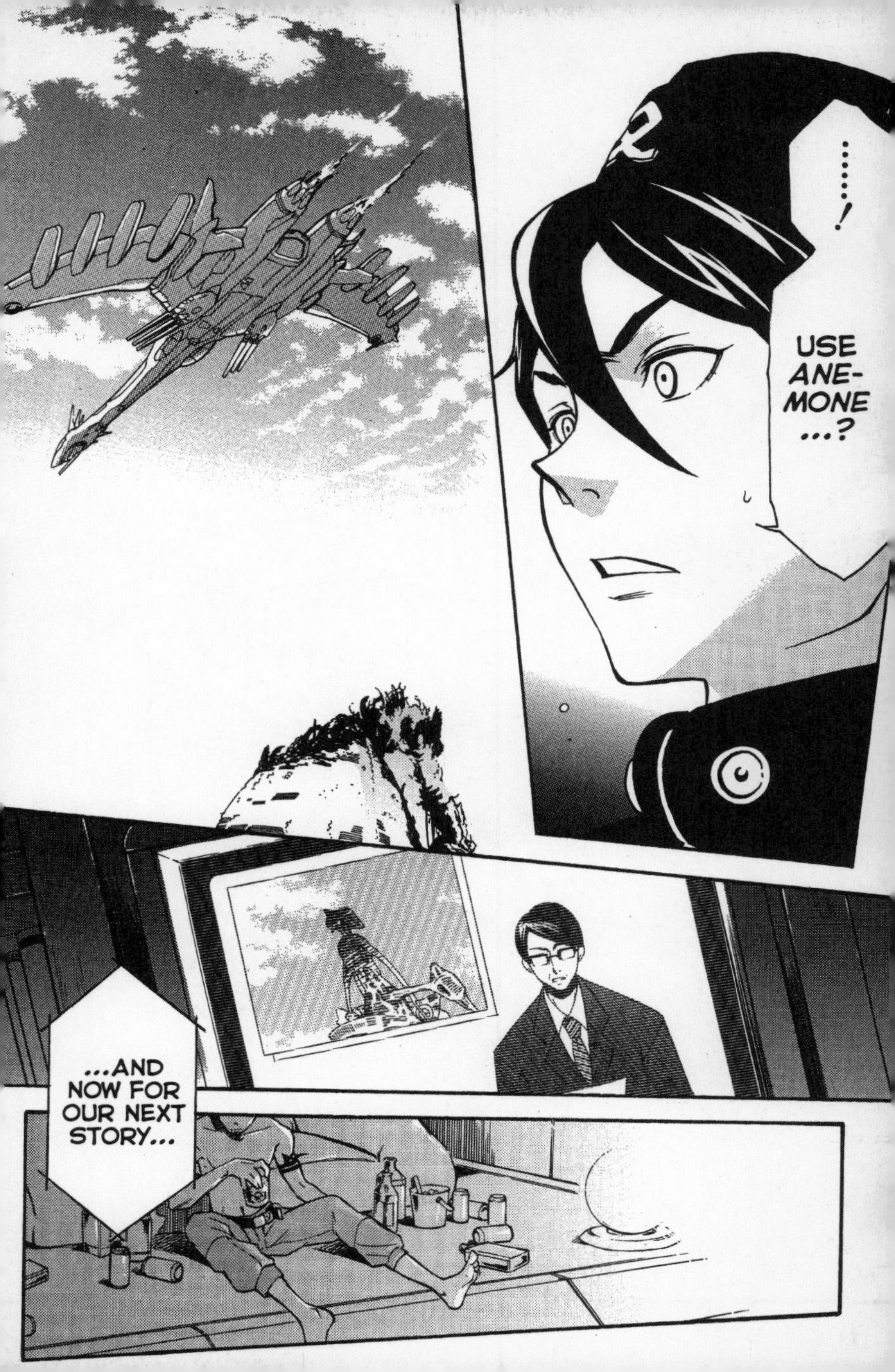
......!
USE ANE-MONE ...?
...AND NOW FOR OUR NEXT STORY...

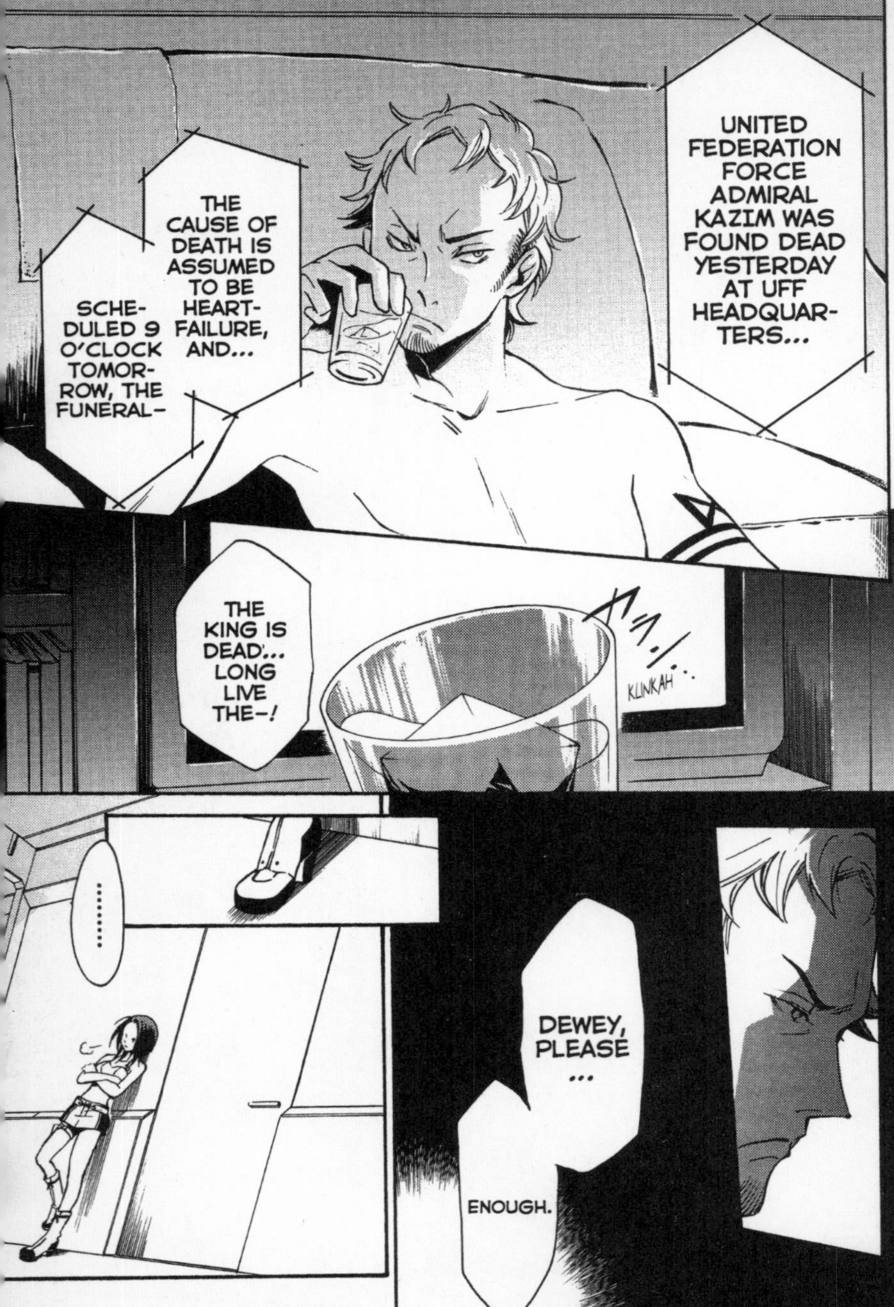
UNITED FEDERATION FORCE ADMIRAL KAZIM WAS FOUND DEAD YESTERDAY AT UFF HEADQUARTERS...
THE CAUSE OF DEATH IS ASSUMED TO BE HEART-FAILURE, AND...
SCHEDULED 9 O'CLOCK TOMORROW, THE FUNERAL-
THE KING IS DEAD... LONG LIVE THE-!
KLINKAH
DEWEY, PLEASE ...
ENOUGH.
....

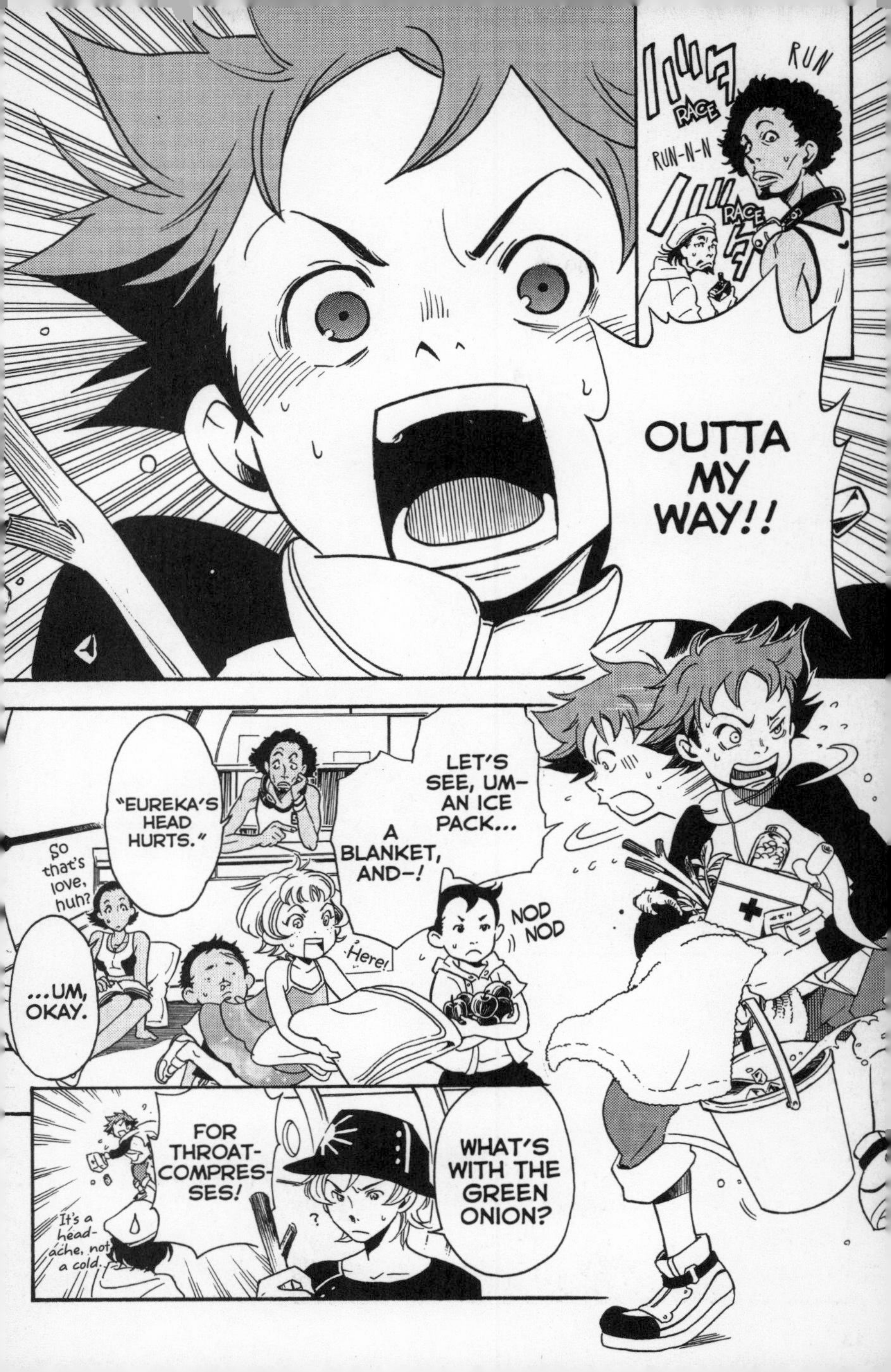
RUN
RAGE
RUN-N-N
RAGE
OUTTA MY WAY!!
LET'S SEE, UM- AN ICE PACK...
A BLANKET, AND-!
NOD NOD
Here!
"EUREKA'S HEAD HURTS."
So that's love, huh?
...UM, OKAY.
WHAT'S WITH THE GREEN ONION?
FOR THROAT-COMPRES-SES!
It's a head-ache, not a cold.

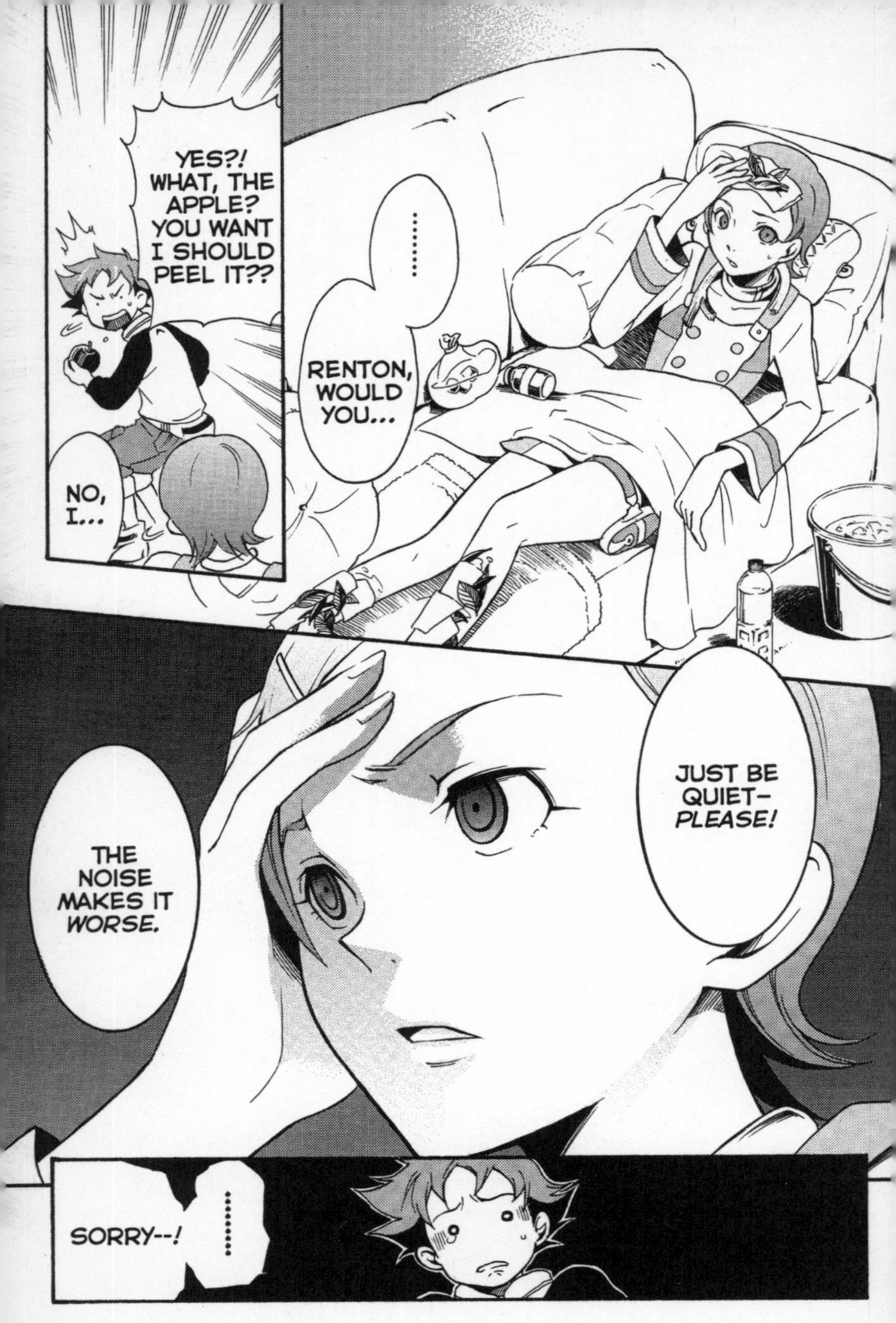
......
RENTON, WOULD YOU...
YES?! WHAT, THE APPLE? YOU WANT I SHOULD PEEL IT??
NO, I...
JUST BE QUIET— PLEASE!
THE NOISE MAKES IT WORSE.
......
SORRY--!

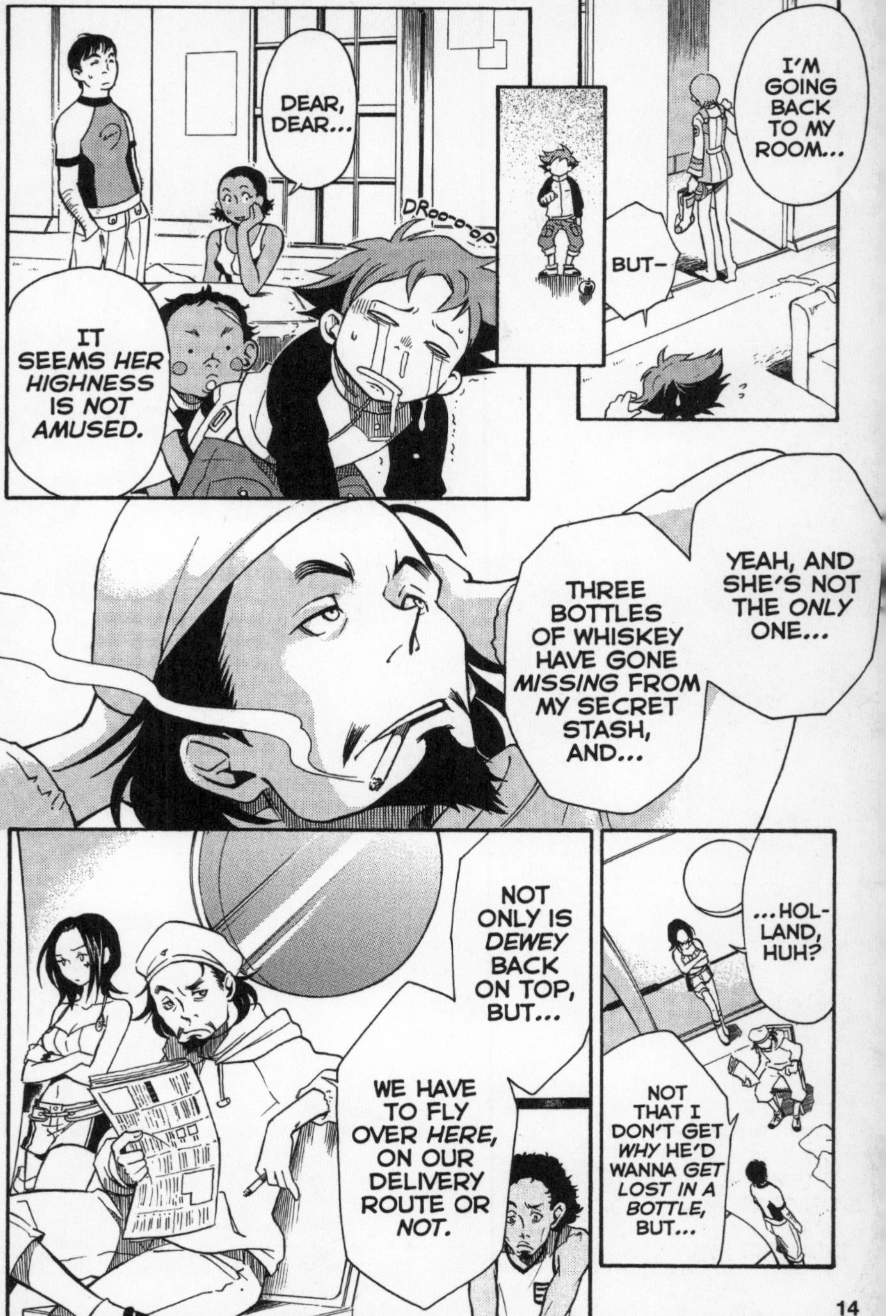
I'M GOING BACK TO MY ROOM...
BUT–
DEAR, DEAR...
DROO-O-OP
IT SEEMS HER HIGHNESS IS NOT AMUSED.
YEAH, AND SHE'S NOT THE ONLY ONE...
THREE BOTTLES OF WHISKEY HAVE GONE MISSING FROM MY SECRET STASH, AND...
...HOL-LAND, HUH?
NOT THAT I DON'T GET WHY HE'D WANNA GET LOST IN A BOTTLE, BUT...
NOT ONLY IS DEWEY BACK ON TOP, BUT...
WE HAVE TO FLY OVER HERE, ON OUR DELIVERY ROUTE OR NOT.

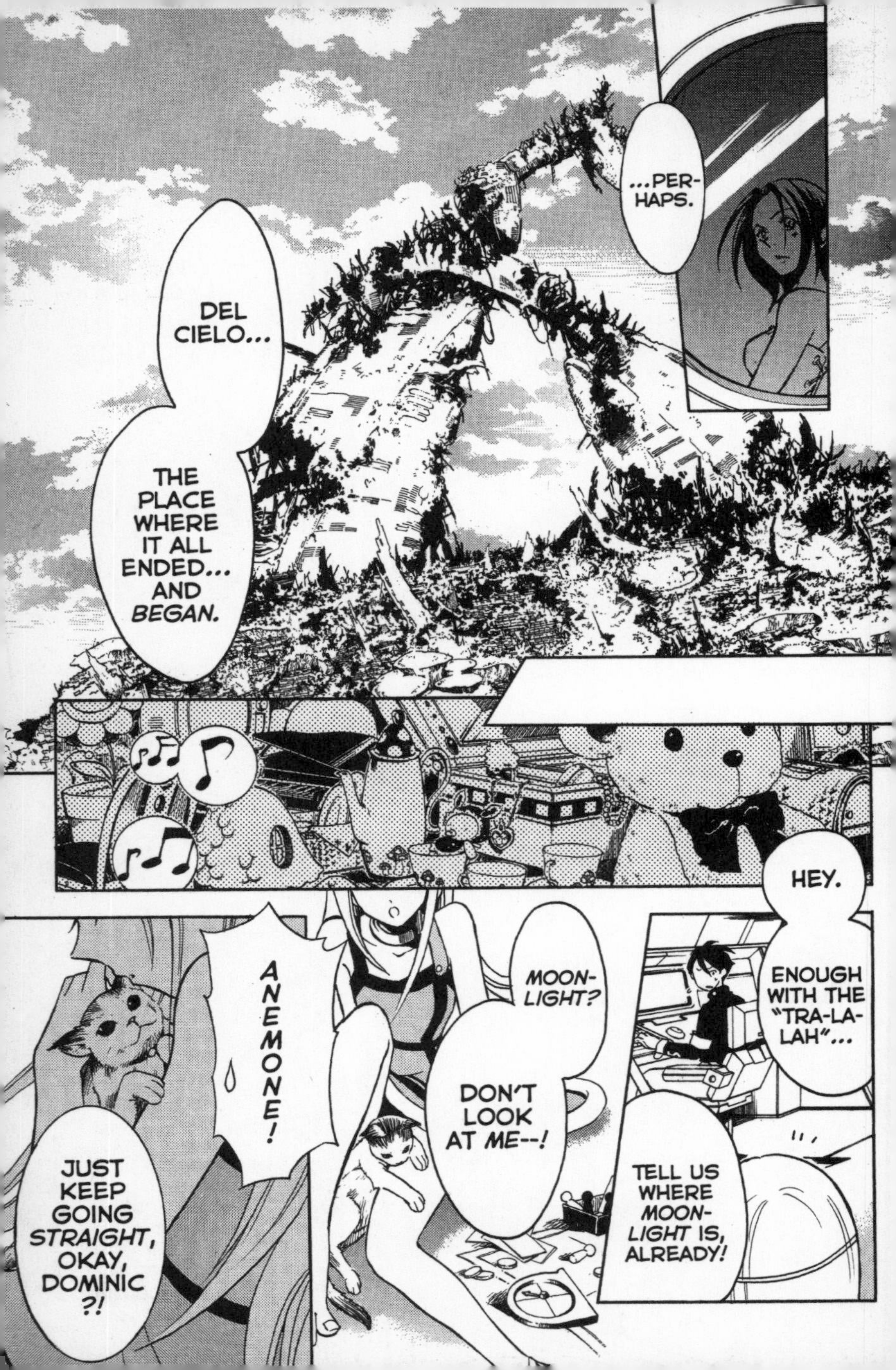
...PER-HAPS.
DEL CIELO...
THE PLACE WHERE IT ALL ENDED... AND *BEGAN.*
HEY.
ENOUGH WITH THE "TRA-LA-LAH"...
TELL US WHERE *MOON-LIGHT* IS, ALREADY!
MOON-LIGHT?
DON'T LOOK AT *ME*--!
ANEMONE!
JUST KEEP GOING *STRAIGHT*, OKAY, DOMINIC?!

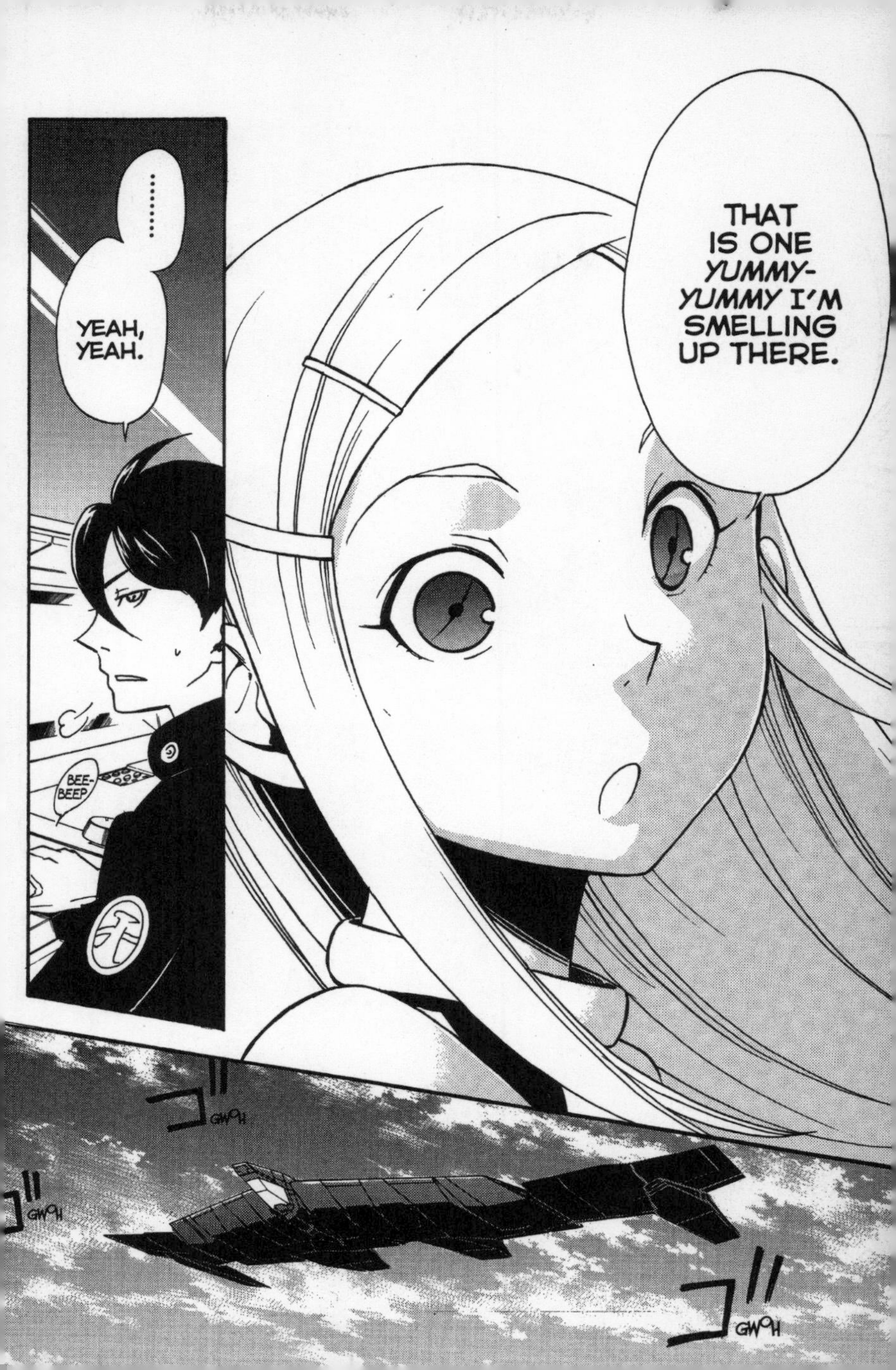
THAT IS ONE *YUMMY-YUMMY* I'M SMELLING UP THERE.
......
YEAH, YEAH.
BEE-BEEP
GWOH
GWOH
GWOH

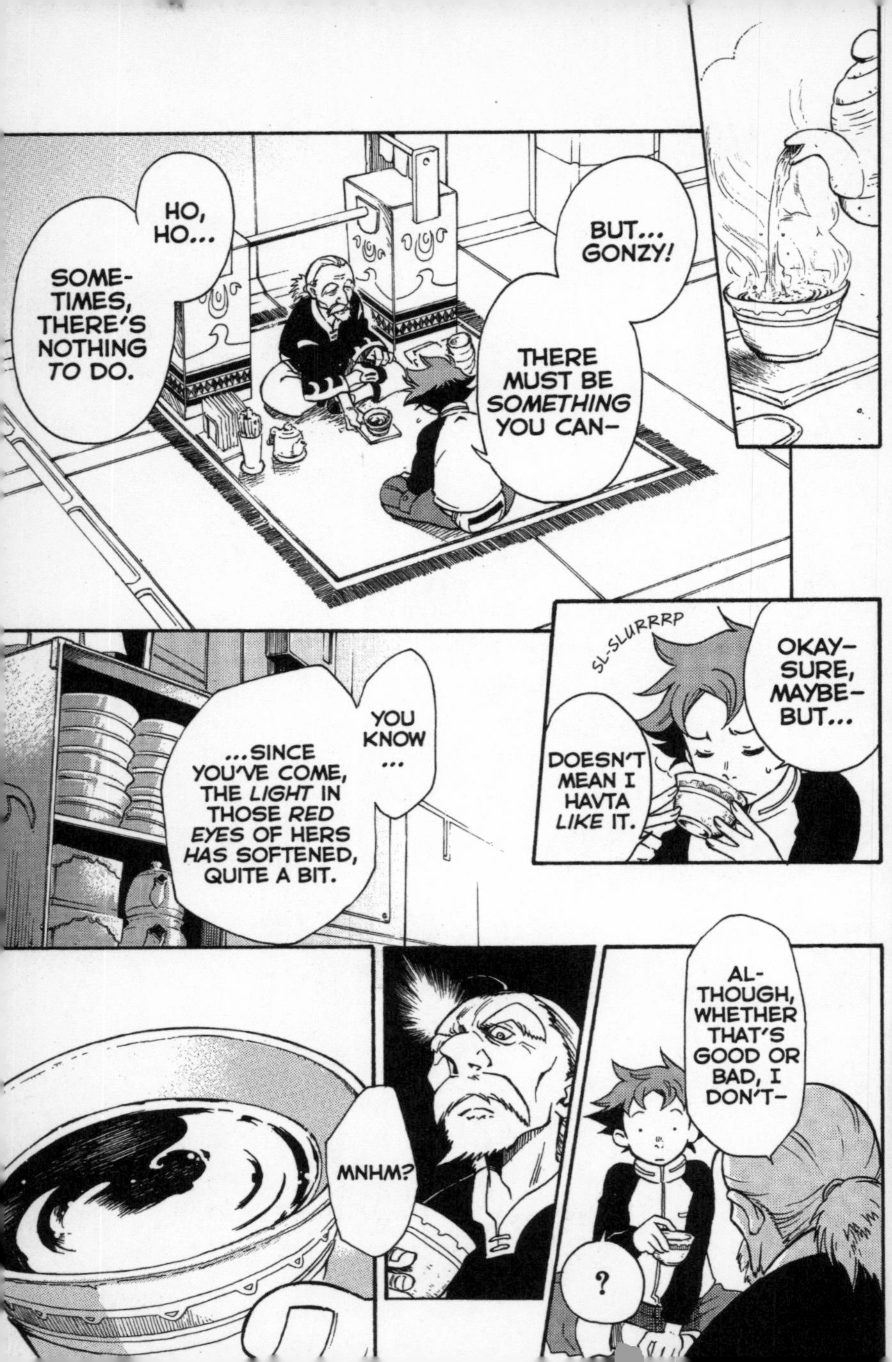
BUT... GONZY!
THERE MUST BE *SOMETHING* YOU CAN-
HO, HO...
SOMETIMES, THERE'S NOTHING *TO DO.*
OKAY-SURE, MAYBE-BUT...
SL-SLURRRP
DOESN'T MEAN I HAVTA *LIKE* IT.
YOU KNOW...
...SINCE YOU'VE COME, THE *LIGHT* IN THOSE *RED EYES* OF HERS *HAS* SOFTENED, QUITE A BIT.
ALTHOUGH, WHETHER THAT'S GOOD OR BAD, I DON'T-
?
MNHM?

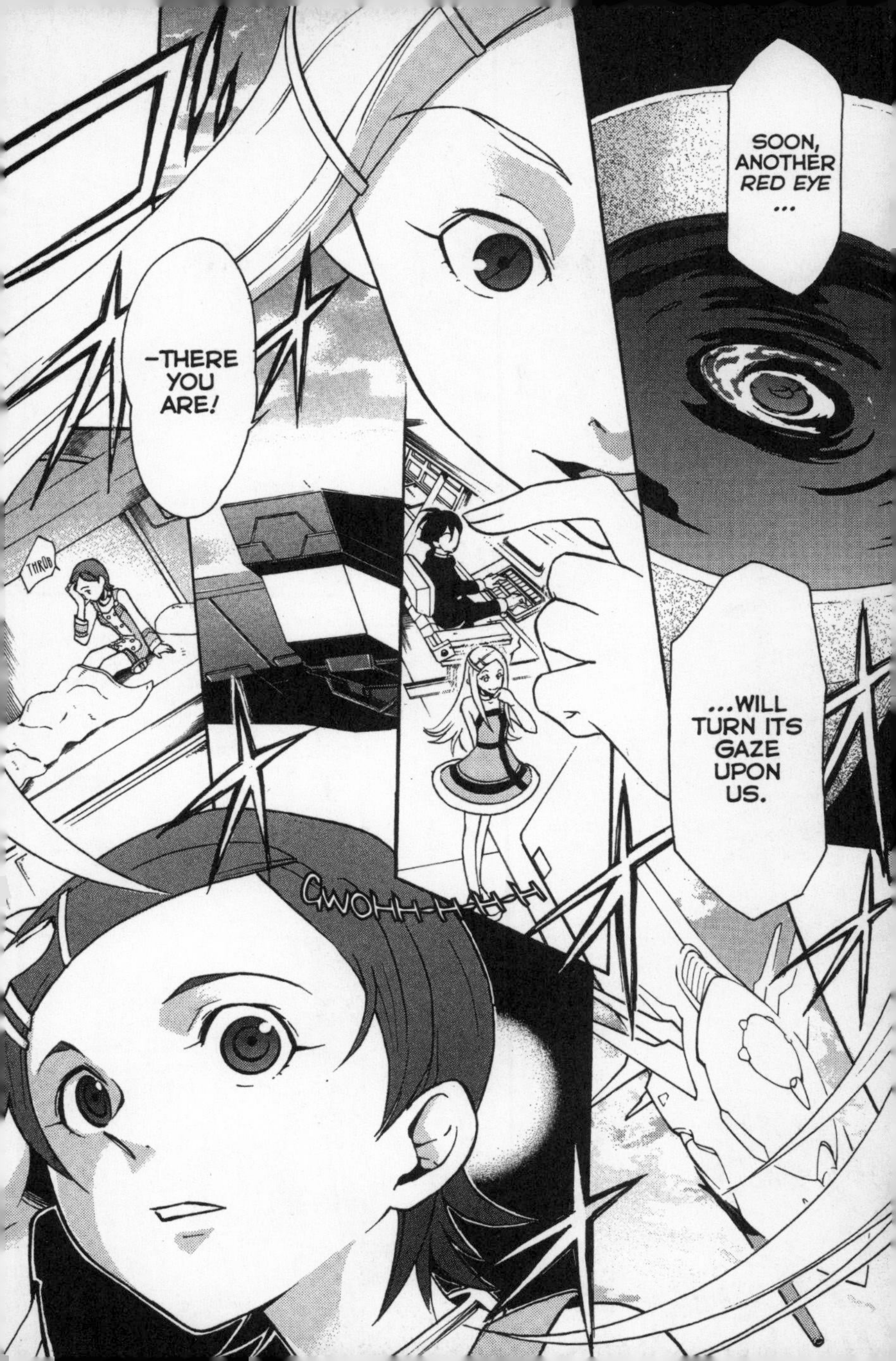
SOON, ANOTHER RED EYE ...
...WILL TURN ITS GAZE UPON US.
-THERE YOU ARE!
THROB
GWOHH-H-H-H

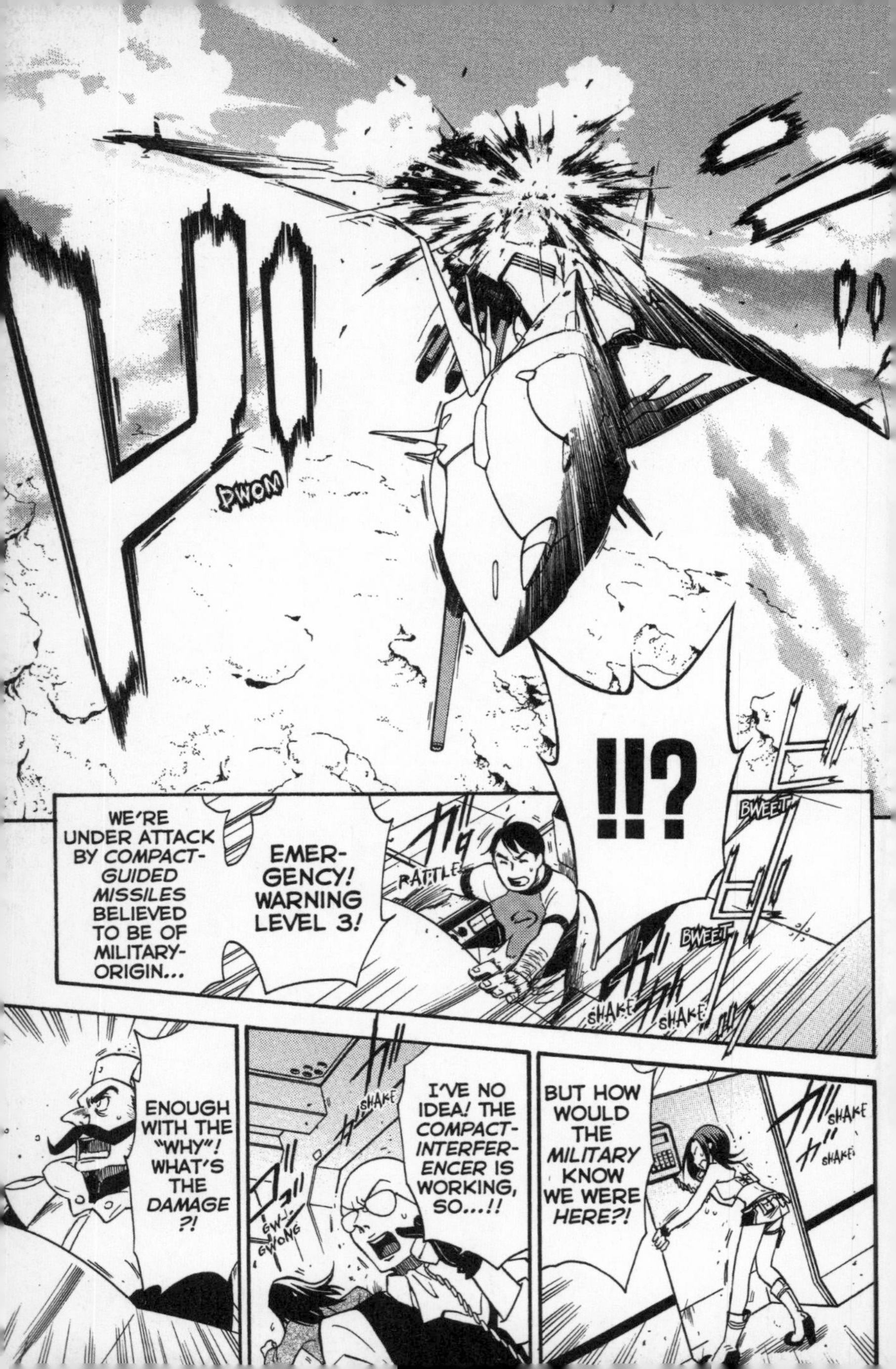
DWOM
!!?
BWEET
EMERGENCY! WARNING LEVEL 3!
RATTLE
WE'RE UNDER ATTACK BY COMPACT-GUIDED MISSILES BELIEVED TO BE OF MILITARY-ORIGIN...
BWEET
SHAKE SHAKE
SHAKE SHAKE
BUT HOW WOULD THE MILITARY KNOW WE WERE HERE?!
SHAKE
I'VE NO IDEA! THE COMPACT-INTERFERENCER IS WORKING, SO...!!
GWJ... GWONG
ENOUGH WITH THE "WHY"! WHAT'S THE DAMAGE?!

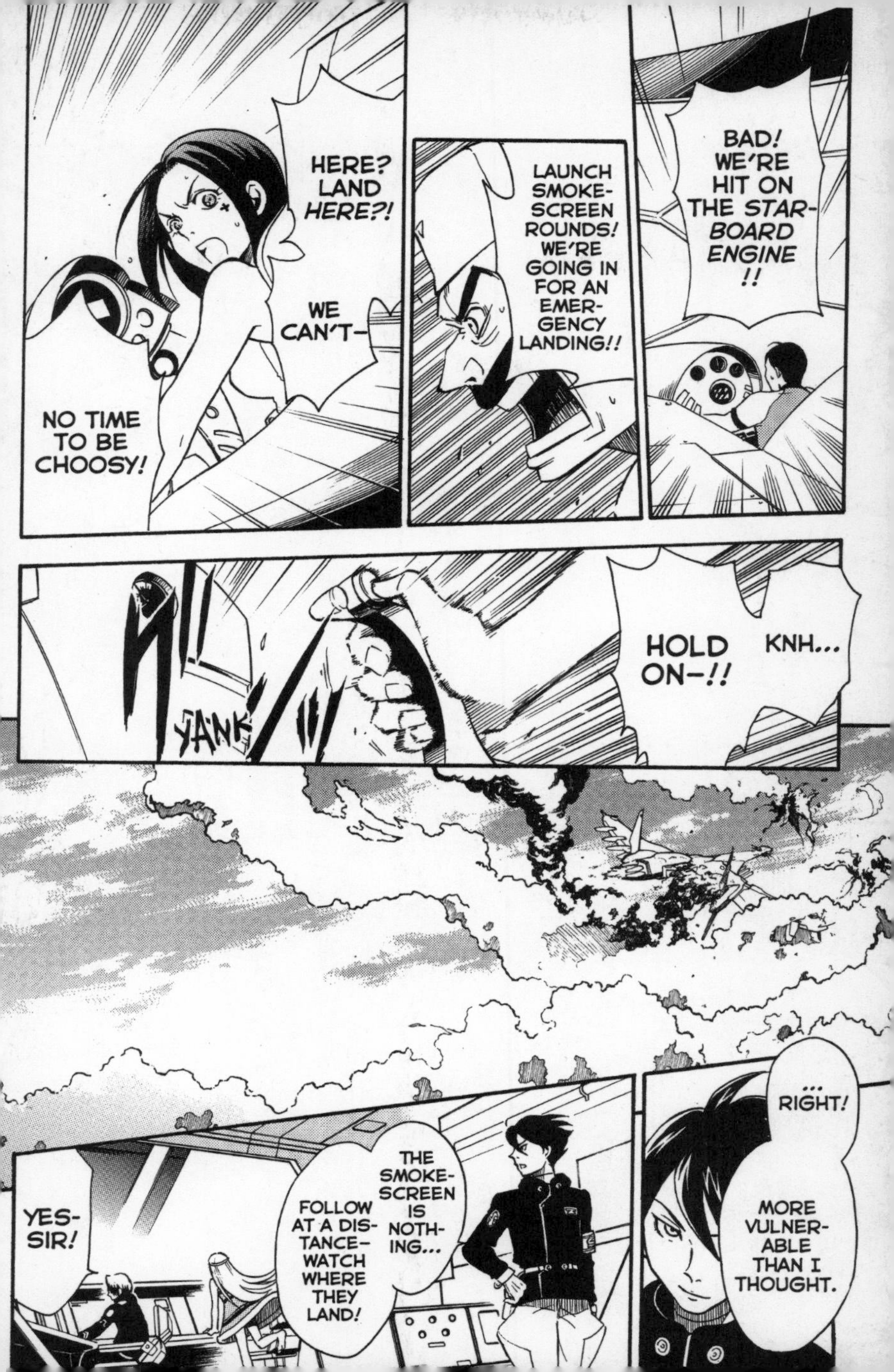
BAD! WE'RE HIT ON THE STARBOARD ENGINE!!
LAUNCH SMOKE-SCREEN ROUNDS! WE'RE GOING IN FOR AN EMERGENCY LANDING!!
HERE? LAND HERE?!
WE CAN'T-
NO TIME TO BE CHOOSY!
KNH...
HOLD ON-!!
YANK
...RIGHT!
MORE VULNERABLE THAN I THOUGHT.
THE SMOKE-SCREEN IS NOTHING...
FOLLOW AT A DISTANCE-WATCH WHERE THEY LAND!
YES-SIR!

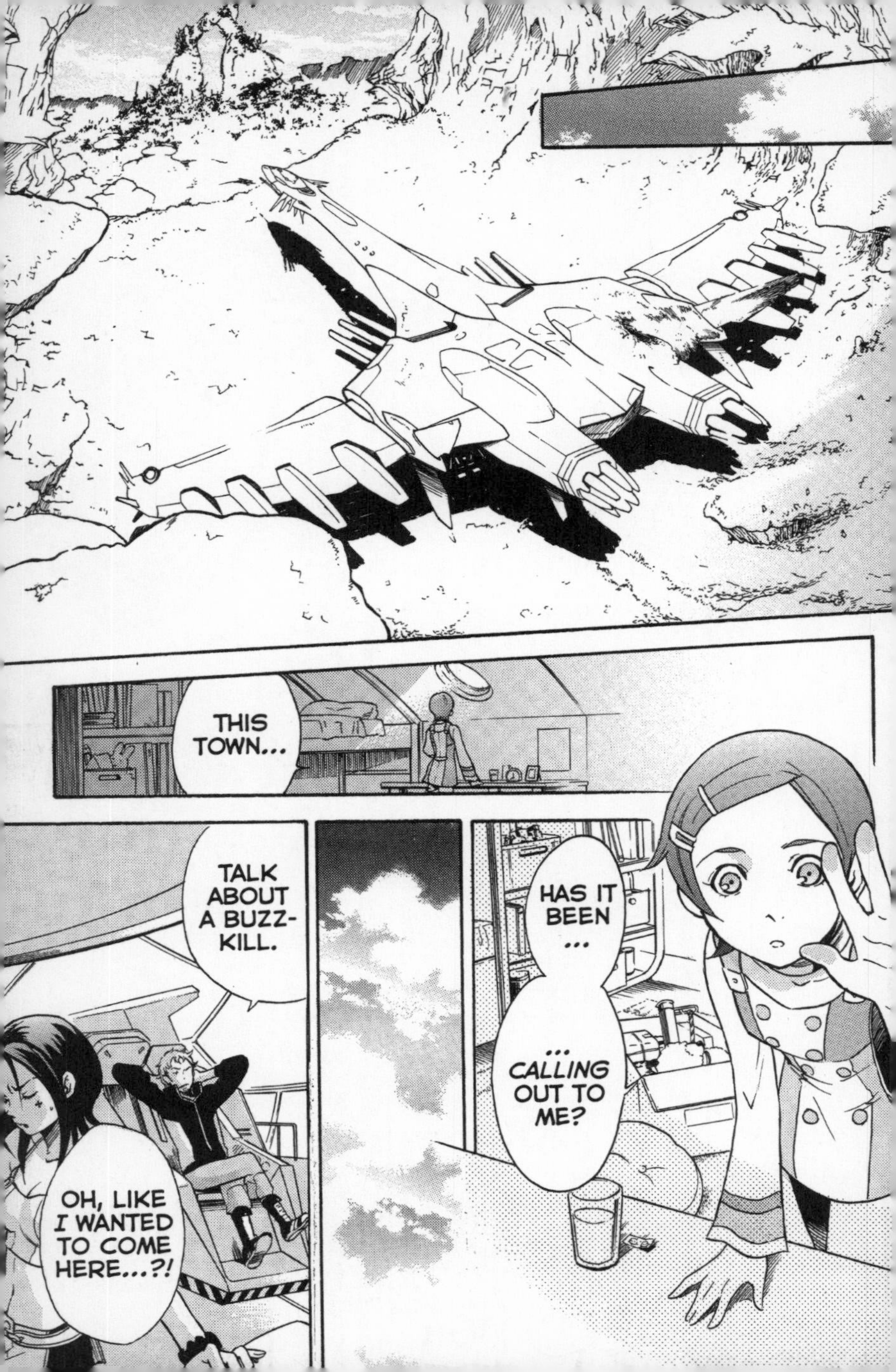
THIS TOWN...
HAS IT BEEN ...
... CALLING OUT TO ME?
TALK ABOUT A BUZZ-KILL.
OH, LIKE *I* WANTED TO COME HERE...?!

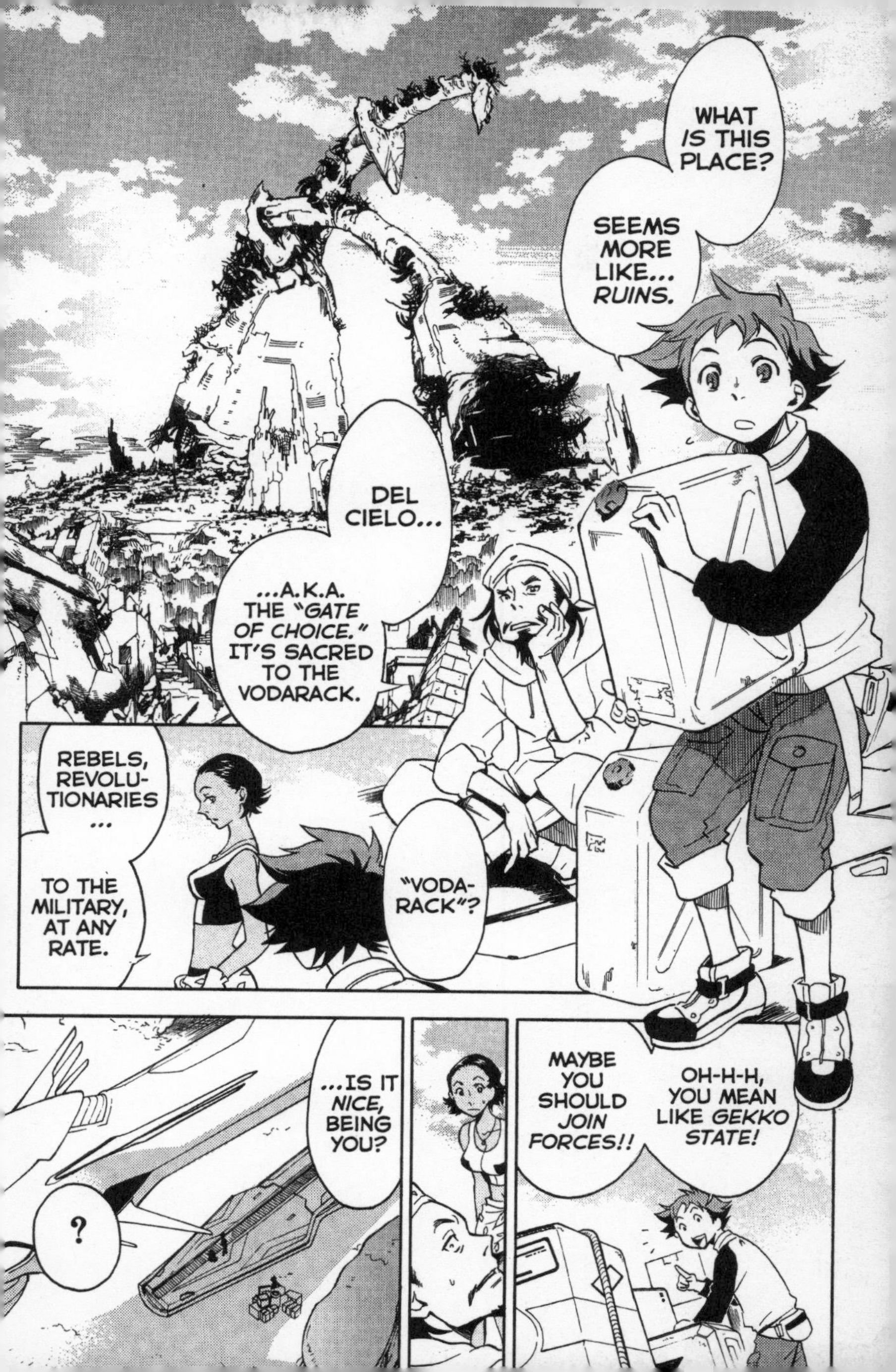
WHAT IS THIS PLACE?
SEEMS MORE LIKE... RUINS.
DEL CIELO...
...A.K.A. THE "GATE OF CHOICE." IT'S SACRED TO THE VODARACK.
"VODA-RACK"?
REBELS, REVOLUTIONARIES ...
TO THE MILITARY, AT ANY RATE.
OH-H-H, YOU MEAN LIKE GEKKO STATE!
MAYBE YOU SHOULD JOIN FORCES!!
...IS IT NICE, BEING YOU?
?

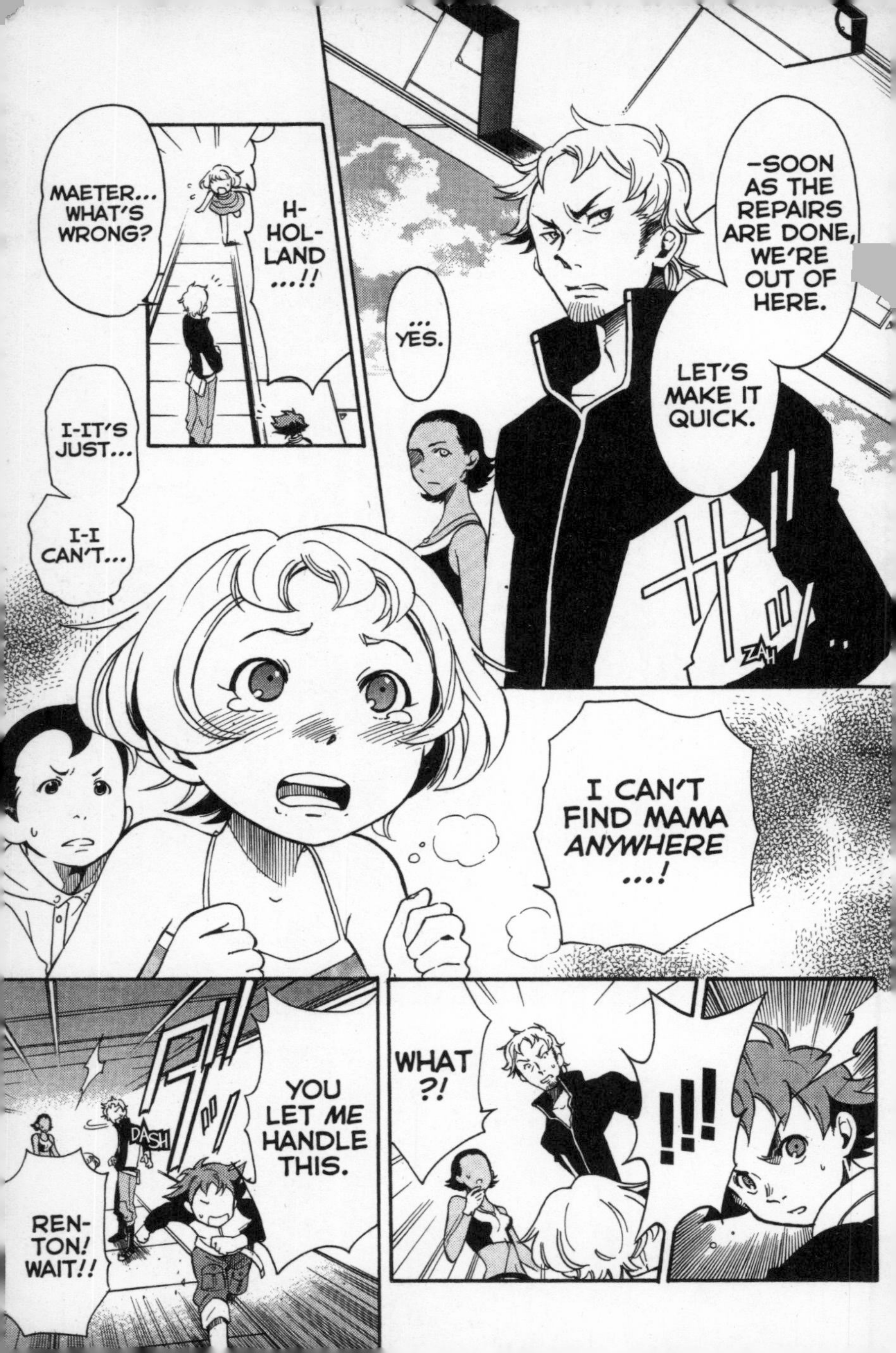
-SOON AS THE REPAIRS ARE DONE, WE'RE OUT OF HERE.
LET'S MAKE IT QUICK.
ZAH
...YES.
H-HOLLAND...!!
MAETER... WHAT'S WRONG?
I-IT'S JUST...
I-I CAN'T...
I CAN'T FIND MAMA *ANYWHERE*...!
!!!
WHAT?!
YOU LET *ME* HANDLE THIS.
DASH
REN-TON! WAIT!!

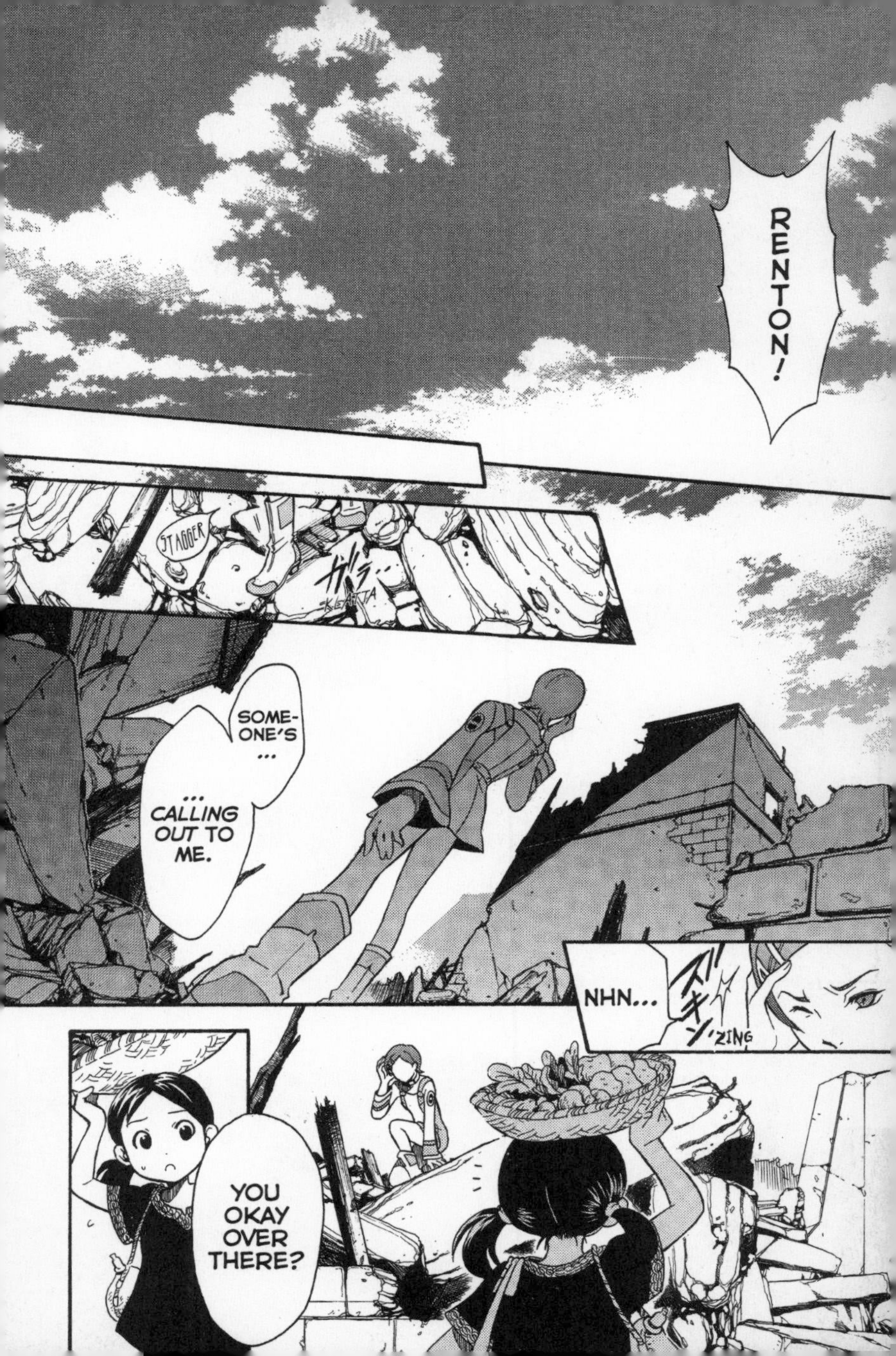

RENTON!
STAGGER
KLATTA
SOME-ONE'S ...
... CALLING OUT TO ME.
NHN...
ZING
YOU OKAY OVER THERE?

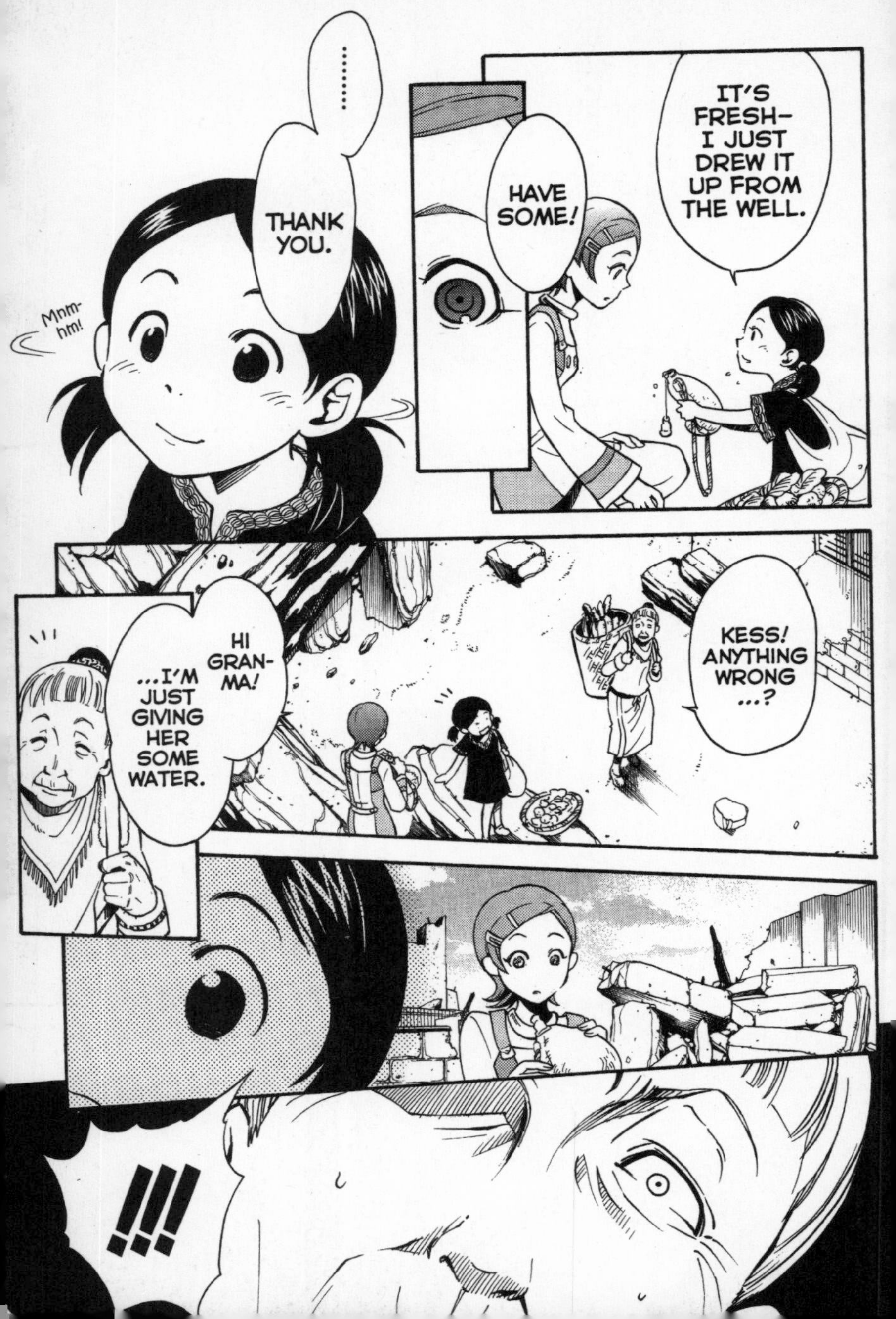
IT'S FRESH— I JUST DREW IT UP FROM THE WELL.
HAVE SOME!
......
THANK YOU.
Mnm-hm!
KESS! ANYTHING WRONG ...?
HI GRAN-MA!
...I'M JUST GIVING HER SOME WATER.
!!!

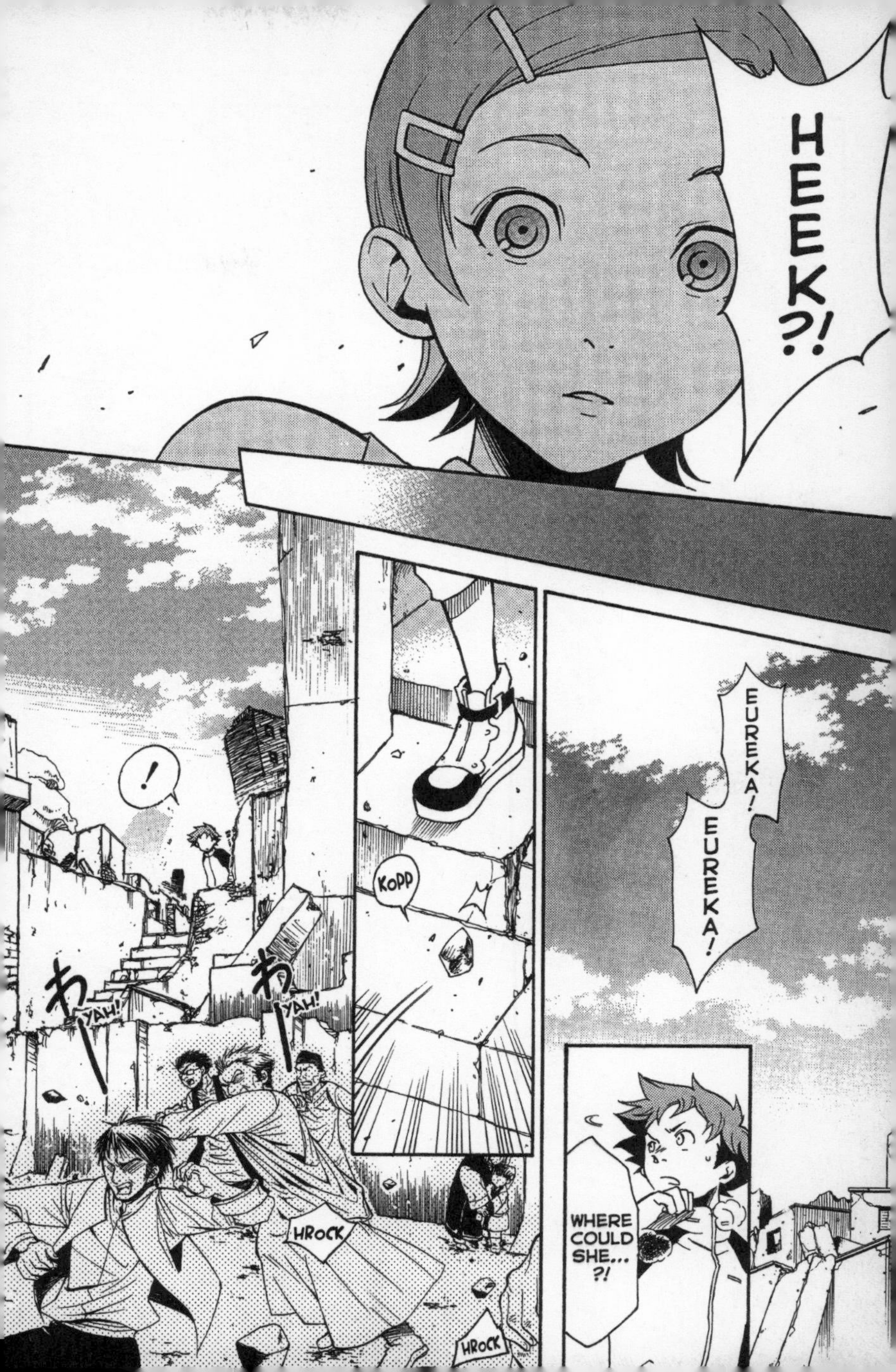
HEEK?!
EUREKA! EUREKA!
WHERE COULD SHE...?!
KOPP
!
わ YAH!
わ YAH!
HROCK
HROCK

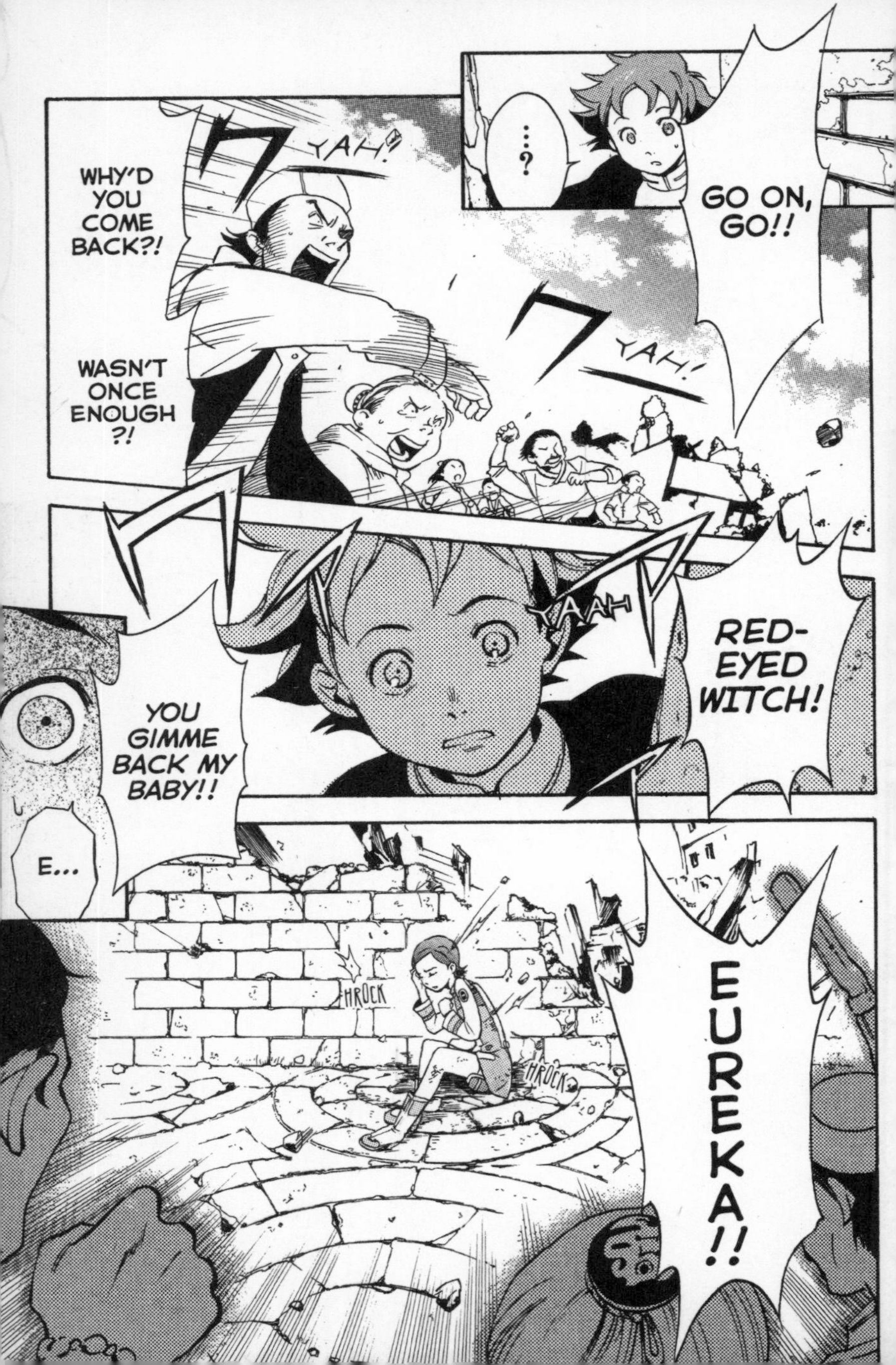
…?
GO ON, GO!!
YAH!
WHY'D YOU COME BACK?!
YAH!
WASN'T ONCE ENOUGH ?!
YAAH
RED-EYED WITCH!
YOU GIMME BACK MY BABY!!
E...
EUREKA!!
HROCK
HROCK

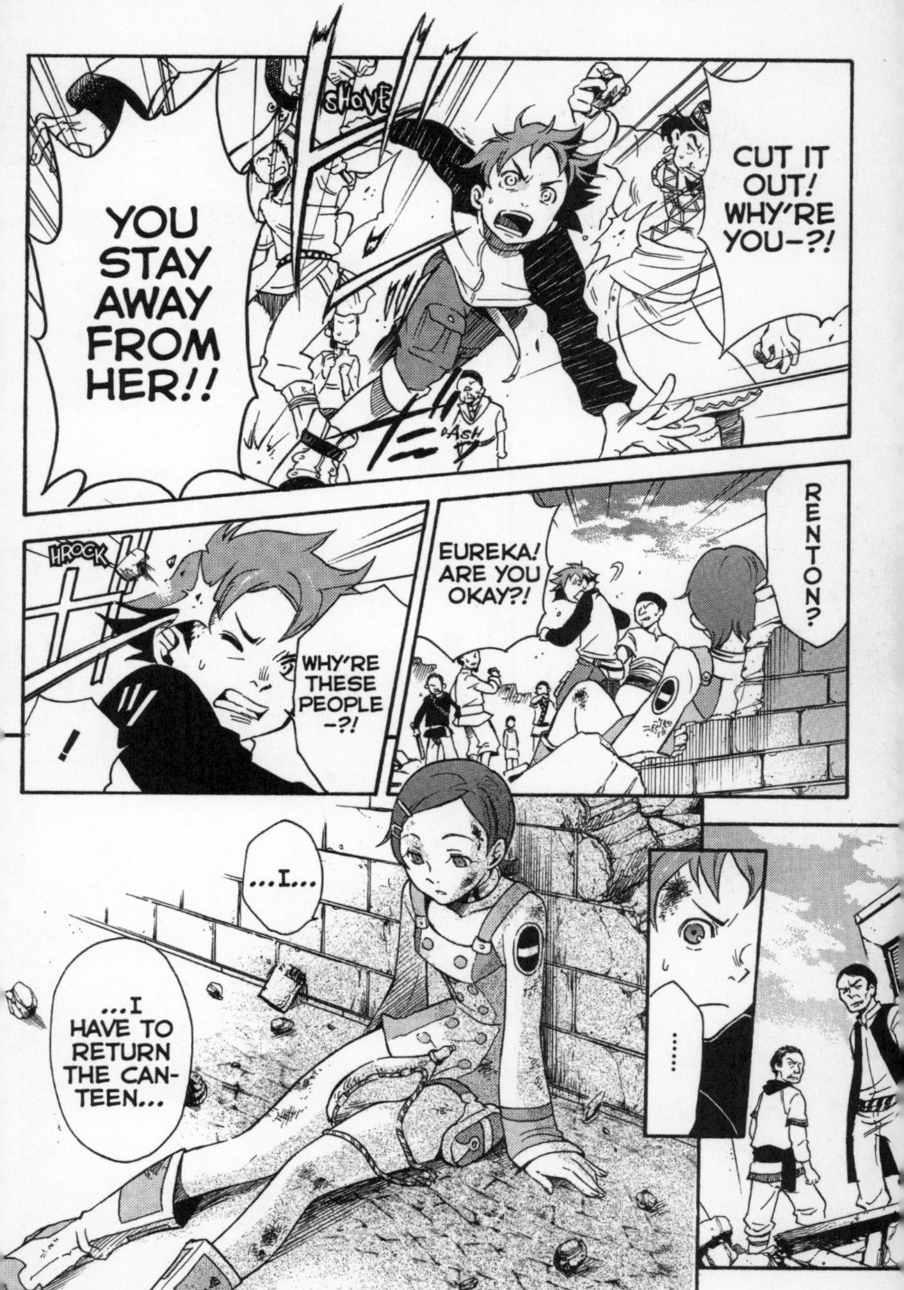
SHOVE
CUT IT OUT! WHY'RE YOU–?!
YOU STAY AWAY FROM HER!!
DASH
RENTON?
EUREKA! ARE YOU OKAY?!
HROCK
WHY'RE THESE PEOPLE –?!
!
......
...I...
...I HAVE TO RETURN THE CAN-TEEN...

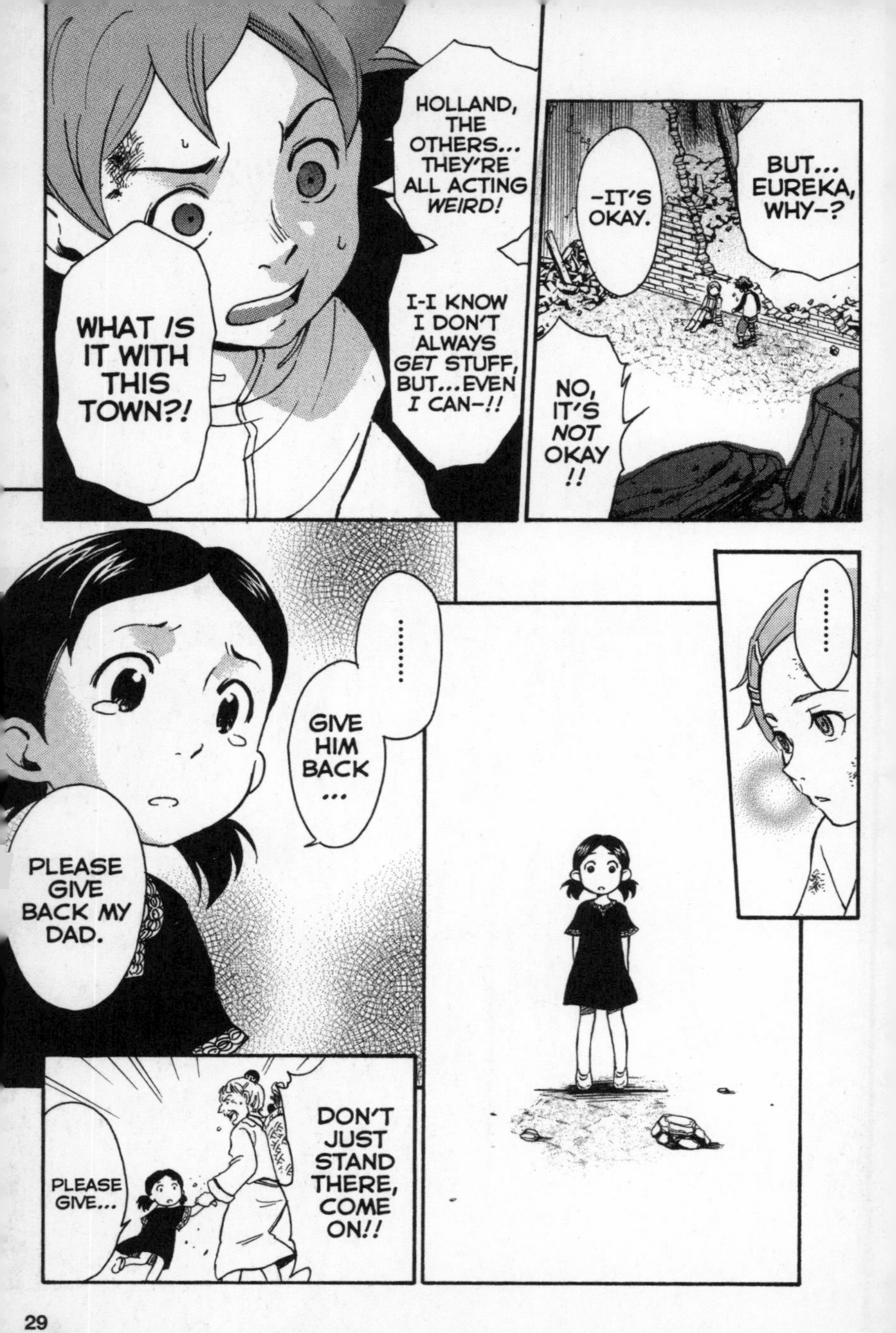
BUT... EUREKA, WHY–?
–IT'S OKAY.
NO, IT'S NOT OKAY!!
HOLLAND, THE OTHERS... THEY'RE ALL ACTING WEIRD!
I-I KNOW I DON'T ALWAYS GET STUFF, BUT...EVEN I CAN–!!
WHAT IS IT WITH THIS TOWN?!
......
....
GIVE HIM BACK ...
PLEASE GIVE BACK MY DAD.
DON'T JUST STAND THERE, COME ON!!
PLEASE GIVE...

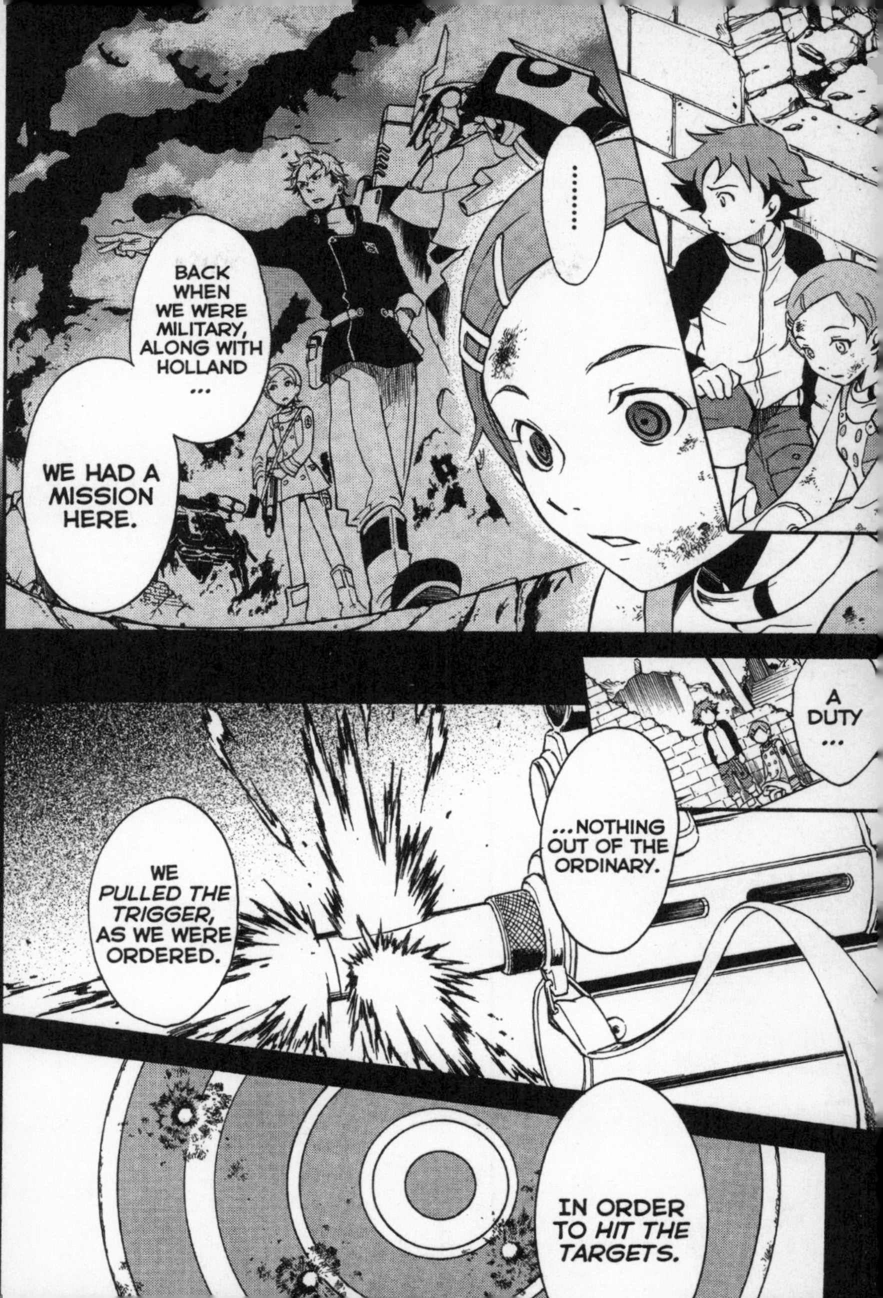
......
BACK WHEN WE WERE MILITARY, ALONG WITH HOLLAND ...
WE HAD A MISSION HERE.
A DUTY ...
...NOTHING OUT OF THE ORDINARY.
WE *PULLED THE TRIGGER*, AS WE WERE ORDERED.
IN ORDER TO *HIT THE TARGETS*.

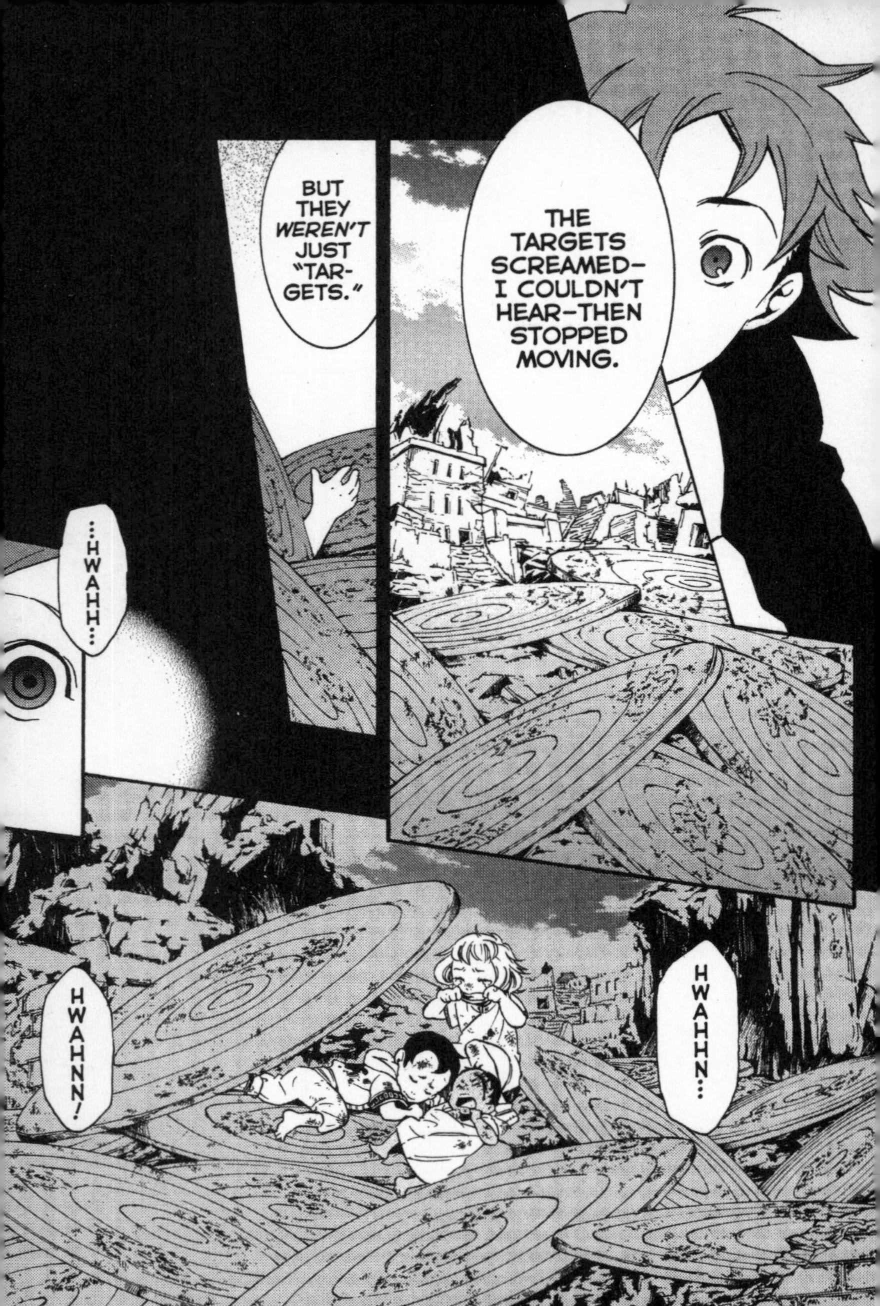
THE TARGETS SCREAMED— I COULDN'T HEAR—THEN STOPPED MOVING.
BUT THEY *WEREN'T* JUST "TARGETS."
...HWAHH...
HWAHHN...
HWAHNN!

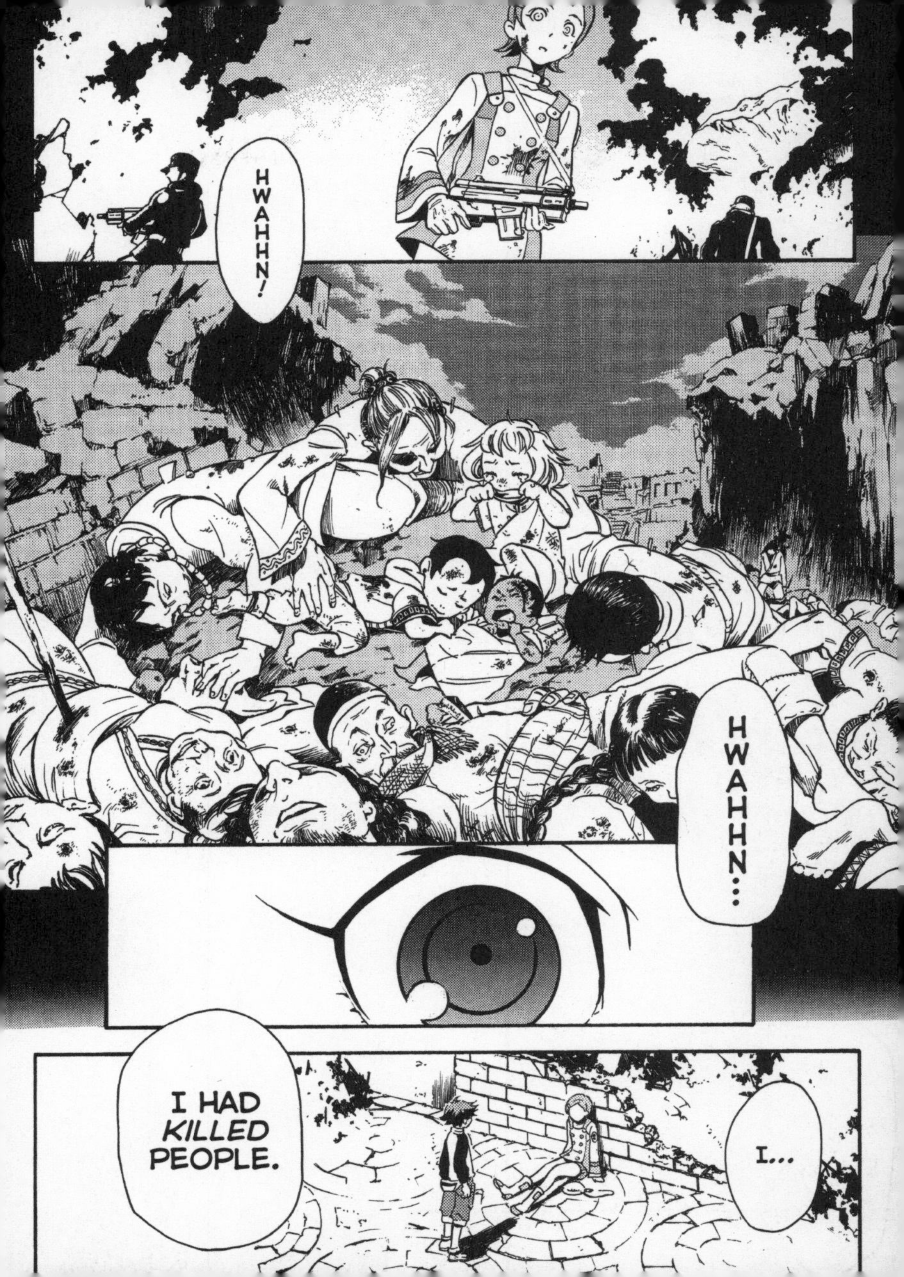
HWAHHN!
HWAHHN...
I...
I HAD KILLED PEOPLE.

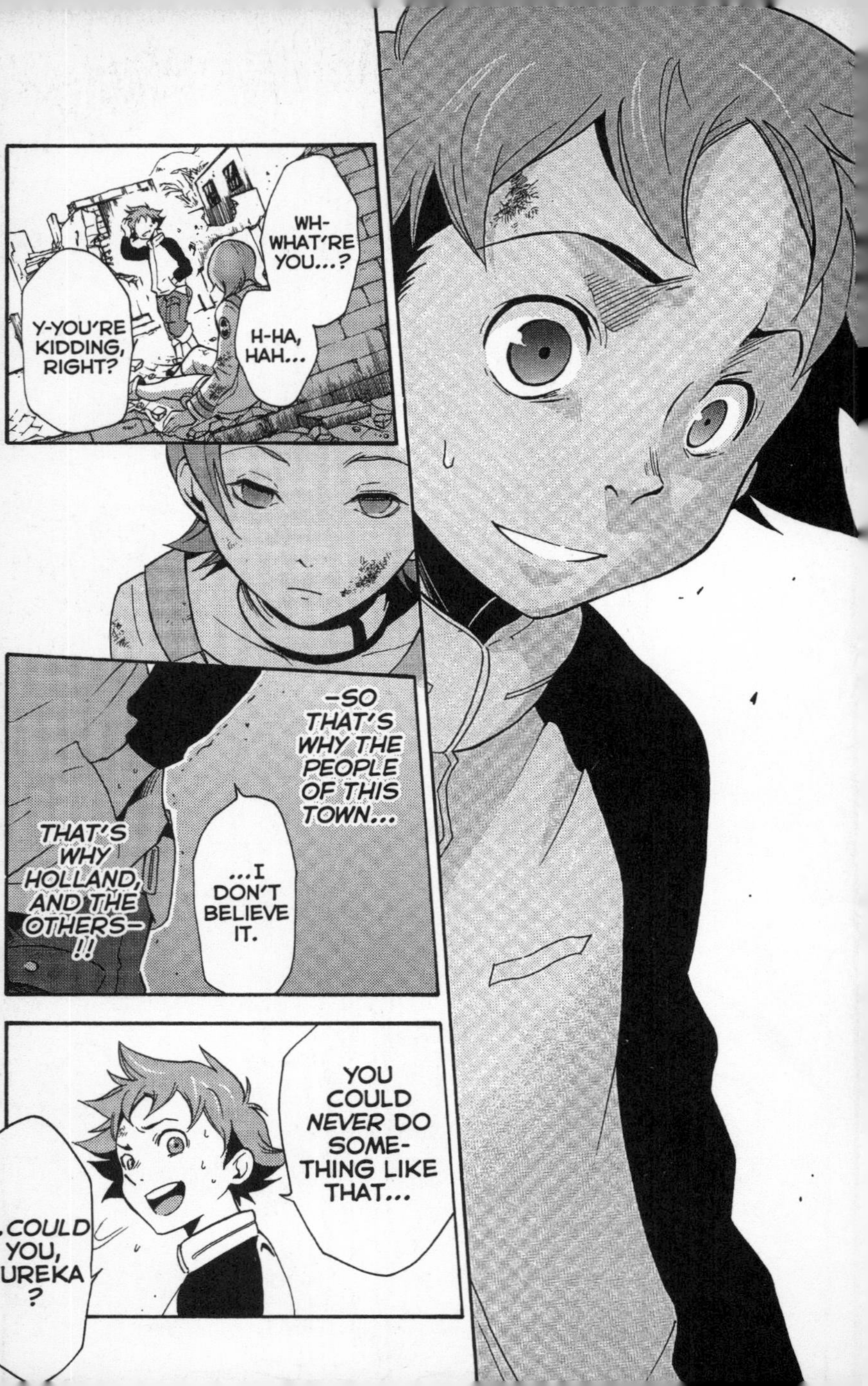
WH- WHAT'RE YOU...?
H-HA, HAH...
Y-YOU'RE KIDDING, RIGHT?
–SO THAT'S WHY THE PEOPLE OF THIS TOWN...
...I DON'T BELIEVE IT.
THAT'S WHY HOLLAND, AND THE OTHERS–!!
YOU COULD *NEVER* DO SOME-THING LIKE THAT...
...COULD YOU, EUREKA?

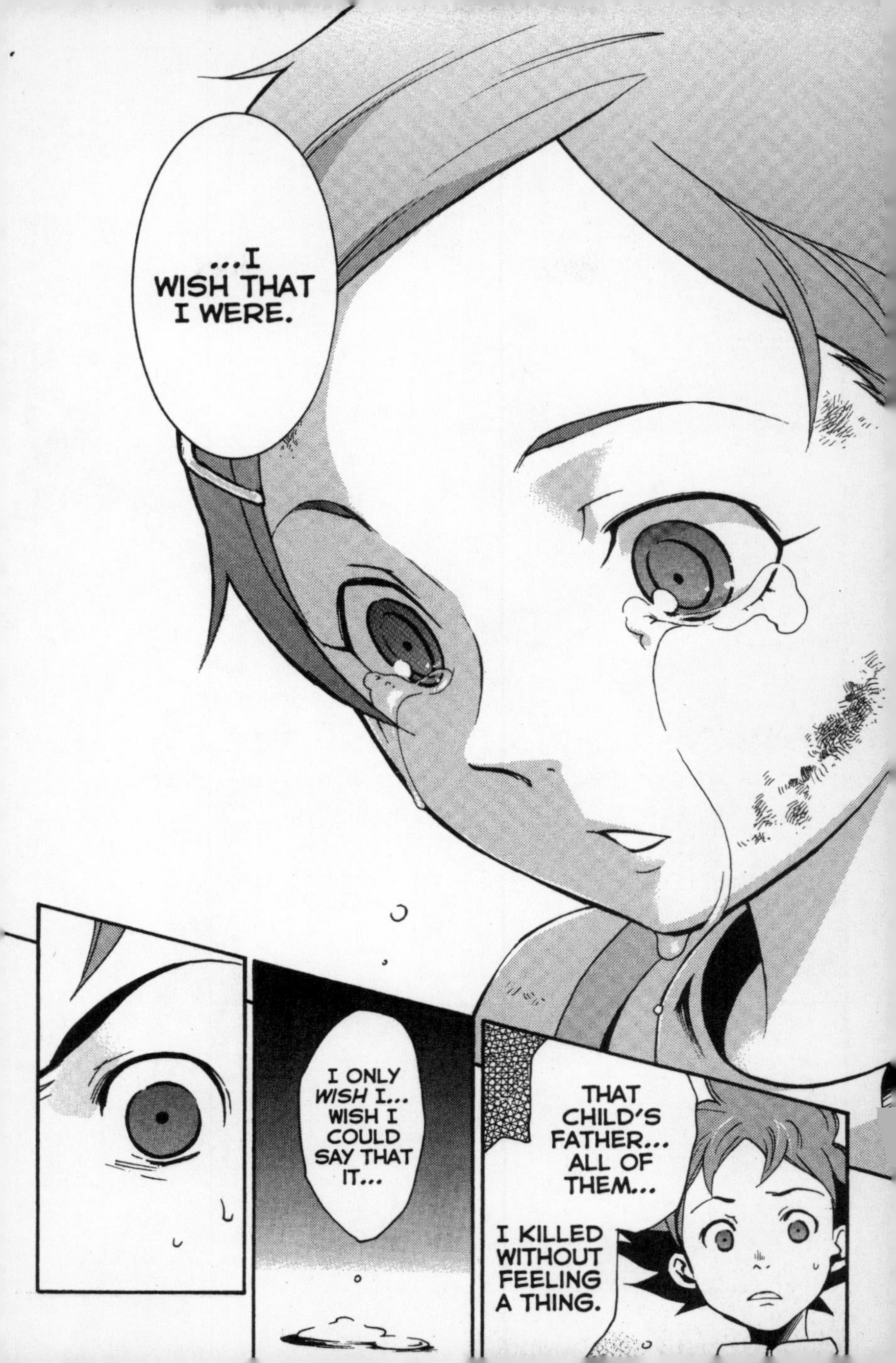
...I WISH THAT I WERE.
THAT CHILD'S FATHER... ALL OF THEM...
I KILLED WITHOUT FEELING A THING.
I ONLY *WISH* I... WISH I COULD SAY THAT IT...

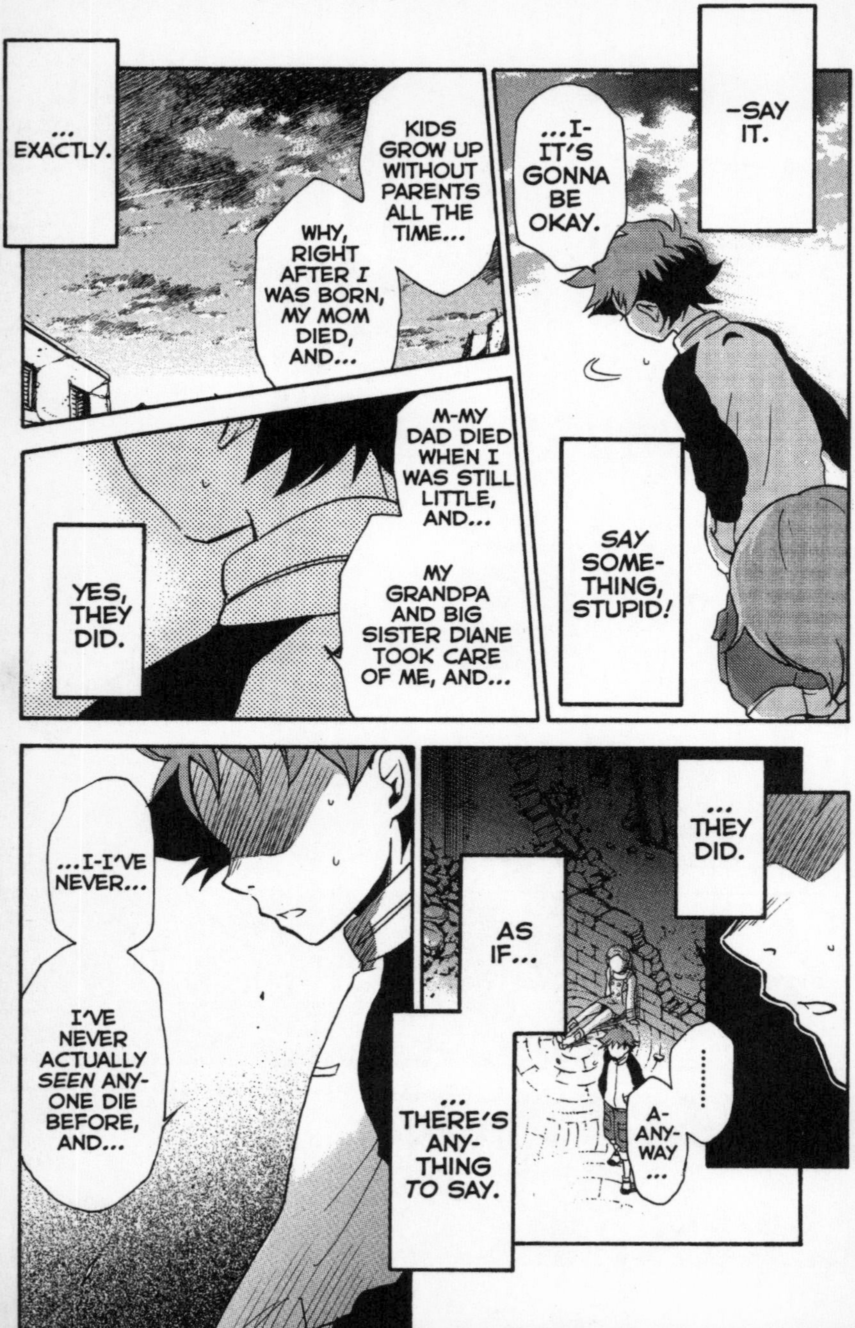
—SAY IT.
...I- IT'S GONNA BE OKAY.
SAY SOME-THING, STUPID!
KIDS GROW UP WITHOUT PARENTS ALL THE TIME...
WHY, RIGHT AFTER I WAS BORN, MY MOM DIED, AND...
...EXACTLY.
M-MY DAD DIED WHEN I WAS STILL LITTLE, AND...
MY GRANDPA AND BIG SISTER DIANE TOOK CARE OF ME, AND...
YES, THEY DID.
...THEY DID.
....
A-ANY-WAY...
AS IF...
...THERE'S ANY-THING TO SAY.
...I-I'VE NEVER...
I'VE NEVER ACTUALLY SEEN ANY-ONE DIE BEFORE, AND...

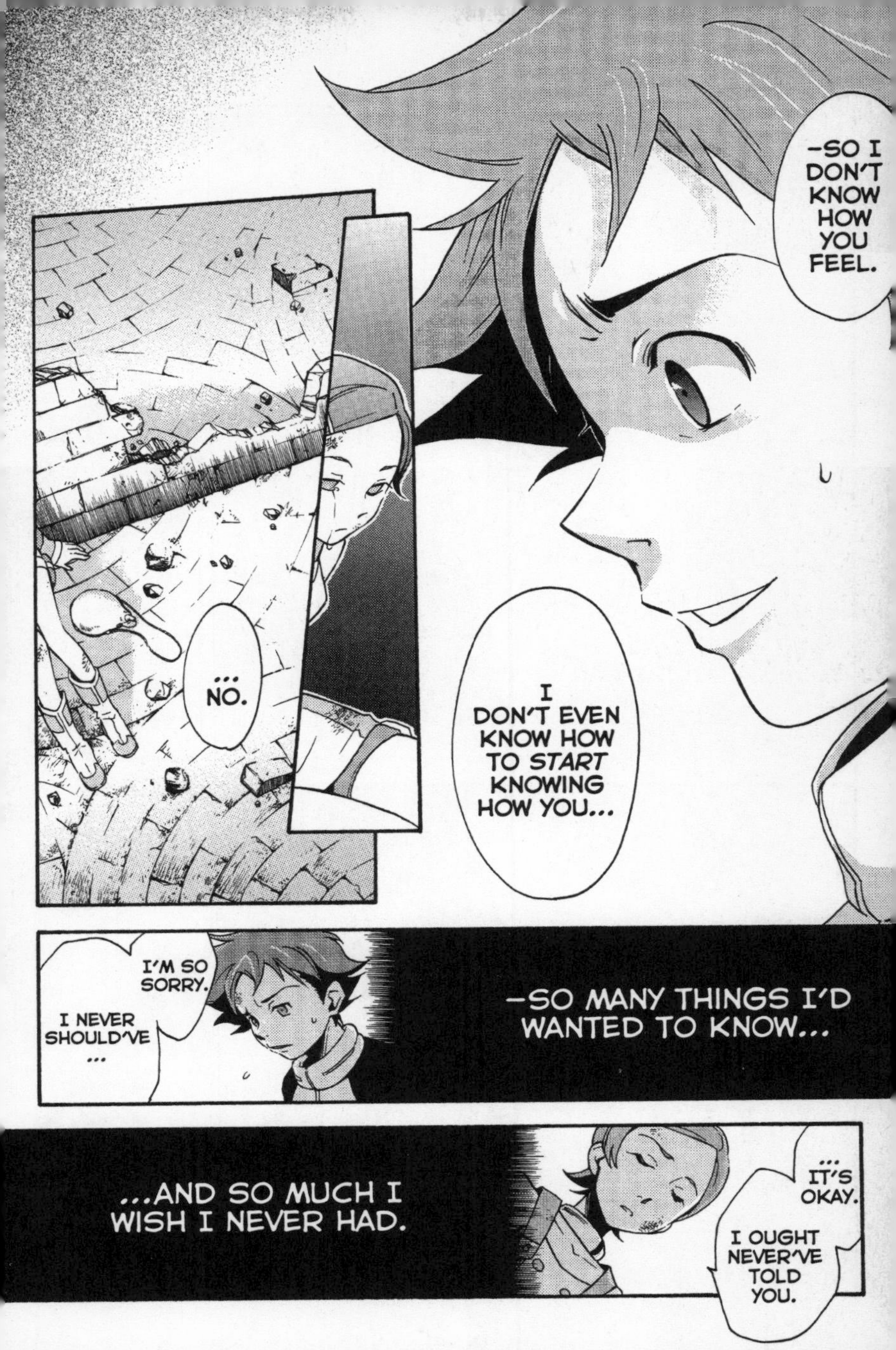
—SO I DON'T KNOW HOW YOU FEEL.
I DON'T EVEN KNOW HOW TO *START* KNOWING HOW YOU...
...NO.
—SO MANY THINGS I'D WANTED TO KNOW...
I'M SO SORRY.
I NEVER SHOULD'VE ...
...IT'S OKAY.
I OUGHT NEVER'VE TOLD YOU.
...AND SO MUCH I WISH I NEVER HAD.

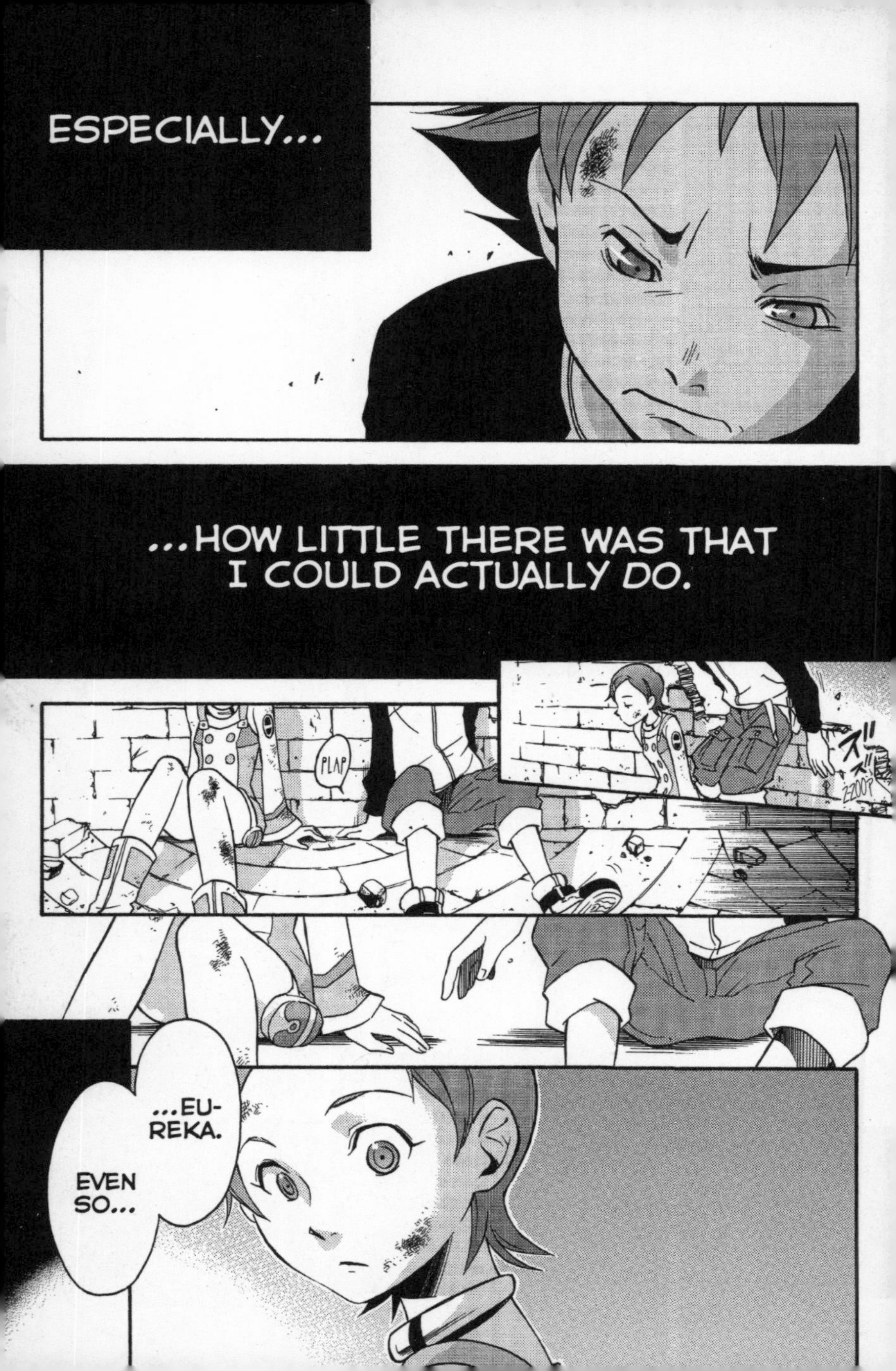
ESPECIALLY...
...HOW LITTLE THERE WAS THAT I COULD ACTUALLY DO.
ZZOOP
PLAP
...EU-REKA.
EVEN SO...

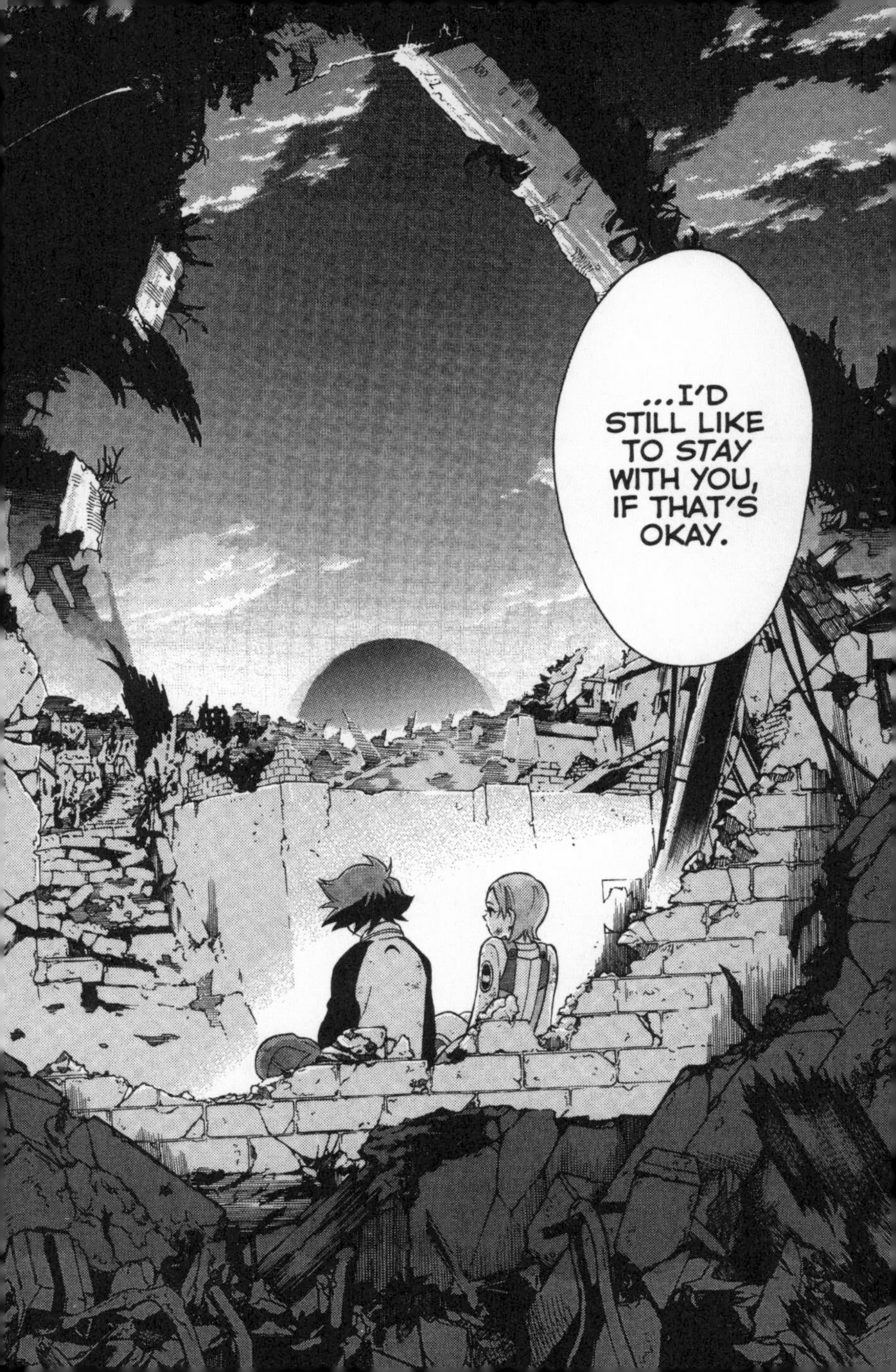
...I'D STILL LIKE TO STAY WITH YOU, IF THAT'S OKAY.

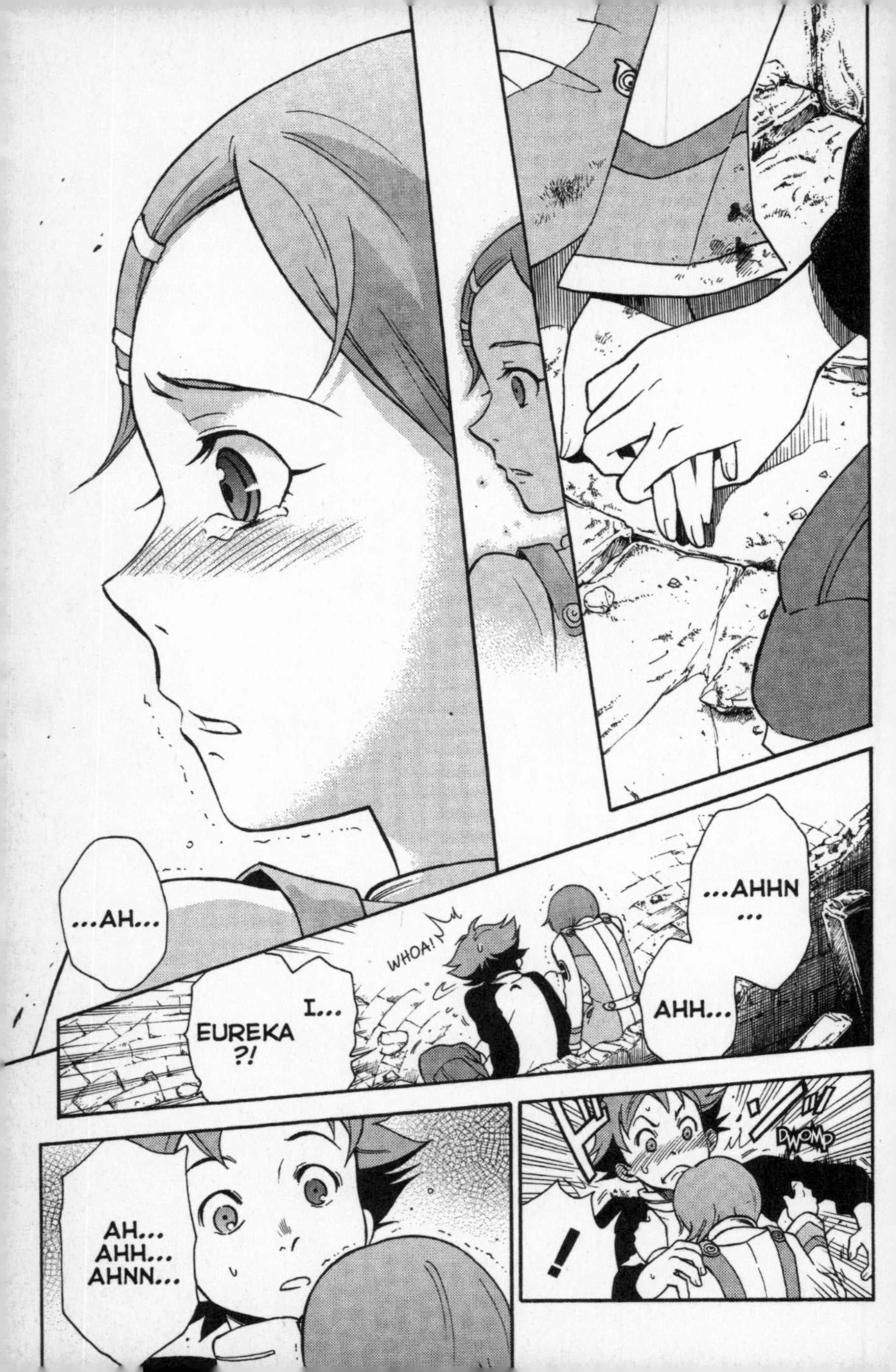
...AH...
...AHHN ...
AHH...
WHOA!
I...
EUREKA ?!
DWOMP
!
AH... AHH... AHNN...

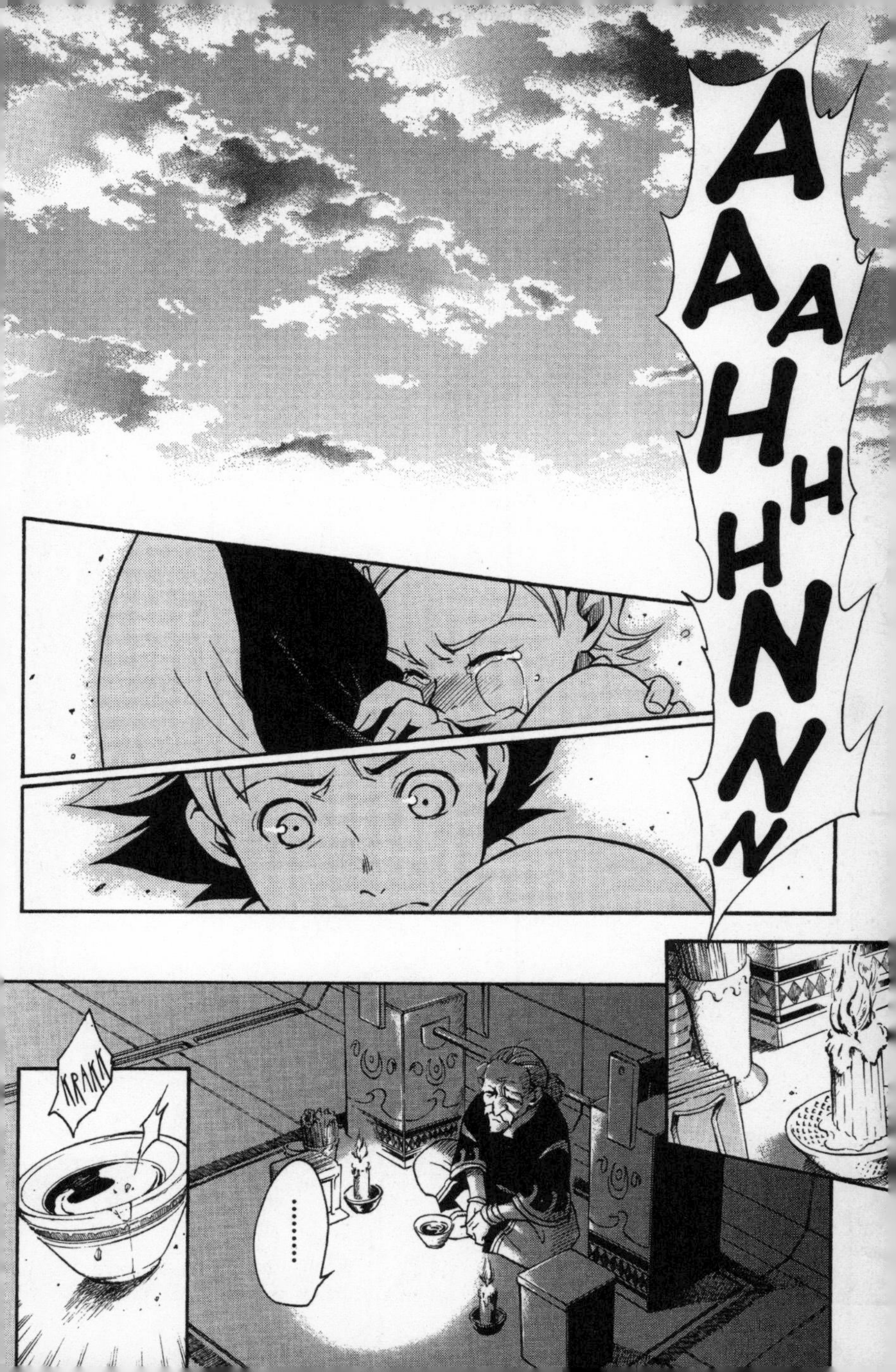
AAAHHHNNNN
....
KRAKK

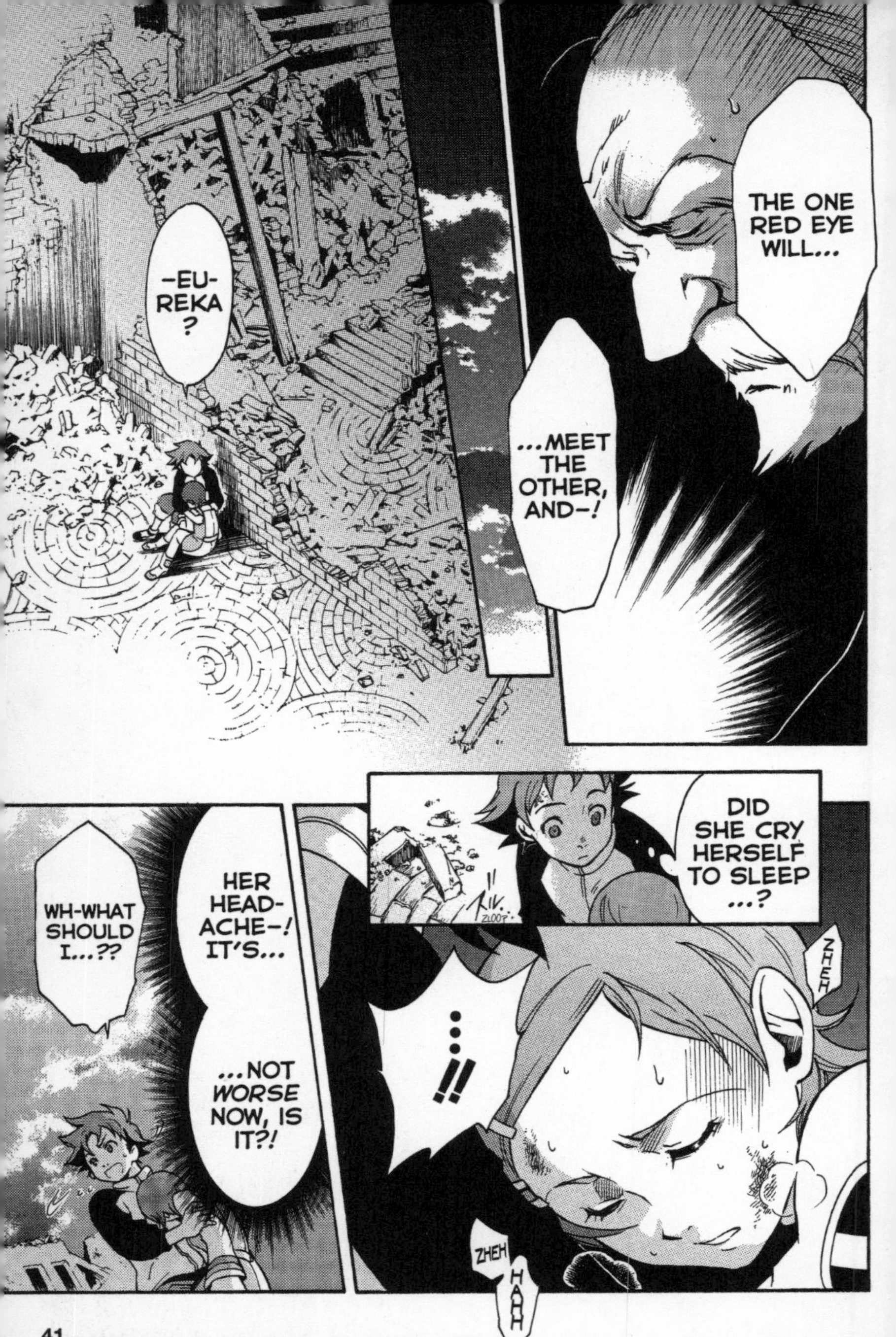
THE ONE RED EYE WILL...
...MEET THE OTHER, AND–!
–EU-REKA?
DID SHE CRY HERSELF TO SLEEP ...?
ZLOOP
ZHEH
...!!
ZHEH
HAHH
HER HEAD-ACHE–! IT'S...
...NOT WORSE NOW, IS IT?!
WH-WHAT SHOULD I...??

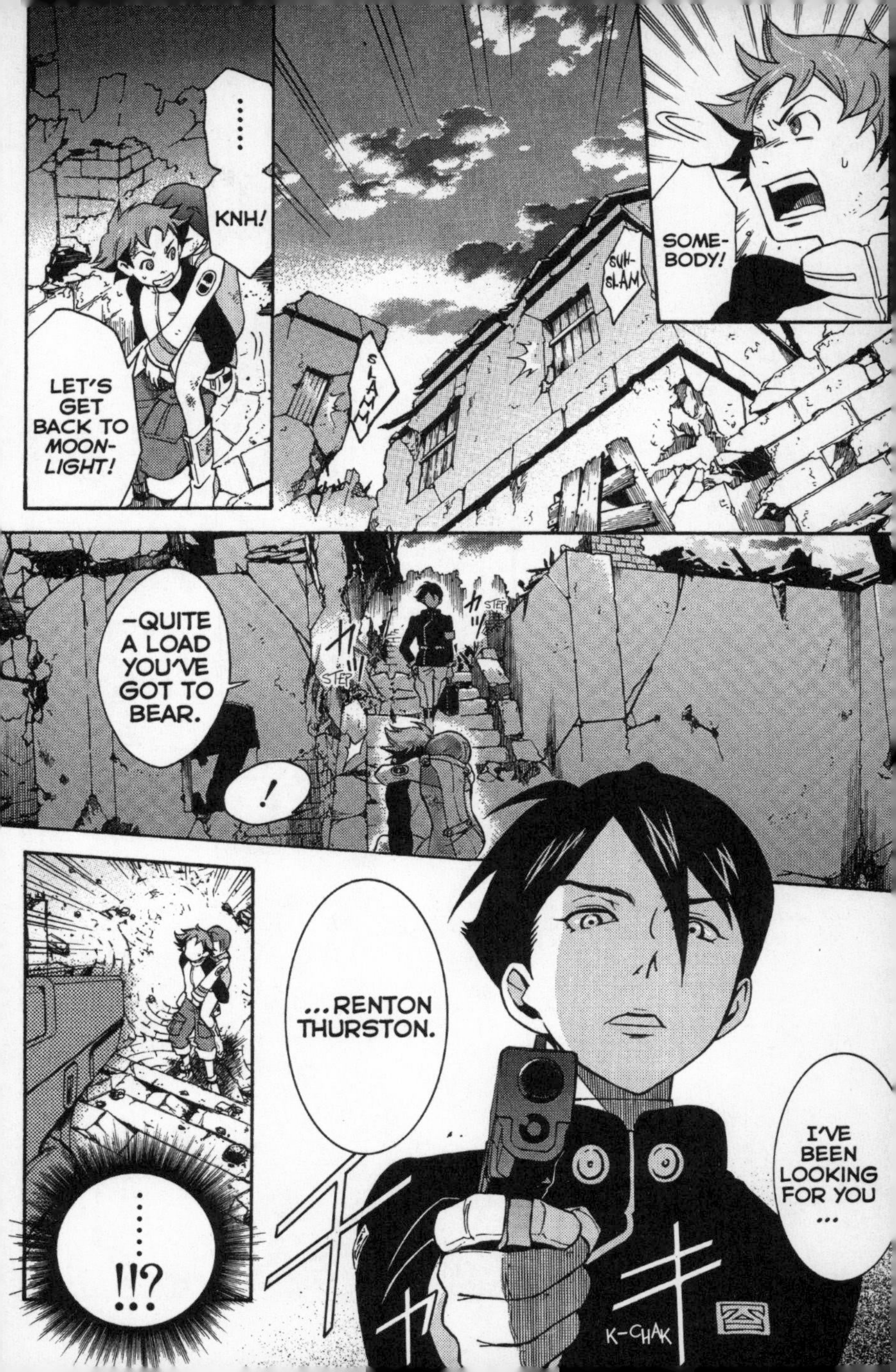
SOME-BODY!
SUH-SLAM
SLAMM
......
KNH!
LET'S GET BACK TO MOON-LIGHT!
-QUITE A LOAD YOU'VE GOT TO BEAR.
STEP
STEP
!
I'VE BEEN LOOKING FOR YOU ...
...RENTON THURSTON.
K-CHAK
......
!!?

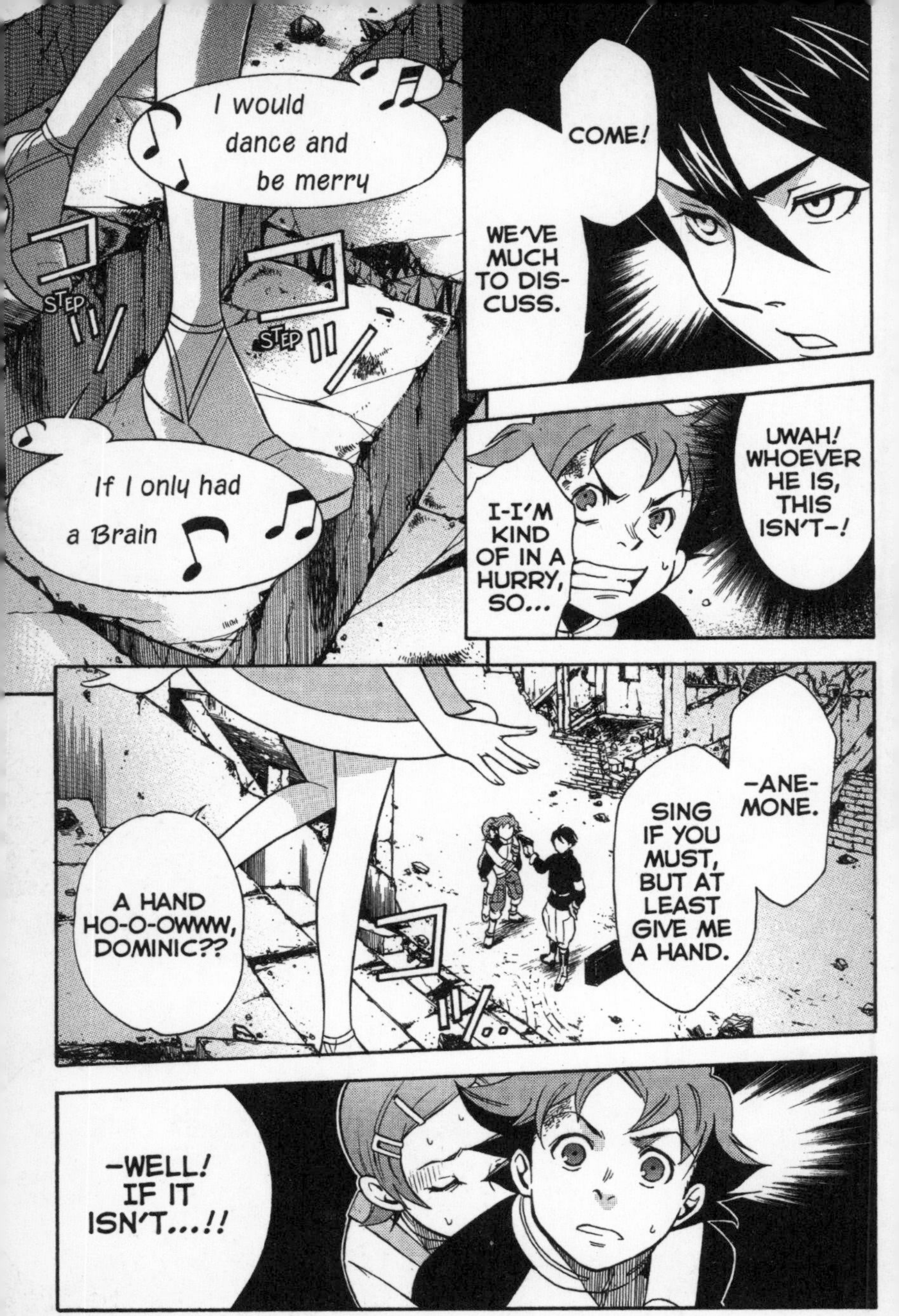
COME!
WE'VE MUCH TO DIS-CUSS.
UWAH! WHOEVER HE IS, THIS ISN'T-!
I-I'M KIND OF IN A HURRY, SO...
I would dance and be merry
STEP
STEP
If I only had a Brain
-ANE-MONE.
SING IF YOU MUST, BUT AT LEAST GIVE ME A HAND.
A HAND HO-O-OWWW, DOMINIC??
-WELL! IF IT ISN'T...!!

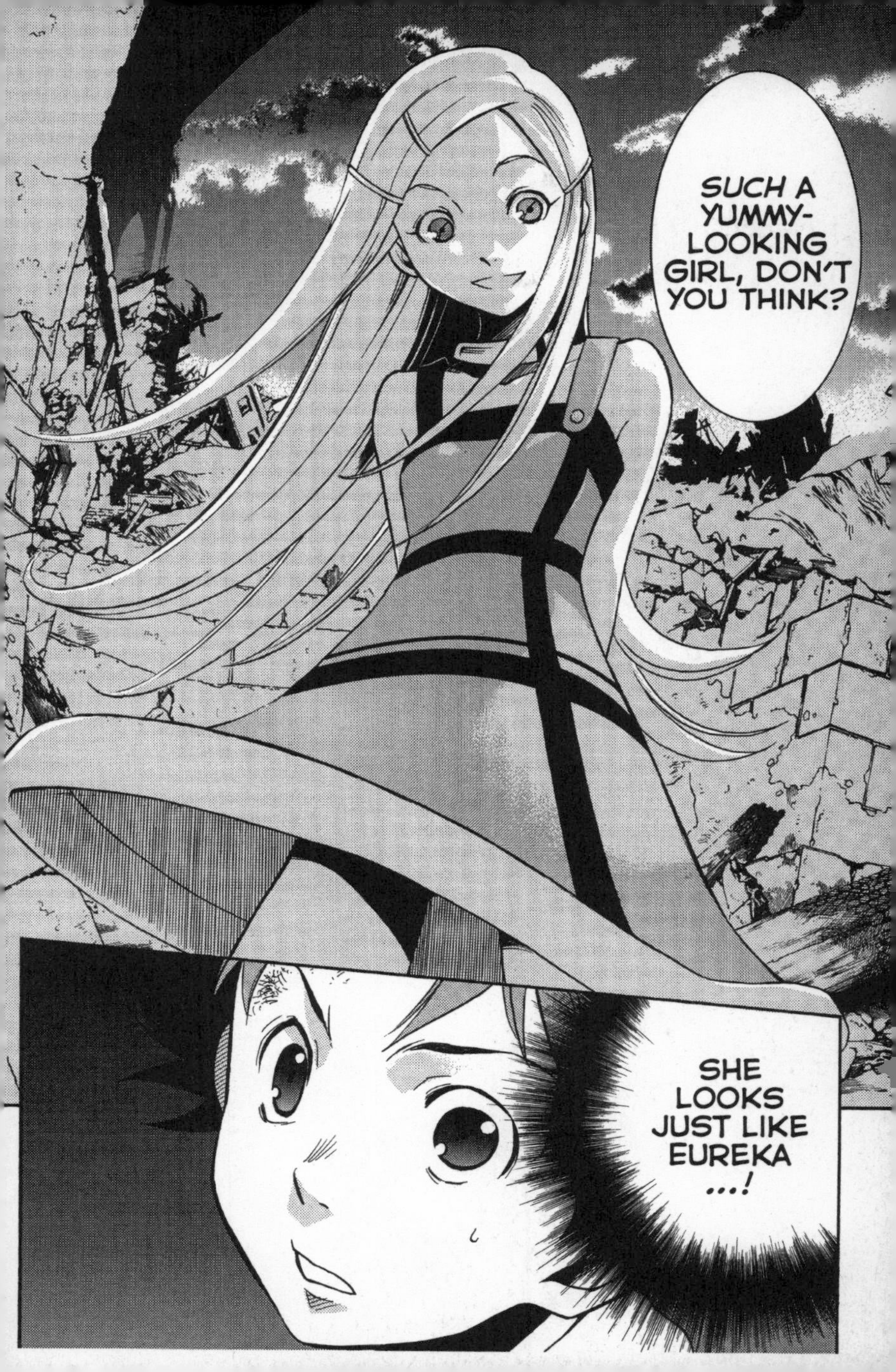
SUCH A YUMMY-LOOKING GIRL, DON'T YOU THINK?
SHE LOOKS JUST LIKE EUREKA ...!

Psalms of
Planet
Eureka seveN

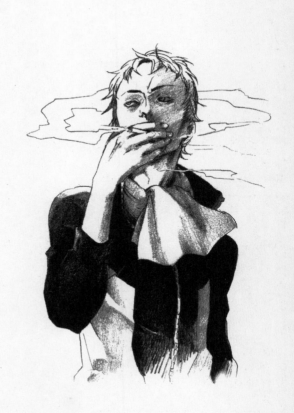

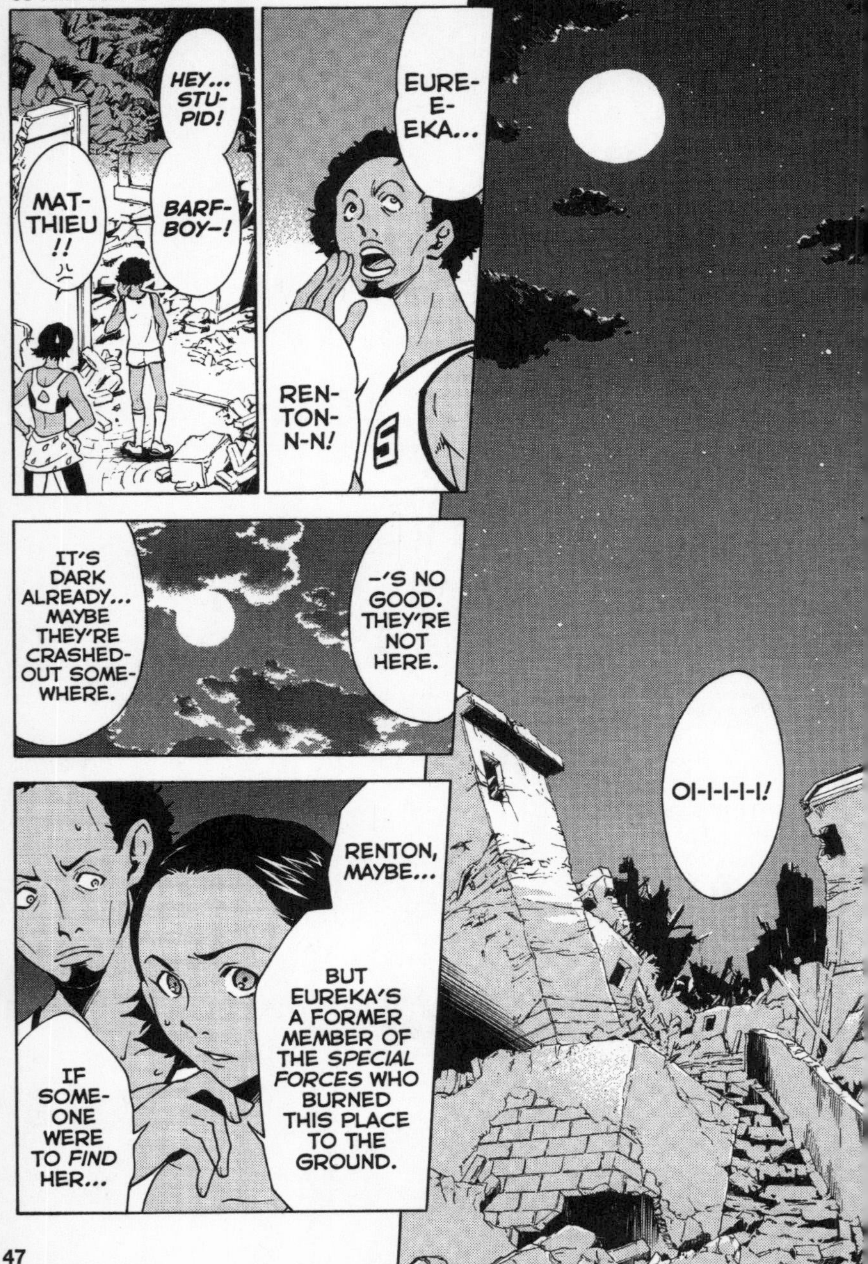
OI-I-I-I-I!
EURE-E-EKA...
RENTON-N-N!
HEY... STUPID!
BARF-BOY–!
MATTHIEU!!
–'S NO GOOD. THEY'RE NOT HERE.
IT'S DARK ALREADY... MAYBE THEY'RE CRASHED-OUT SOMEWHERE.
RENTON, MAYBE...
BUT EUREKA'S A FORMER MEMBER OF THE *SPECIAL FORCES* WHO BURNED THIS PLACE TO THE GROUND.
IF SOMEONE WERE TO *FIND* HER...

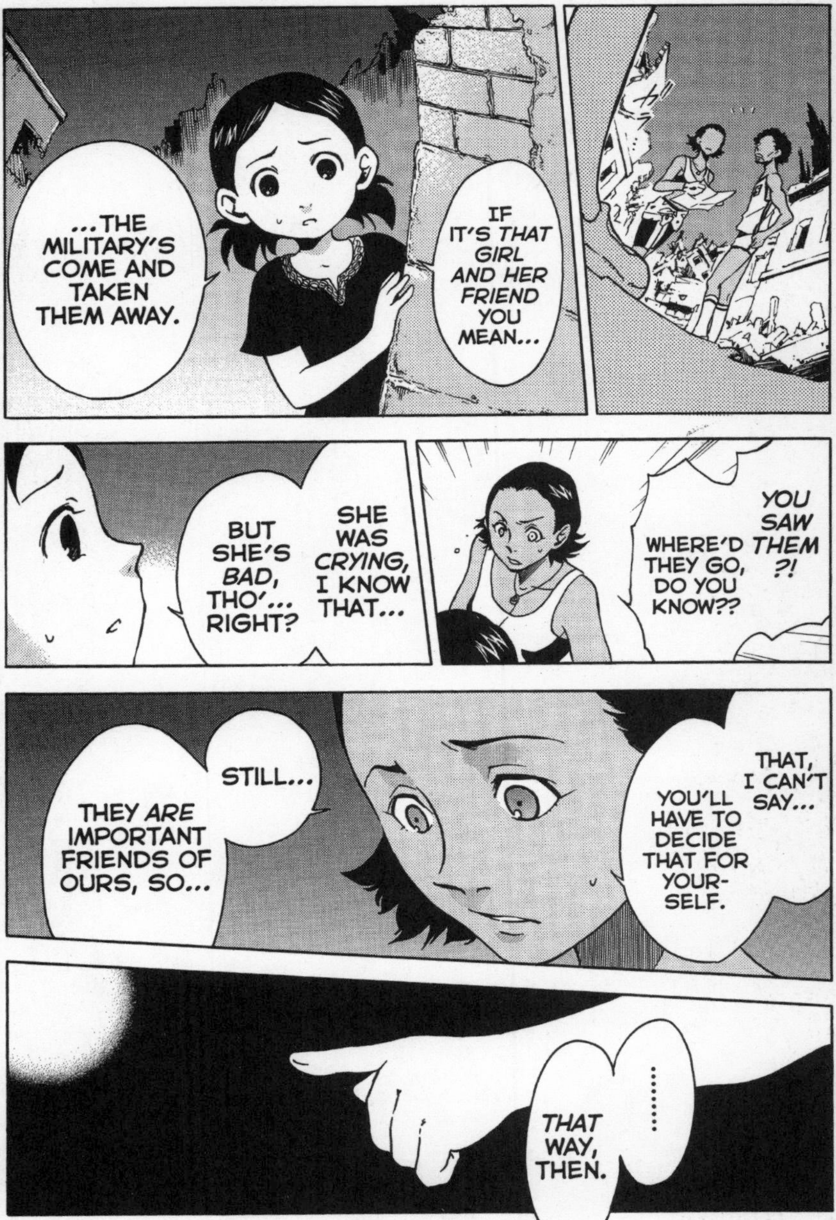
IF IT'S *THAT* GIRL AND HER FRIEND YOU MEAN...
...THE MILITARY'S COME AND TAKEN THEM AWAY.
YOU SAW THEM ?!
WHERE'D THEY GO, DO YOU KNOW??
SHE WAS *CRYING*, I KNOW THAT...
BUT SHE'S *BAD*, THO'... RIGHT?
THAT, I CAN'T SAY...
YOU'LL HAVE TO DECIDE THAT FOR YOUR-SELF.
STILL...
THEY *ARE* IMPORTANT FRIENDS OF OURS, SO...
......
THAT WAY, THEN.

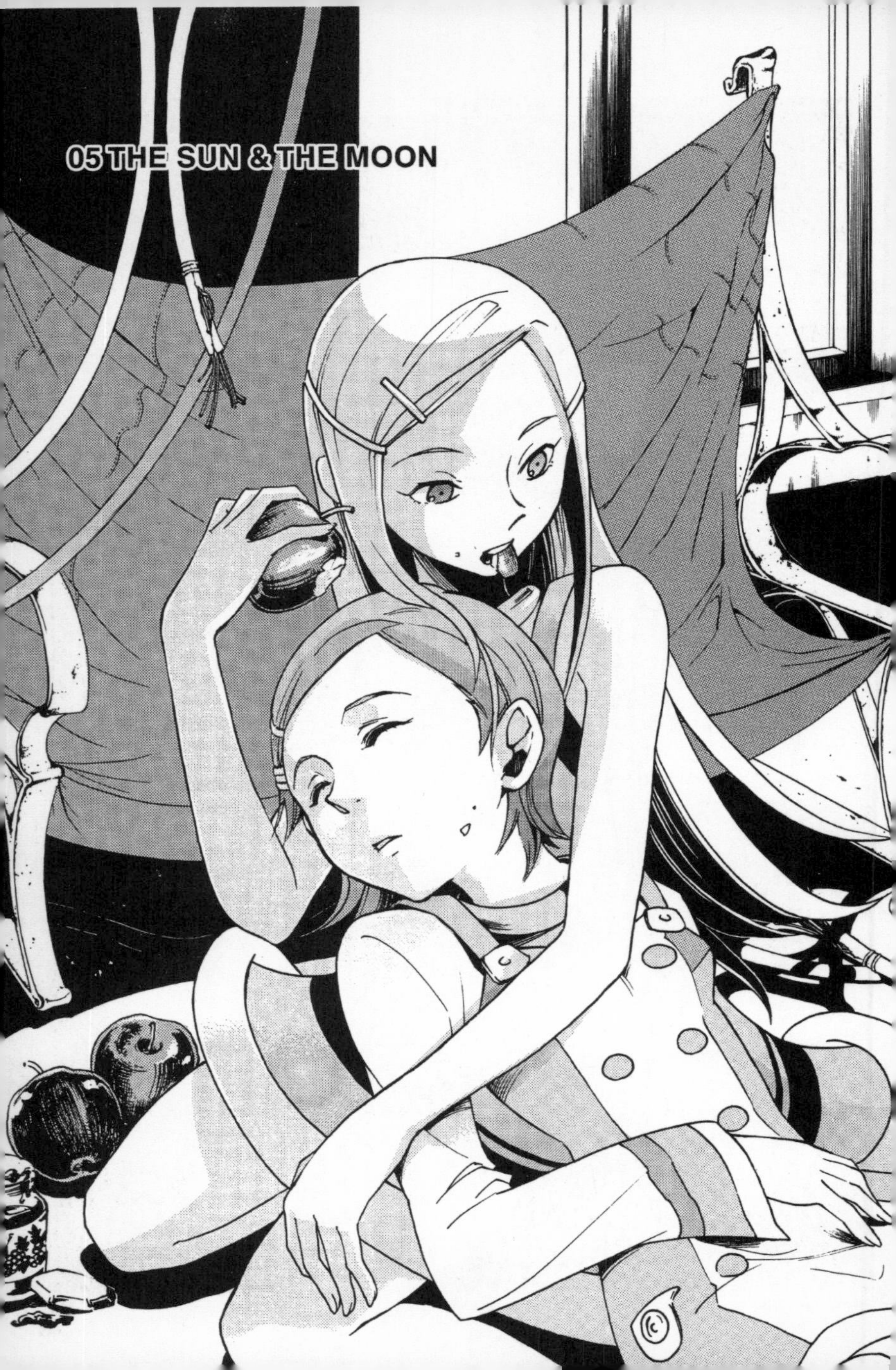
05 THE SUN & THE MOON

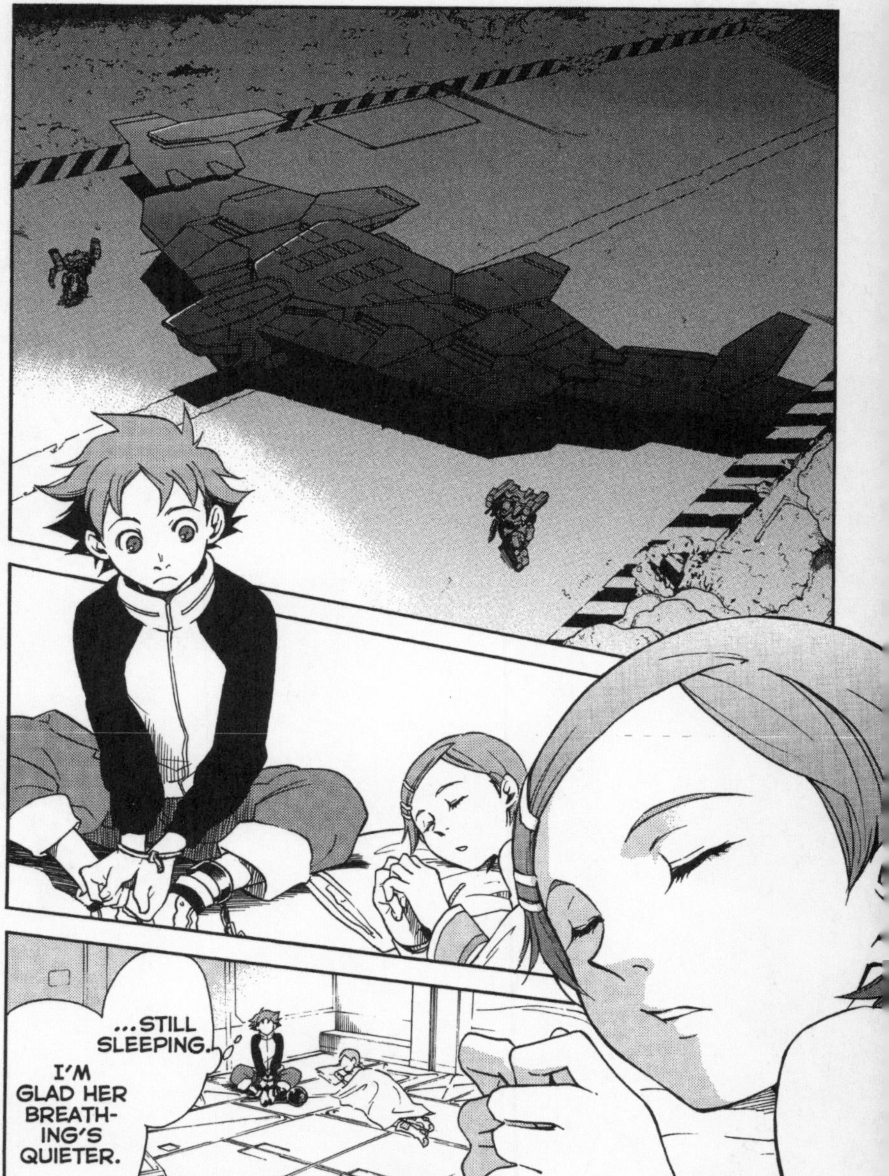
...STILL SLEEPING.
I'M GLAD HER BREATH-ING'S QUIETER.

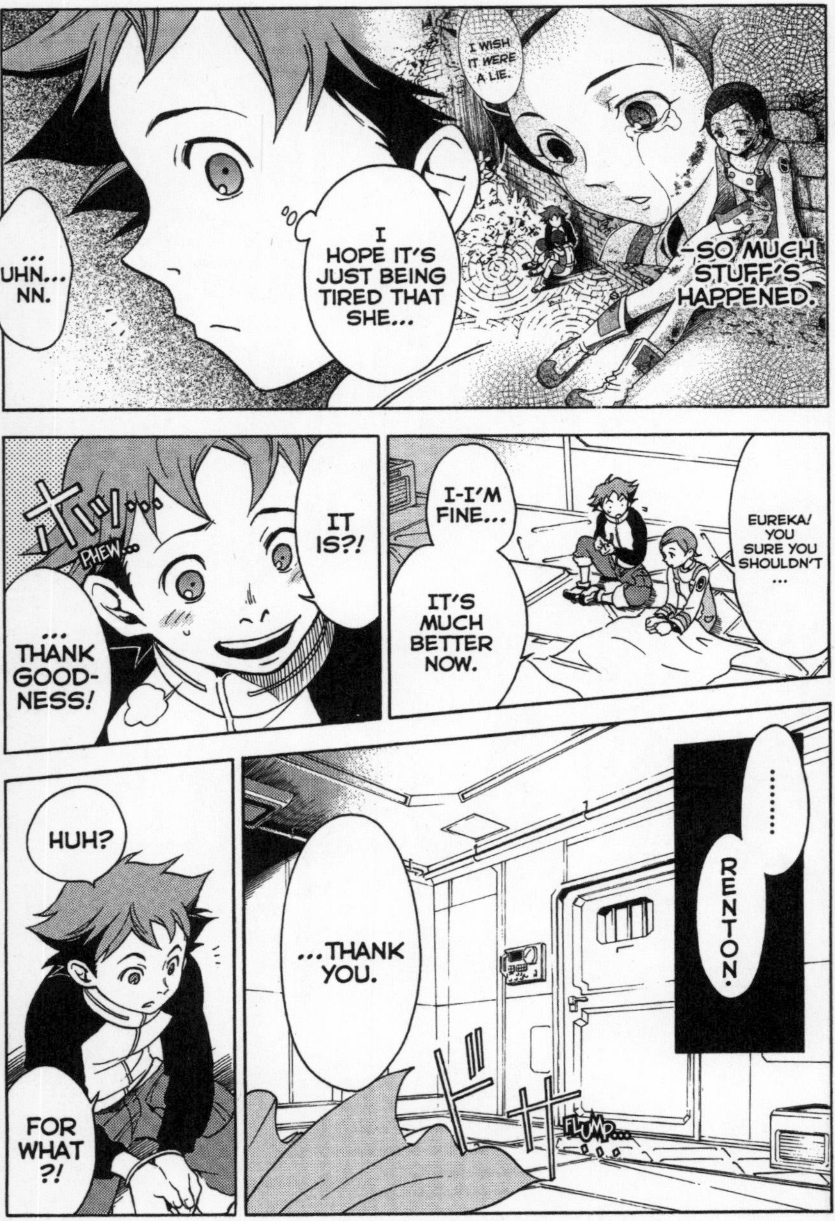
I WISH IT WERE A LIE.
—SO MUCH STUFF'S HAPPENED.
I HOPE IT'S JUST BEING TIRED THAT SHE...
... UHN... NN.
EUREKA! YOU SURE YOU SHOULDN'T ...
I-I'M FINE...
IT'S MUCH BETTER NOW.
IT IS?!
PHEW...
... THANK GOODNESS!
...... RENTON.
...THANK YOU.
FLUMP...
HUH?
FOR WHAT ?!

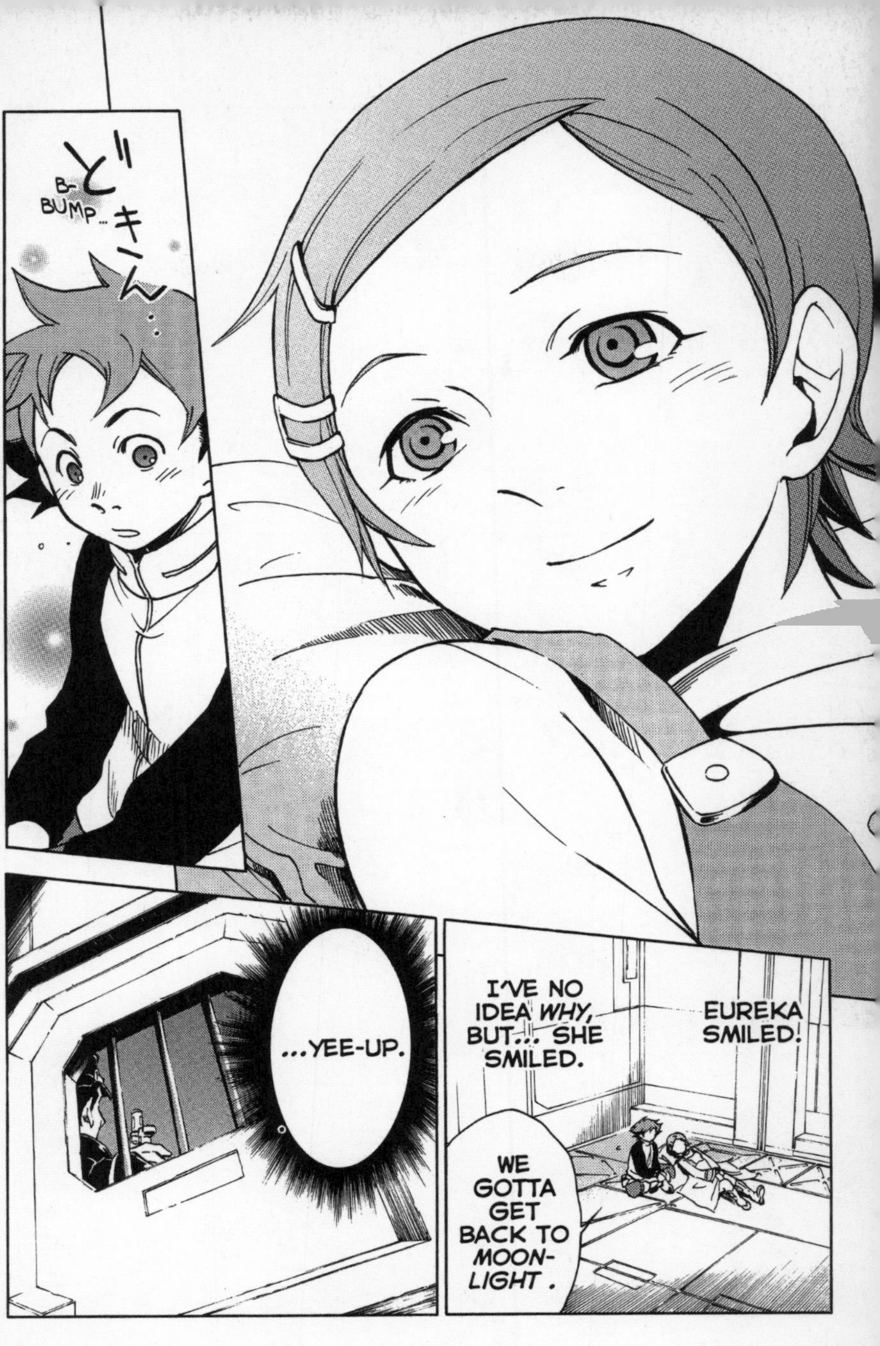
どきん
B-BUMP...
EUREKA SMILED!
I'VE NO IDEA WHY, BUT... SHE SMILED.
WE GOTTA GET BACK TO MOONLIGHT.
...YEE-UP.

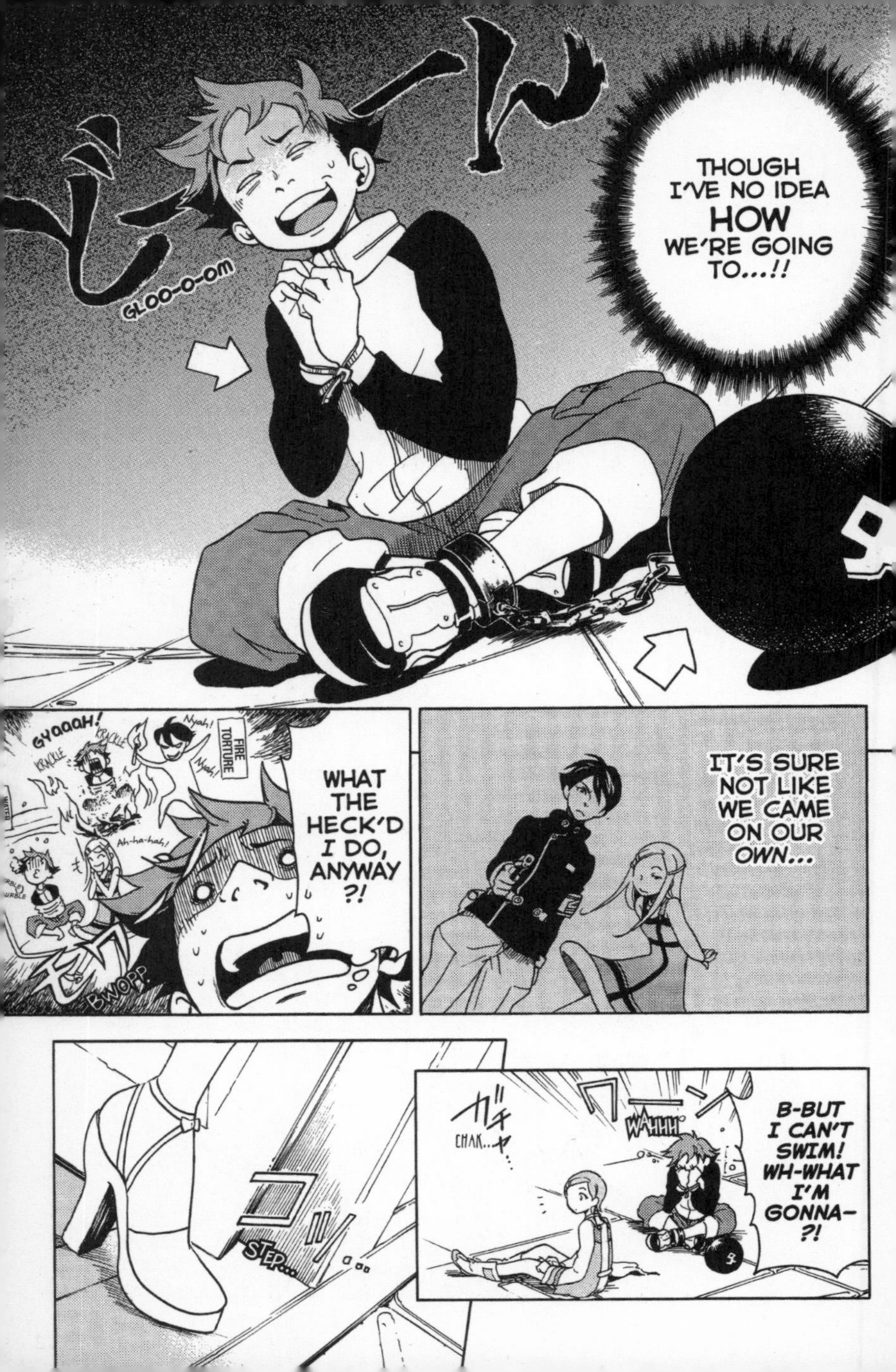
GLOO-O-OM
THOUGH I'VE NO IDEA HOW WE'RE GOING TO...!!
IT'S SURE NOT LIKE WE CAME ON OUR OWN...
WHAT THE HECK'D I DO, ANYWAY ?!
GYAAAH!
KRACKLE
KRACKLE
Nyah!
Nyah!
FIRE TORTURE
Ah-ha-hah!
BWOPP
B-BUT I CAN'T SWIM! WH-WHAT I'M GONNA- ?!
WAHHH
CHAK...
STEP...

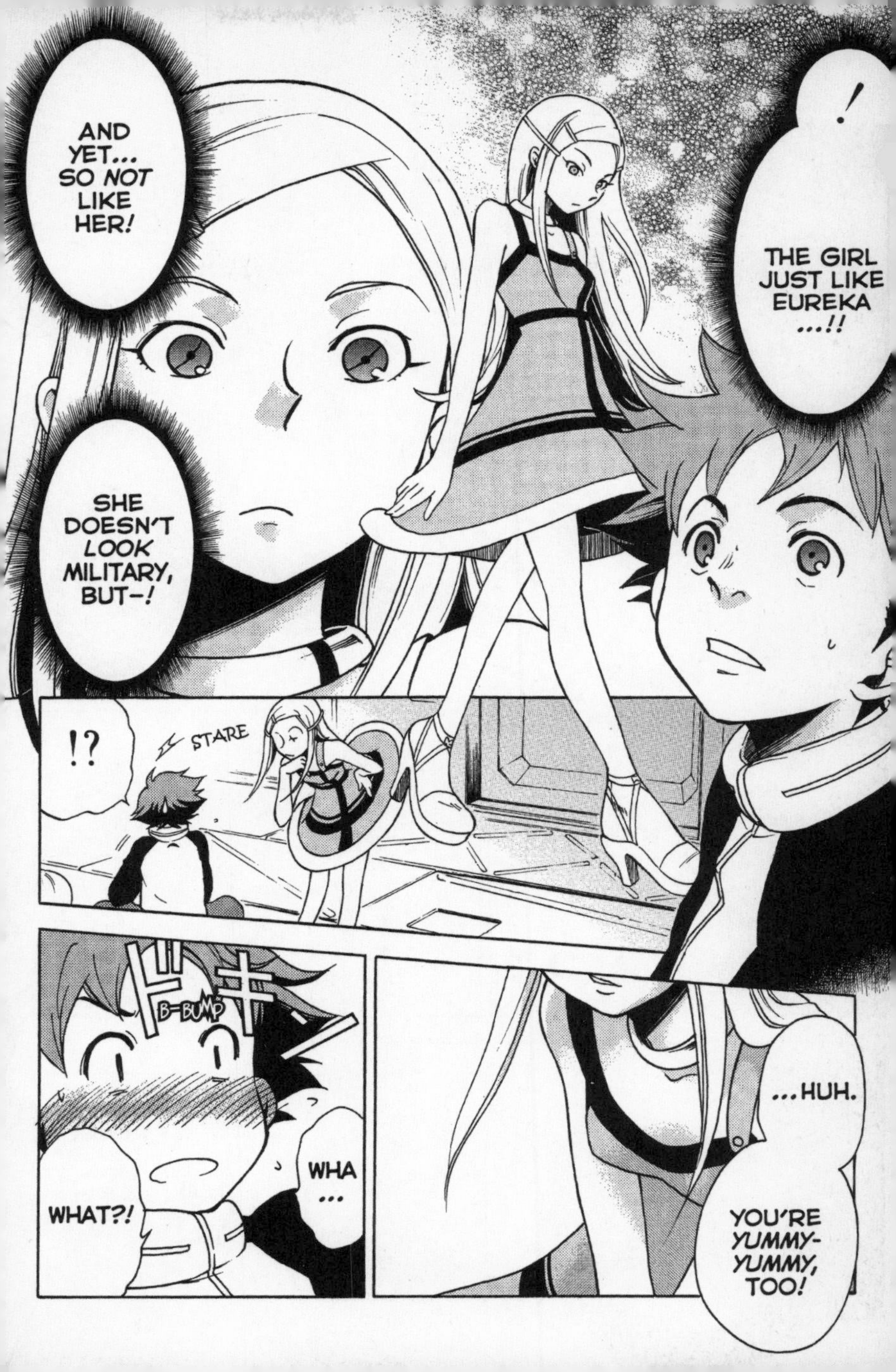
!
THE GIRL JUST LIKE EUREKA ...!!
AND YET... SO *NOT* LIKE HER!
SHE DOESN'T *LOOK* MILITARY, BUT-!
STARE
!?
...HUH.
YOU'RE *YUMMY-YUMMY,* TOO!
B-BUMP
WHA ...
WHAT?!

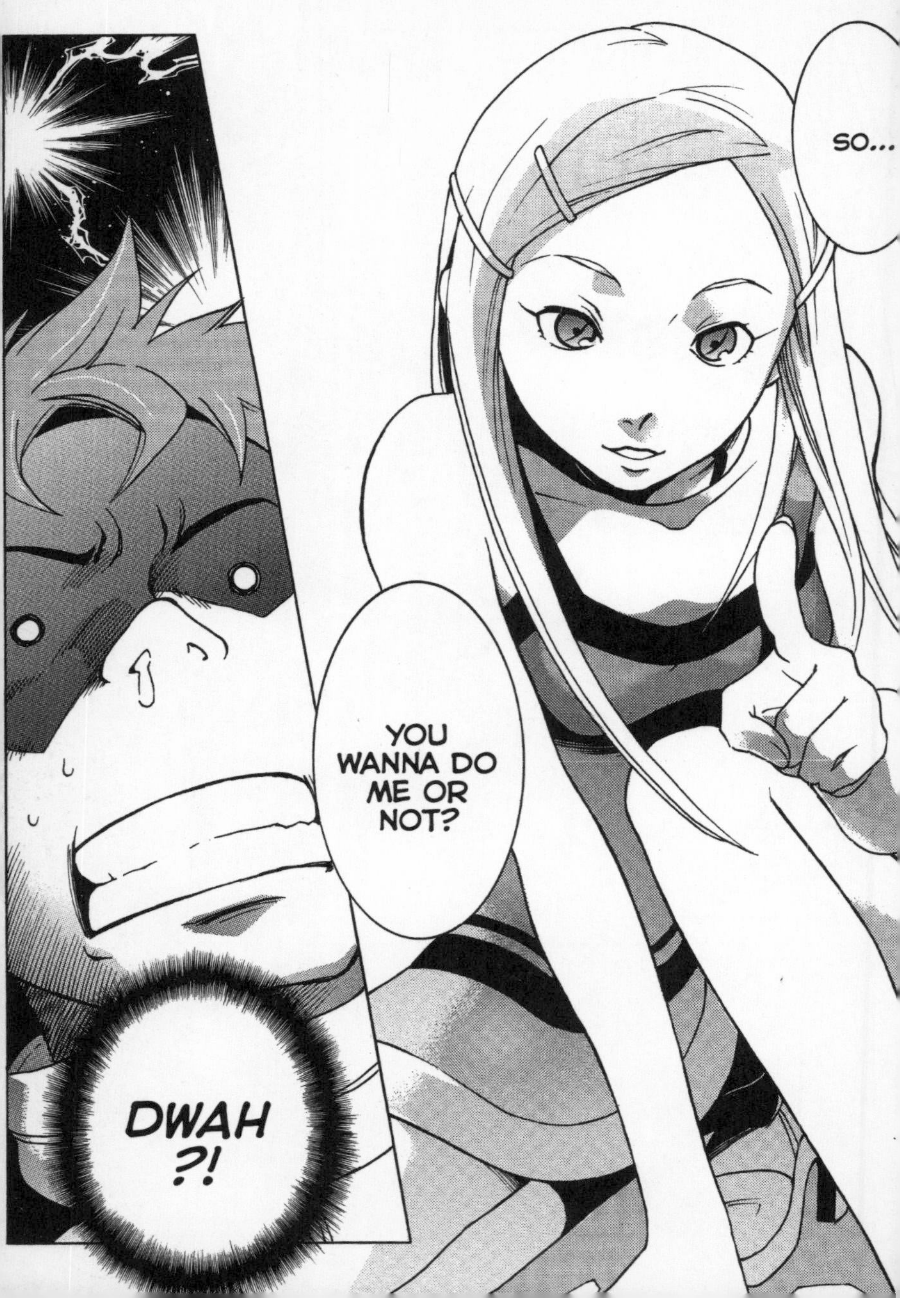
SO...
YOU WANNA DO ME OR NOT?
DWAH ?!

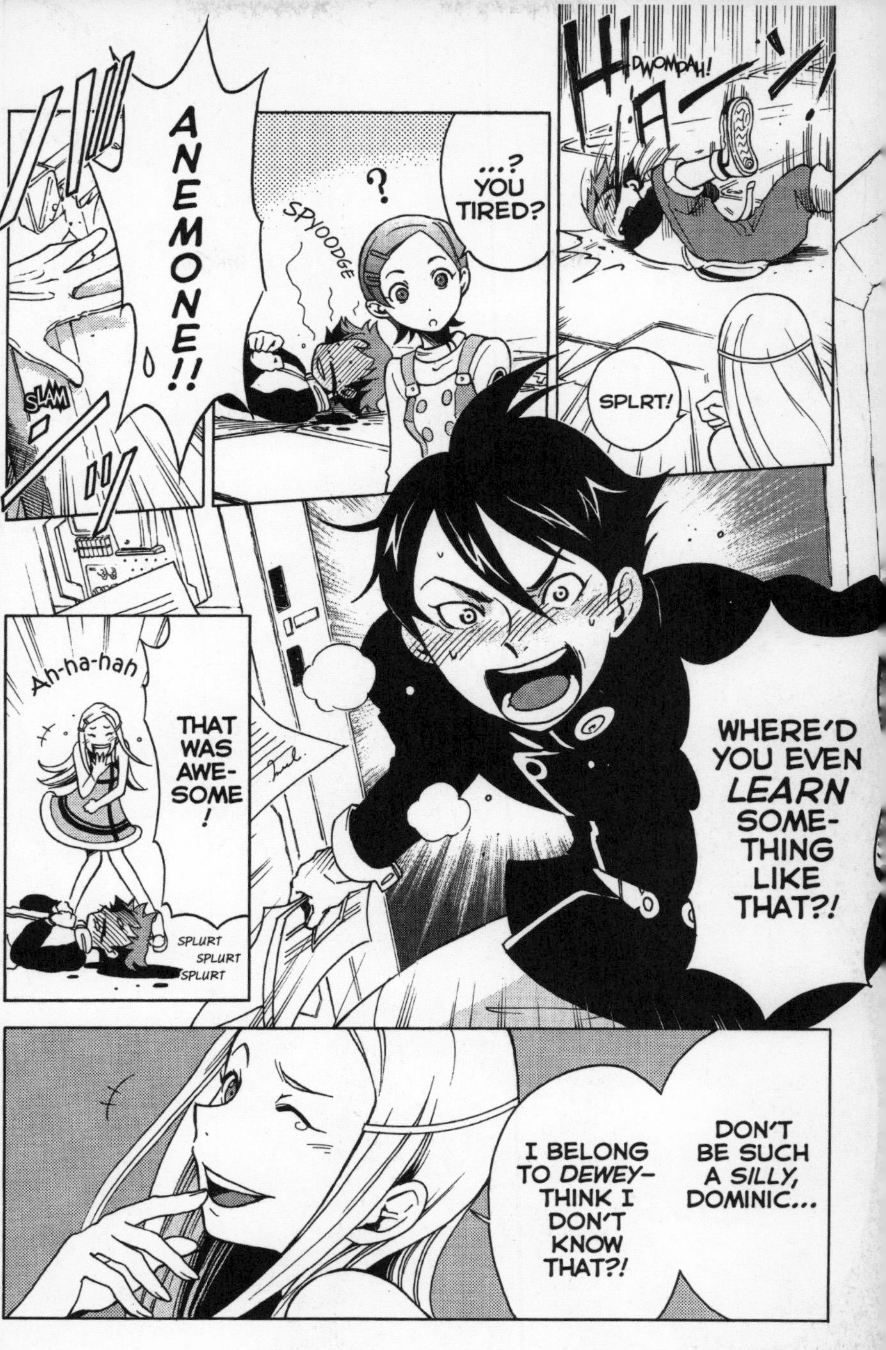
HI-A—!
DWOMPAH!
SPLRT!
?
SPYOODGE
...? YOU TIRED?
ANEMONE!!
SLAM
WHERE'D YOU EVEN LEARN SOMETHING LIKE THAT?!
Ah-ha-hah
THAT WAS AWE-SOME!
SPLURT SPLURT SPLURT
DON'T BE SUCH A SILLY, DOMINIC...
I BELONG TO DEWEY— THINK I DON'T KNOW THAT?!

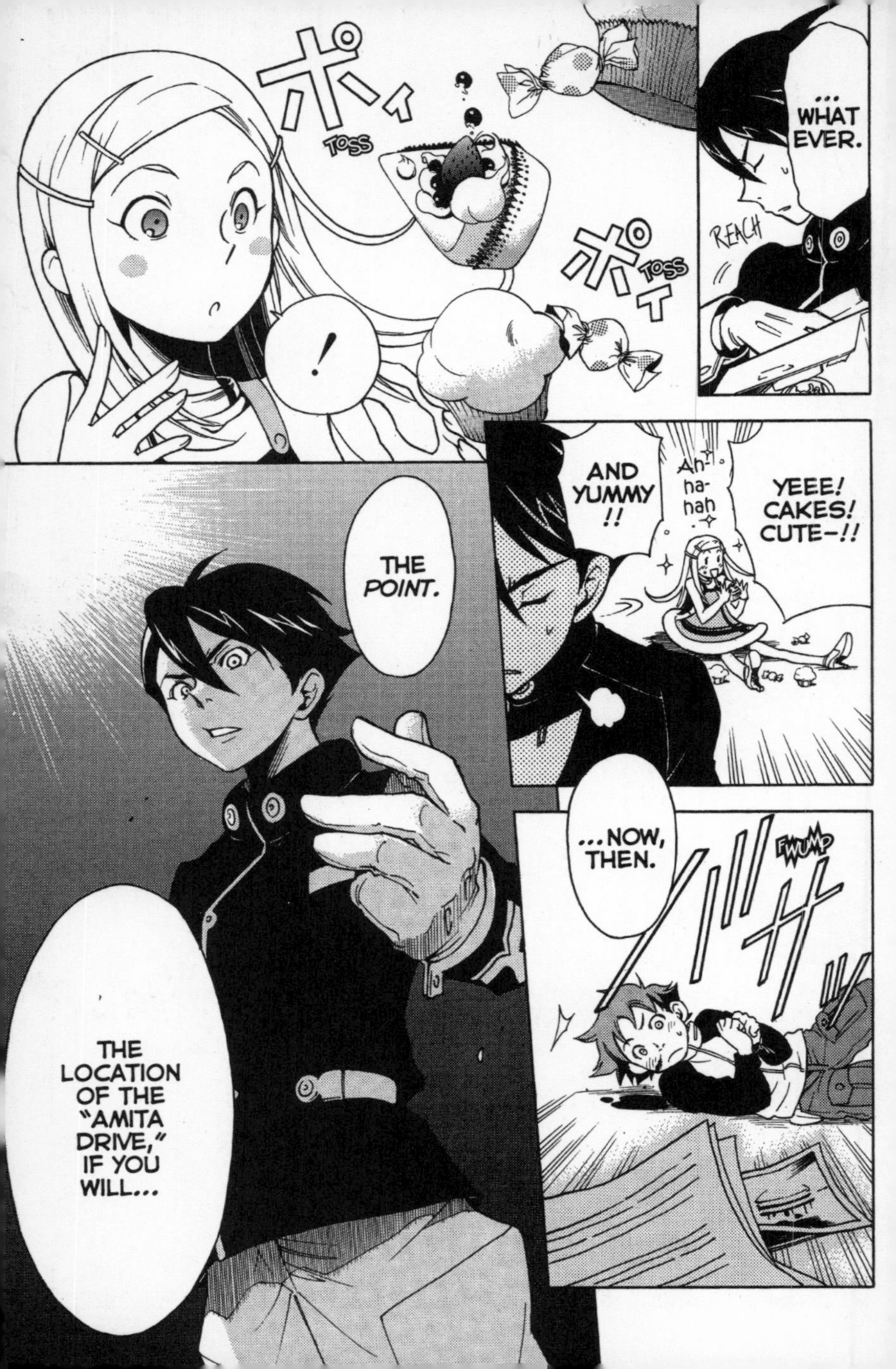

...WHAT EVER.
REACH
ポイ
TOSS
ポイ
TOSS
!
YEEE! CAKES! CUTE-!!
Ah-ha-hah
AND YUMMY!!
...NOW, THEN.
FWUMP
THE POINT.
THE LOCATION OF THE "AMITA DRIVE," IF YOU WILL...

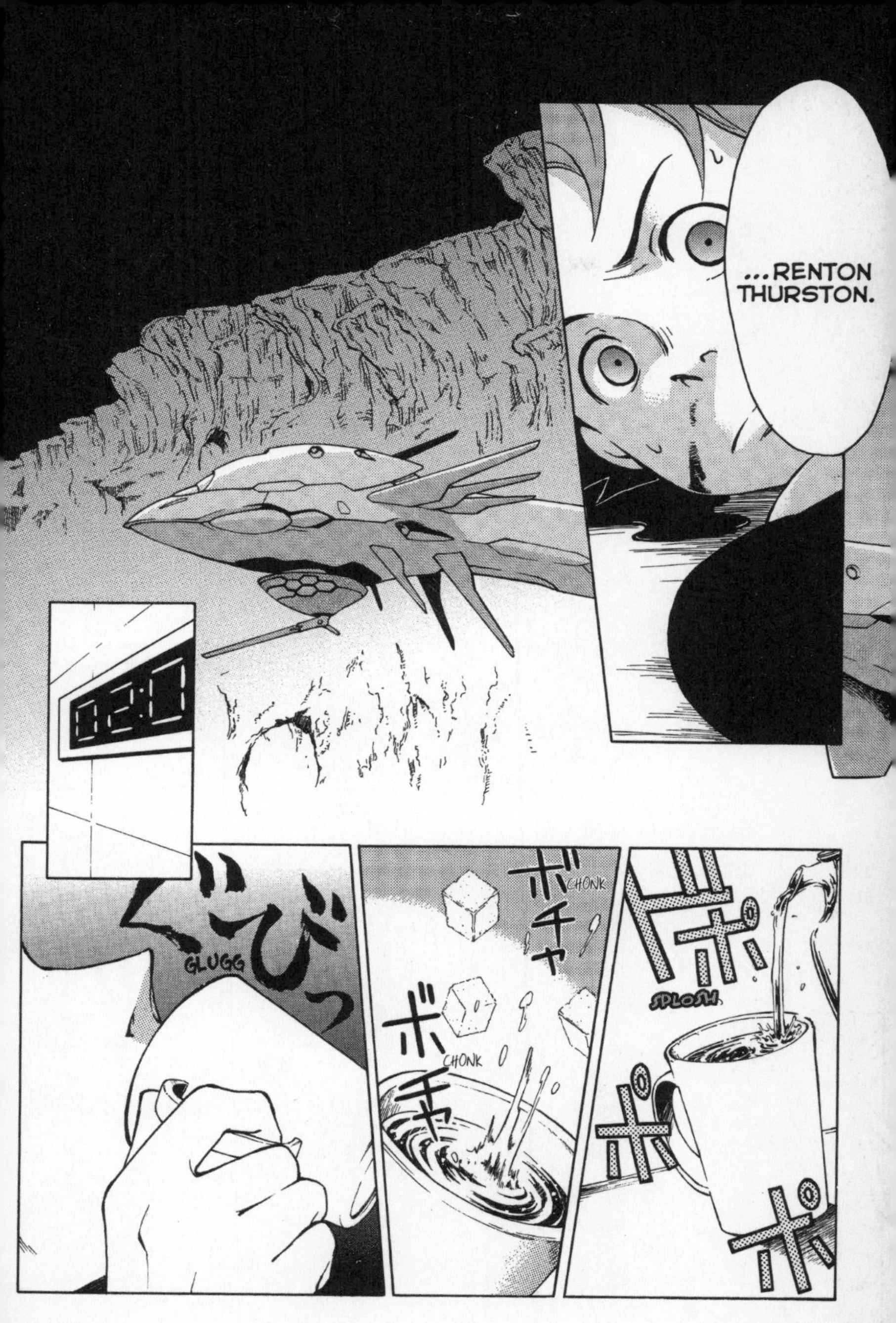
...RENTON THURSTON.
ドポ!
SPLOSH
ポポ
ボチャ
CHONK
ボチャ
CHONK
ぐびっ
GLUGG

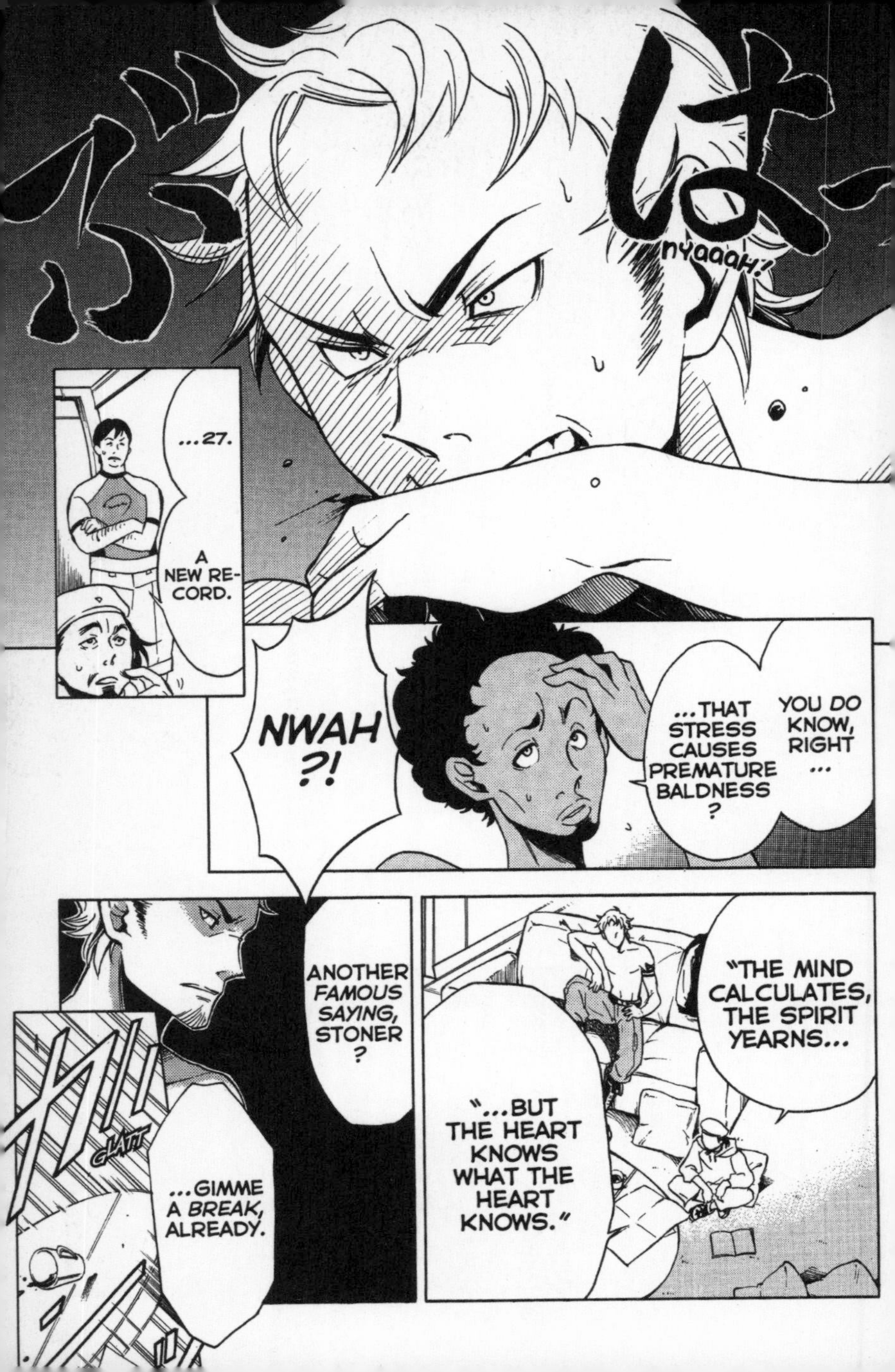
NYAAAH!
...27.
A NEW RE-CORD.
YOU DO KNOW, RIGHT ...
...THAT STRESS CAUSES PREMATURE BALDNESS ?
NWAH ?!
"THE MIND CALCULATES, THE SPIRIT YEARNS...
"...BUT THE HEART KNOWS WHAT THE HEART KNOWS."
ANOTHER FAMOUS SAYING, STONER ?
GLATT
...GIMME A BREAK, ALREADY.

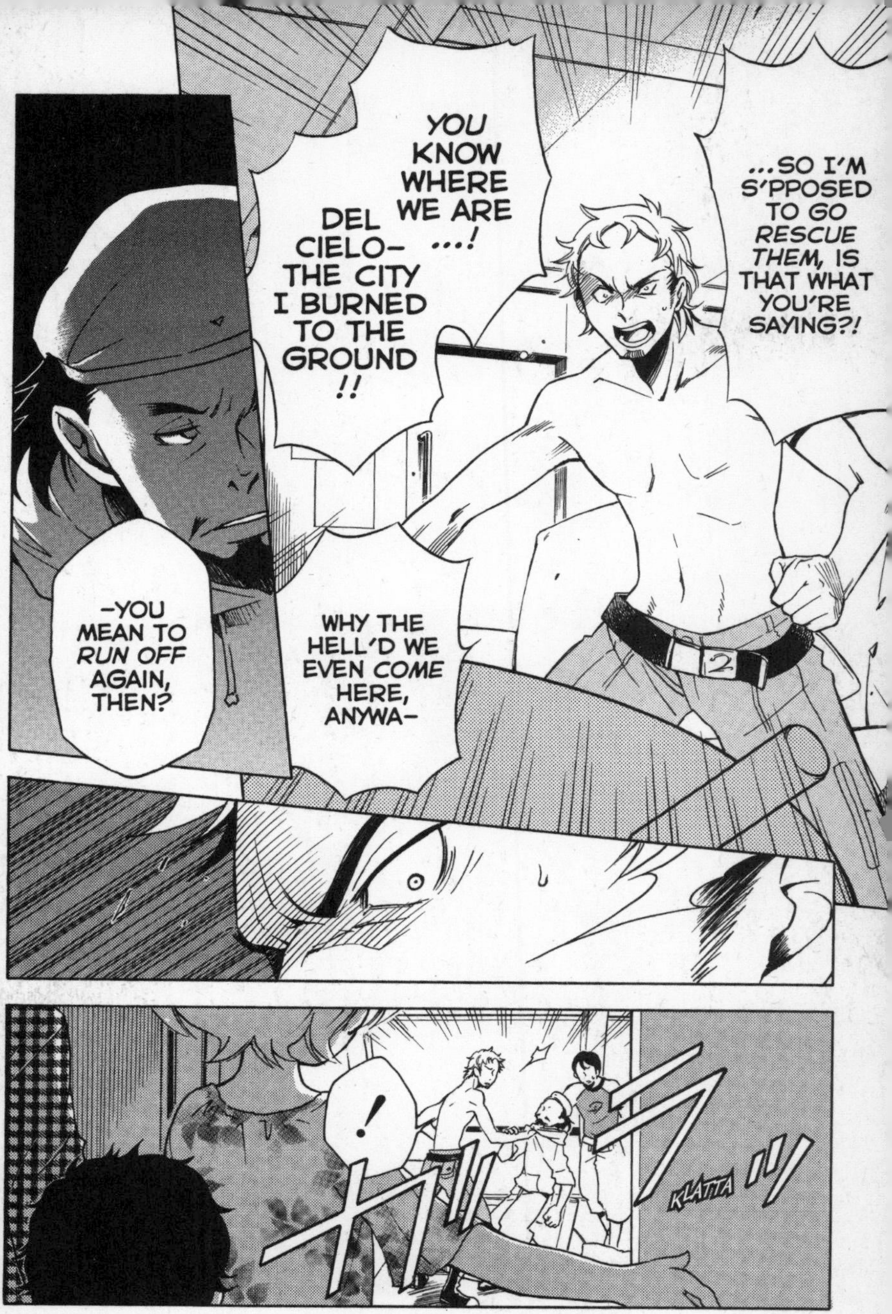
...SO I'M S'PPOSED TO GO RESCUE THEM, IS THAT WHAT YOU'RE SAYING?!
YOU KNOW WHERE WE ARE ...!
DEL CIELO— THE CITY I BURNED TO THE GROUND !!
WHY THE HELL'D WE EVEN COME HERE, ANYWA—
—YOU MEAN TO RUN OFF AGAIN, THEN?
!
KLATTA

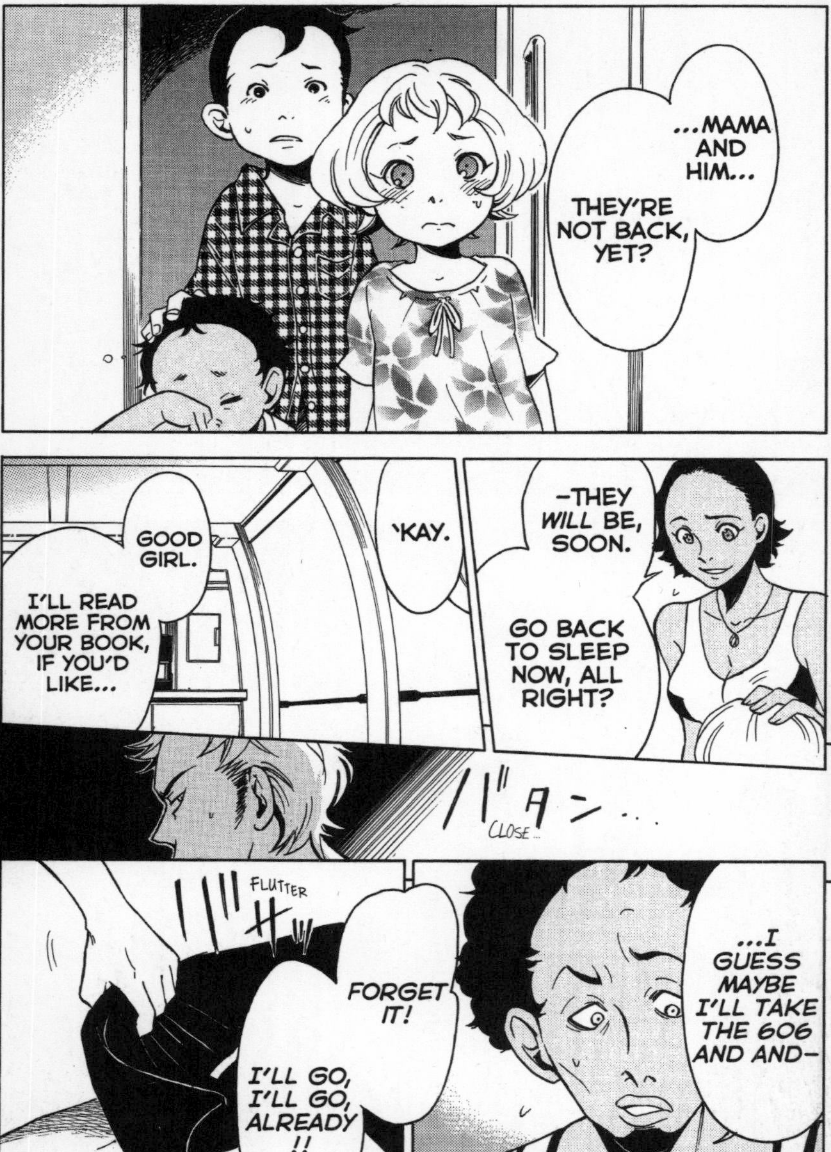
...MAMA AND HIM...
THEY'RE NOT BACK, YET?
—THEY WILL BE, SOON.
GO BACK TO SLEEP NOW, ALL RIGHT?
'KAY.
GOOD GIRL.
I'LL READ MORE FROM YOUR BOOK, IF YOU'D LIKE...
バタン...
CLOSE...
...I GUESS MAYBE I'LL TAKE THE 606 AND AND—
FLUTTER
FORGET IT!
I'LL GO, I'LL GO, ALREADY!!

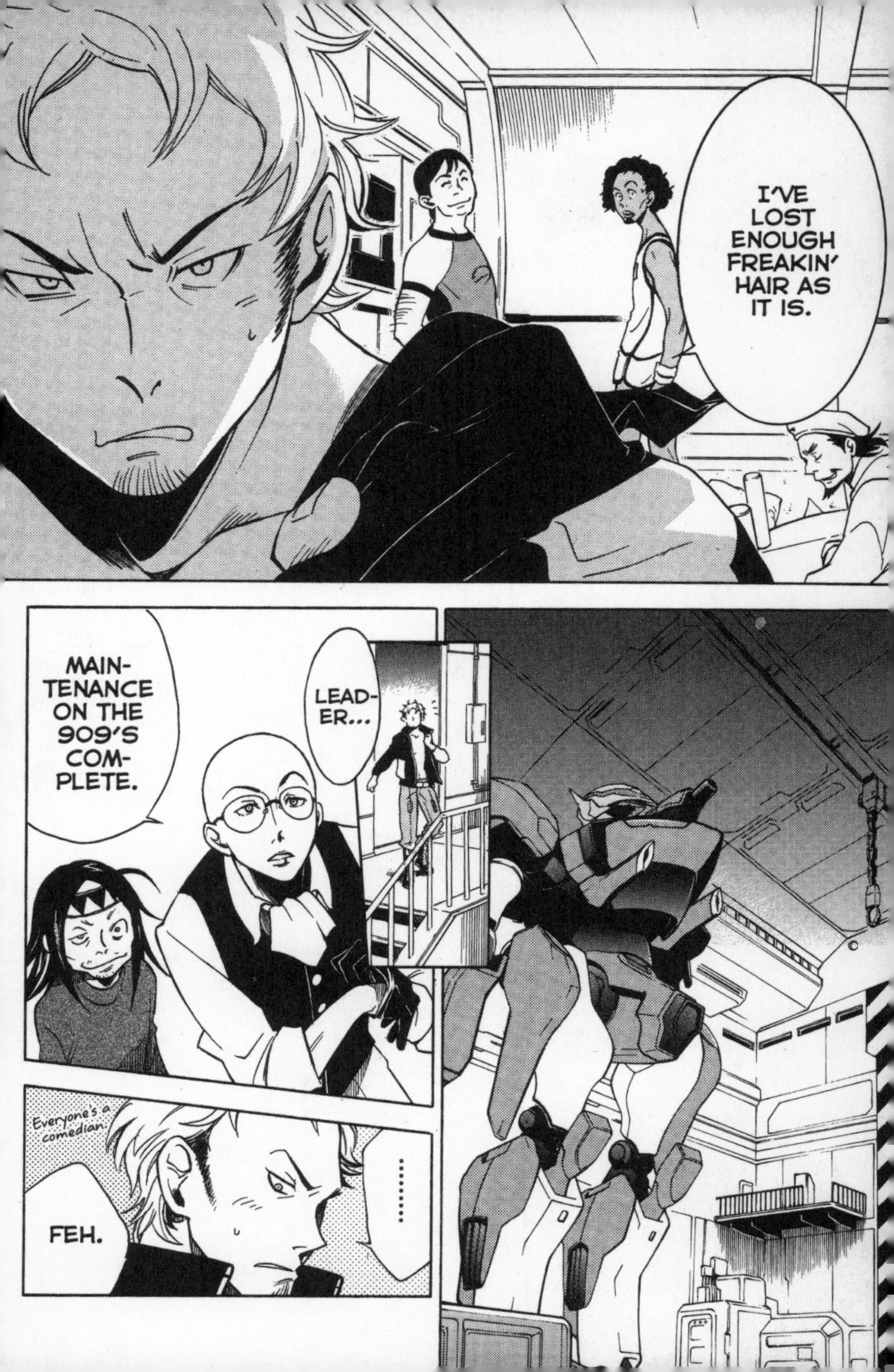
I'VE LOST ENOUGH FREAKIN' HAIR AS IT IS.
LEAD-ER...
MAIN-TENANCE ON THE 909'S COM-PLETE.
......
Everyone's a comedian.
FEH.

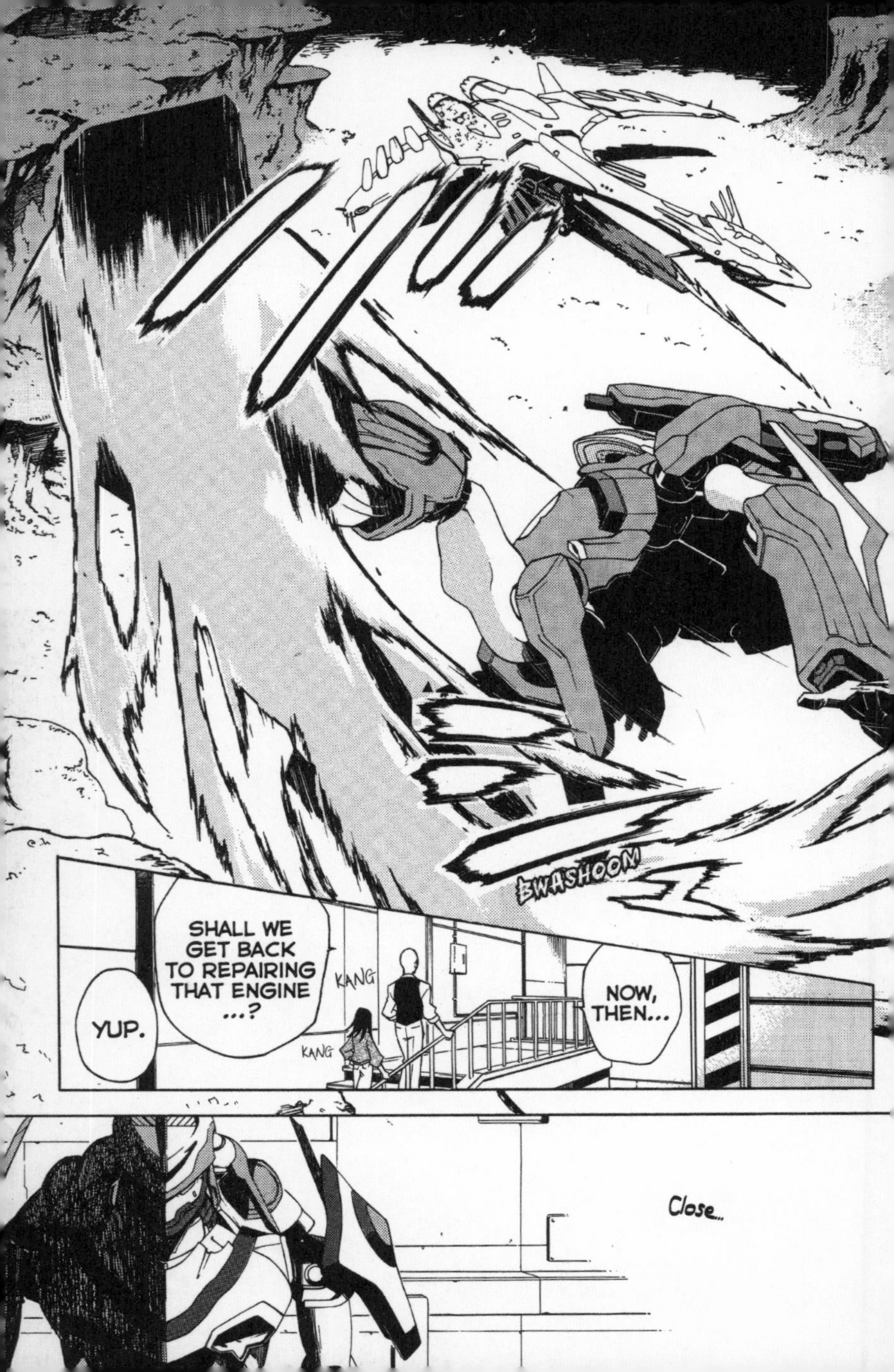
BWASHOOM
NOW, THEN...
KANG
SHALL WE GET BACK TO REPAIRING THAT ENGINE ...?
KANG
YUP.
Close...

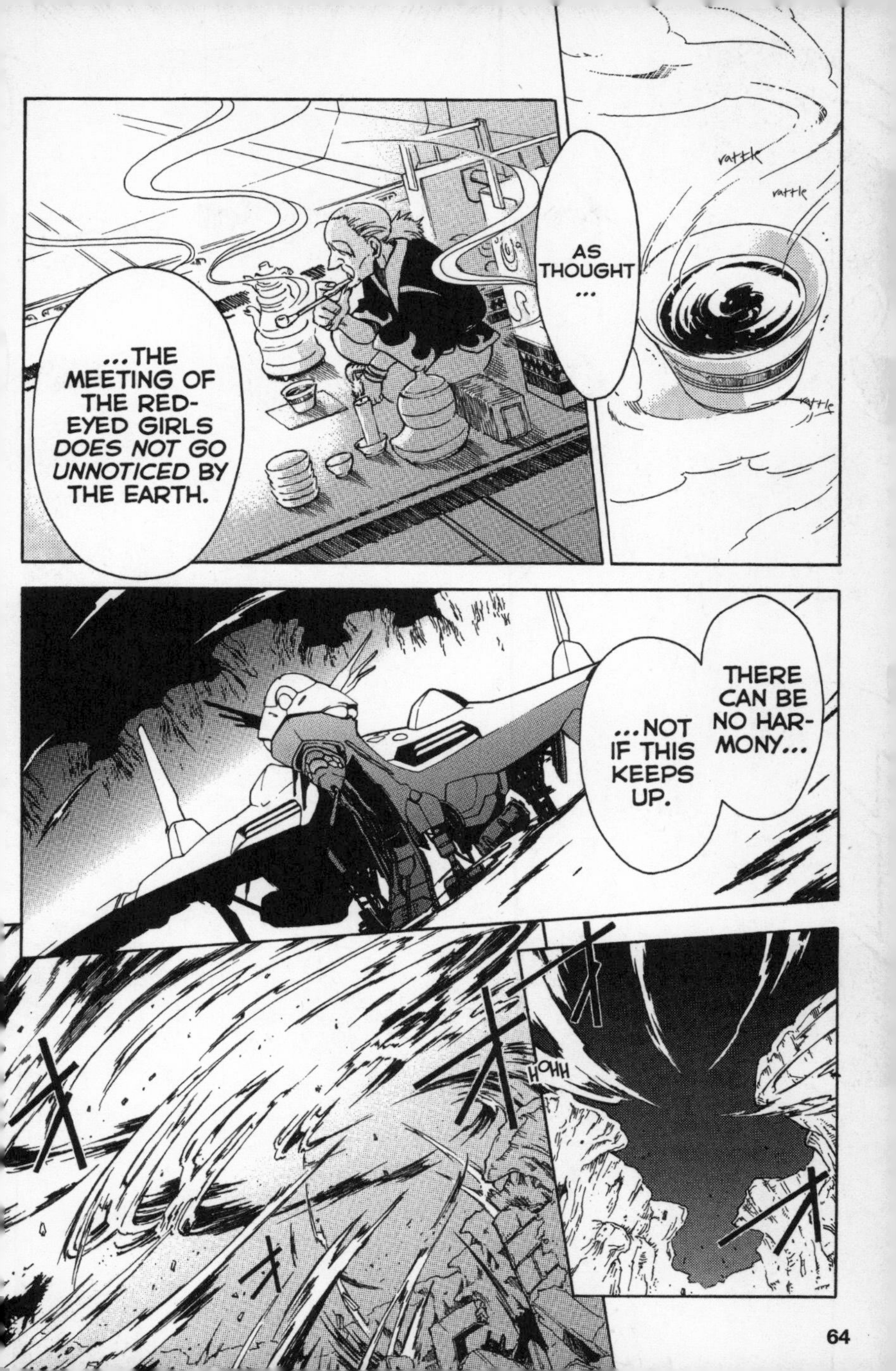

rattle
rattle
rattle
AS THOUGHT ...
...THE MEETING OF THE RED-EYED GIRLS *DOES NOT GO UNNOTICED* BY THE EARTH.
THERE CAN BE NO HARMONY...
...NOT IF THIS KEEPS UP.
HOHH

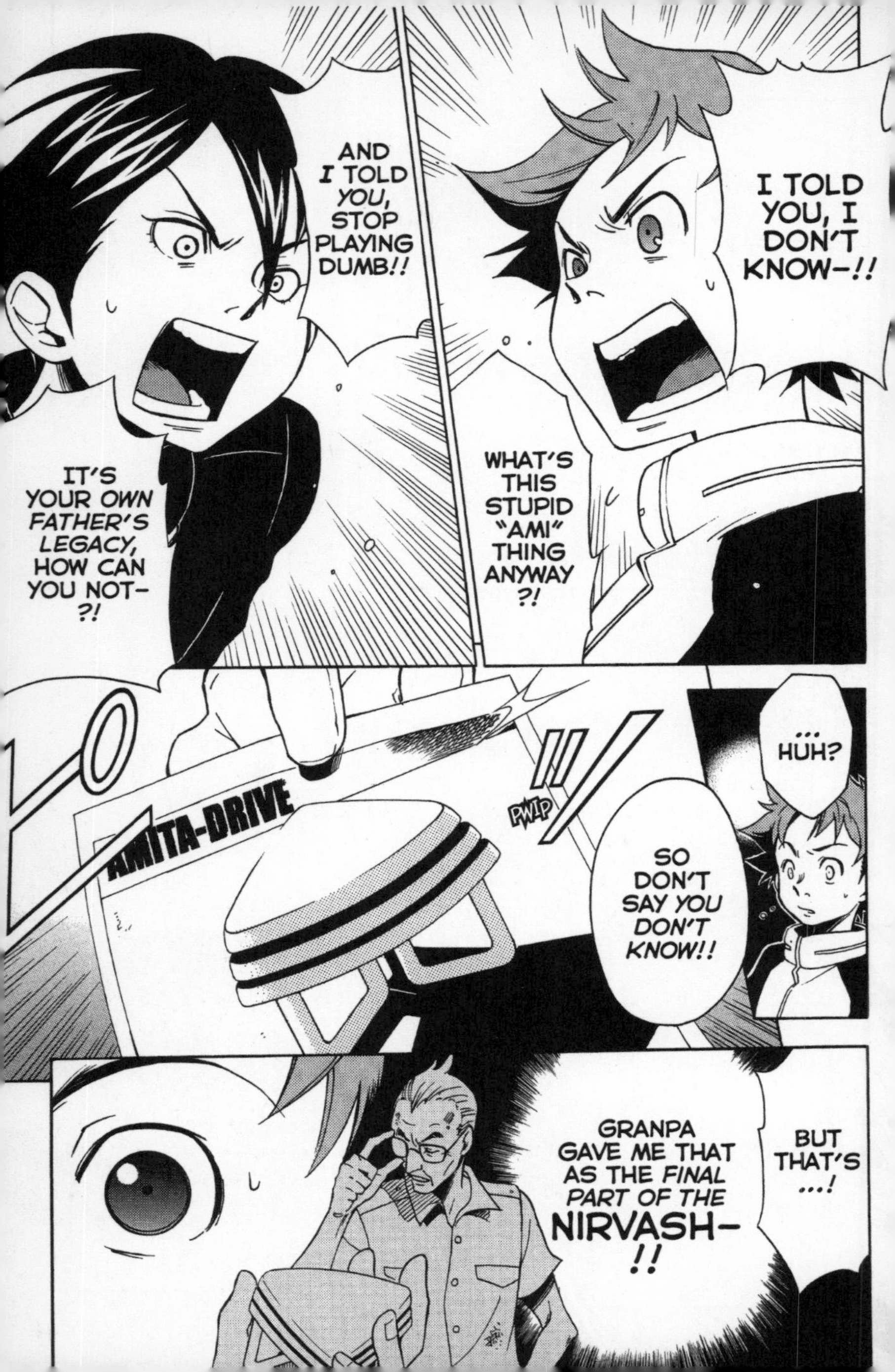
I TOLD YOU, I DON'T KNOW-!!
WHAT'S THIS STUPID "AMI" THING ANYWAY?!
AND *I* TOLD *YOU*, STOP PLAYING DUMB!!
IT'S YOUR *OWN FATHER'S LEGACY*, HOW CAN YOU NOT-?!
... HUH?
SO DON'T SAY *YOU* DON'T KNOW!!
PWIP
AMITA-DRIVE
BUT THAT'S ...!
GRANPA GAVE ME THAT AS THE *FINAL PART OF THE* NIRVASH-!!

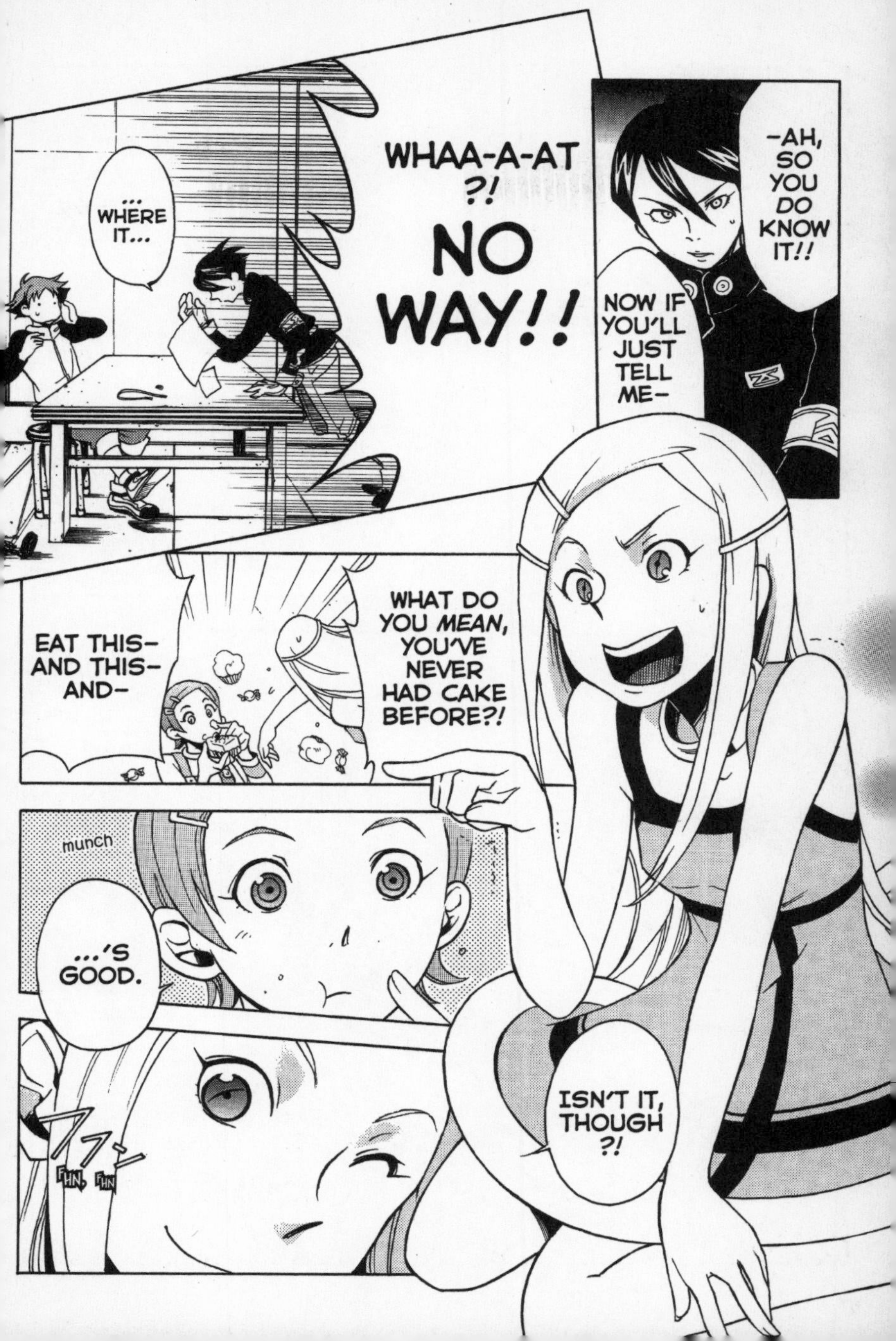
-AH, SO YOU DO KNOW IT!!
NOW IF YOU'LL JUST TELL ME-
WHAA-A-AT ?! NO WAY!!
... WHERE IT...
WHAT DO YOU MEAN, YOU'VE NEVER HAD CAKE BEFORE?!
EAT THIS- AND THIS- AND-
munch
...'S GOOD.
ISN'T IT, THOUGH ?!
FHN, FHN

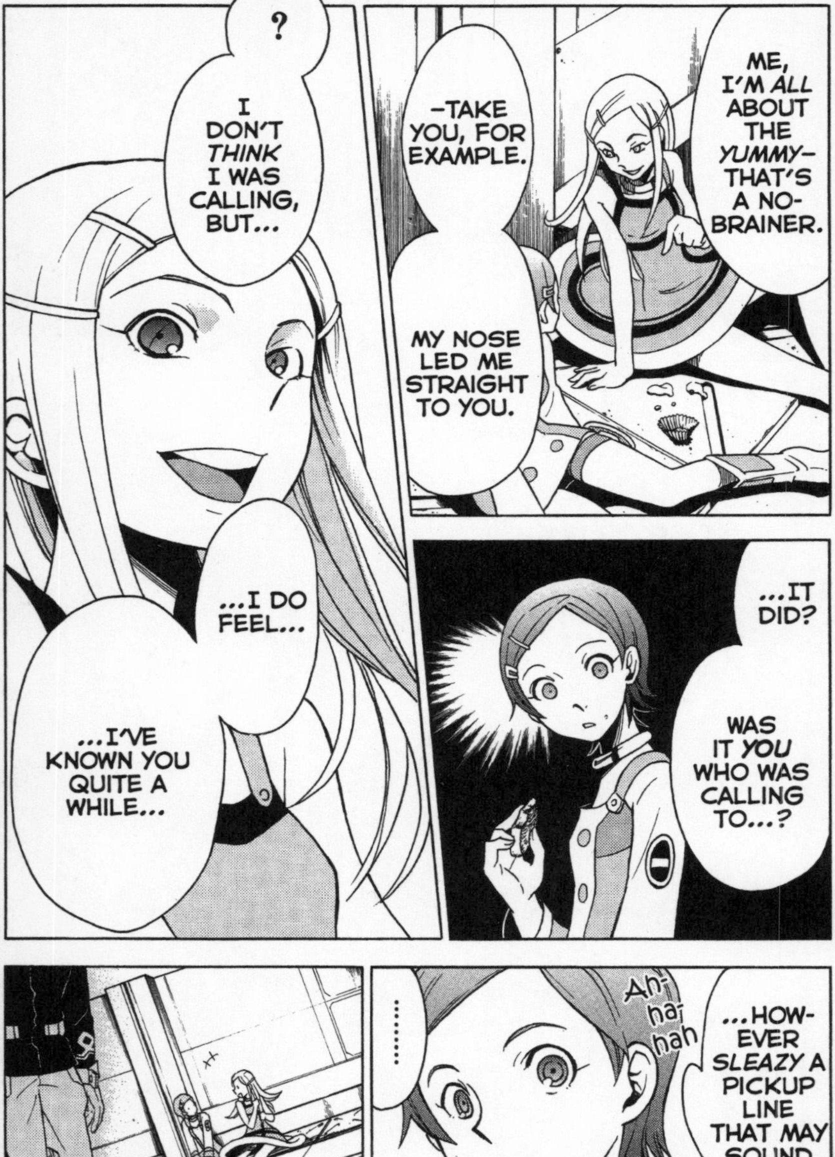
ME, I'M *ALL* ABOUT THE *YUMMY*—THAT'S A NO-BRAINER.
—TAKE YOU, FOR EXAMPLE.
MY NOSE LED ME STRAIGHT TO YOU.
...IT DID?
WAS IT *YOU* WHO WAS CALLING TO...?
?
I DON'T *THINK* I WAS CALLING, BUT...
...I DO FEEL...
...I'VE KNOWN YOU QUITE A WHILE...
...HOW-EVER *SLEAZY* A PICKUP LINE THAT MAY SOUND !!
Ah-ha-hah
......

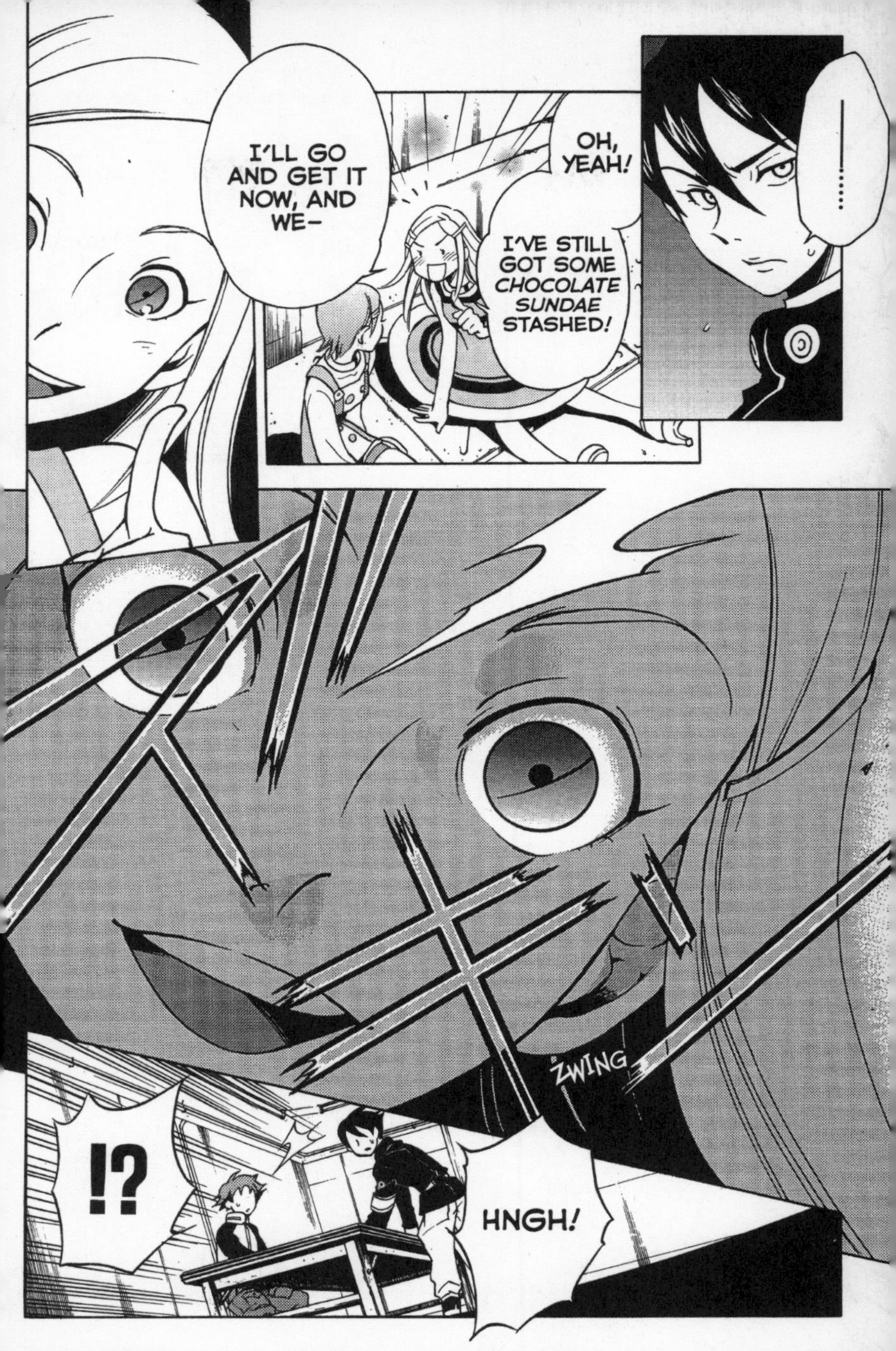
......
OH, YEAH!
I'VE STILL GOT SOME *CHOCOLATE SUNDAE* STASHED!
I'LL GO AND GET IT NOW, AND WE–
ZWING
HNGH!
!?

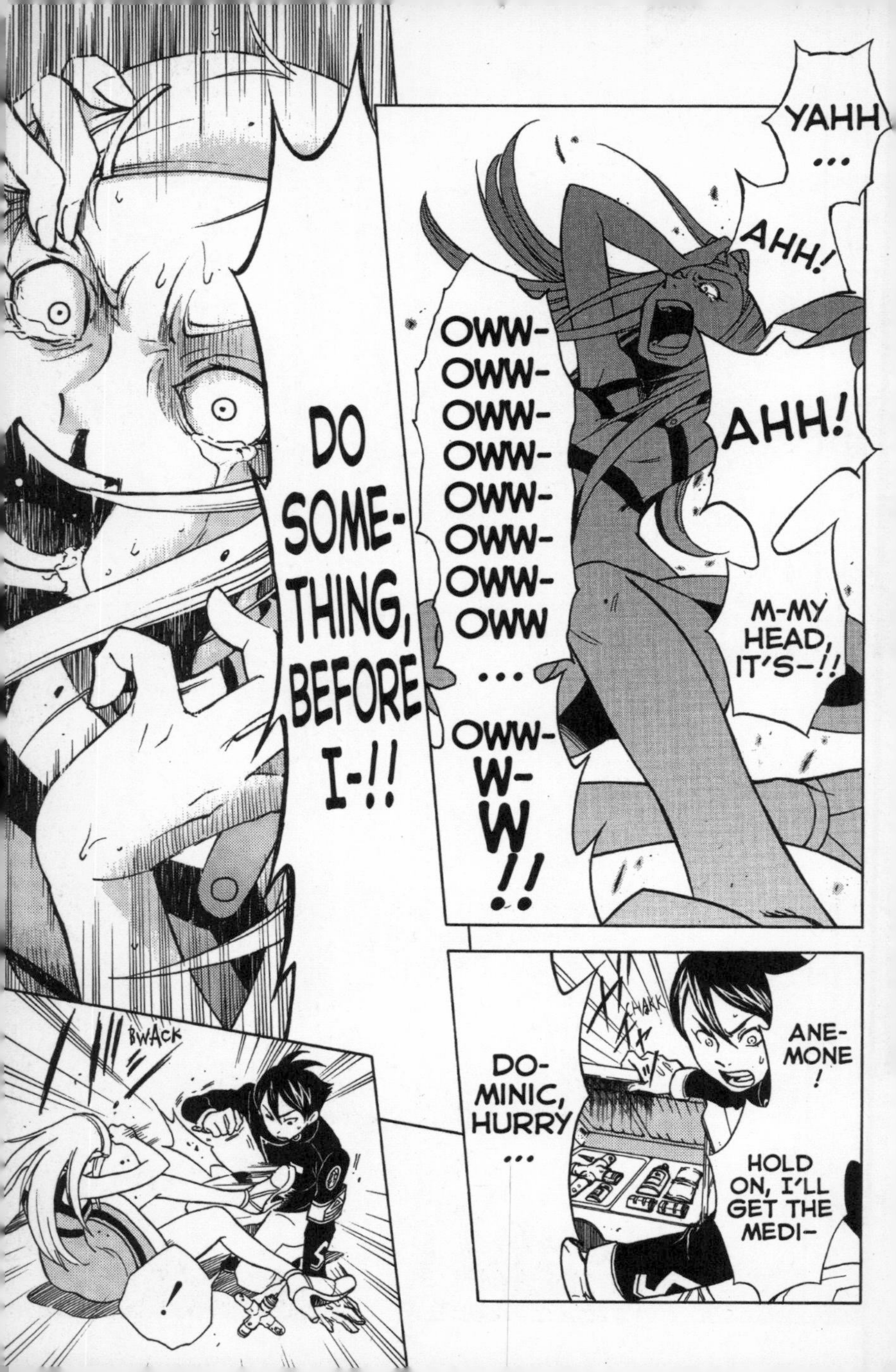
YAHH ...
AHH!
AHH!
M-MY HEAD, IT'S-!!
OWW-OWW-OWW-OWW-OWW-OWW-OWW-OWW ... OWW-W-W!!
DO SOME-THING, BEFORE I-!!
CHAKK
ANE-MONE!
DO-MINIC, HURRY ...
HOLD ON, I'LL GET THE MEDI-
BWACK
!

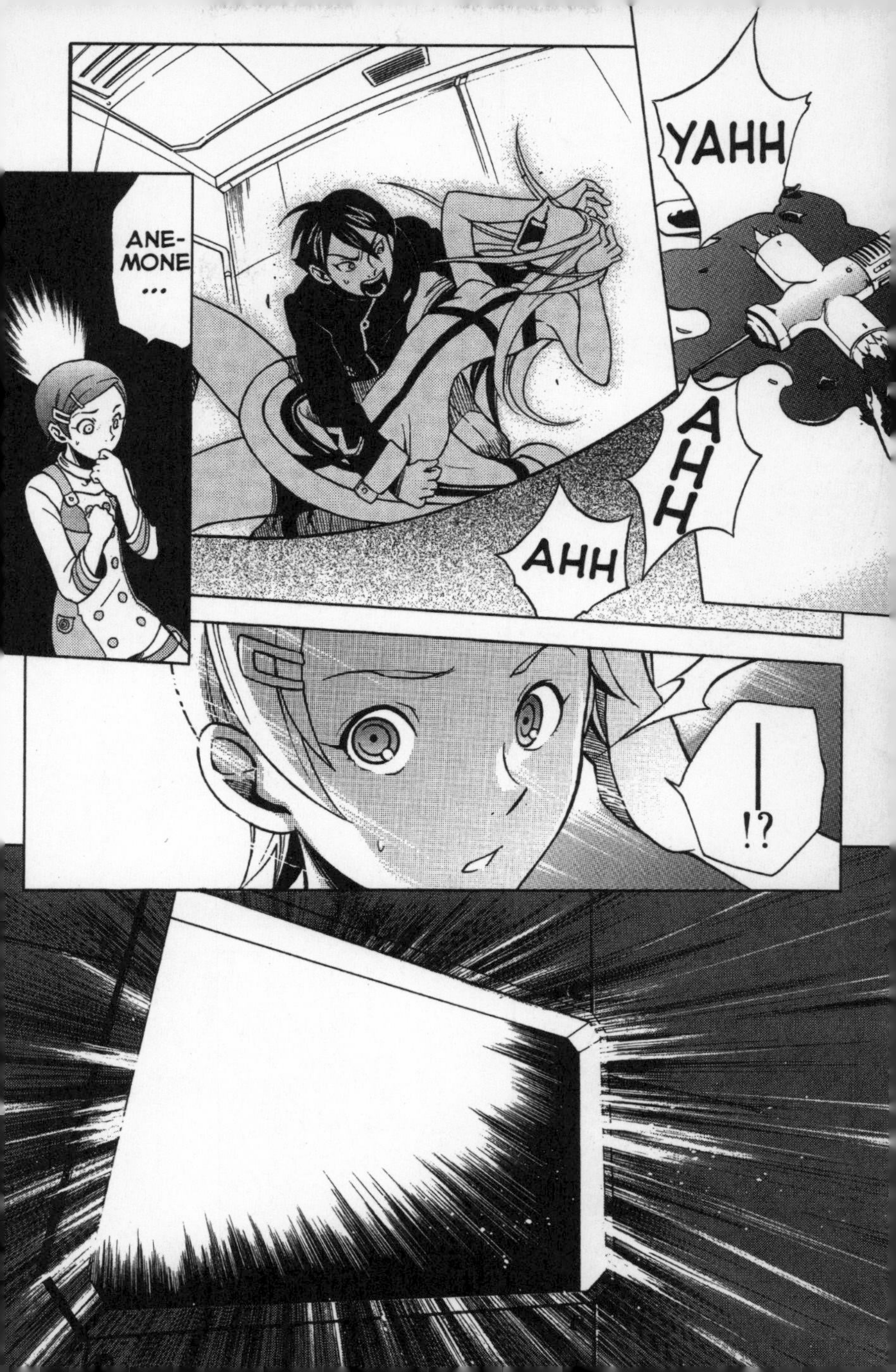
YAHH
AHHH
AHH
ANE-MONE ...
—!?

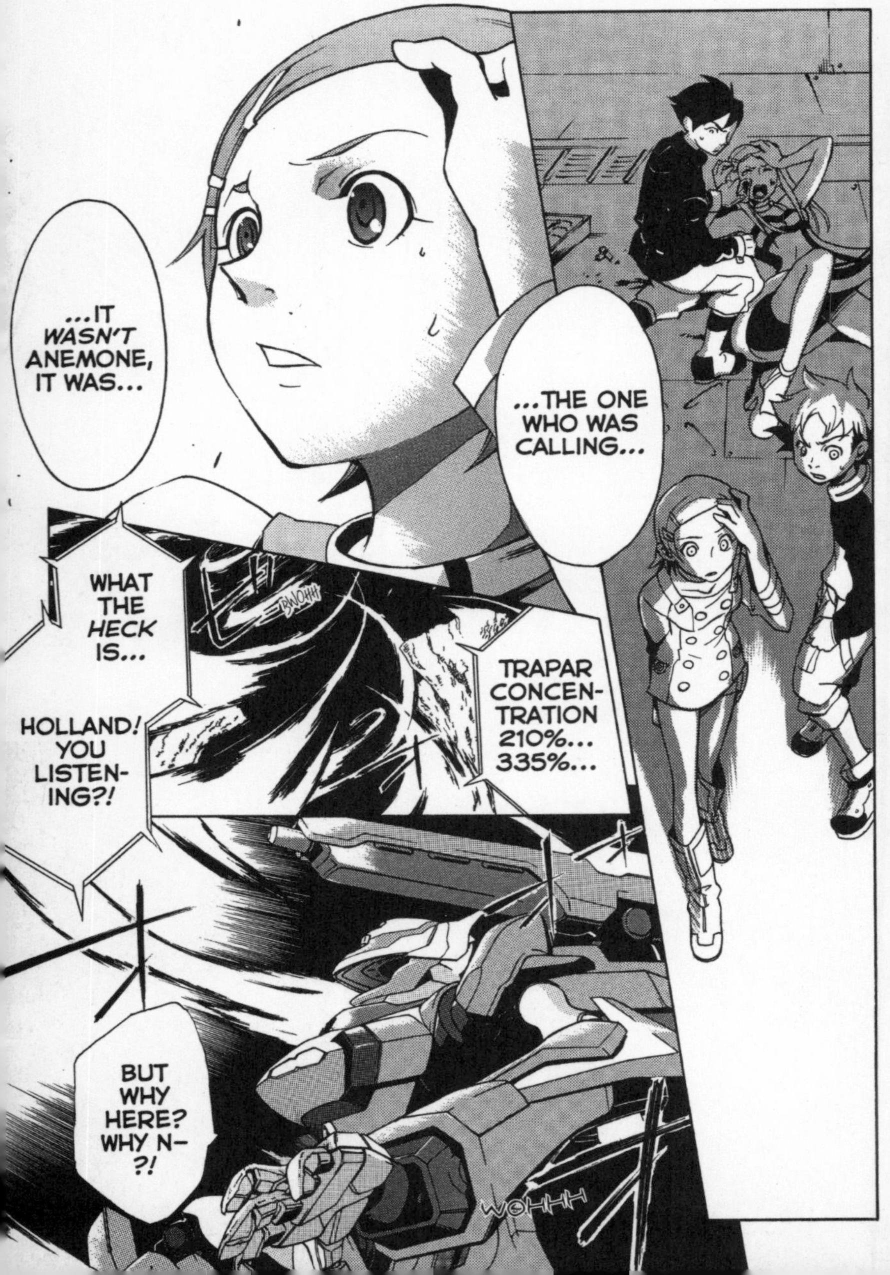
...THE ONE WHO WAS CALLING...
...IT WASN'T ANEMONE, IT WAS...
BWOHH
TRAPAR CONCENTRATION 210%... 335%...
WHAT THE HECK IS...
HOLLAND! YOU LISTENING?!
BUT WHY HERE? WHY N-?!
WOHHH

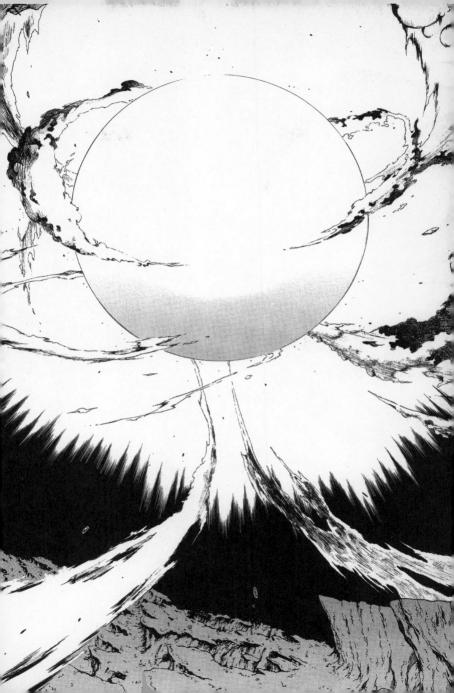

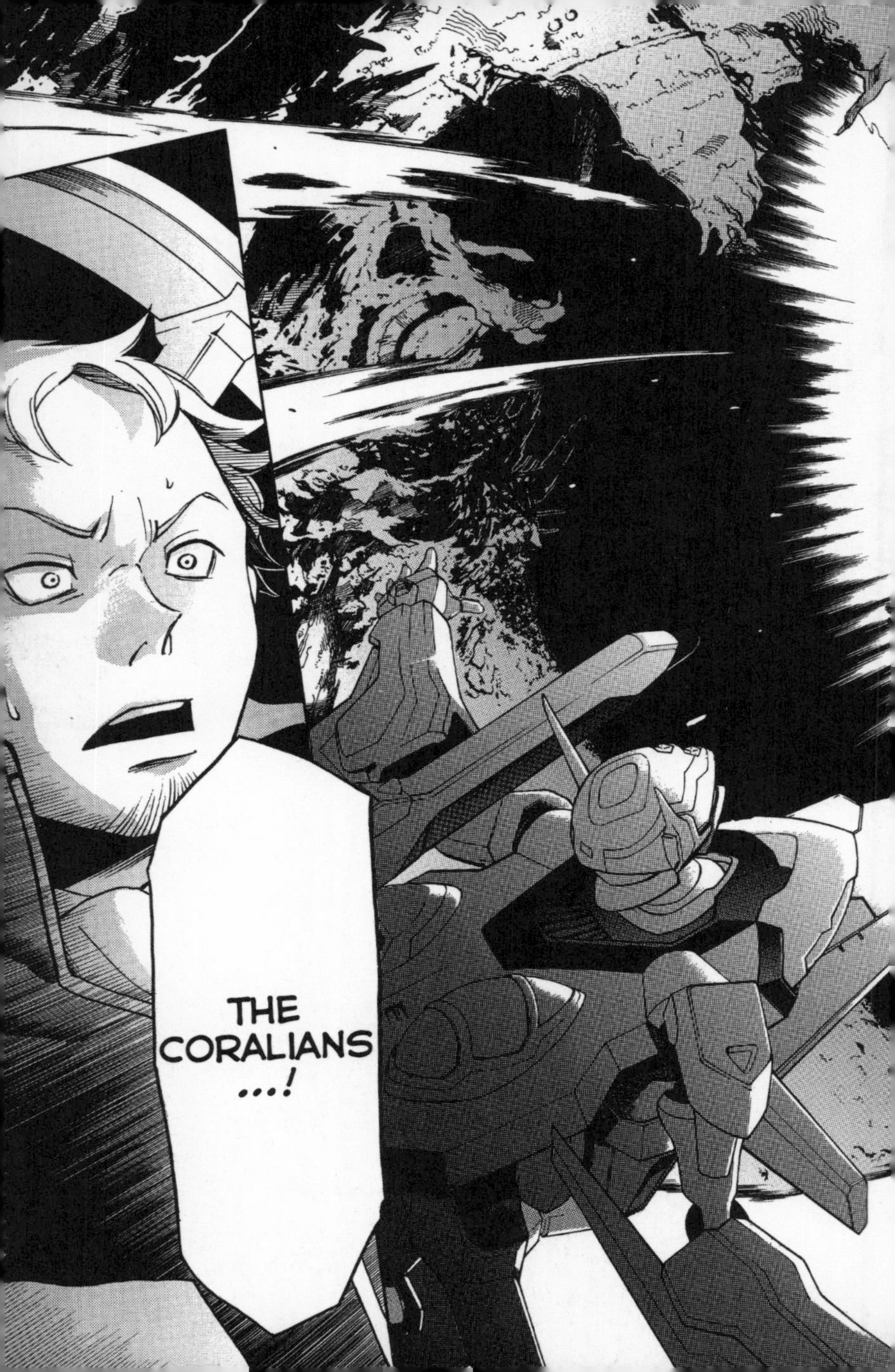
THE CORALIANS ...!

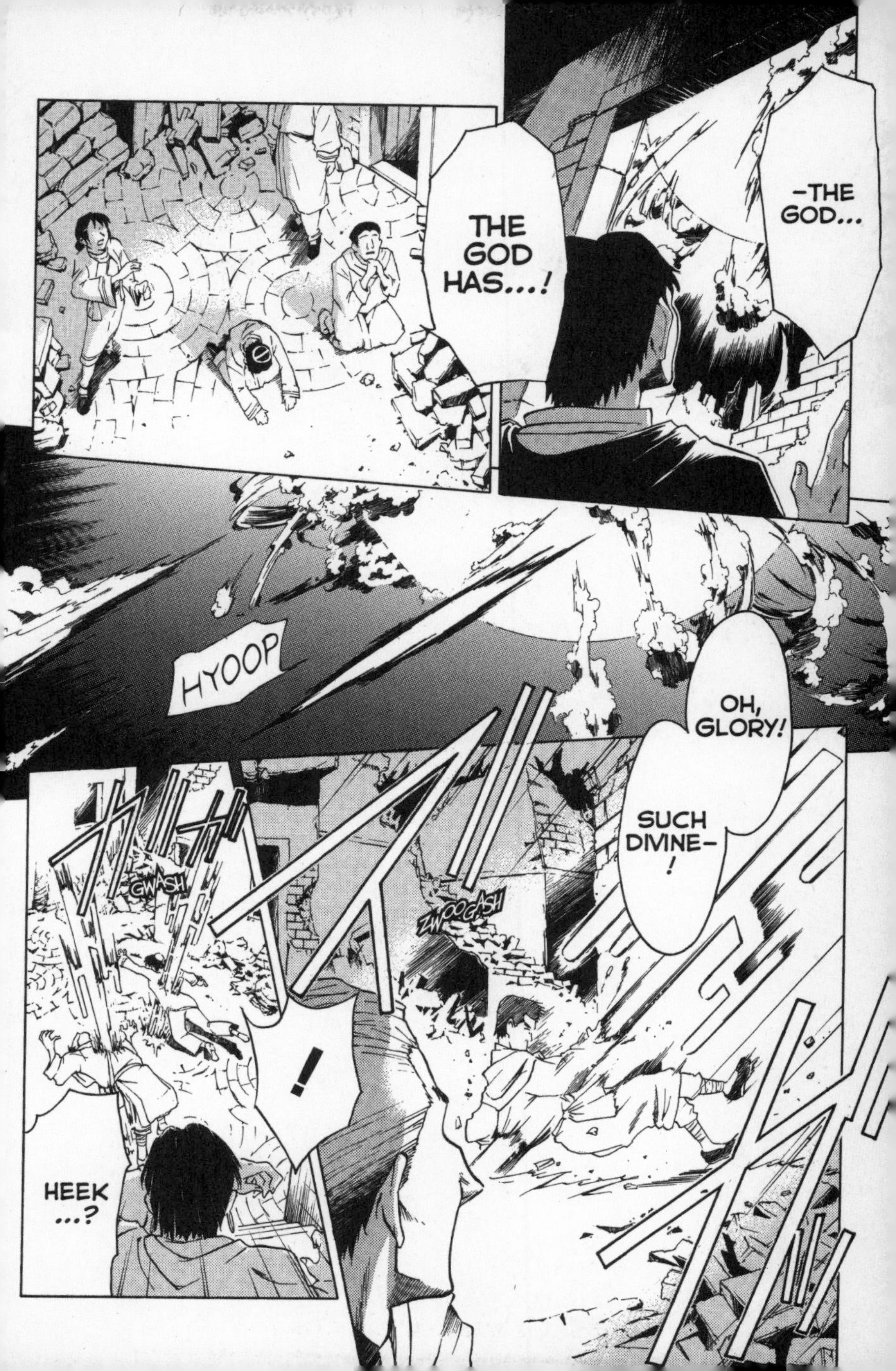
-THE GOD...
THE GOD HAS...!
HYOOP
OH, GLORY!
SUCH DIVINE-!
ZWOOGASH
GWASH
!
HEEK...?

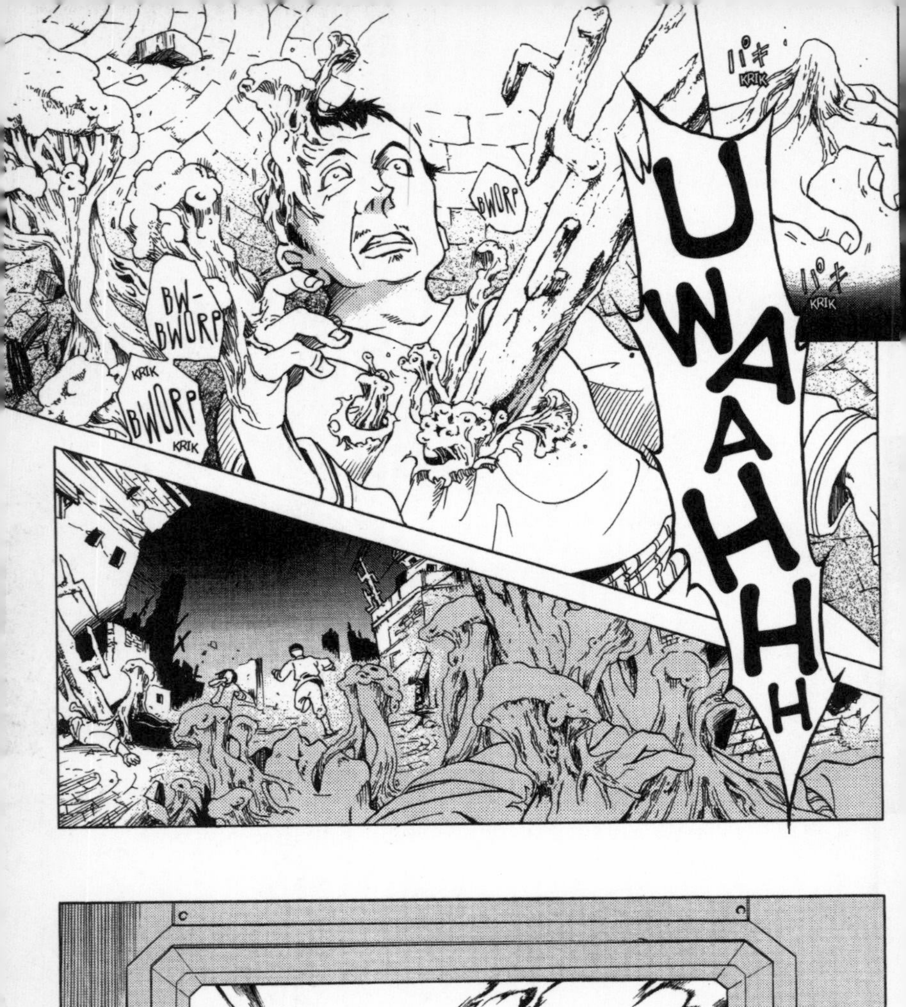
パキ
KRIK
UWAHHH
パキ
KRIK
BWORP
BW-BWORP
KRIK
BWORP
KRIK
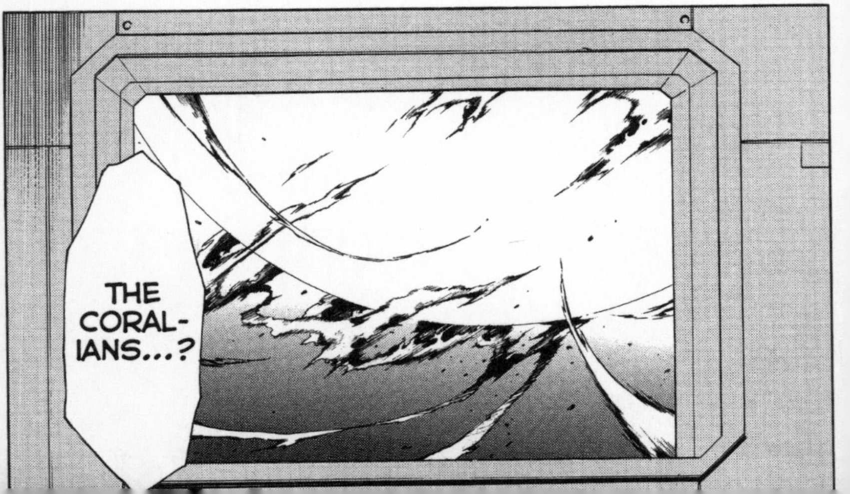
THE CORAL-IANS...?

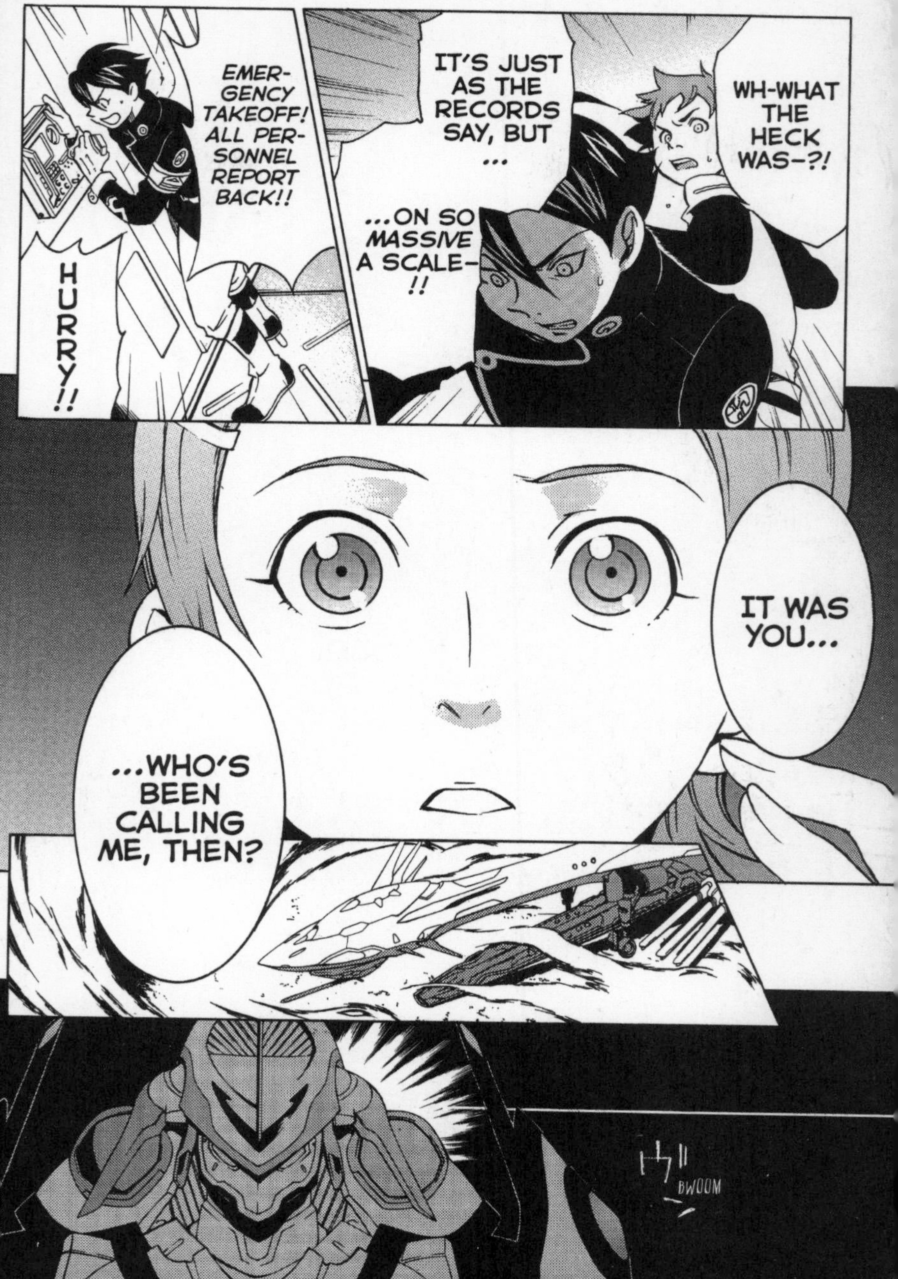
WH-WHAT THE HECK WAS-?!
IT'S JUST AS THE RECORDS SAY, BUT ...
...ON SO MASSIVE A SCALE-!!
EMER-GENCY TAKEOFF! ALL PER-SONNEL REPORT BACK!!
HURRY!!
IT WAS YOU...
...WHO'S BEEN CALLING ME, THEN?
...
BWOOM

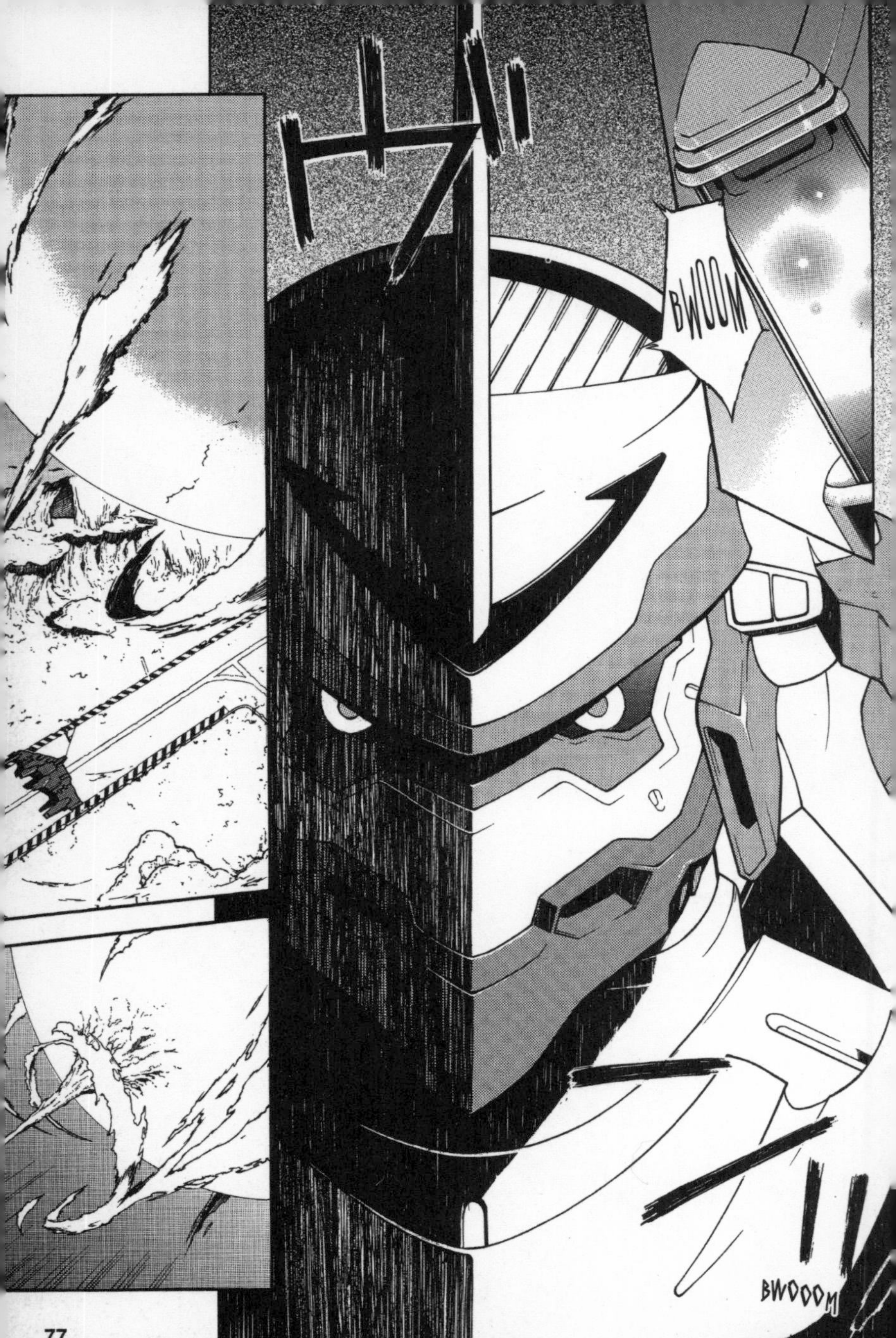
BWOOM
BWOOOM

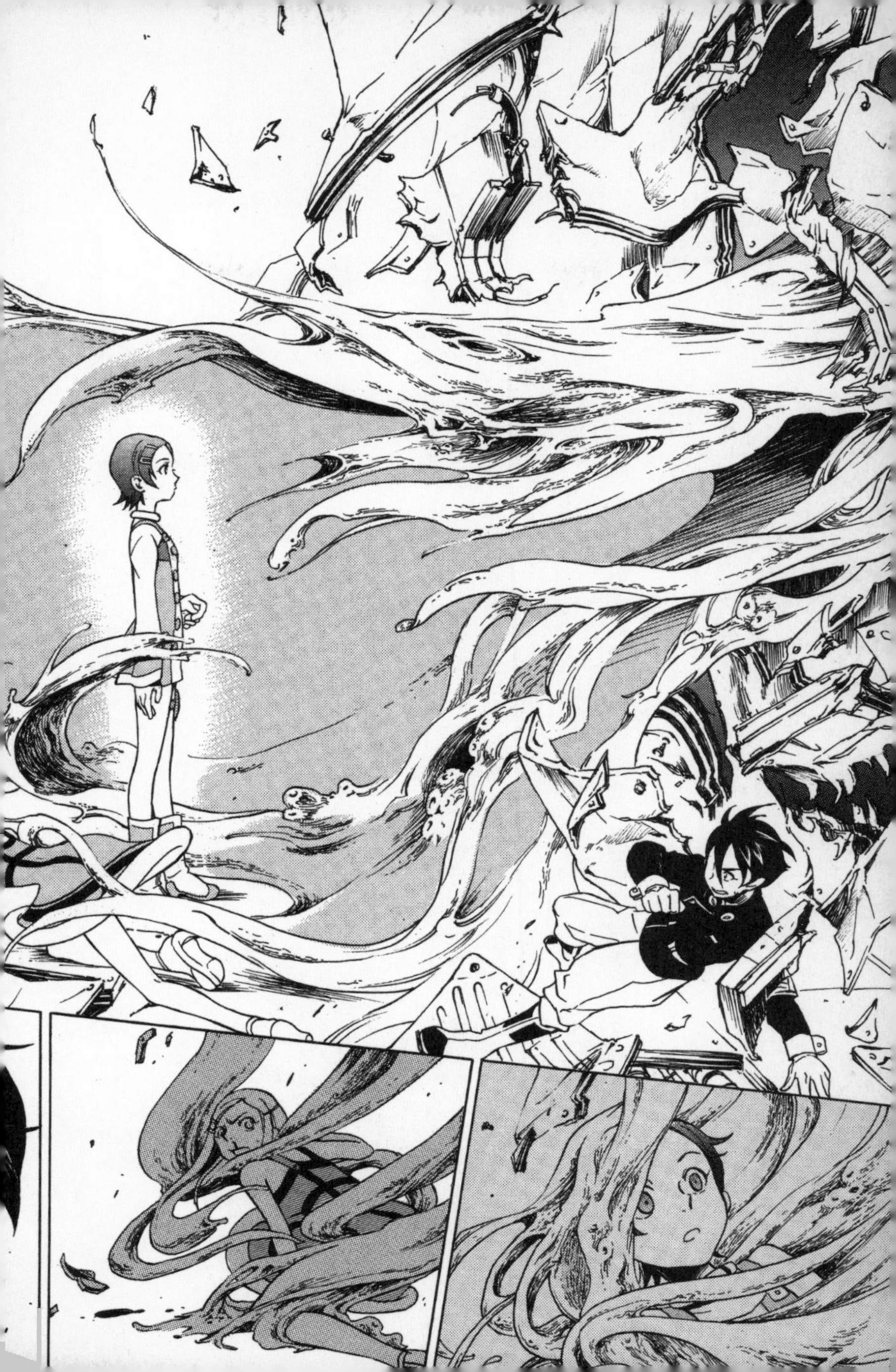

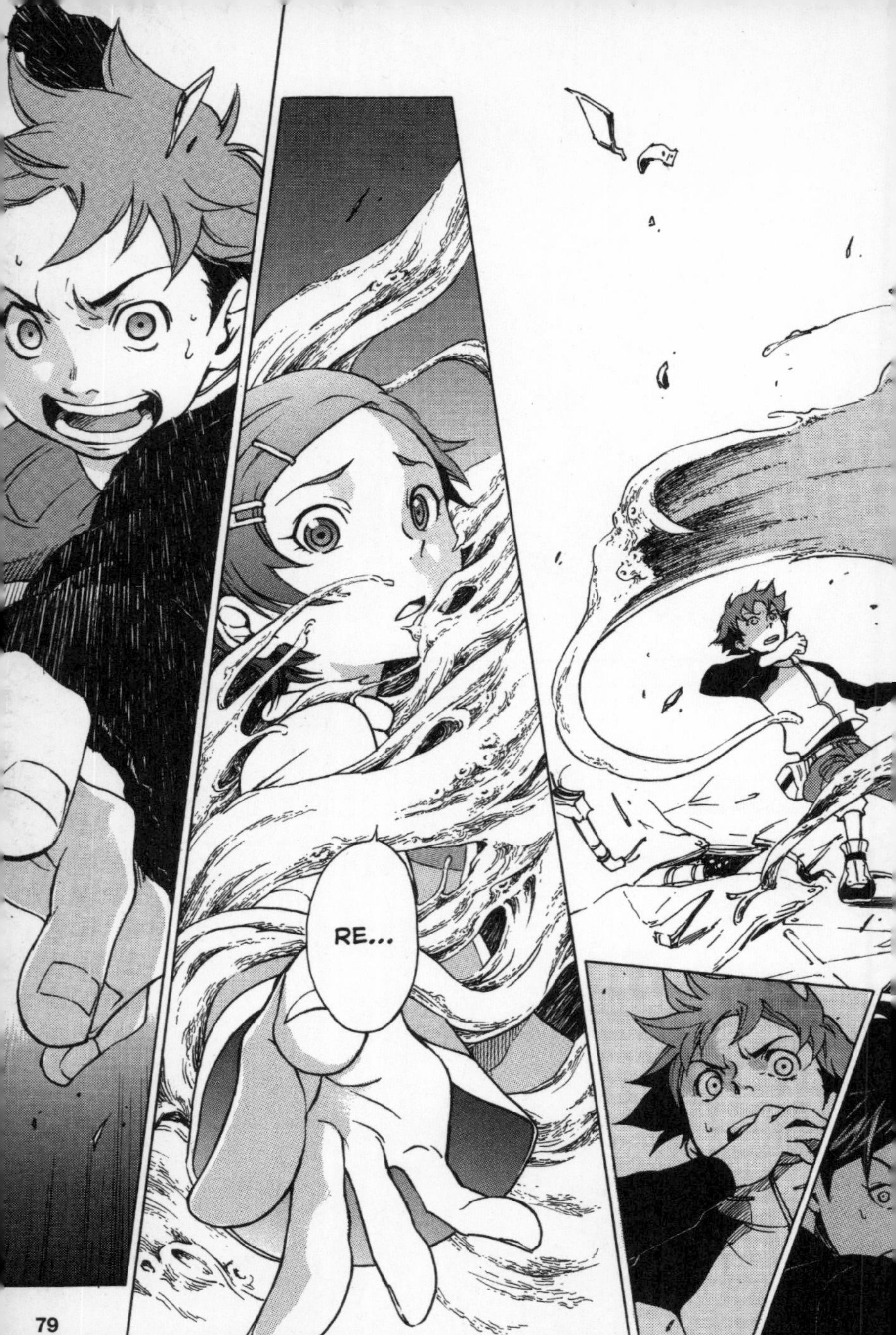
RE...

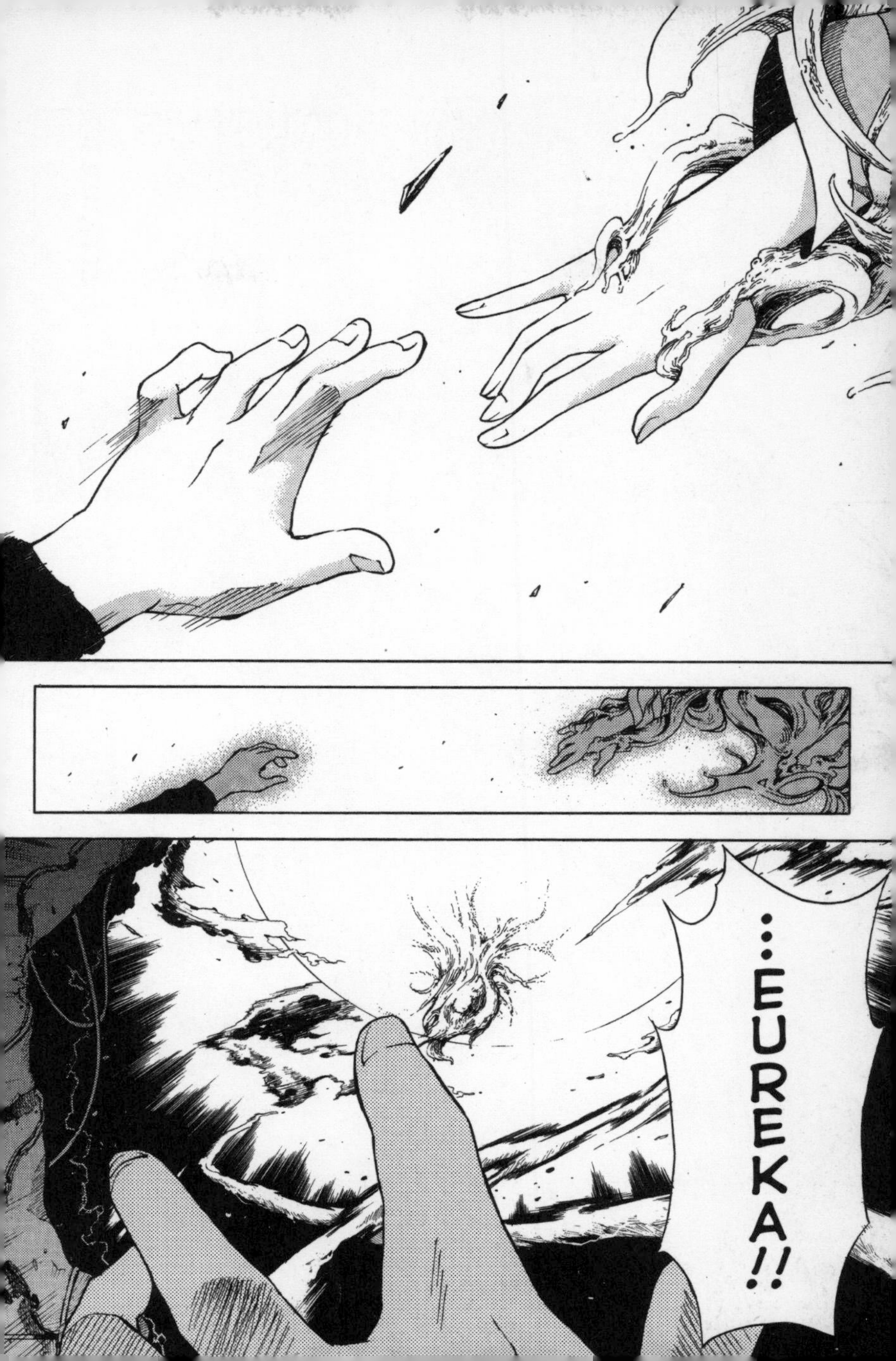
...EUREKA!!

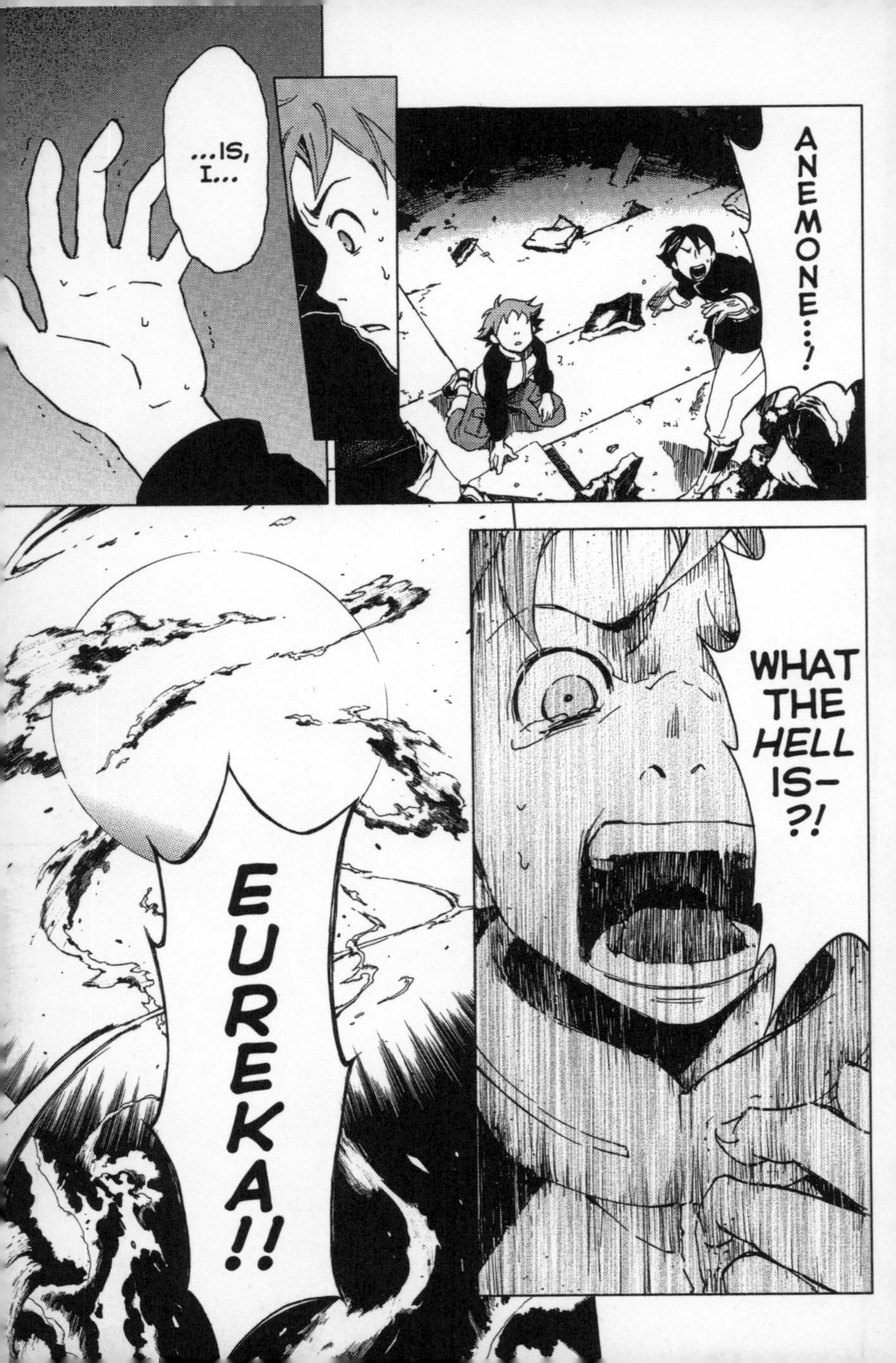
ANEMONE...!
...IS, I...
WHAT THE HELL IS—?!
EUREKA!!

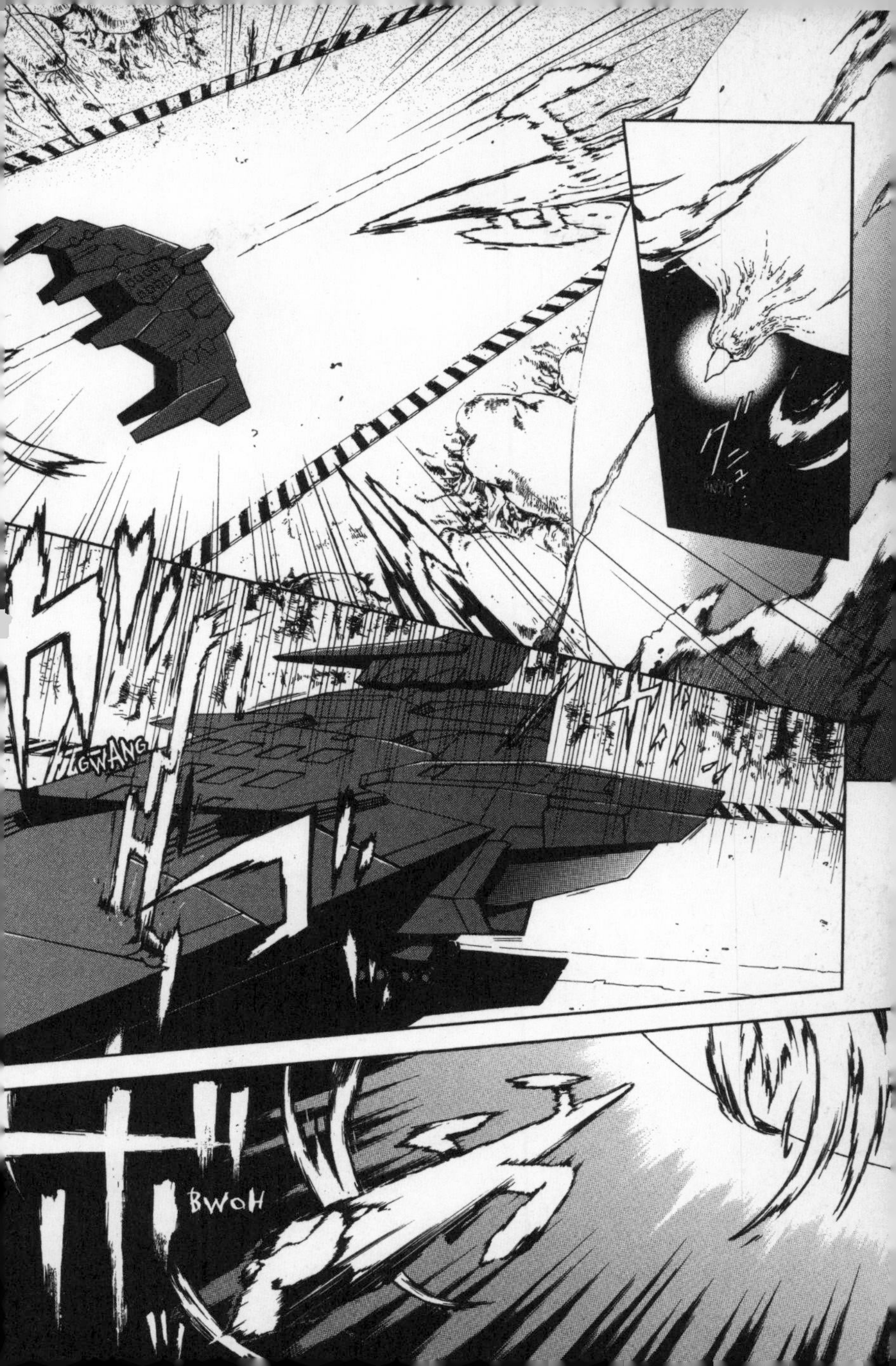
グニュ…
GWANG
BWOH

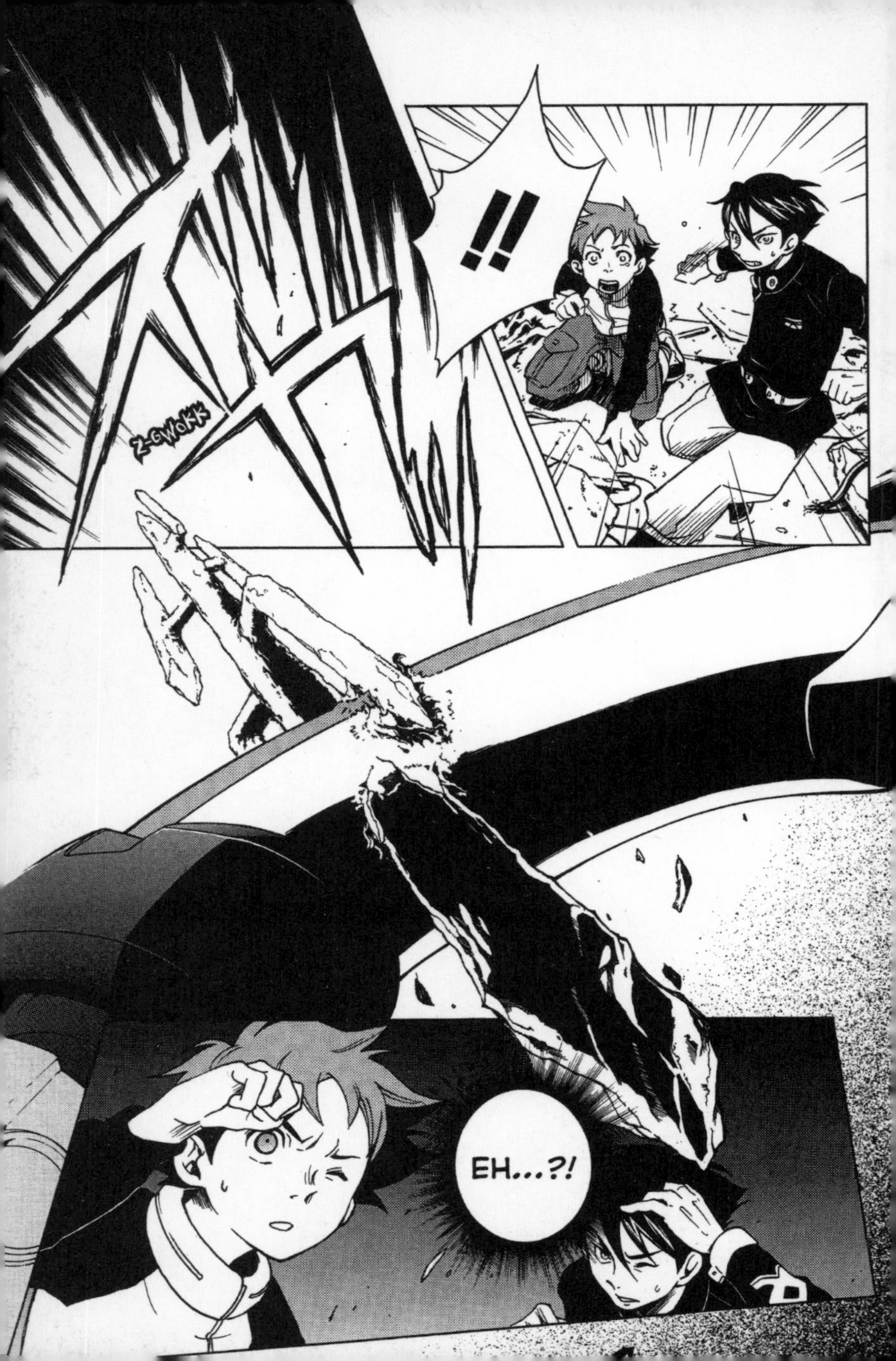
!!
Z-GWOKK
EH...?!

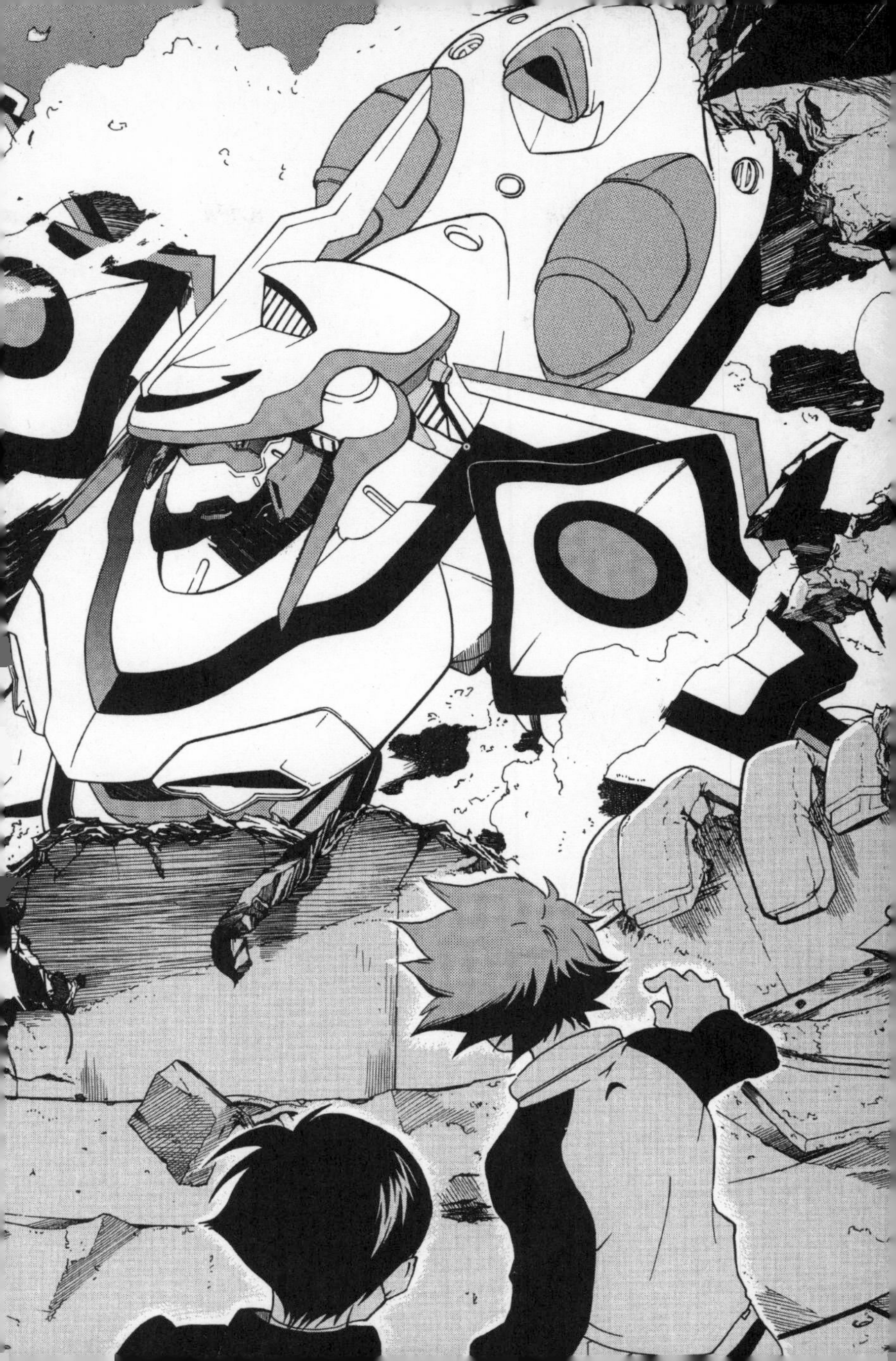

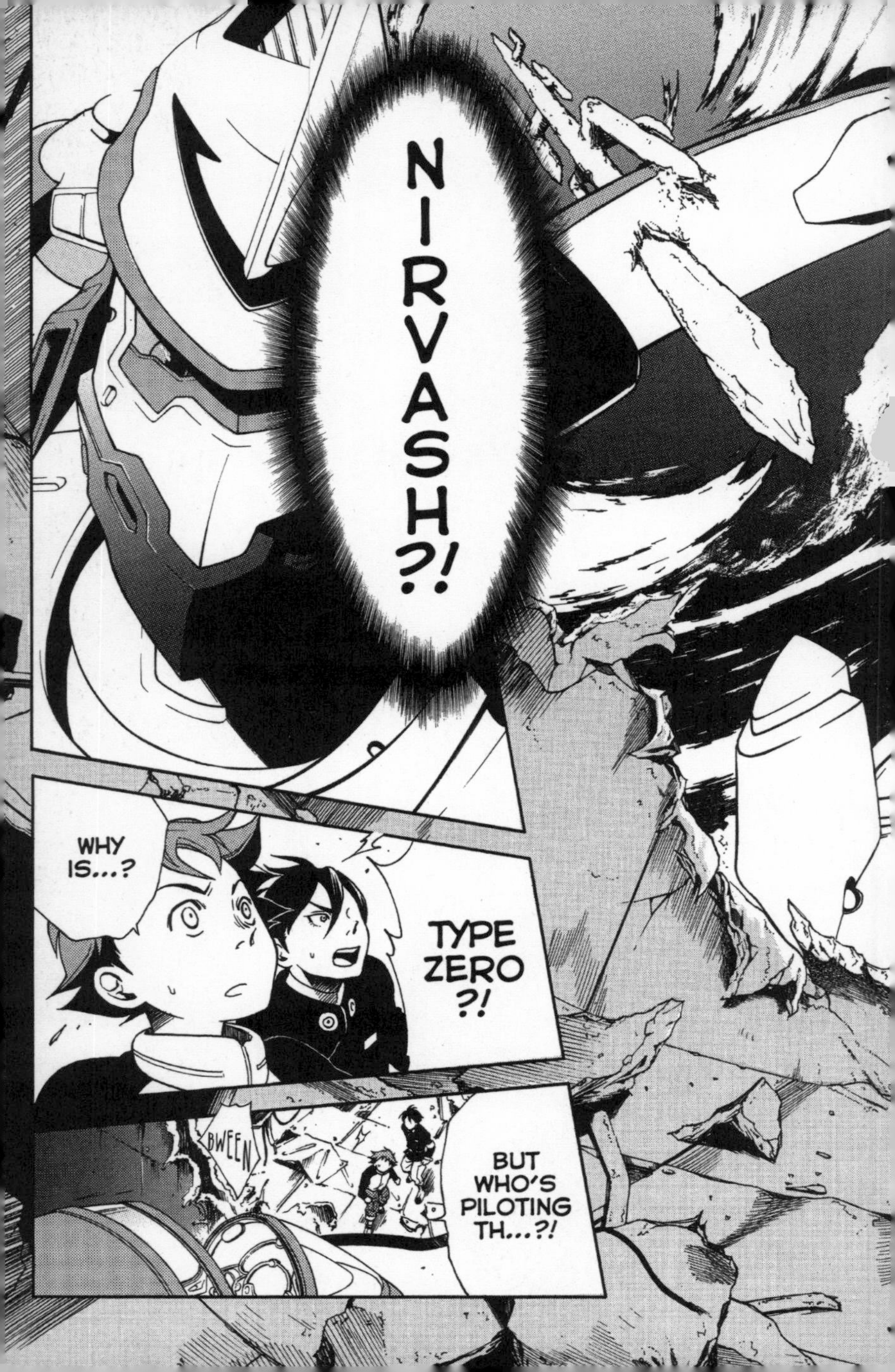
NIRVASH?!
WHY IS...?
TYPE ZERO?!
BUT WHO'S PILOTING TH...?!
BWEEN

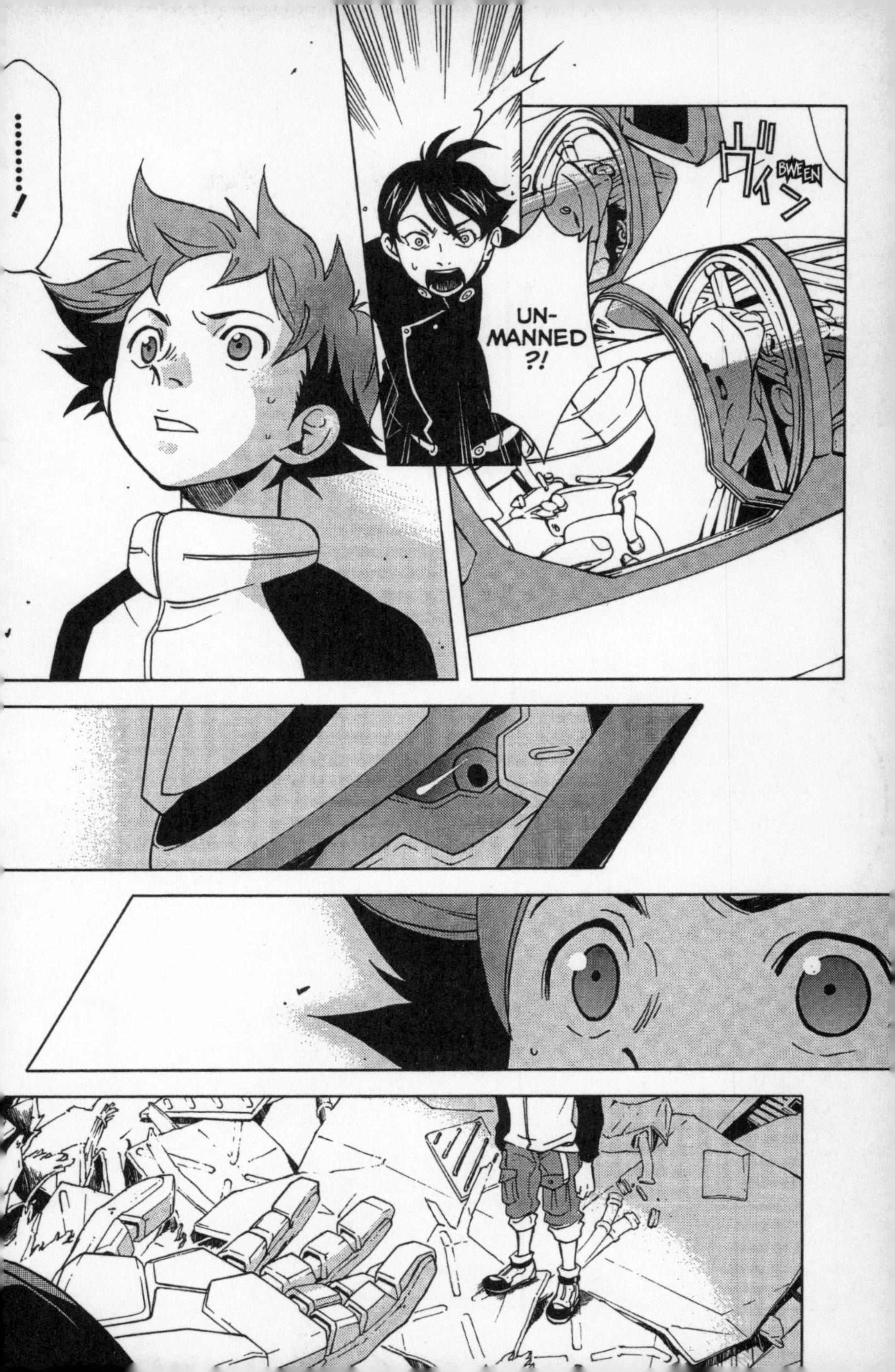
ヴィン
BWEEN
UN-MANNED?!
......!

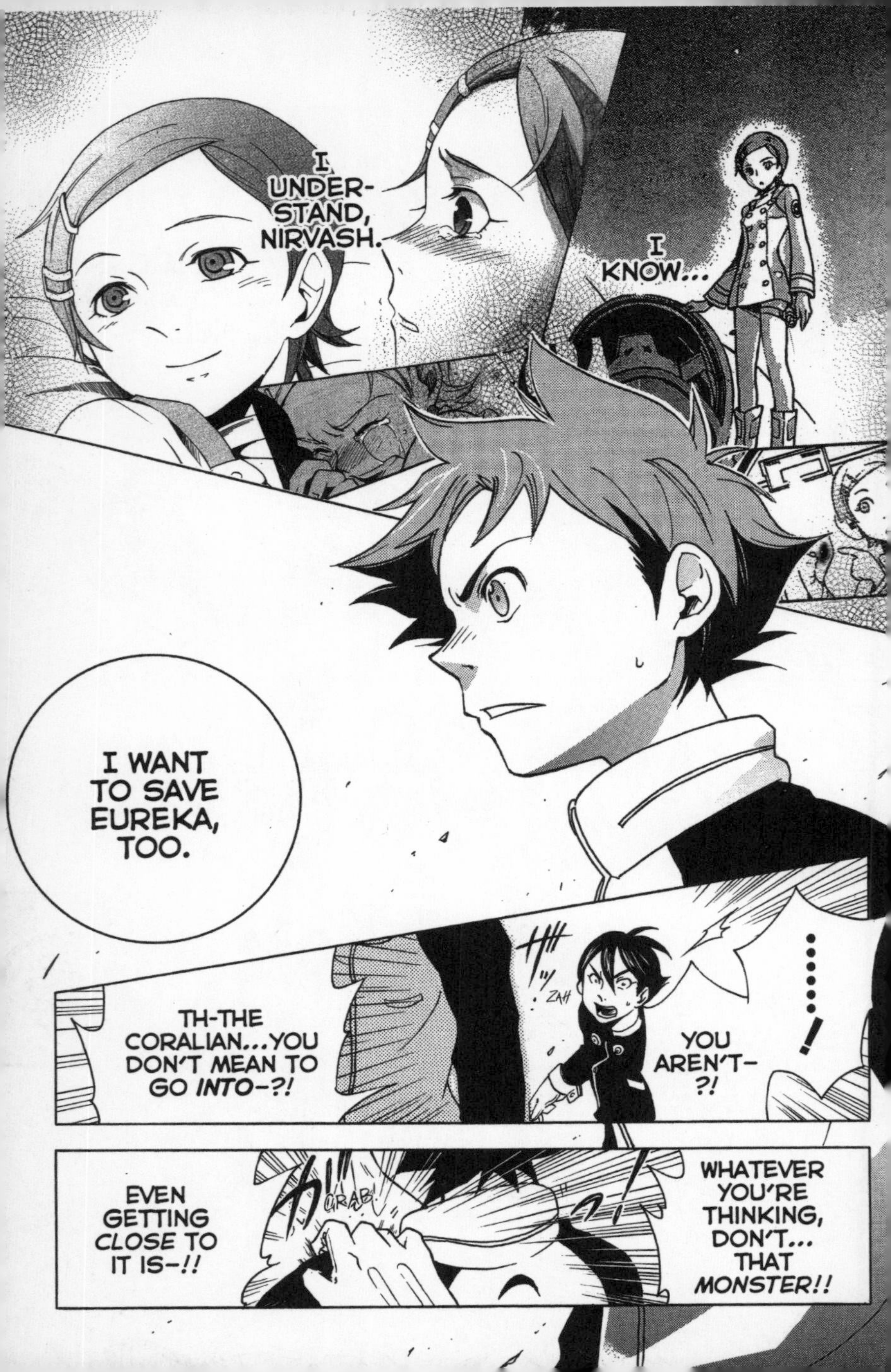
I KNOW...
I UNDERSTAND, NIRVASH.
I WANT TO SAVE EUREKA, TOO.
......!
YOU AREN'T-?!
ZAH
TH-THE CORALIAN...YOU DON'T MEAN TO GO *INTO*-?!
WHATEVER YOU'RE THINKING, DON'T... THAT *MONSTER*!!
GRAB
EVEN GETTING *CLOSE* TO IT IS-!!

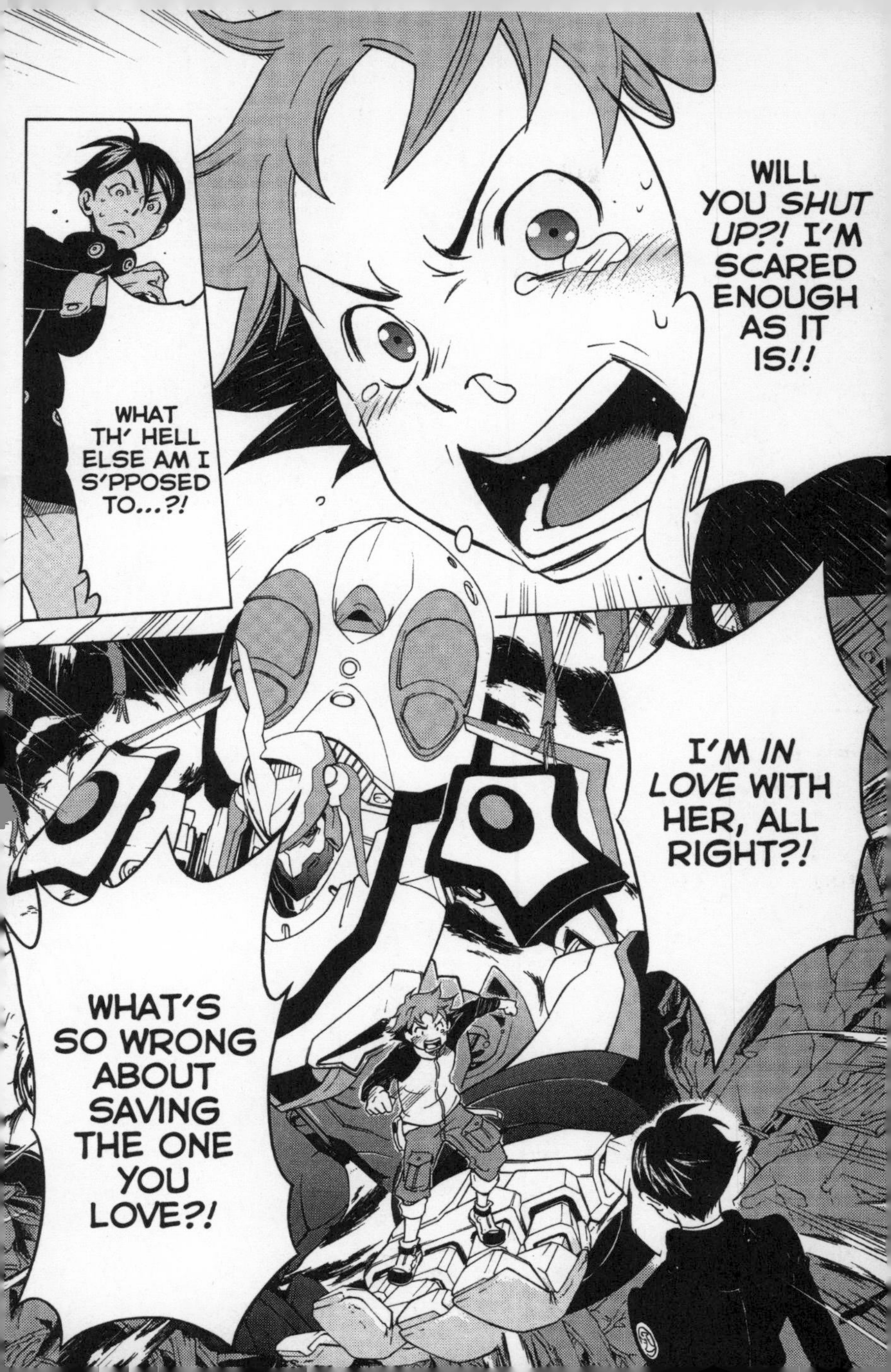
WILL YOU SHUT UP?! I'M SCARED ENOUGH AS IT IS!!
WHAT TH' HELL ELSE AM I S'PPOSED TO...?!
I'M IN LOVE WITH HER, ALL RIGHT?!
WHAT'S SO WRONG ABOUT SAVING THE ONE YOU LOVE?!

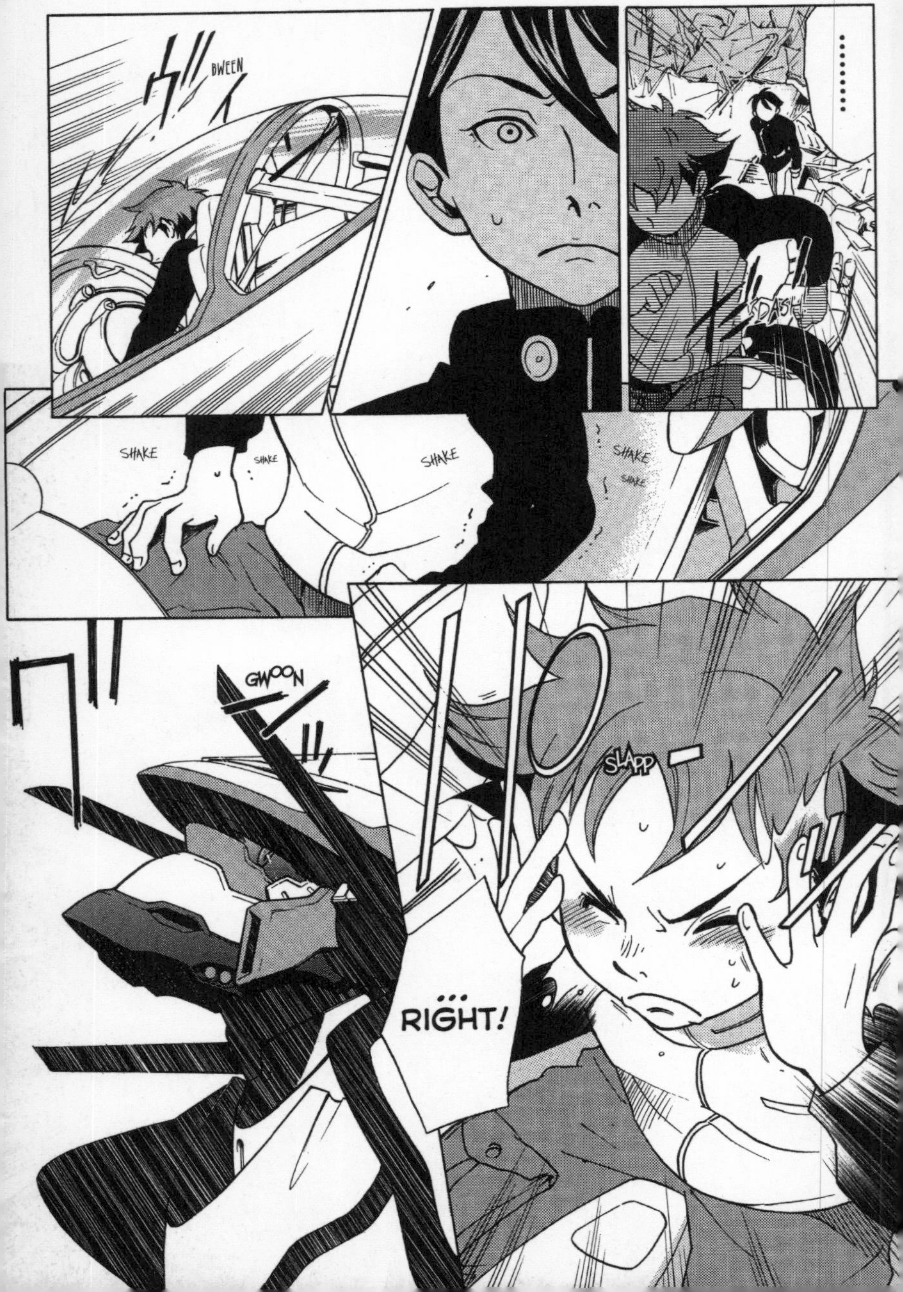
......
DASH!
BWEEN
SHAKE
SHAKE
SHAKE
SHAKE
SHAKE
SLAPP
...RIGHT!
GWOON

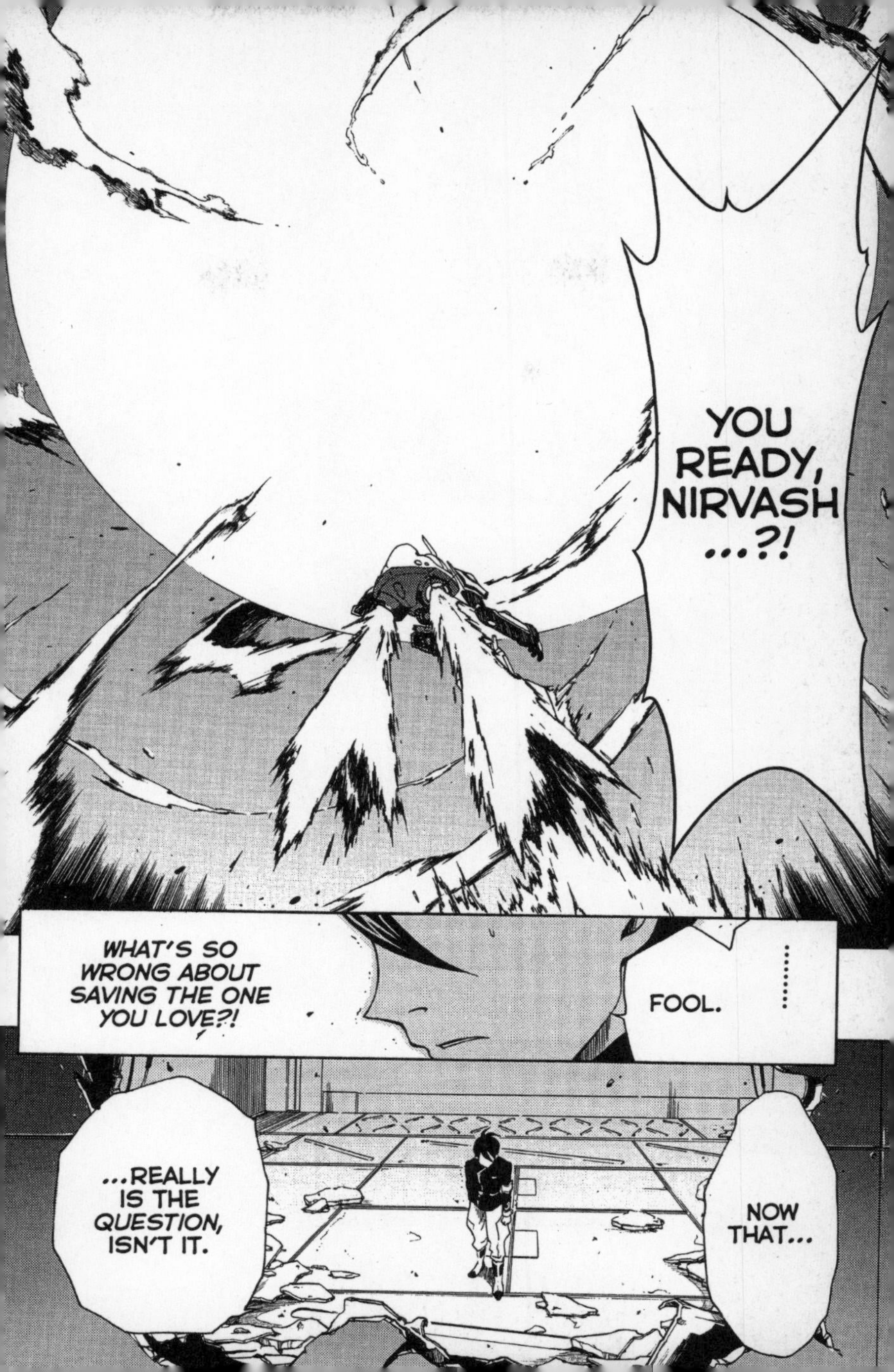
YOU READY, NIRVASH ...?!
......
FOOL.
WHAT'S SO WRONG ABOUT SAVING THE ONE YOU LOVE?!
NOW THAT...
...REALLY IS THE QUESTION, ISN'T IT.

Psalms of
Planet
Eureka seveN

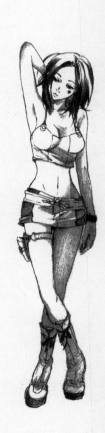

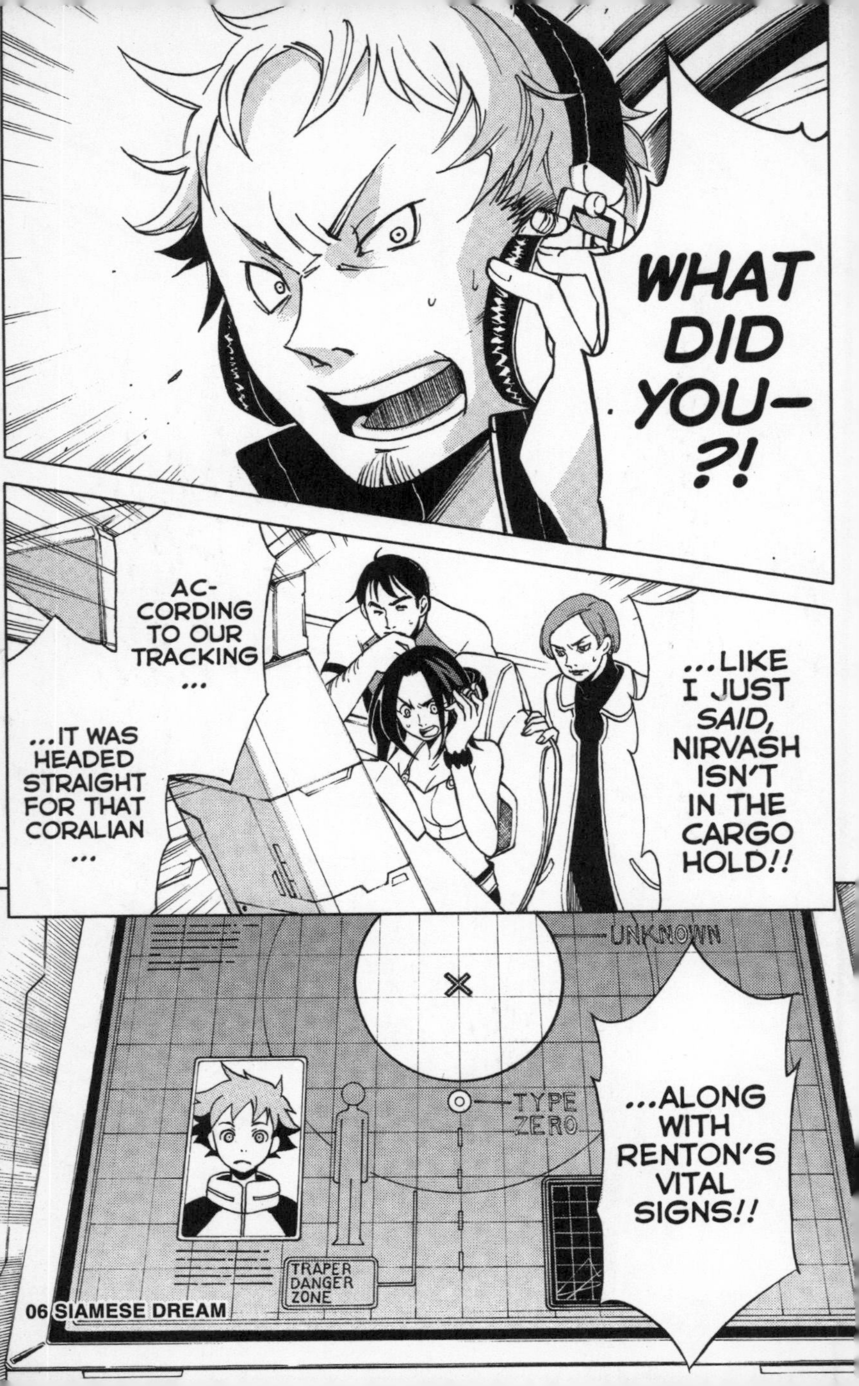
WHAT DID YOU—?!
...LIKE I JUST *SAID*, NIRVASH ISN'T IN THE CARGO HOLD!!
AC-CORDING TO OUR TRACKING...
...IT WAS HEADED STRAIGHT FOR THAT CORALIAN...
UNKNOWN
...ALONG WITH RENTON'S VITAL SIGNS!!
TYPE ZERO
TRAPER DANGER ZONE

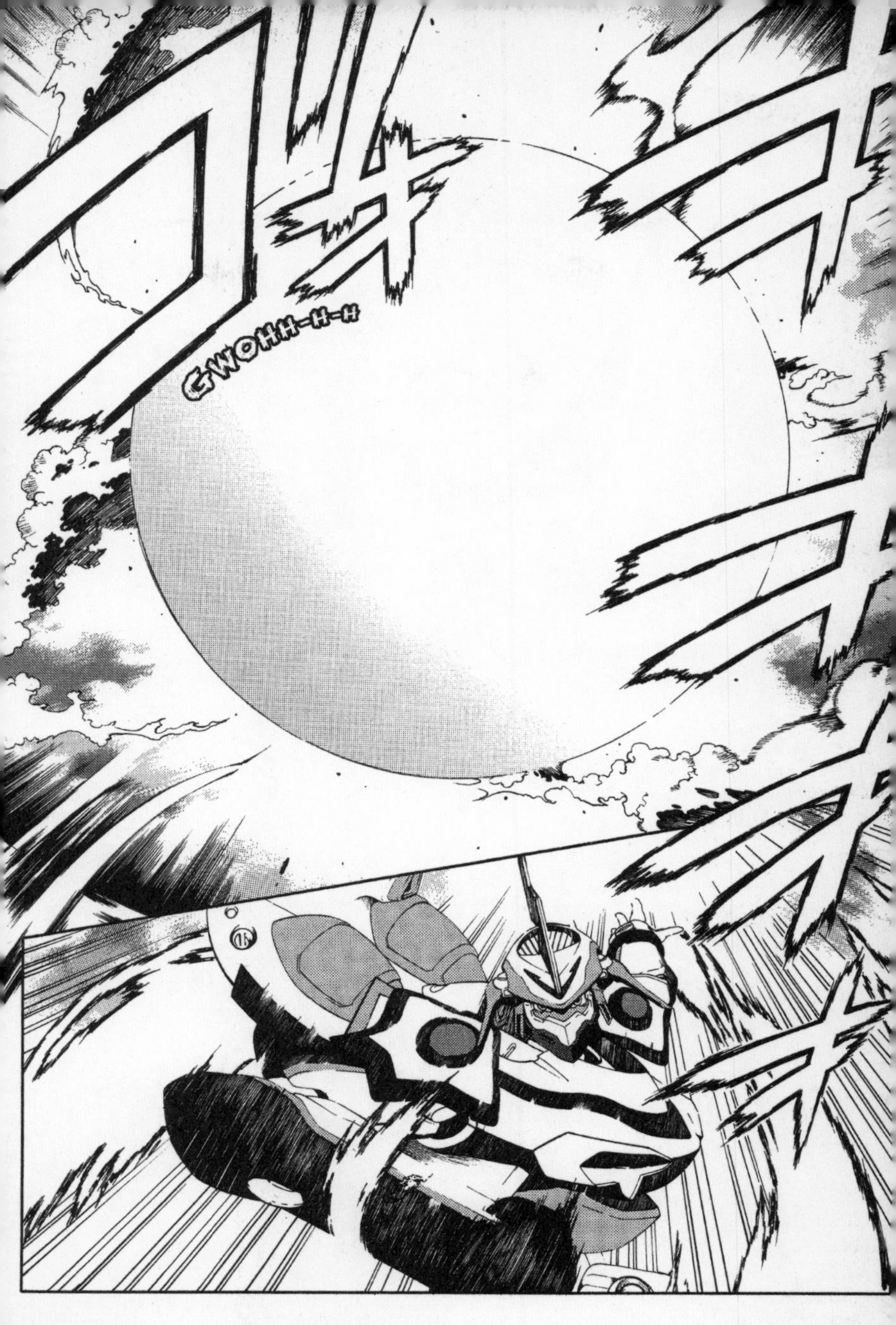
GWOHH-H-H

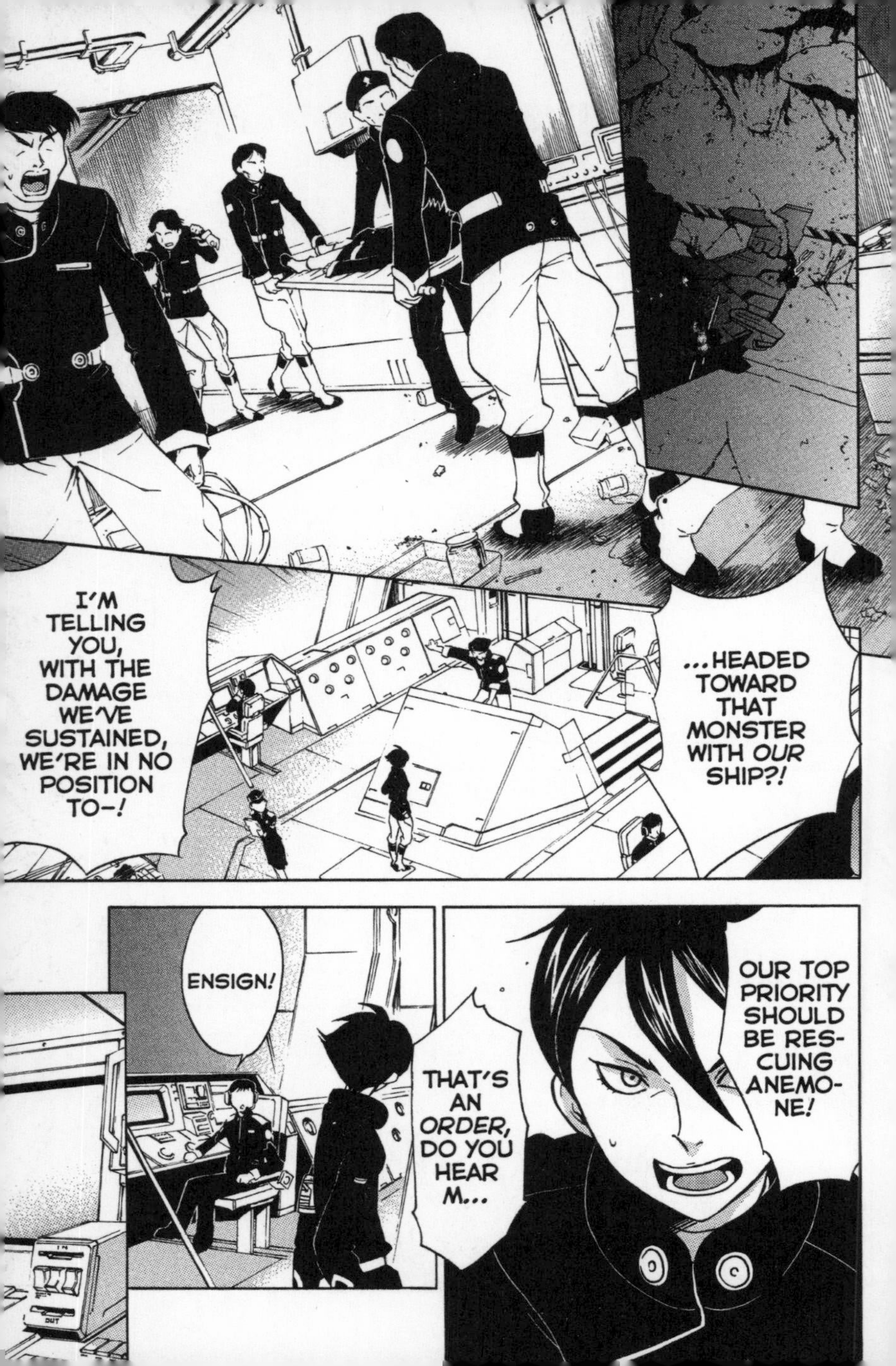
...HEADED TOWARD THAT MONSTER WITH *OUR* SHIP?!
I'M TELLING YOU, WITH THE DAMAGE WE'VE SUSTAINED, WE'RE IN NO POSITION TO-!
OUR TOP PRIORITY SHOULD BE RESCUING ANEMONE!
THAT'S AN *ORDER*, DO YOU HEAR M...
ENSIGN!

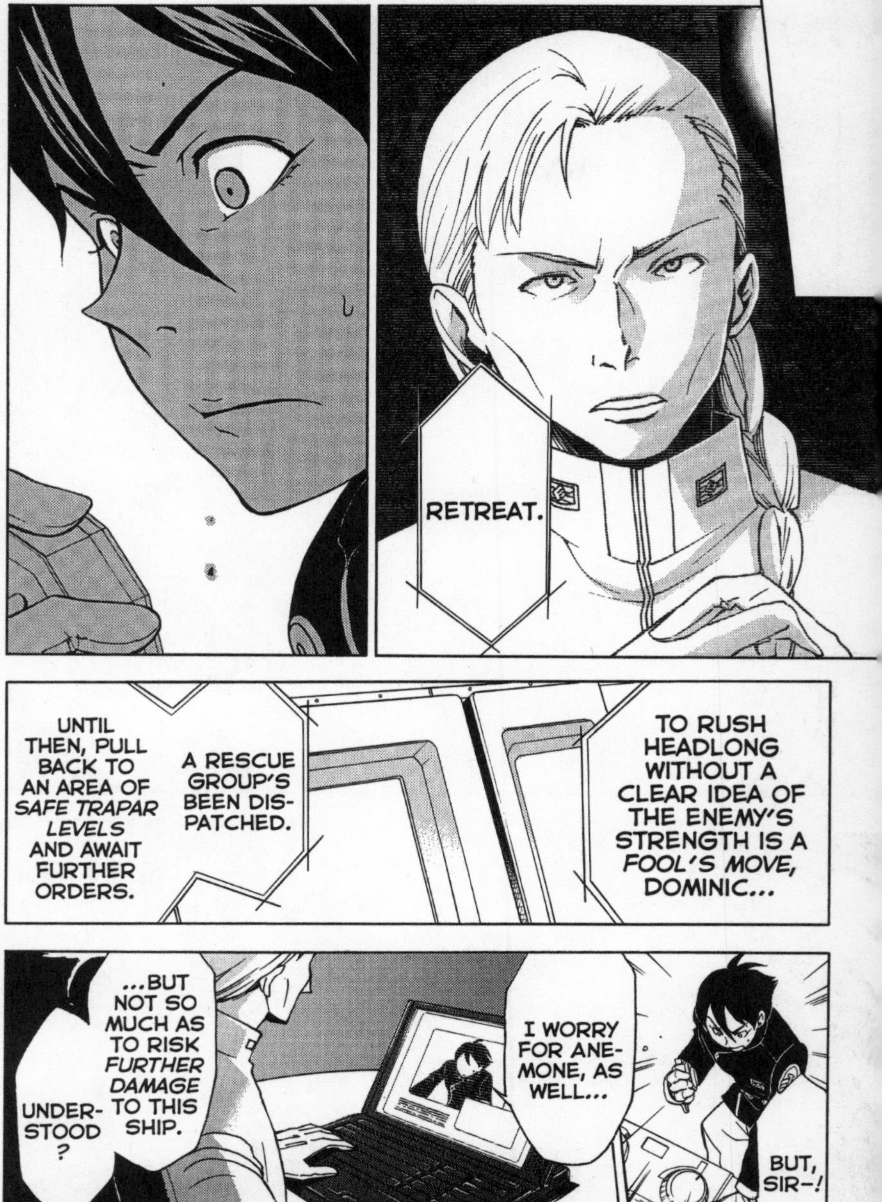
RETREAT.
TO RUSH HEADLONG WITHOUT A CLEAR IDEA OF THE ENEMY'S STRENGTH IS A *FOOL'S MOVE,* DOMINIC...
A RESCUE GROUP'S BEEN DIS-PATCHED.
UNTIL THEN, PULL BACK TO AN AREA OF *SAFE TRAPAR LEVELS* AND AWAIT FURTHER ORDERS.
BUT, SIR–!
I WORRY FOR ANE-MONE, AS WELL...
...BUT NOT SO MUCH AS TO RISK *FURTHER DAMAGE* TO THIS SHIP.
UNDER-STOOD?

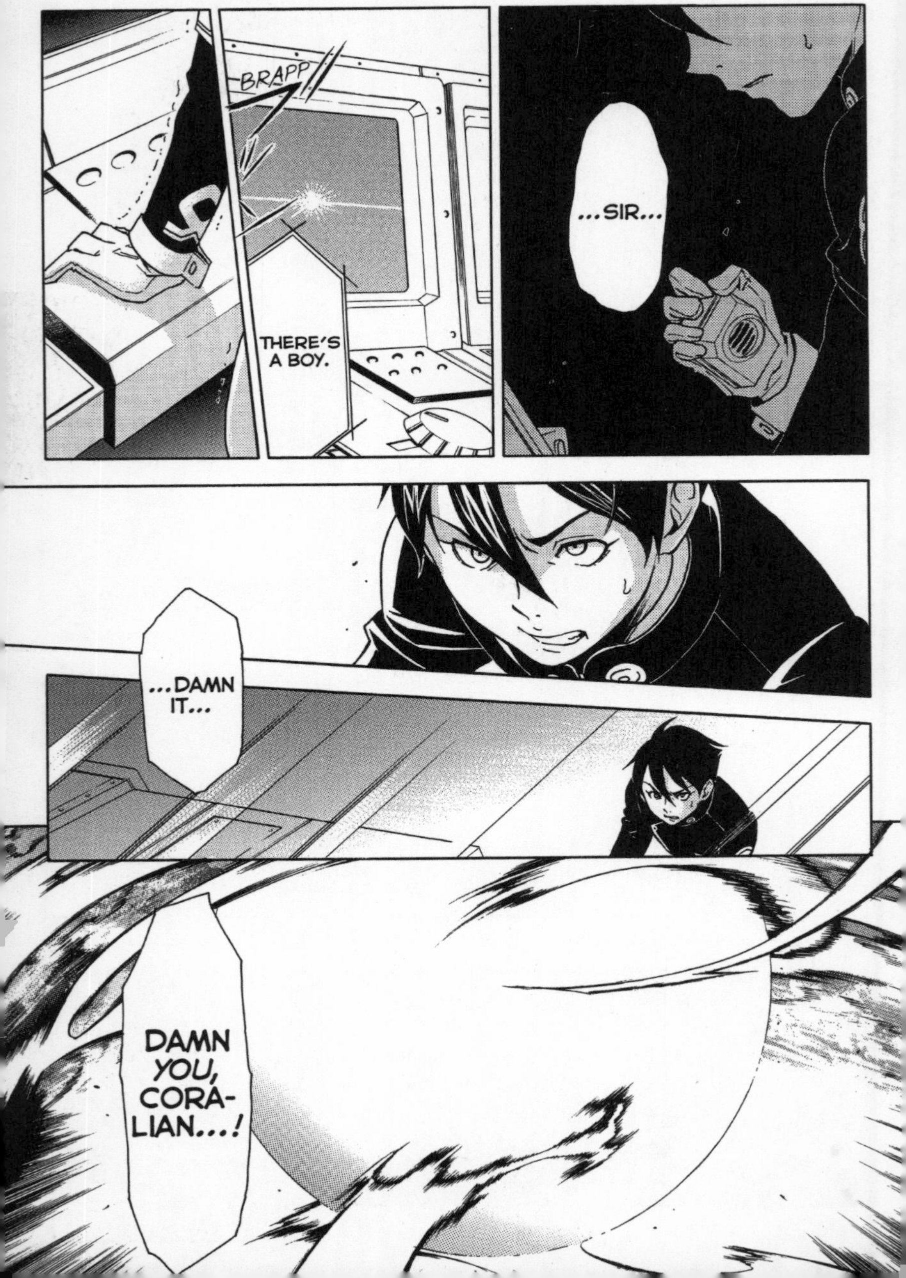
...SIR...
BRAPP
THERE'S A BOY.
...DAMN IT...
DAMN YOU, CORA-LIAN...!

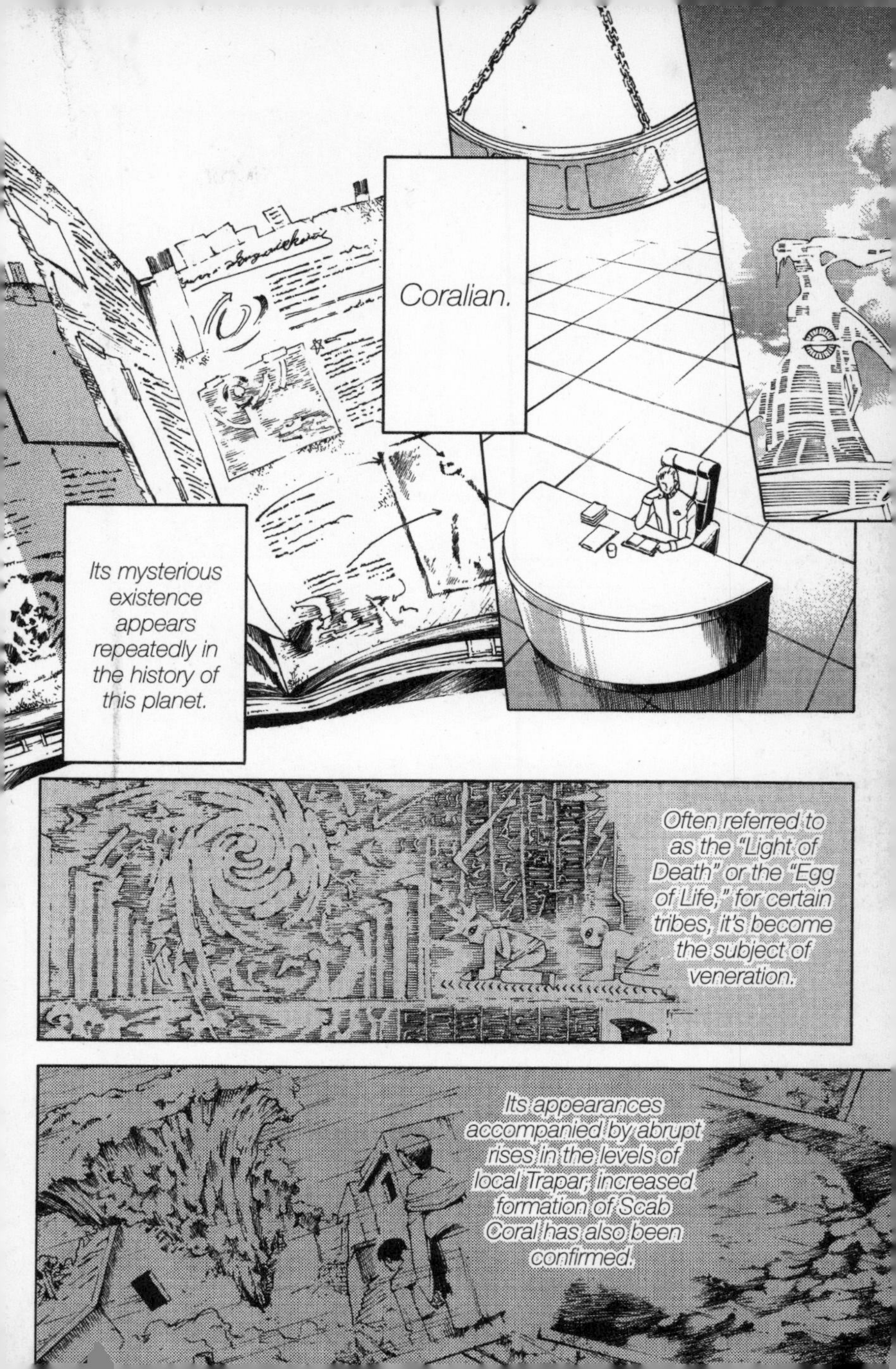
Coralian.
Its mysterious existence appears repeatedly in the history of this planet.
Often referred to as the "Light of Death" or the "Egg of Life," for certain tribes, it's become the subject of veneration.
Its appearances accompanied by abrupt rises in the levels of local Trapar, increased formation of Scab Coral has also been confirmed.

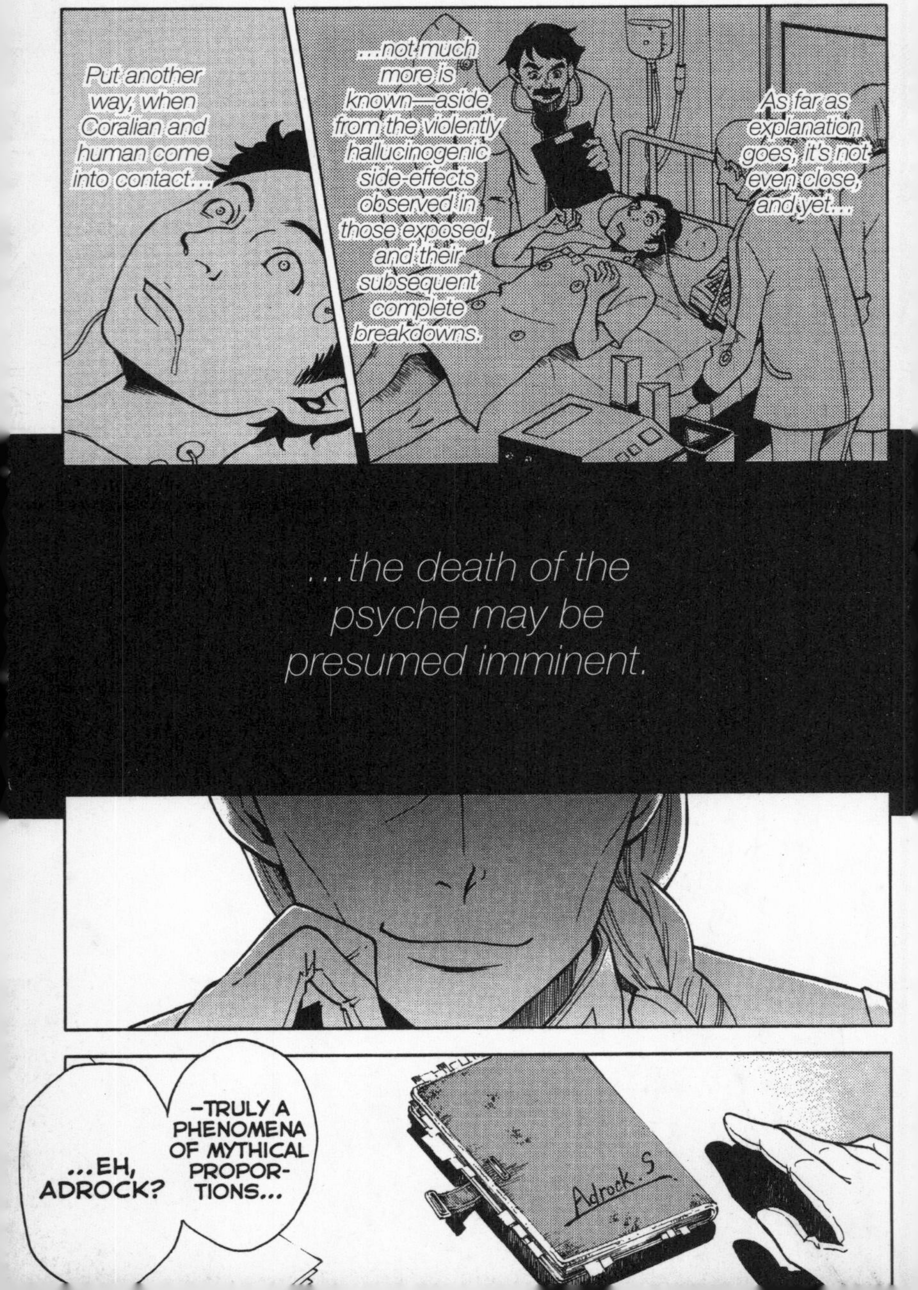
Put another way, when Coralian and human come into contact...
...not much more is known—aside from the violently hallucinogenic side-effects observed in those exposed, and their subsequent complete breakdowns.
As far as explanation goes, it's not even close, and yet...
...the death of the psyche may be presumed imminent.
-TRULY A PHENOMENA OF MYTHICAL PROPOR-TIONS...
...EH, ADROCK?
Adrock S

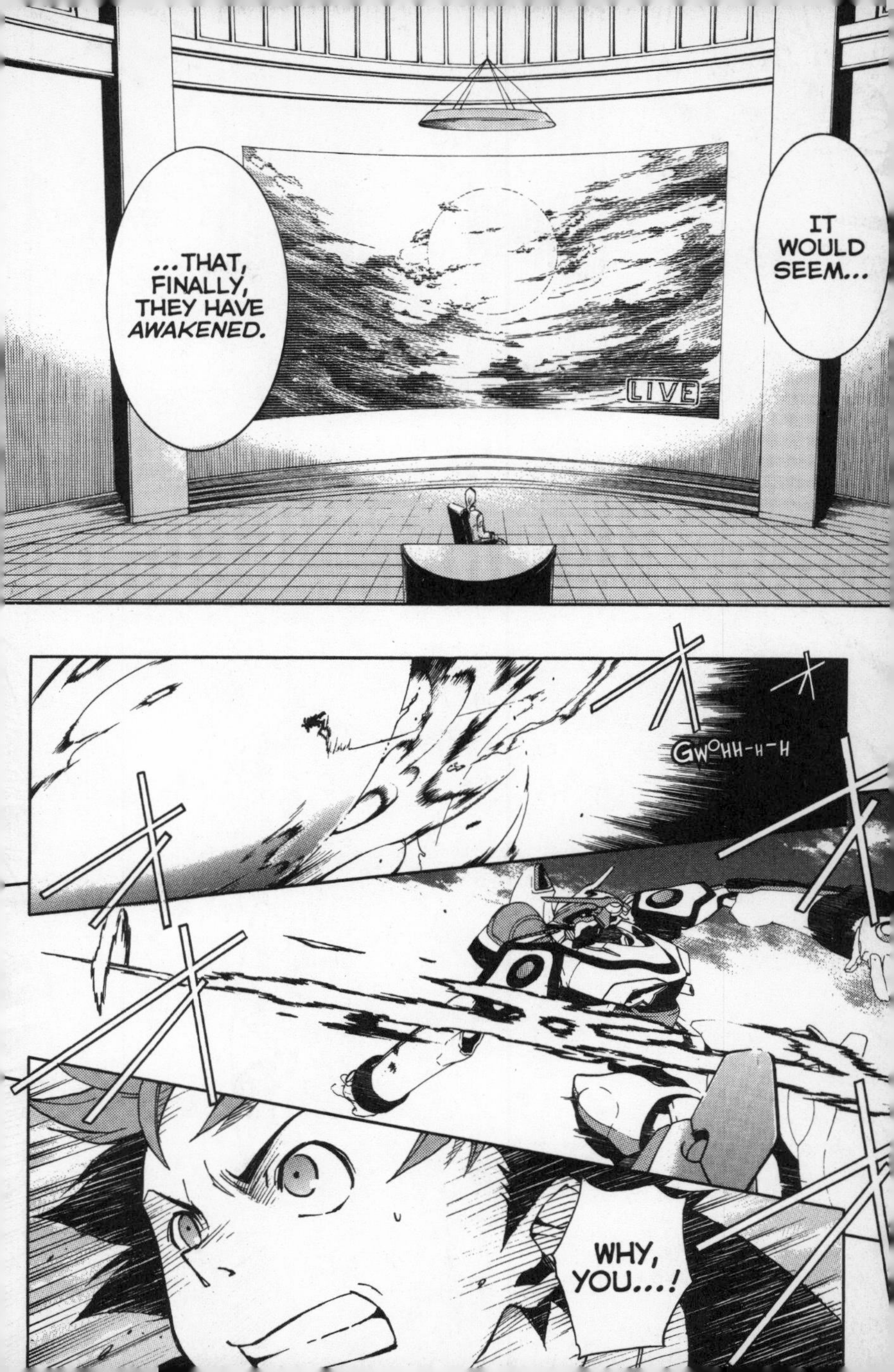
IT WOULD SEEM...
...THAT, FINALLY, THEY HAVE *AWAKENED.*
LIVE
GWOHH-H-H
WHY, YOU...!

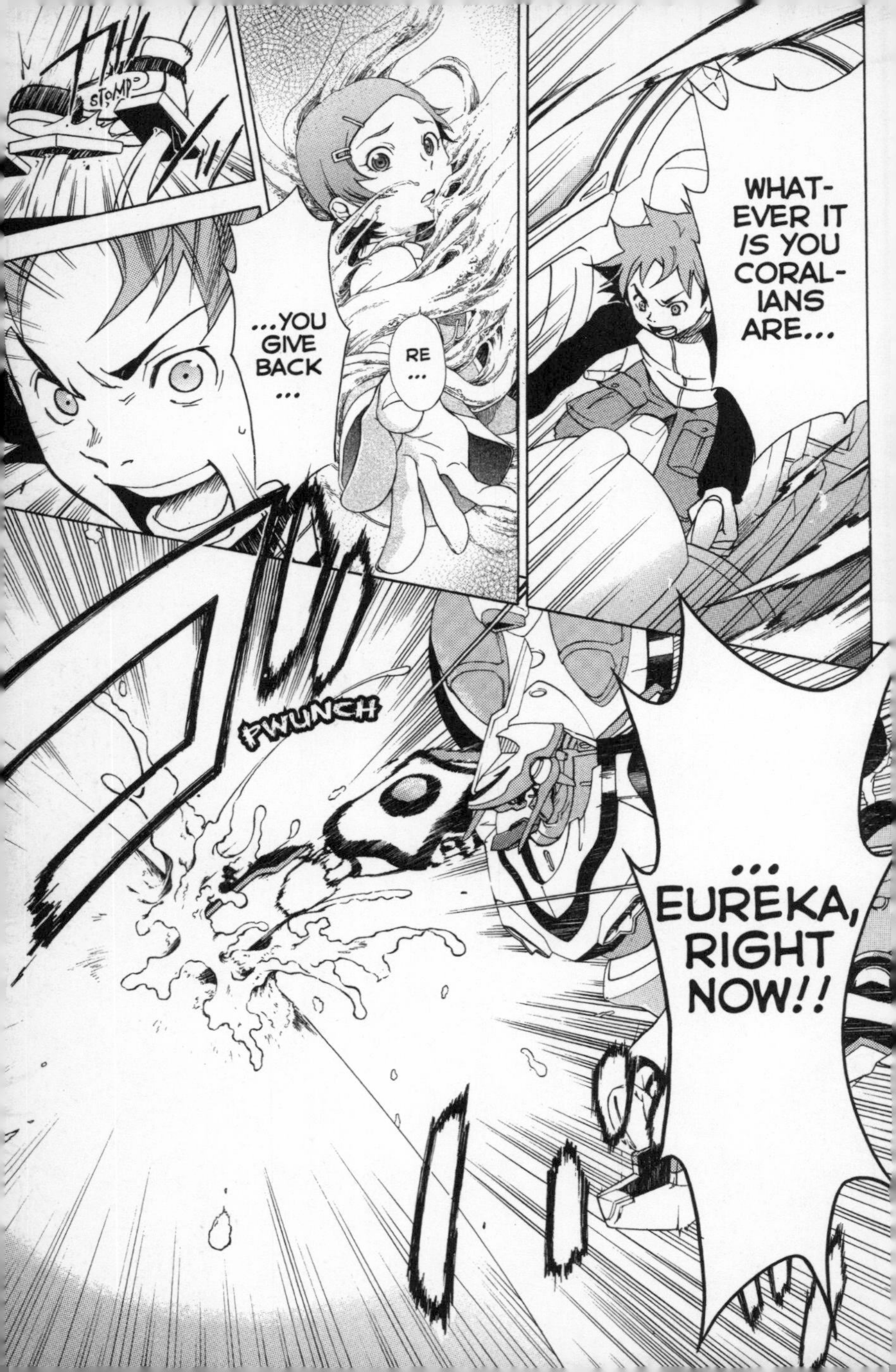
WHAT-EVER IT IS YOU CORAL-IANS ARE...
RE...
STOMP
...YOU GIVE BACK...
PWUNCH
...EUREKA, RIGHT NOW!!

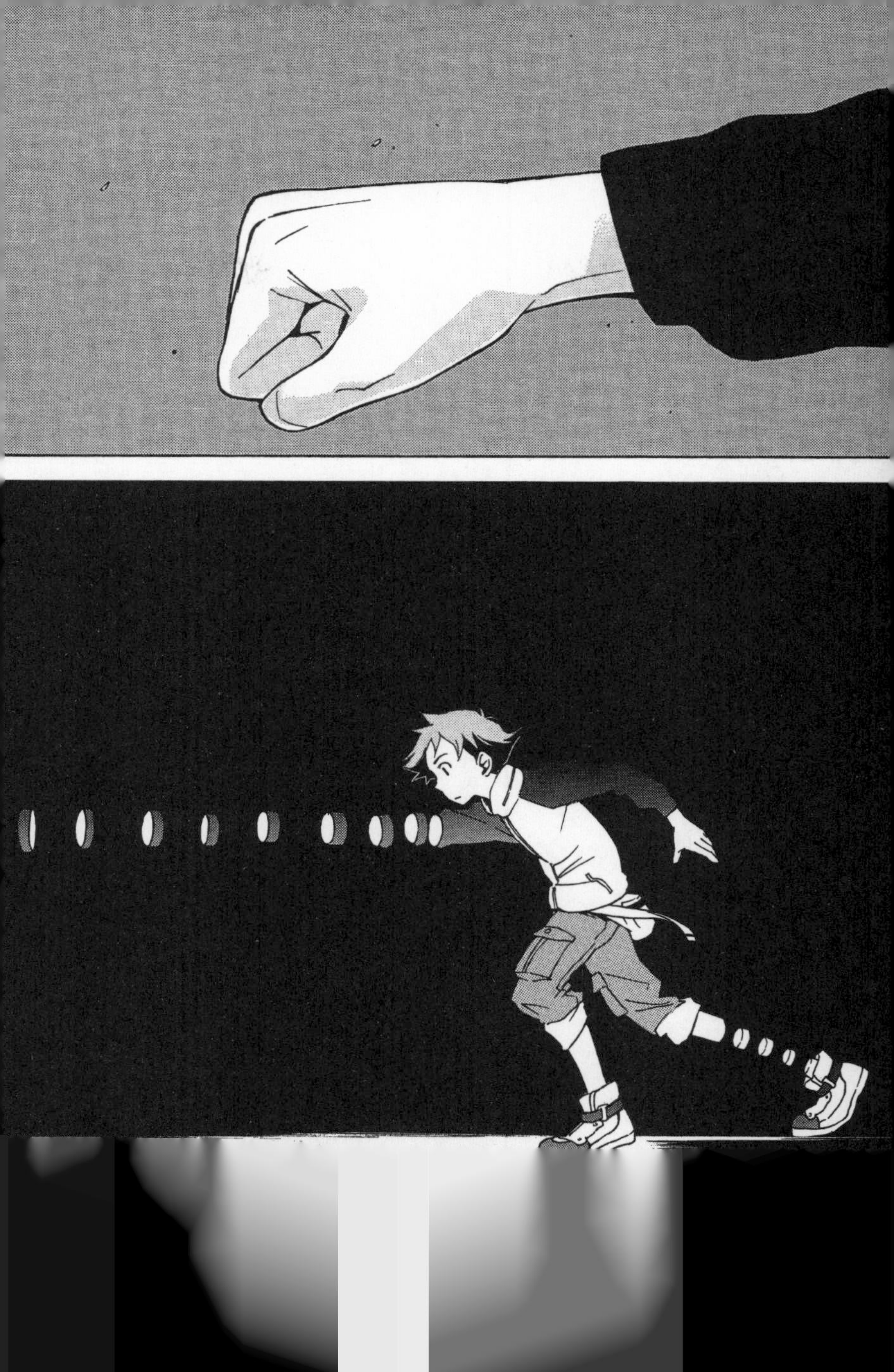

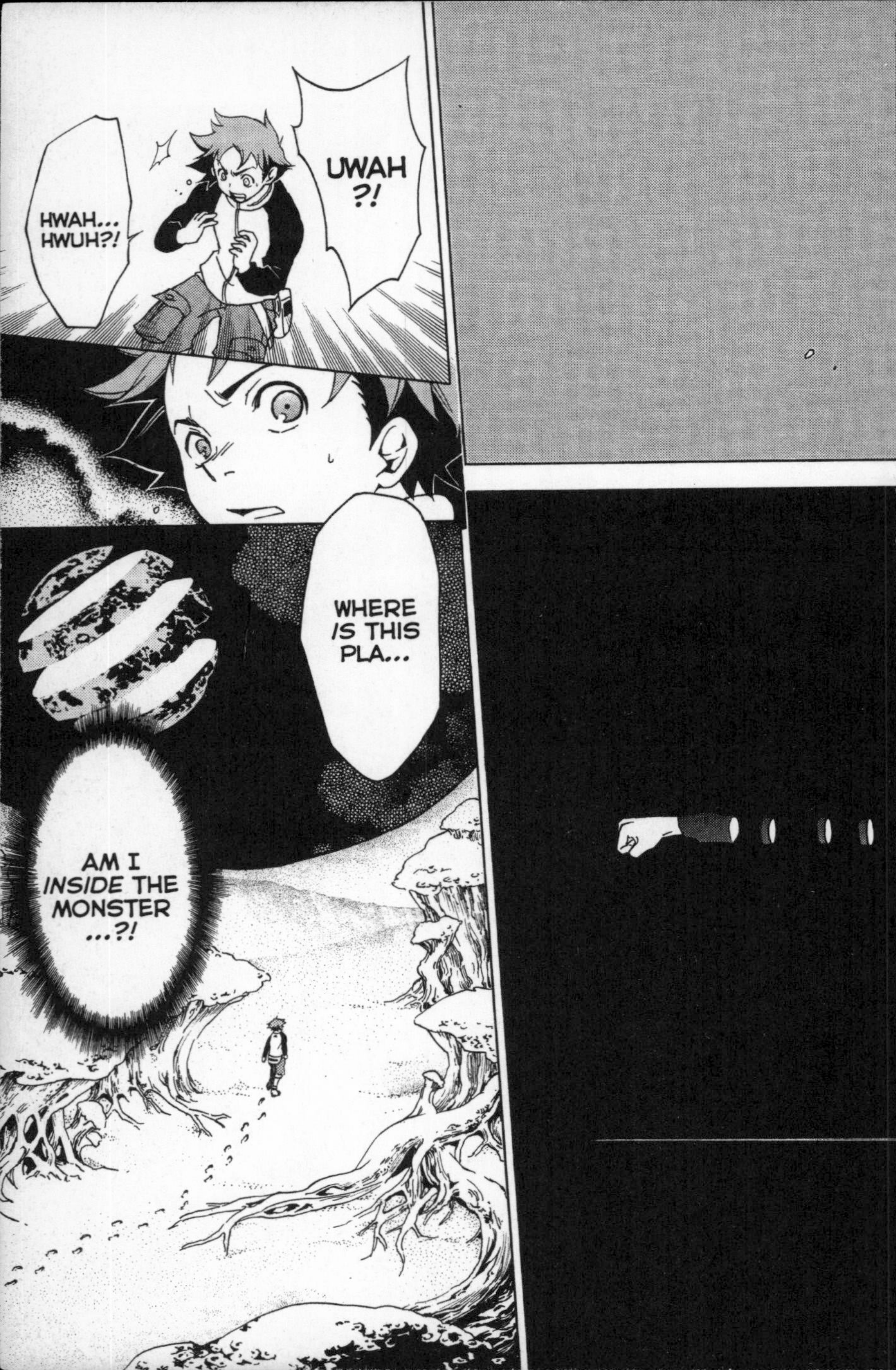
UWAH ?!
HWAH... HWUH?!
WHERE IS THIS PLA...
AM I INSIDE THE MONSTER ...?!

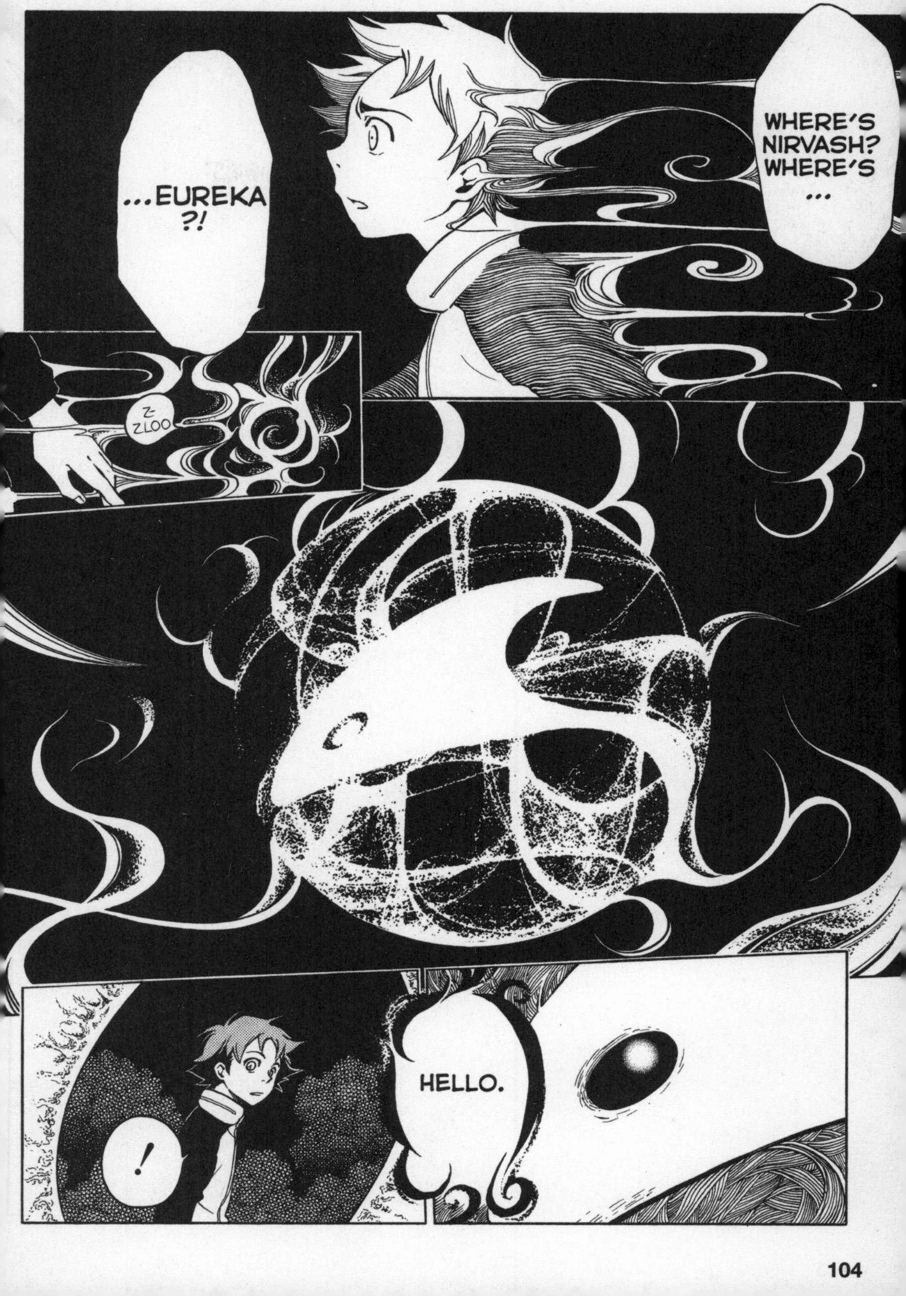
WHERE'S NIRVASH? WHERE'S ...
...EUREKA ?!
Z- ZLOO
HELLO.
!

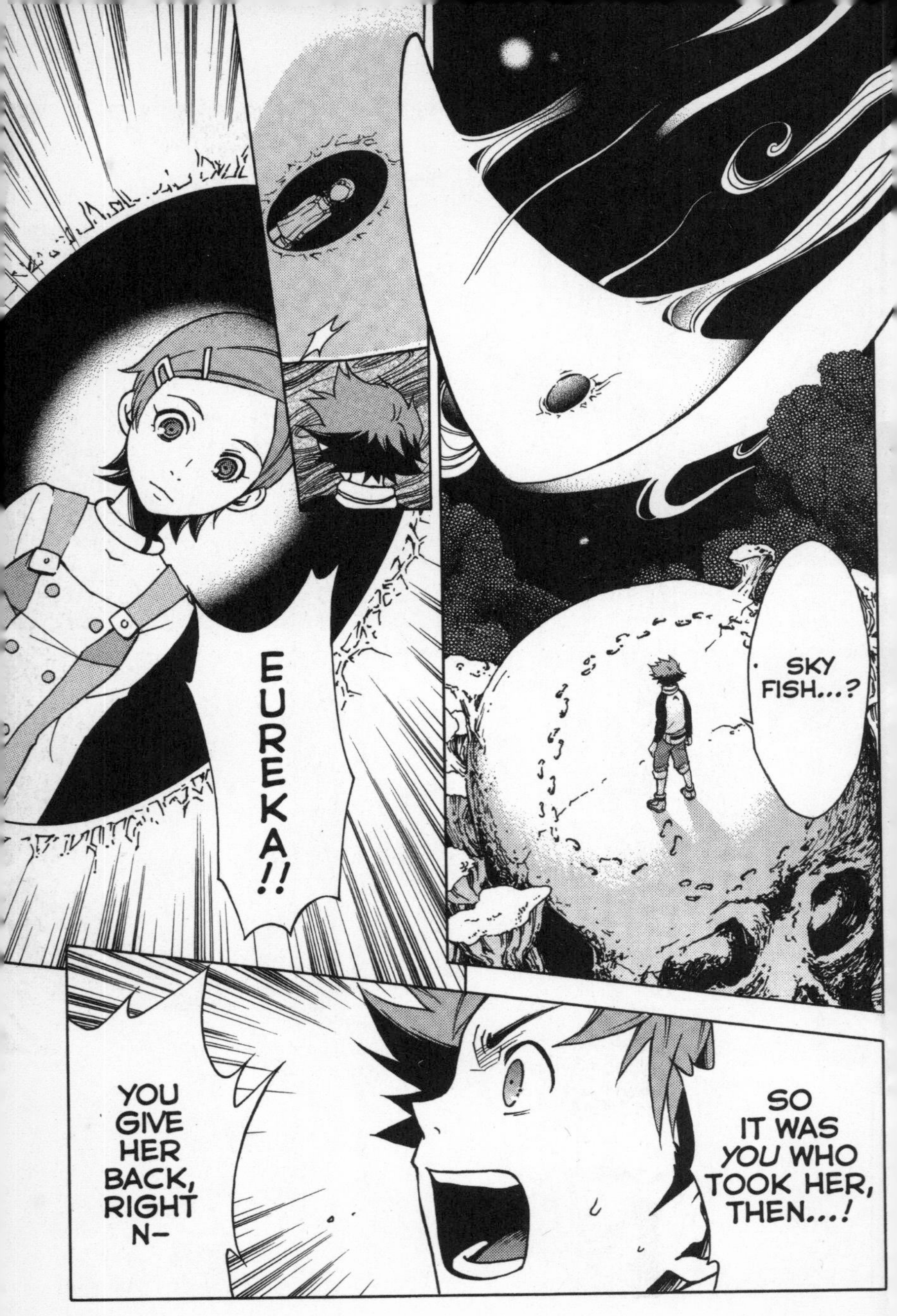
SKY FISH...?
EUREKA!!
SO IT WAS *YOU* WHO TOOK HER, THEN...!
YOU GIVE HER BACK, RIGHT N—

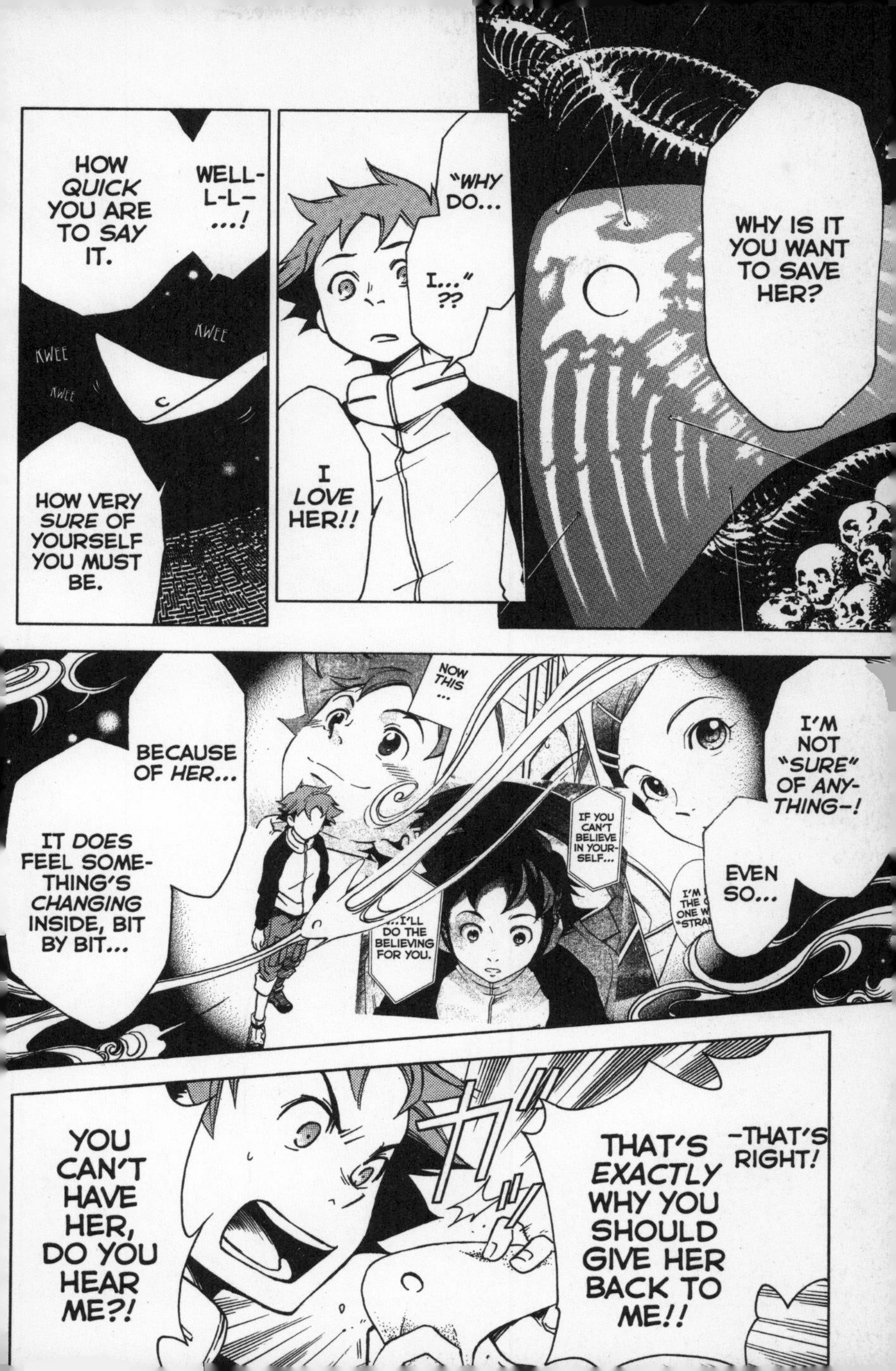
WHY IS IT YOU WANT TO SAVE HER?
"WHY DO... I..."
??
I LOVE HER!!
WELL-L-L-...!
HOW QUICK YOU ARE TO SAY IT.
KWEE
KWEE
KWEE
HOW VERY SURE OF YOURSELF YOU MUST BE.
I'M NOT "SURE" OF ANY-THING-!
EVEN SO...
IF YOU CAN'T BELIEVE IN YOUR-SELF...
...I'LL DO THE BELIEVING FOR YOU.
NOW THIS ...
BECAUSE OF HER...
IT DOES FEEL SOME-THING'S CHANGING INSIDE, BIT BY BIT...
-THAT'S RIGHT!
THAT'S EXACTLY WHY YOU SHOULD GIVE HER BACK TO ME!!
YOU CAN'T HAVE HER, DO YOU HEAR ME?!

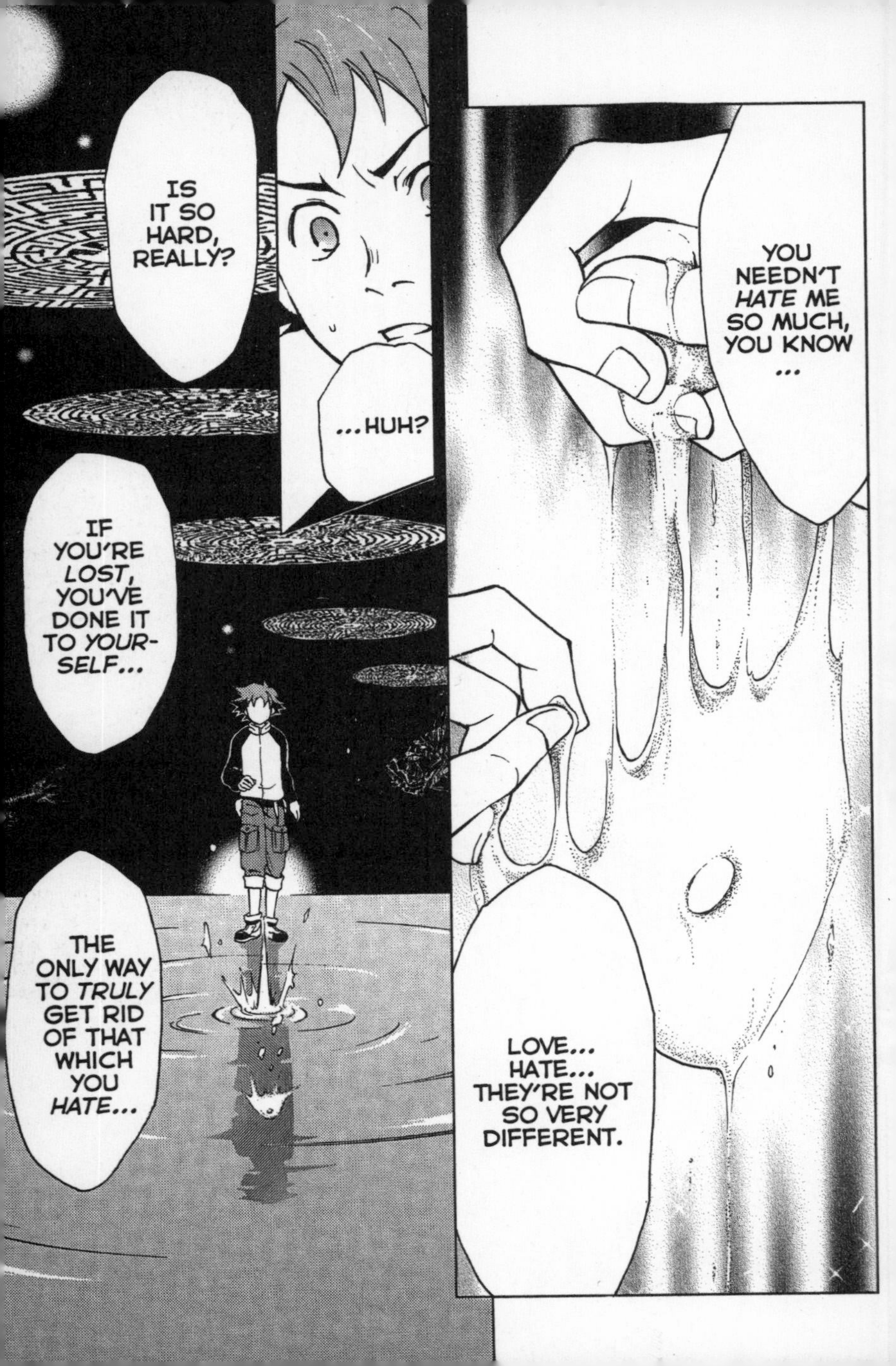
YOU NEEDN'T *HATE* ME SO MUCH, YOU KNOW ...
LOVE... HATE... THEY'RE NOT SO VERY DIFFERENT.
IS IT SO HARD, REALLY?
...HUH?
IF YOU'RE *LOST*, YOU'VE DONE IT TO *YOURSELF*...
THE ONLY WAY TO *TRULY* GET RID OF THAT WHICH YOU *HATE*...

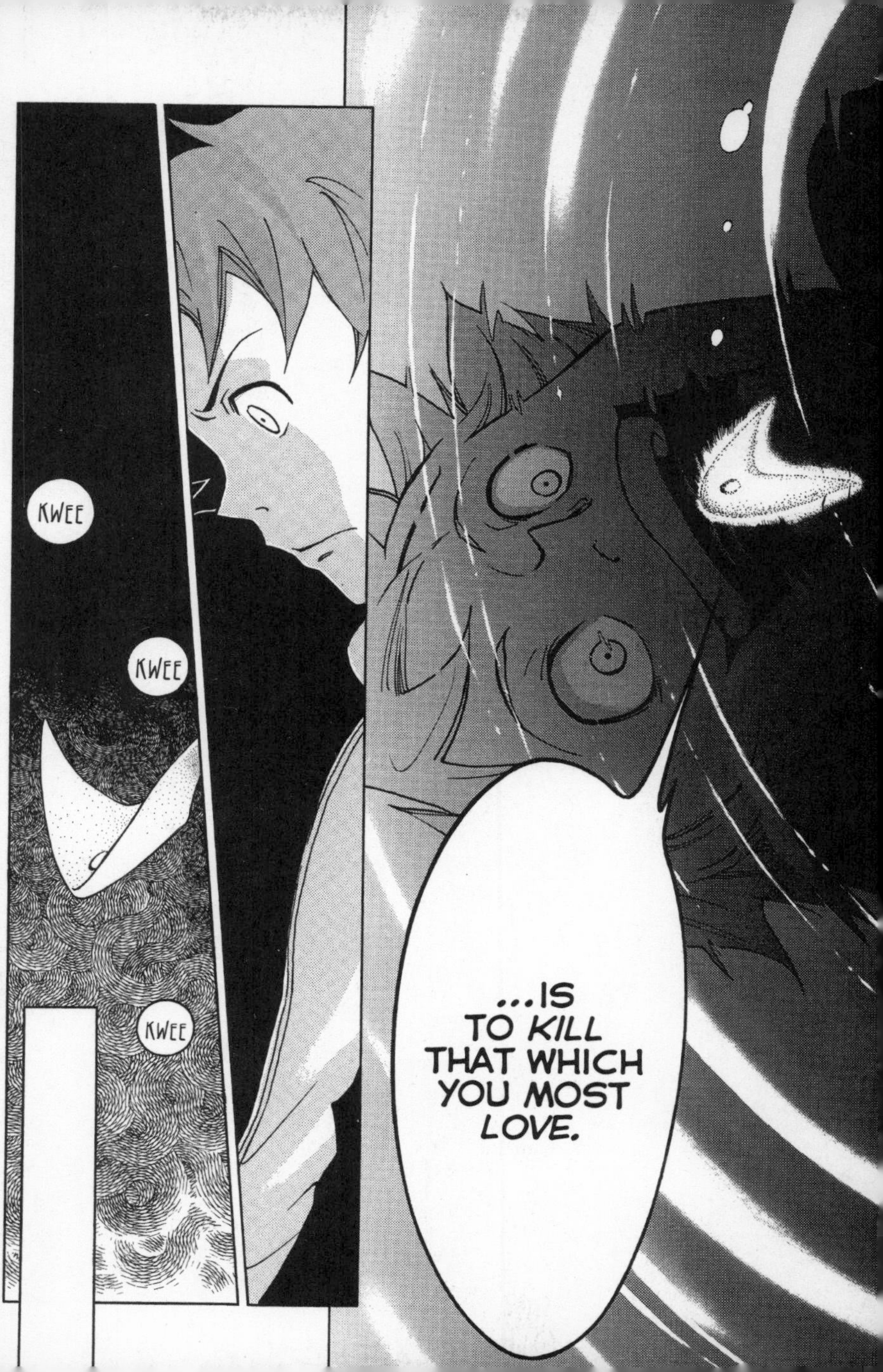
...IS TO *KILL* THAT WHICH YOU MOST *LOVE.*
KWEE
KWEE
KWEE

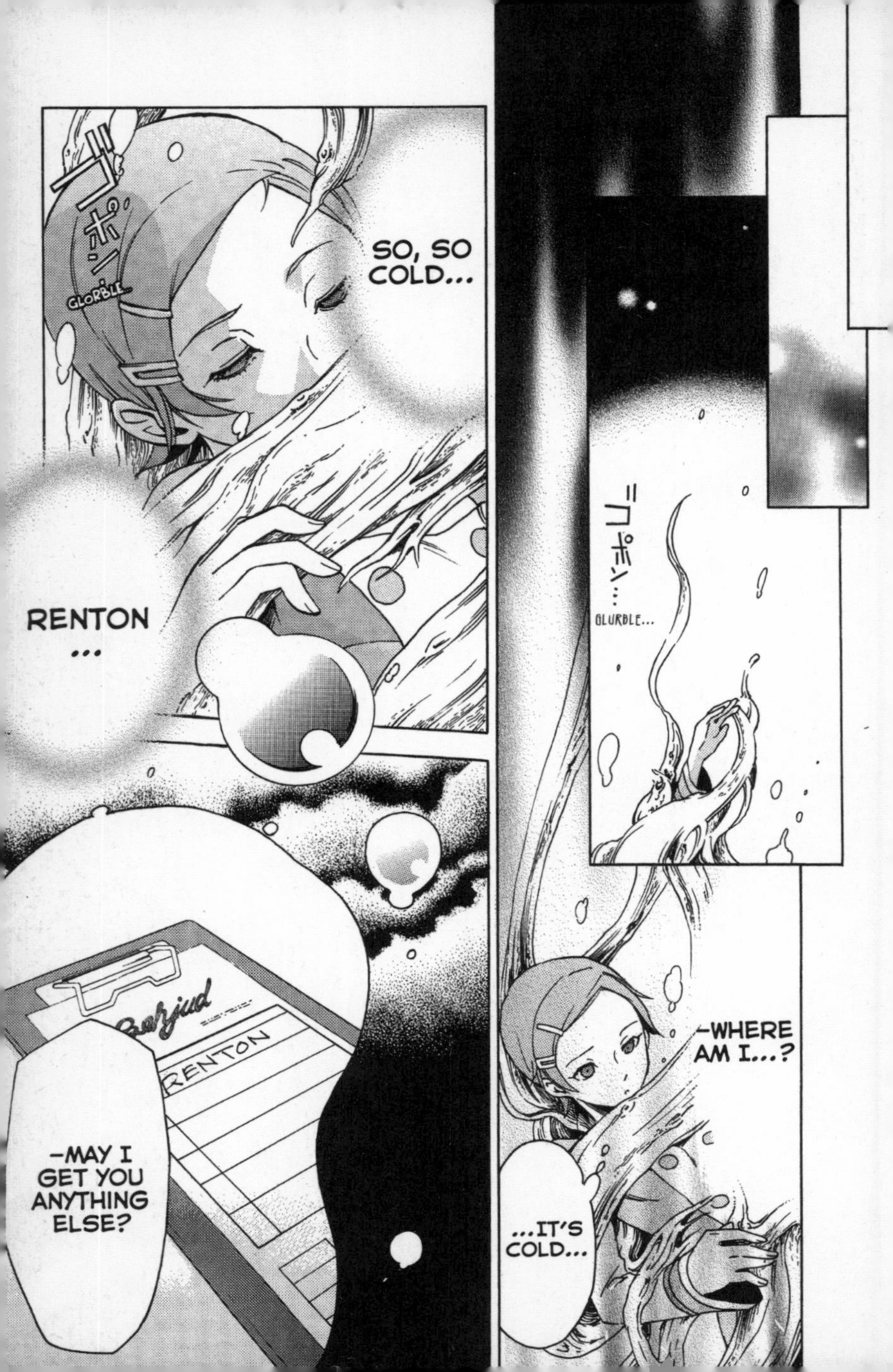
ゴポン…
GLURBLE...
-WHERE AM I...?
...IT'S COLD...
ゴポン
GLORBLE
SO, SO COLD...
RENTON ...
RENTON
RENTON
-MAY I GET YOU ANYTHING ELSE?

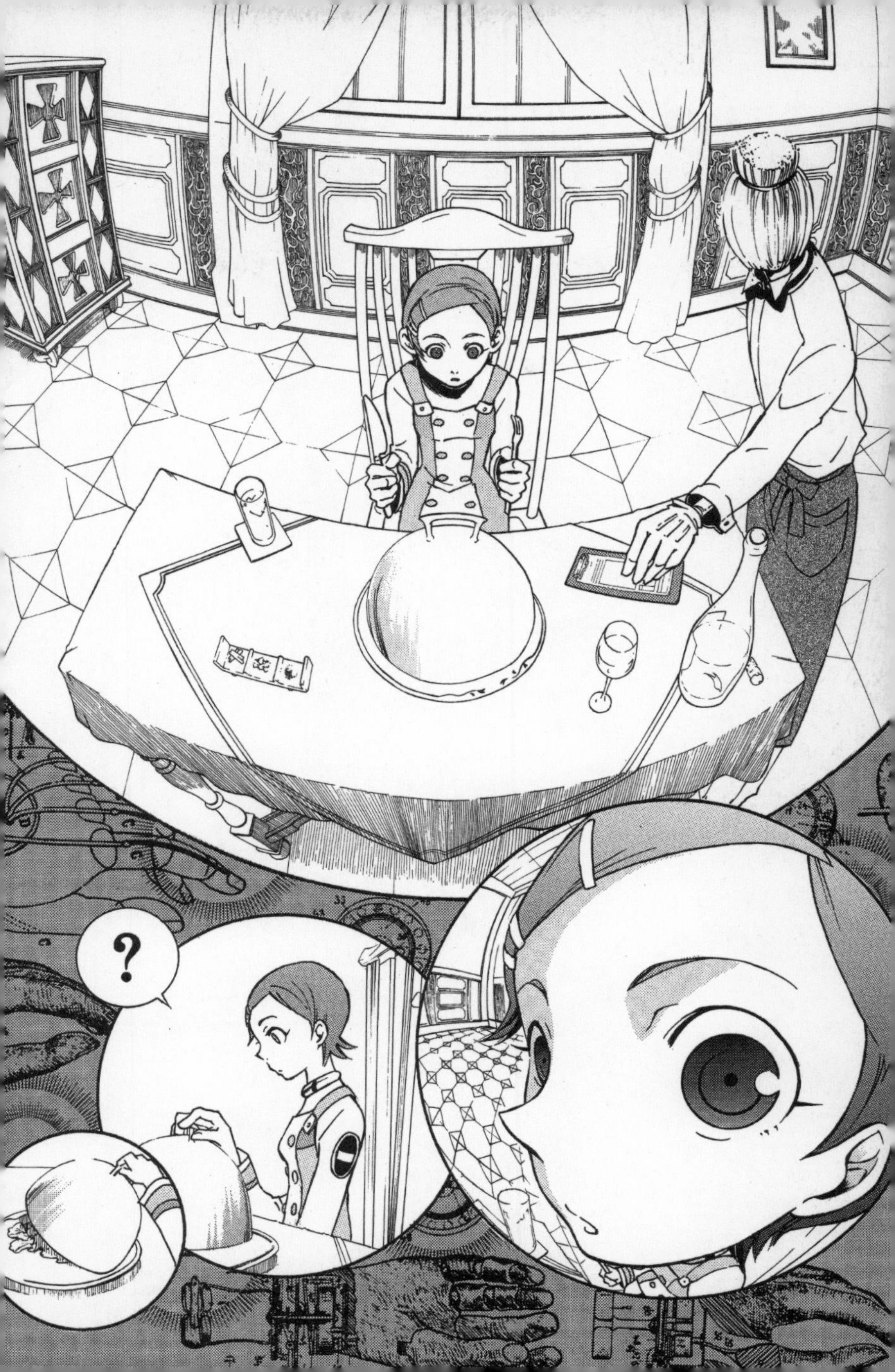
?

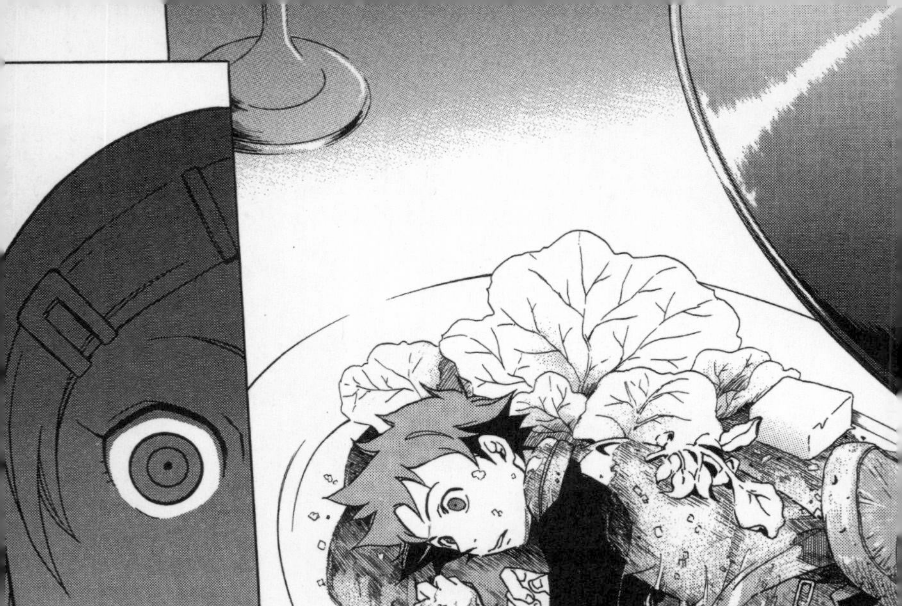

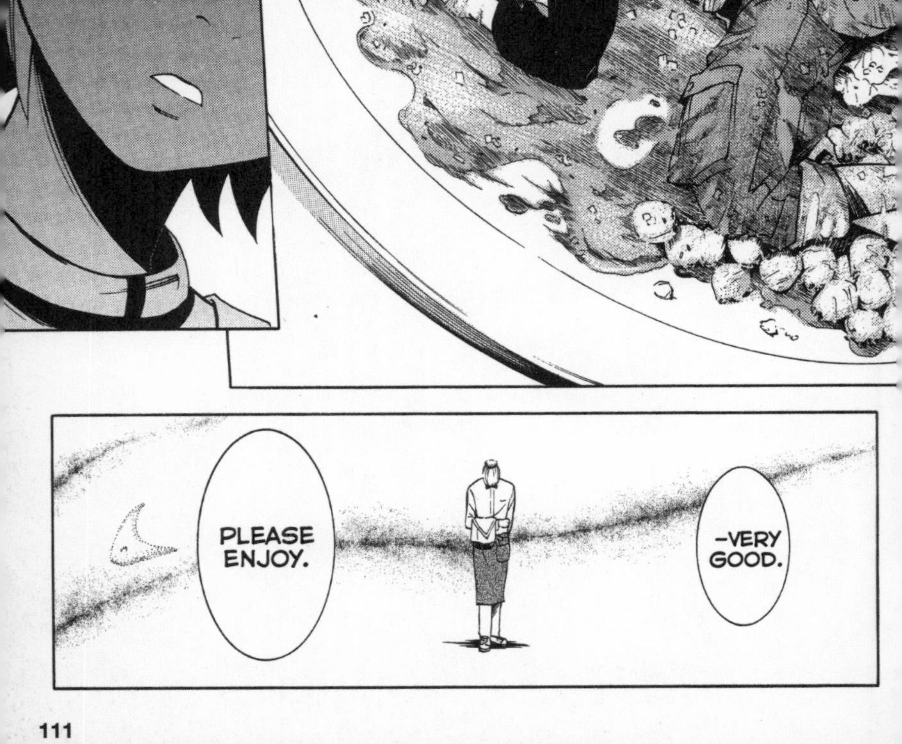
—VERY GOOD.
PLEASE ENJOY.

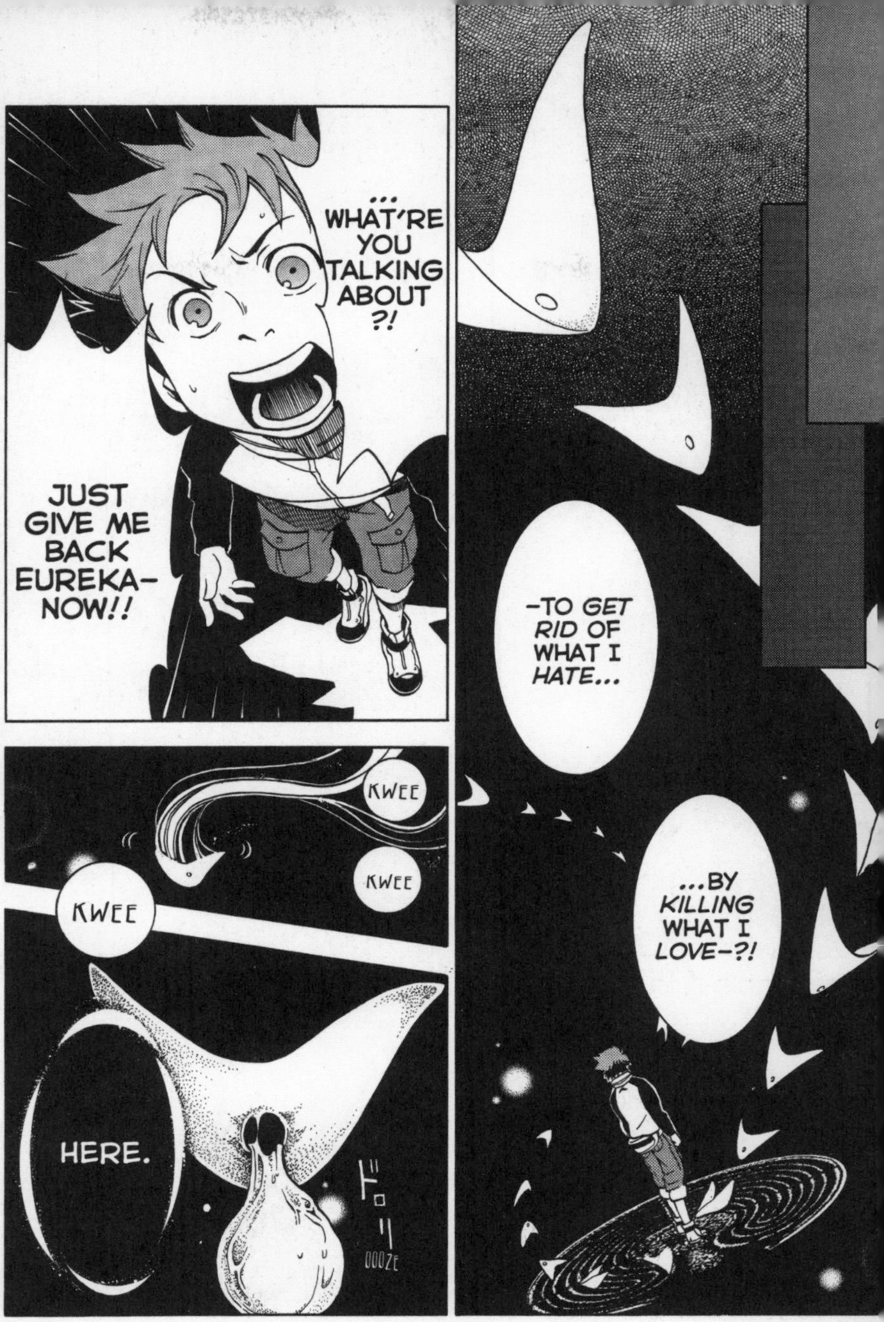
-TO GET RID OF WHAT I HATE...
...BY KILLING WHAT I LOVE-?!
...WHAT'RE YOU TALKING ABOUT?!
JUST GIVE ME BACK EUREKA-NOW!!
KWEE
KWEE
KWEE
HERE.
ドロリ
OOOZE

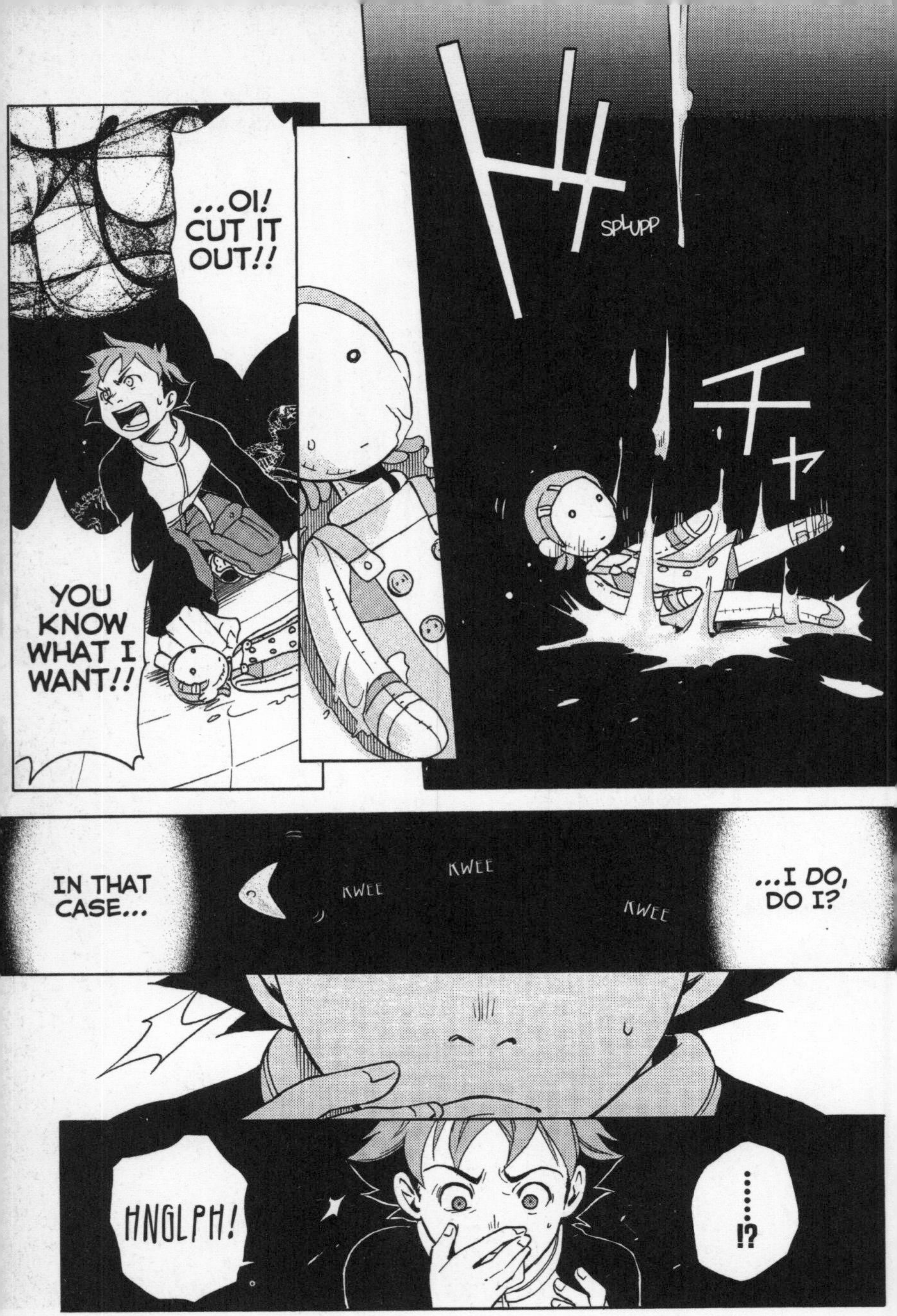
SPLUPP
チャ
...OI! CUT IT OUT!!
YOU KNOW WHAT I WANT!!
...I DO, DO I?
KWEE
KWEE
KWEE
IN THAT CASE...
......!?
HNGLPH!

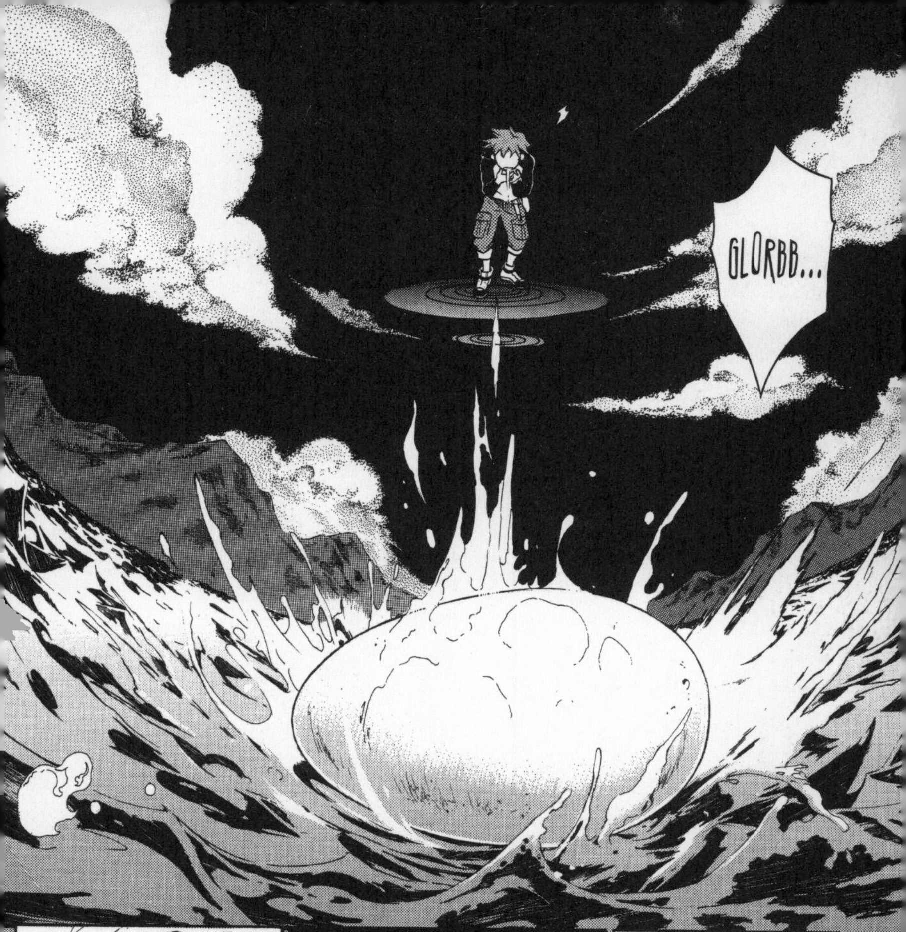
GLORBB...
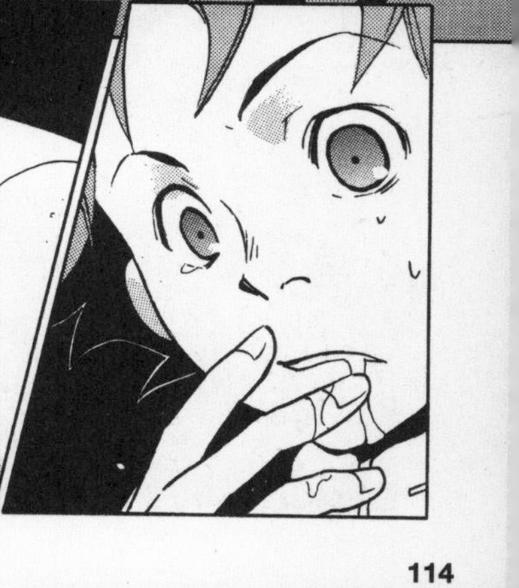
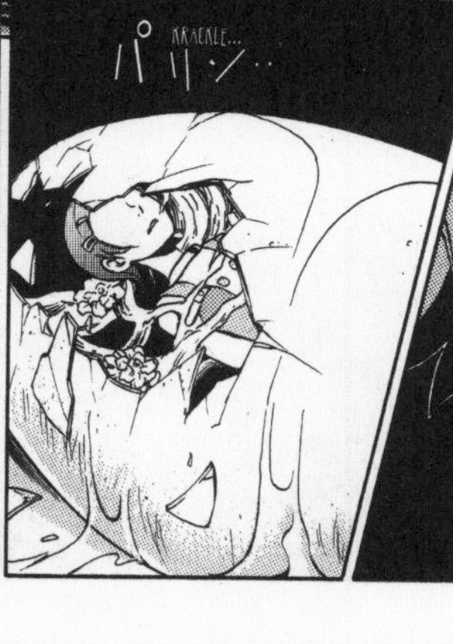
パリッ‥
KRACKLE...
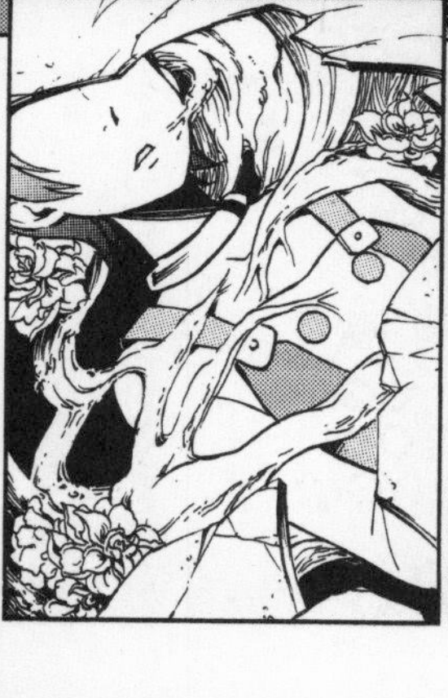

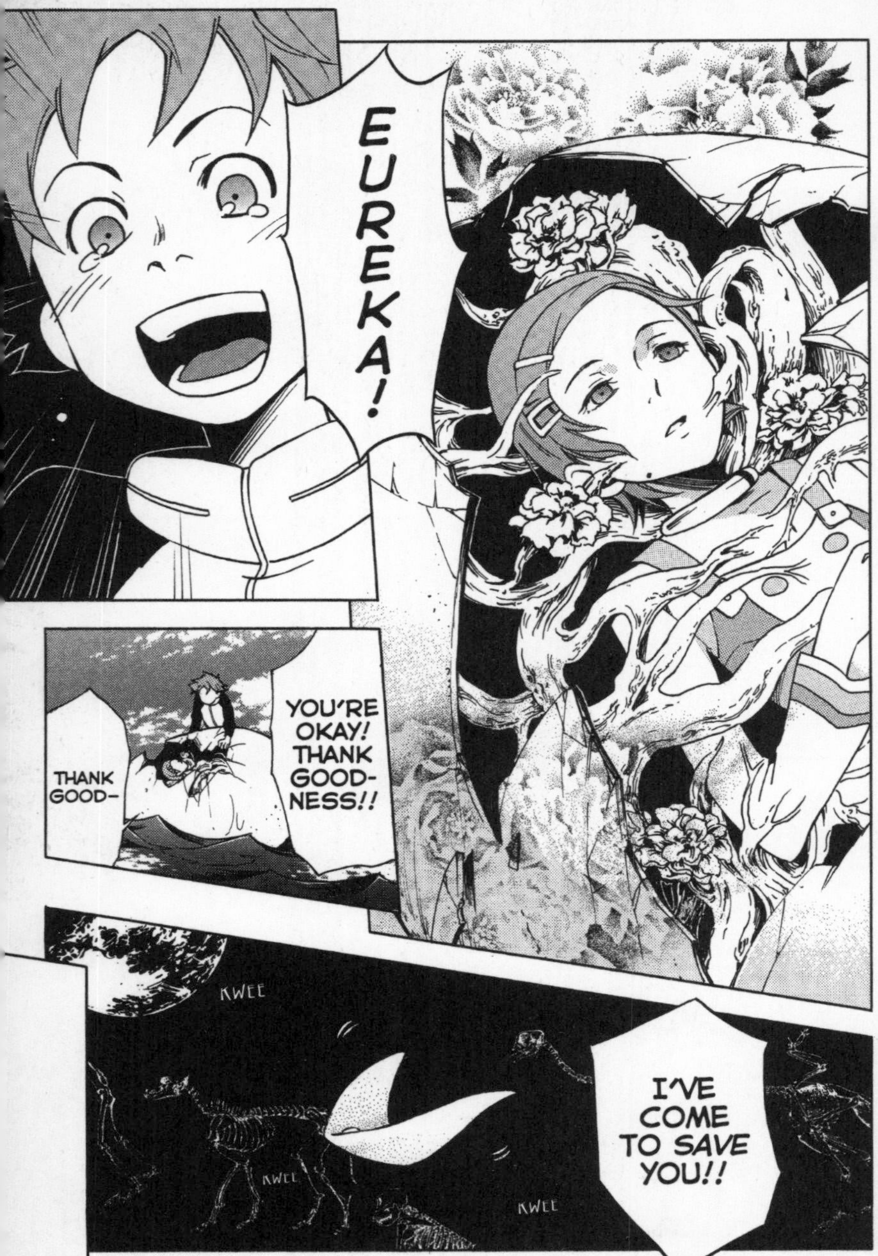
EUREKA!
YOU'RE OKAY! THANK GOODNESS!!
THANK GOOD-
KWEE
I'VE COME TO SAVE YOU!!
KWEE
KWEE

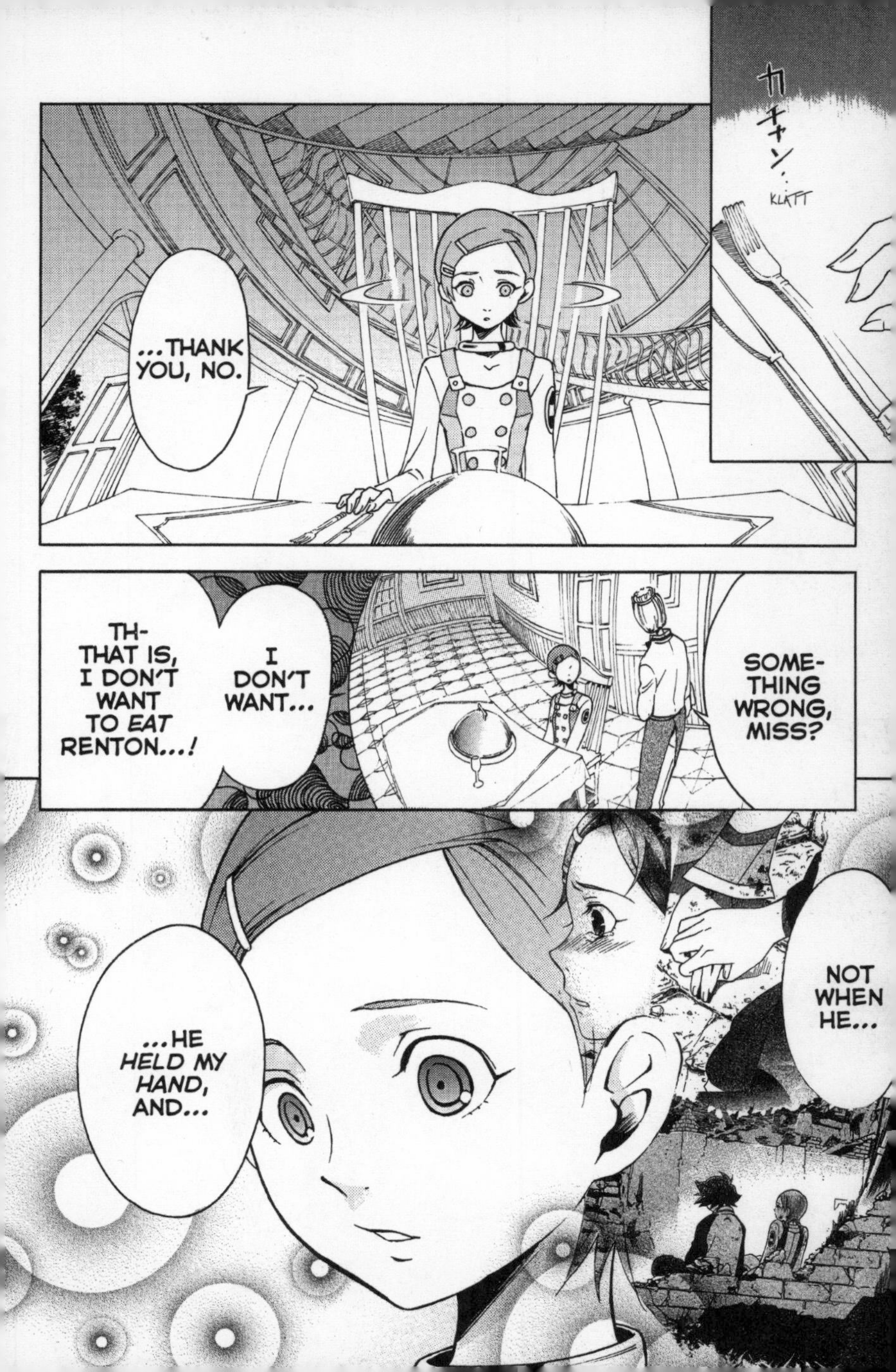

カチャン…
KLATT
...THANK YOU, NO.
SOME-THING WRONG, MISS?
I DON'T WANT...
TH- THAT IS, I DON'T WANT TO *EAT* RENTON...!
NOT WHEN HE...
...HE *HELD MY HAND,* AND...

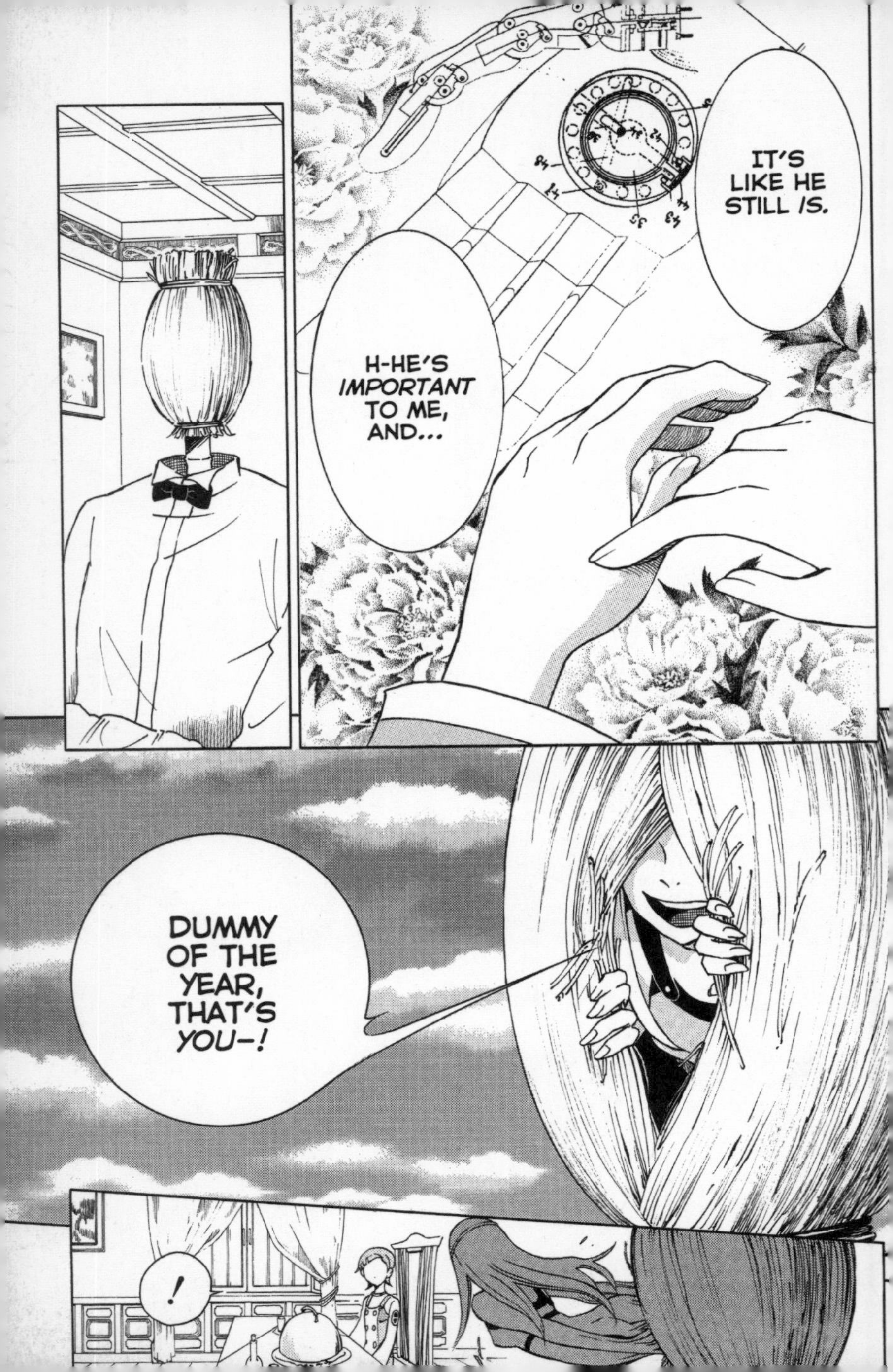
IT'S LIKE HE STILL *IS*.
H-HE'S *IMPORTANT* TO ME, AND...
DUMMY OF THE YEAR, THAT'S *YOU*-!
!

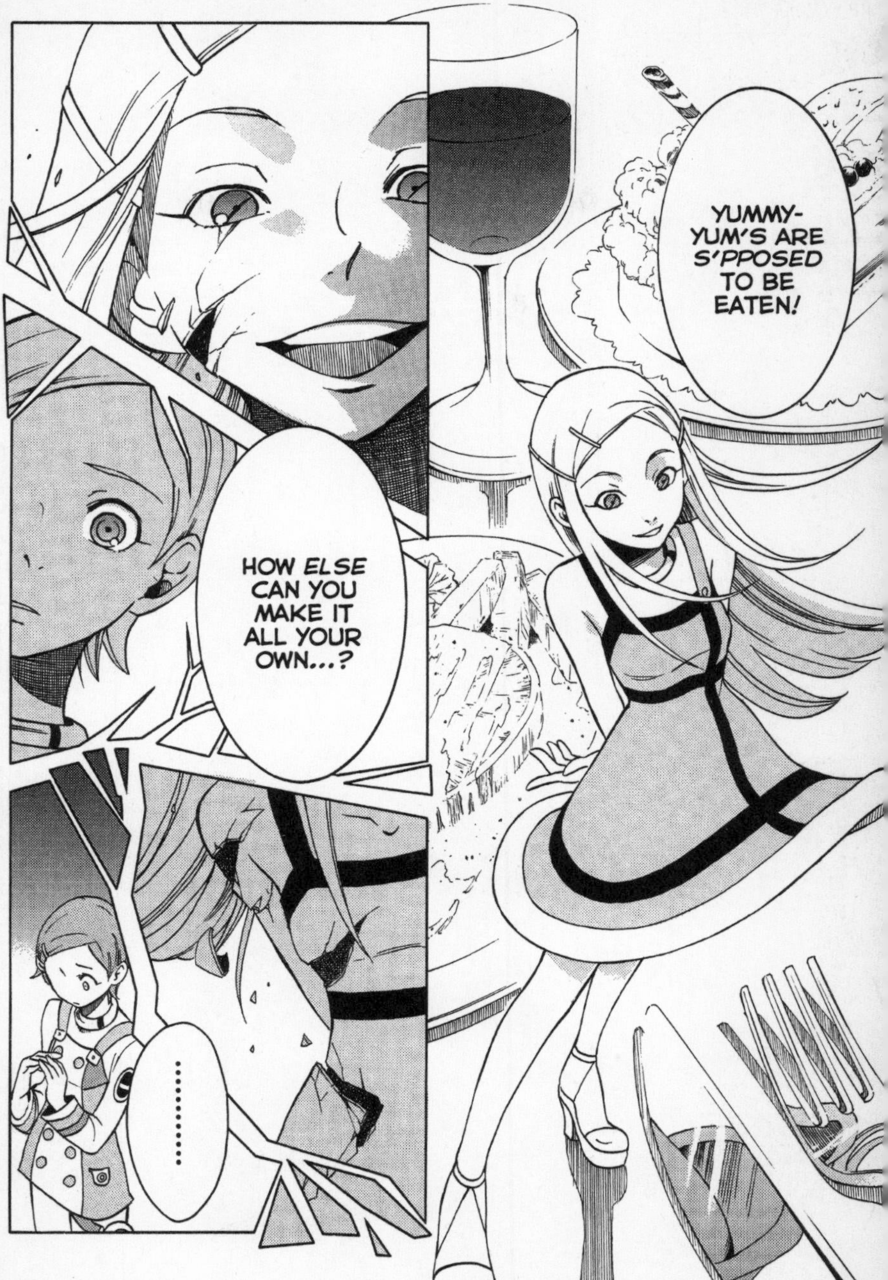
YUMMY-YUM'S ARE S'PPOSED TO BE EATEN!
HOW ELSE CAN YOU MAKE IT ALL YOUR OWN...?
....

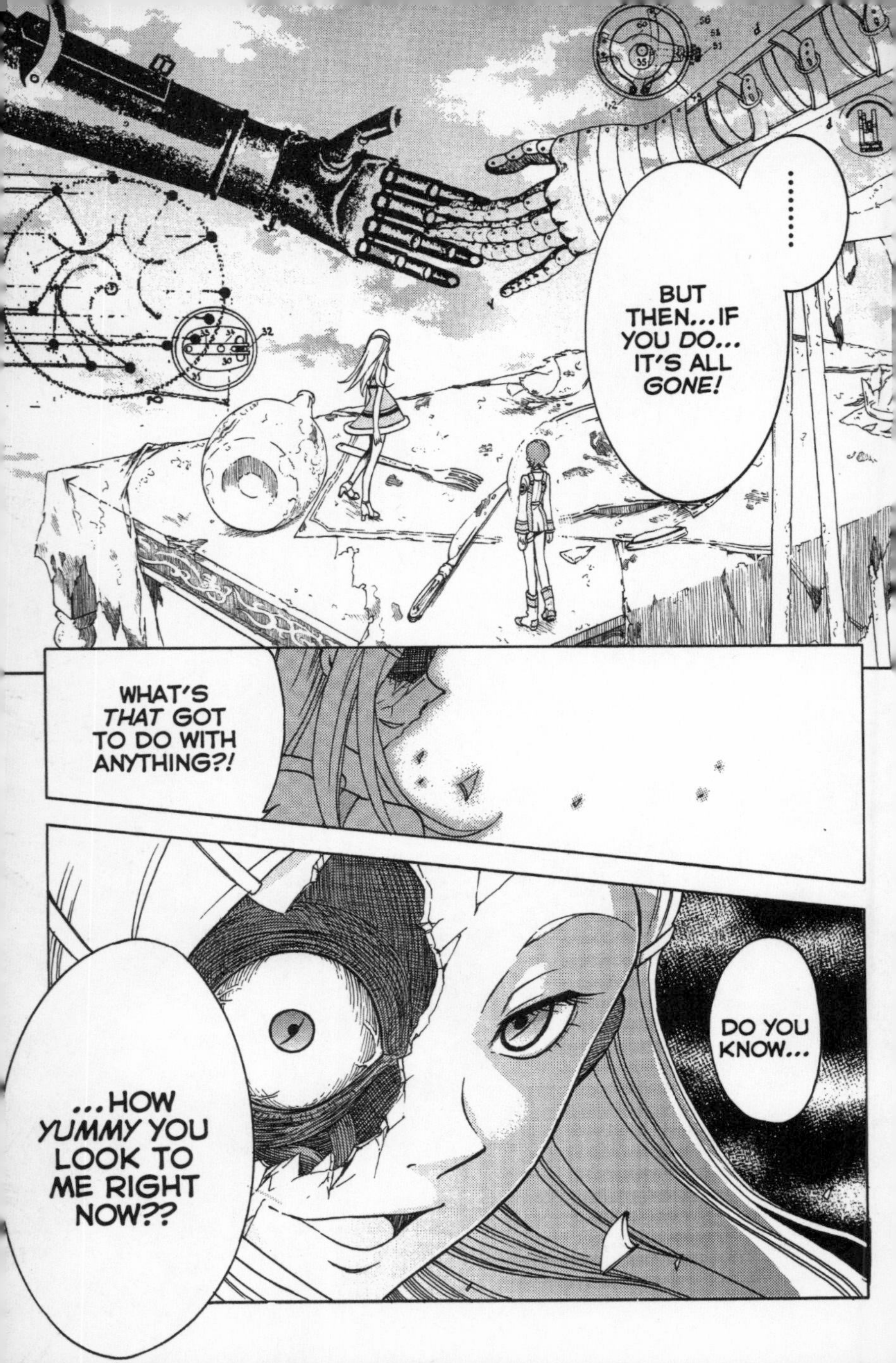
......
BUT THEN...IF YOU *DO*... IT'S ALL *GONE!*
WHAT'S *THAT* GOT TO DO WITH ANYTHING?!
DO YOU KNOW...
...HOW *YUMMY* YOU LOOK TO ME RIGHT NOW??

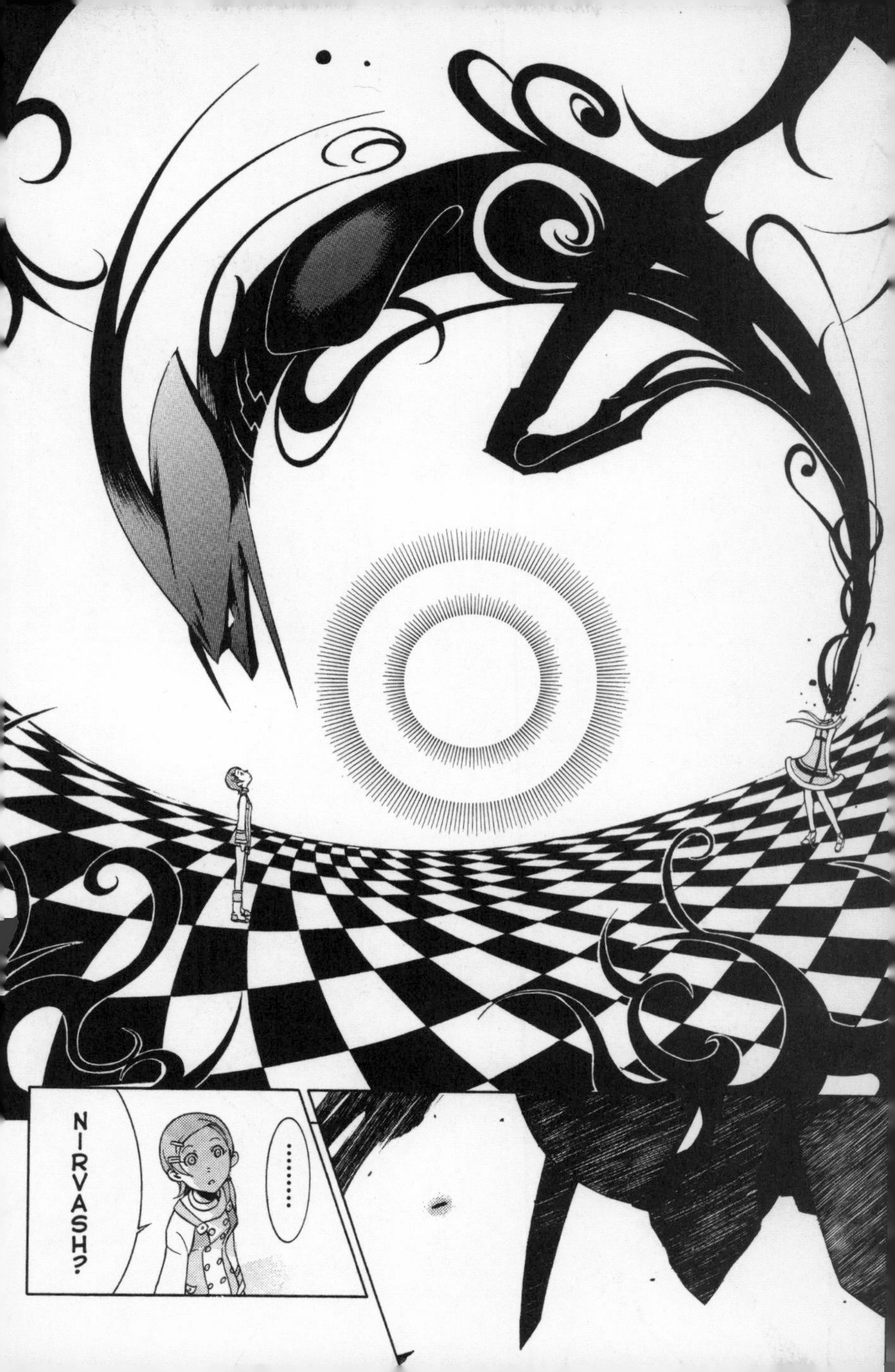
......
NIRVASH?

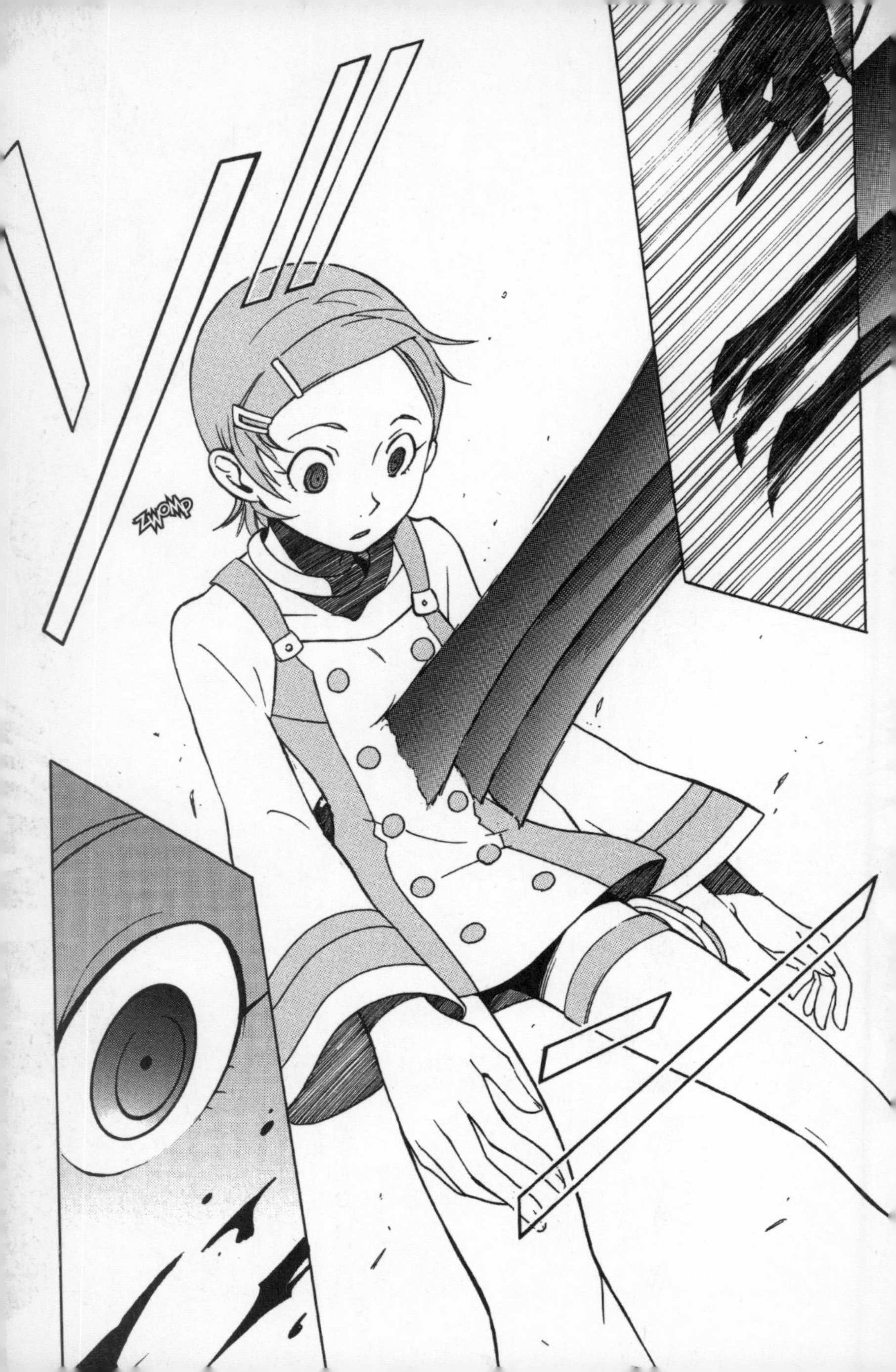
ZWOMP

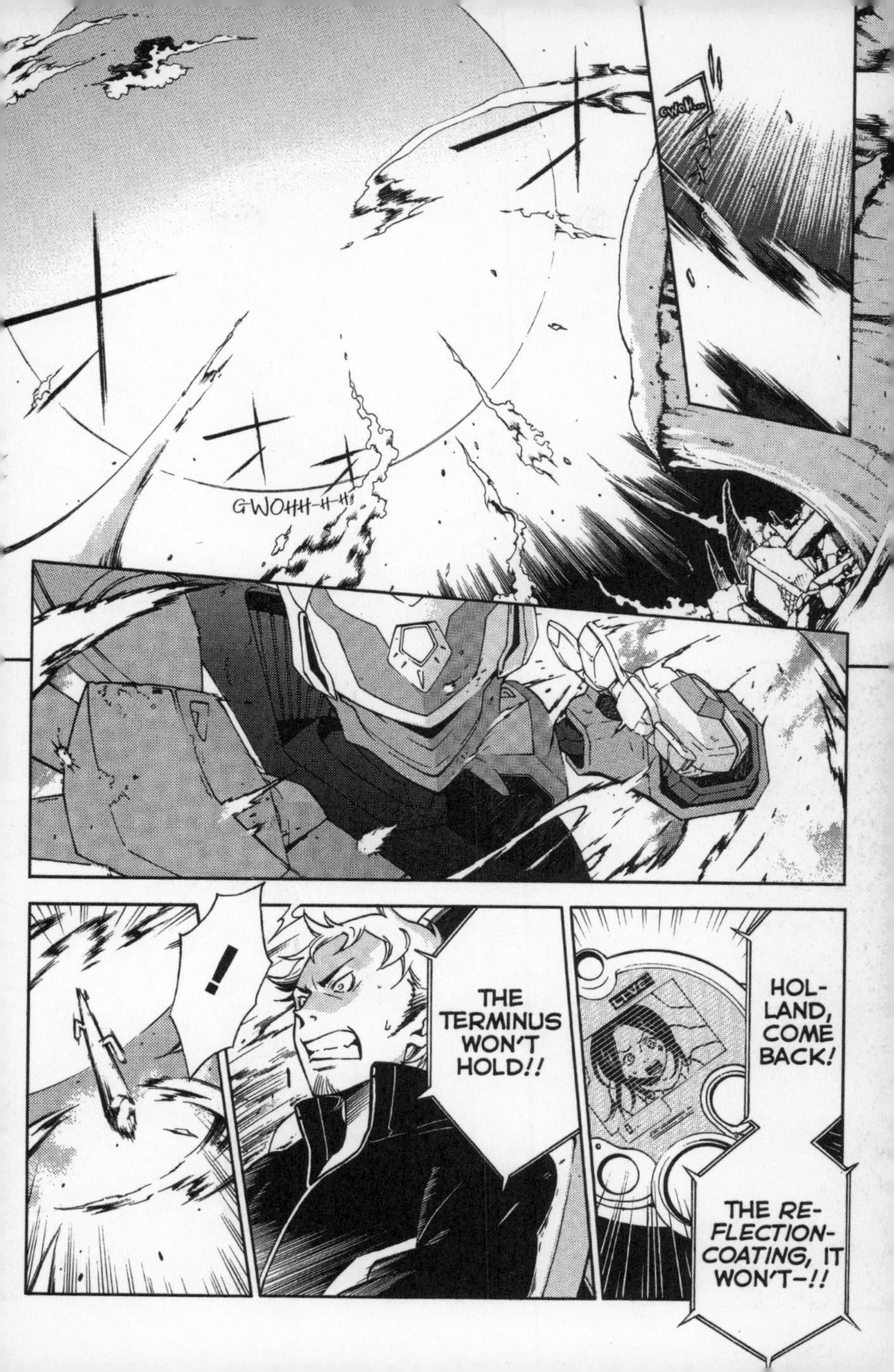
GWOH...
GWOHH-H-H
HOL-LAND, COME BACK!
THE RE-FLECTION-COATING, IT WON'T-!!
THE TERMINUS WON'T HOLD!!
!

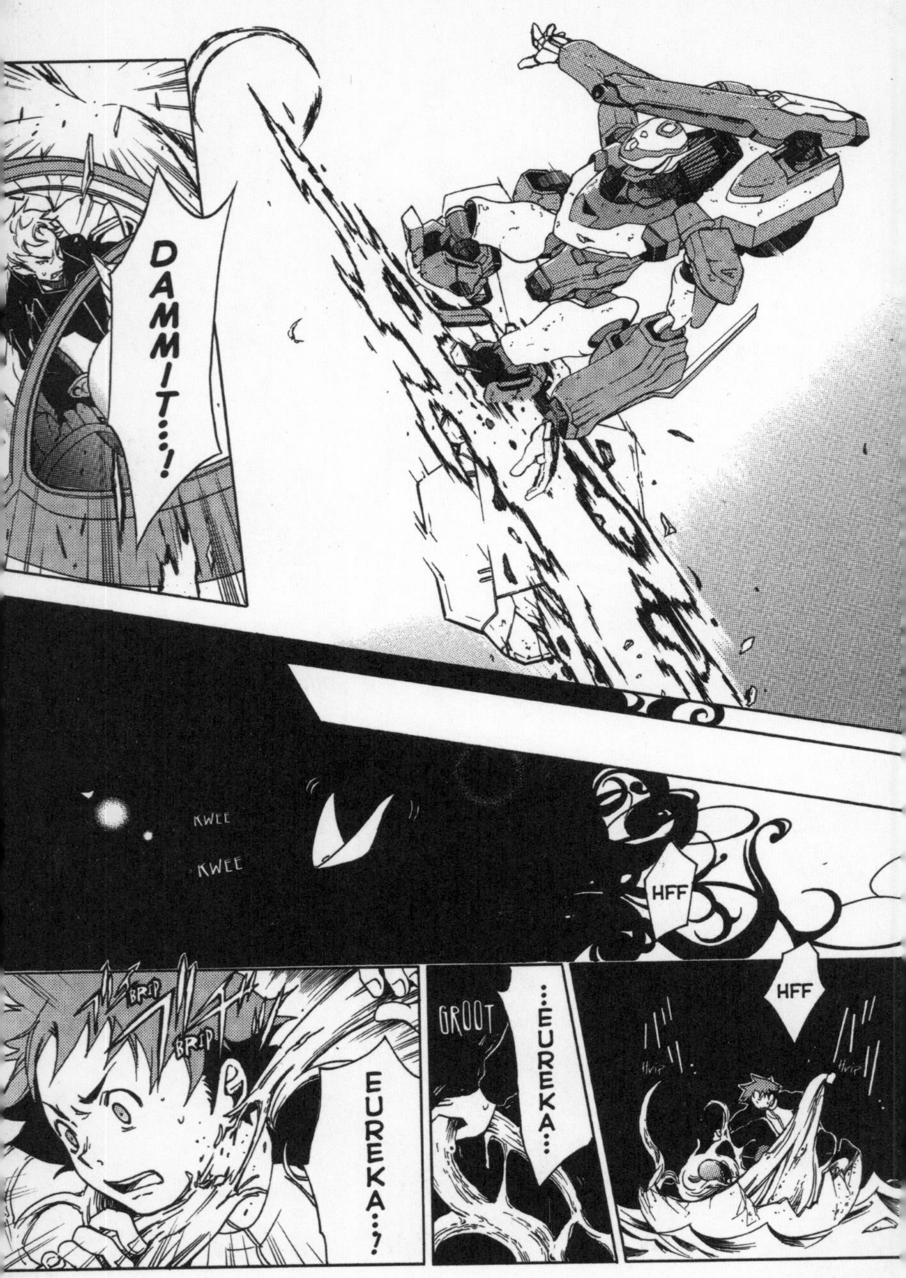
DAMMIT...!
HFF
KWEE
KWEE
HFF
...EUREKA...
GROOT
BRIP
BRIP
EUREKA...?

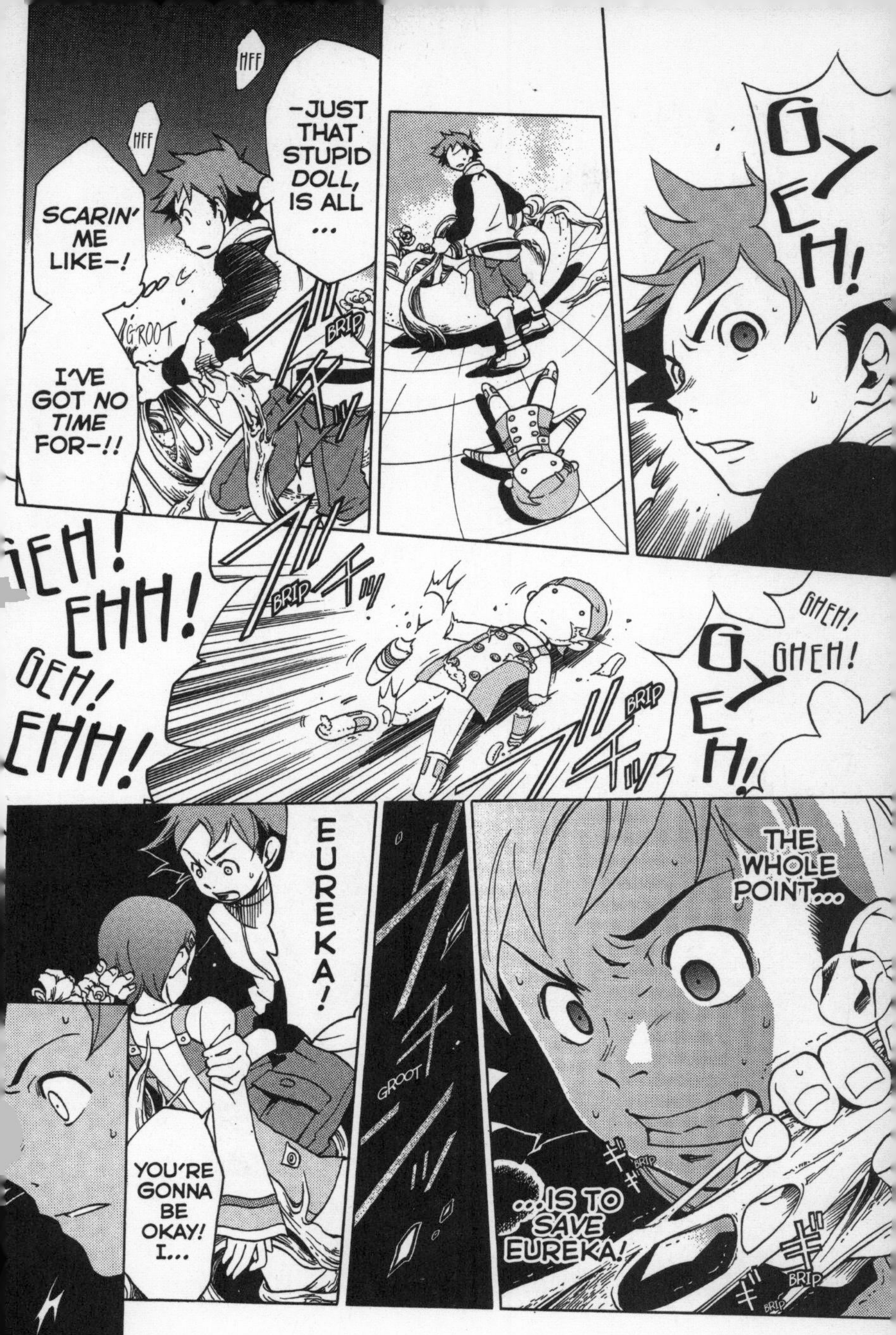
GYEH!
HFF
-JUST THAT STUPID DOLL, IS ALL ...
HFF
SCARIN' ME LIKE-!
GROOT
BRIP
I'VE GOT NO TIME FOR-!!
GHEH!
GHEH!
GYEH!
BRIP
BRIP
EH! EHH!
GEH!
EHH!
THE WHOLE POINT...
BRIP
...IS TO SAVE EUREKA!
BRIP
BRIP
GROOT
EUREKA!
YOU'RE GONNA BE OKAY! I...

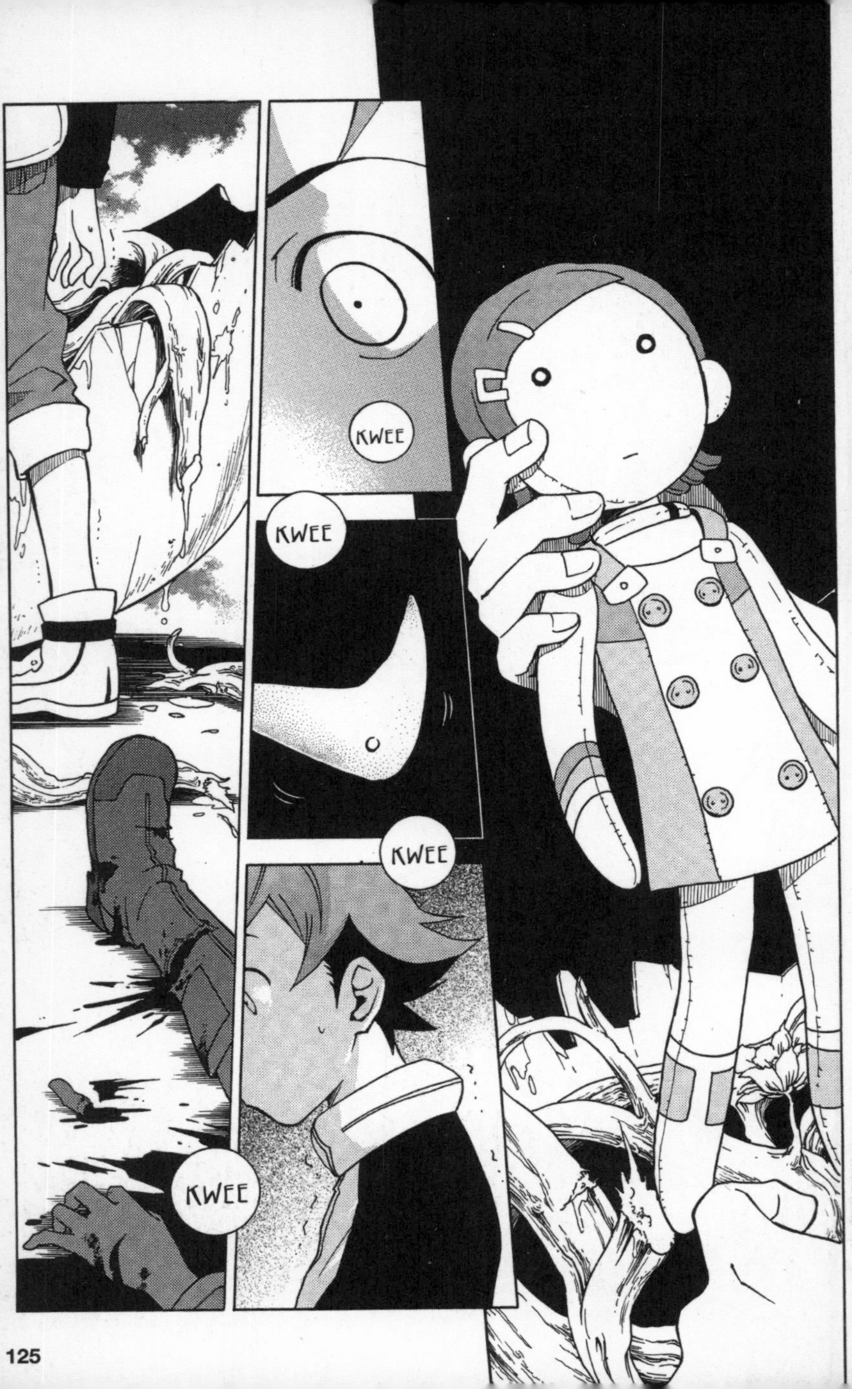
KWEE
KWEE
KWEE
KWEE

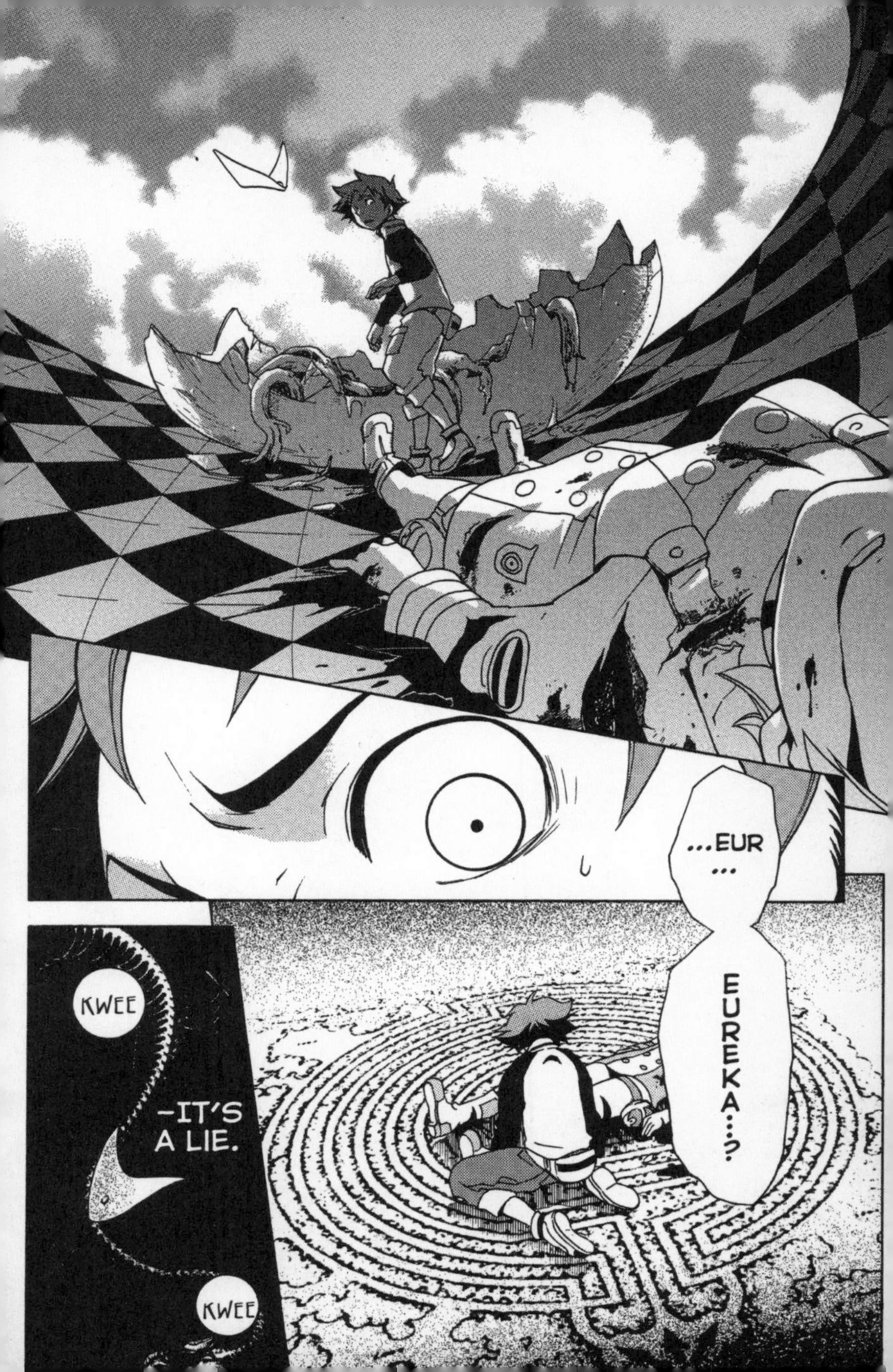
...EUR ...
EUREKA...?
KWEE
-IT'S A LIE.
KWEE

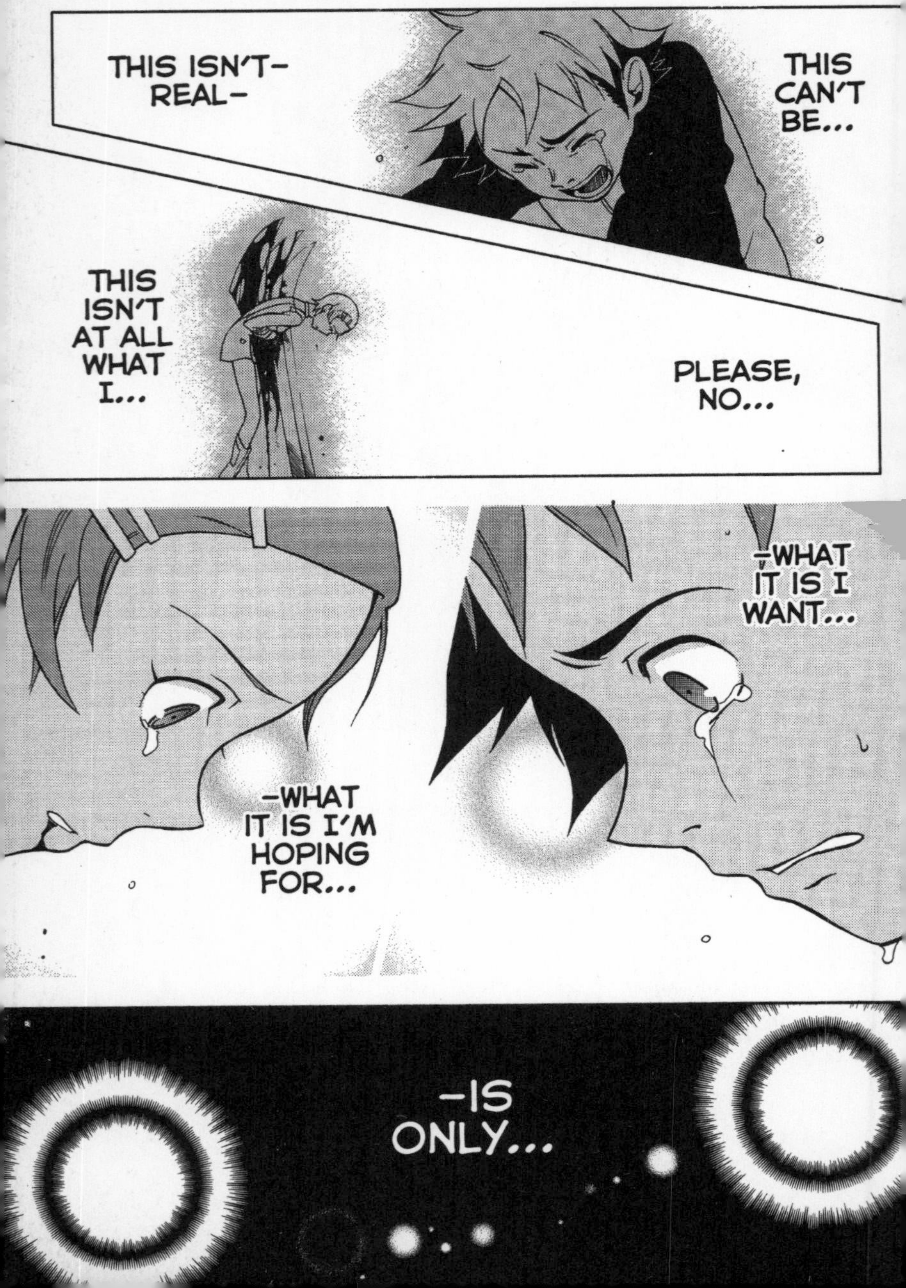
THIS CAN'T BE...
THIS ISN'T- REAL-
PLEASE, NO...
THIS ISN'T AT ALL WHAT I...
-WHAT IT IS I WANT...
-WHAT IT IS I'M HOPING FOR...
-IS ONLY...

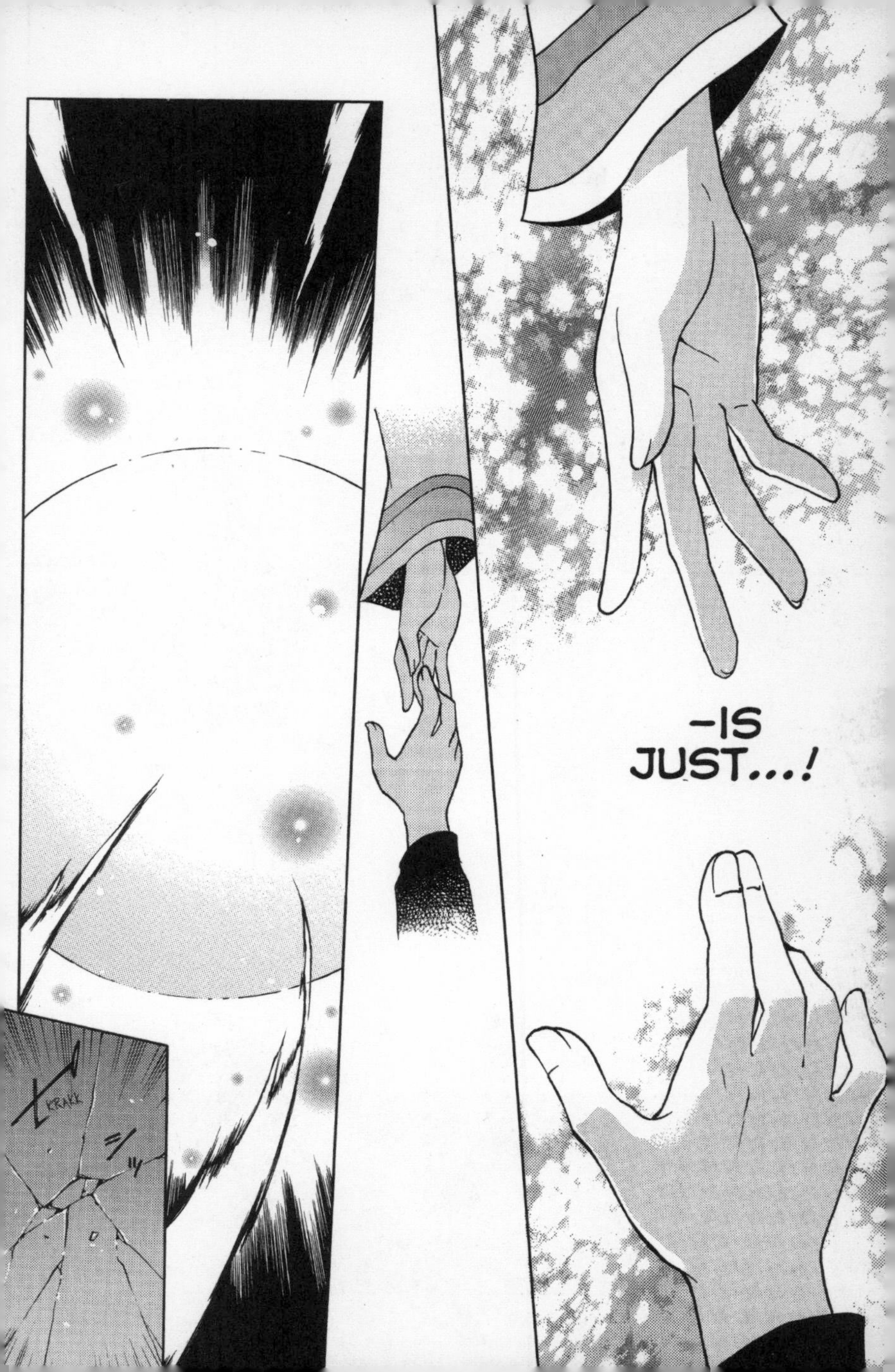
–IS JUST...!
KRAKK

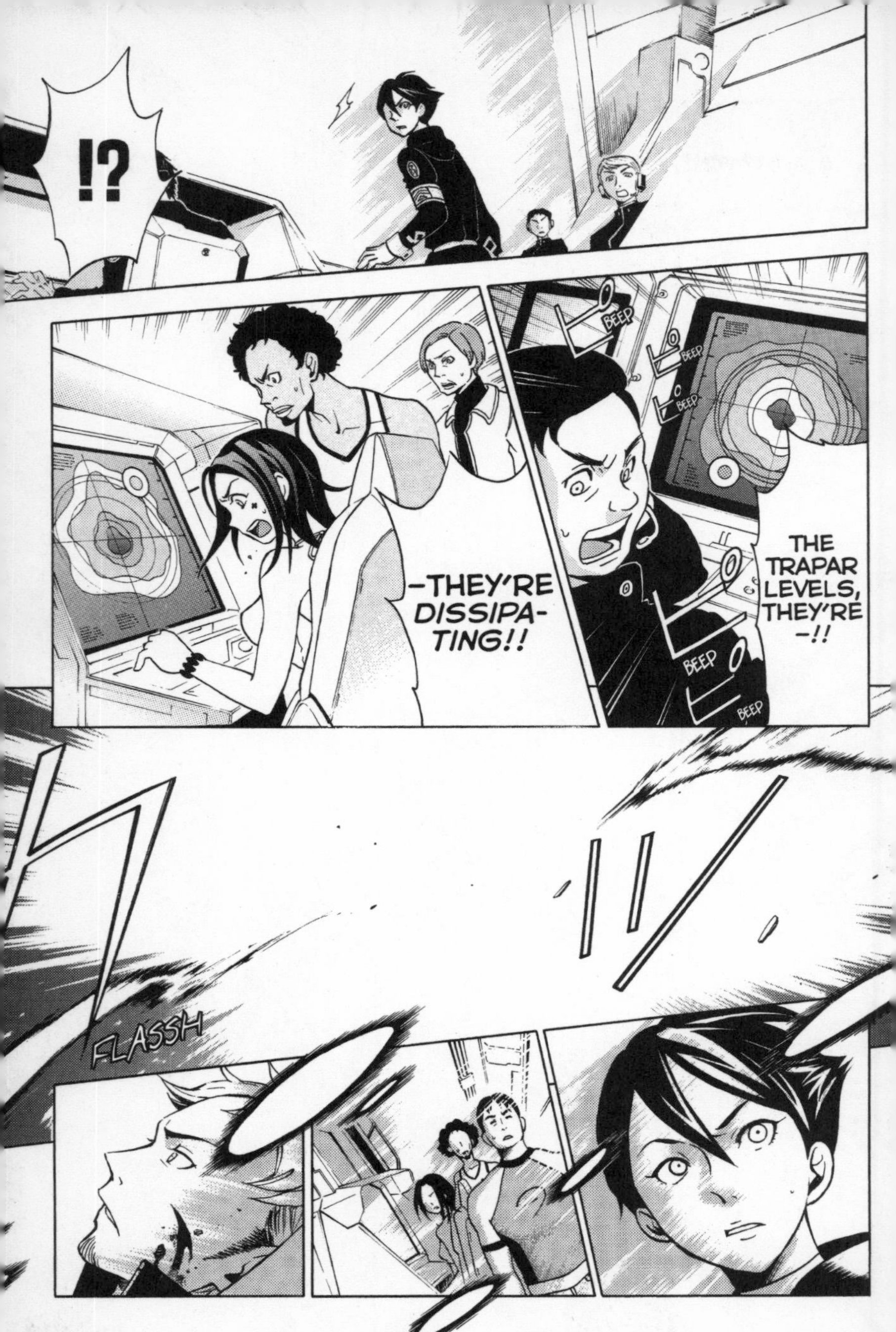
!?
BEEP
BEEP
BEEP
THE TRAPAR LEVELS, THEY'RE -!!
BEEP
BEEP
-THEY'RE DISSIPA-TING!!
FLASSH

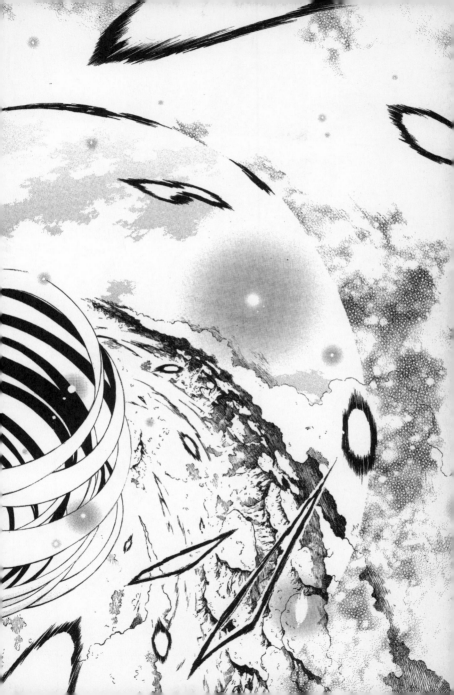

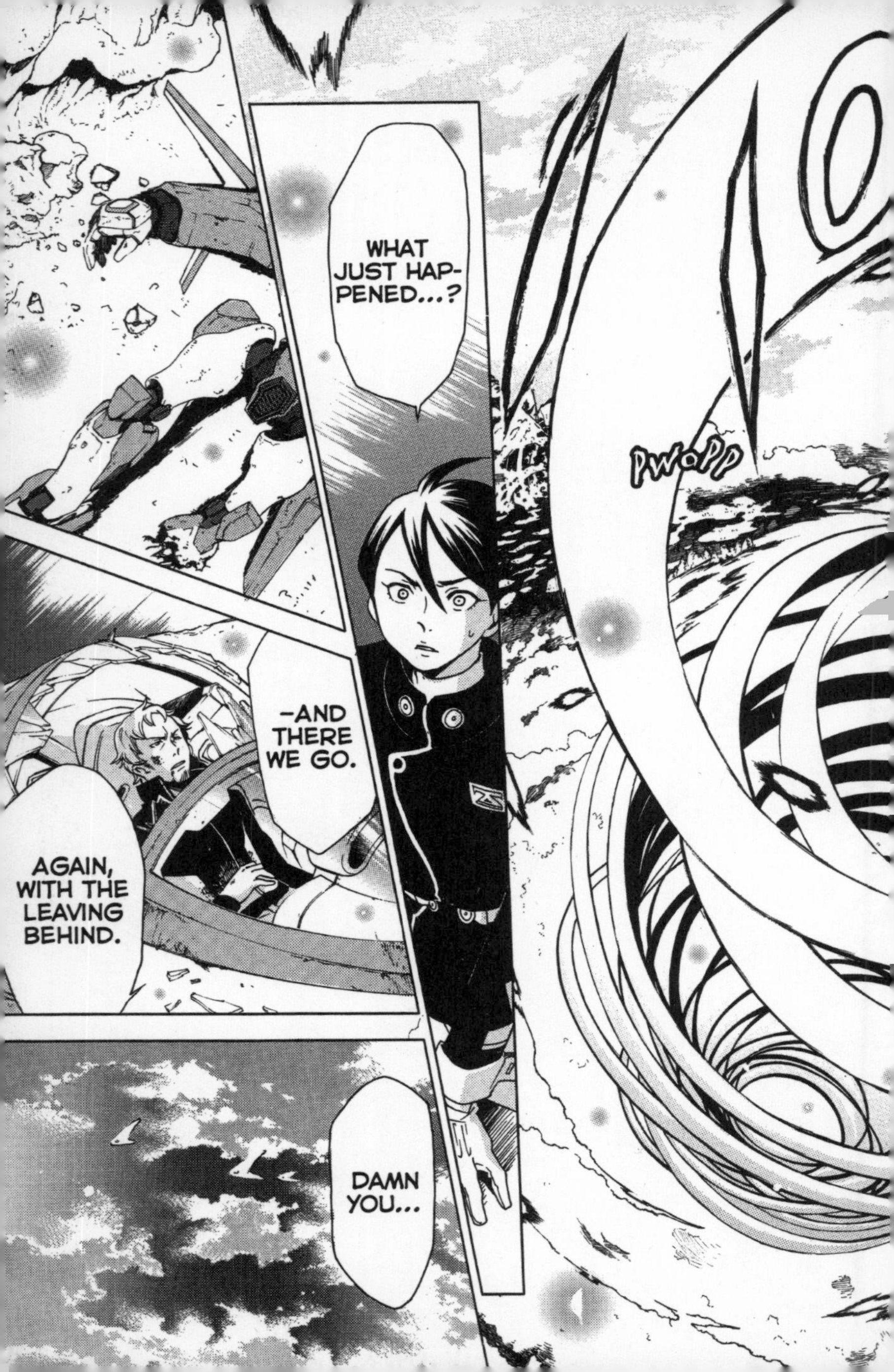
PWAPP
WHAT JUST HAPPENED...?
-AND THERE WE GO.
AGAIN, WITH THE LEAVING BEHIND.
DAMN YOU...

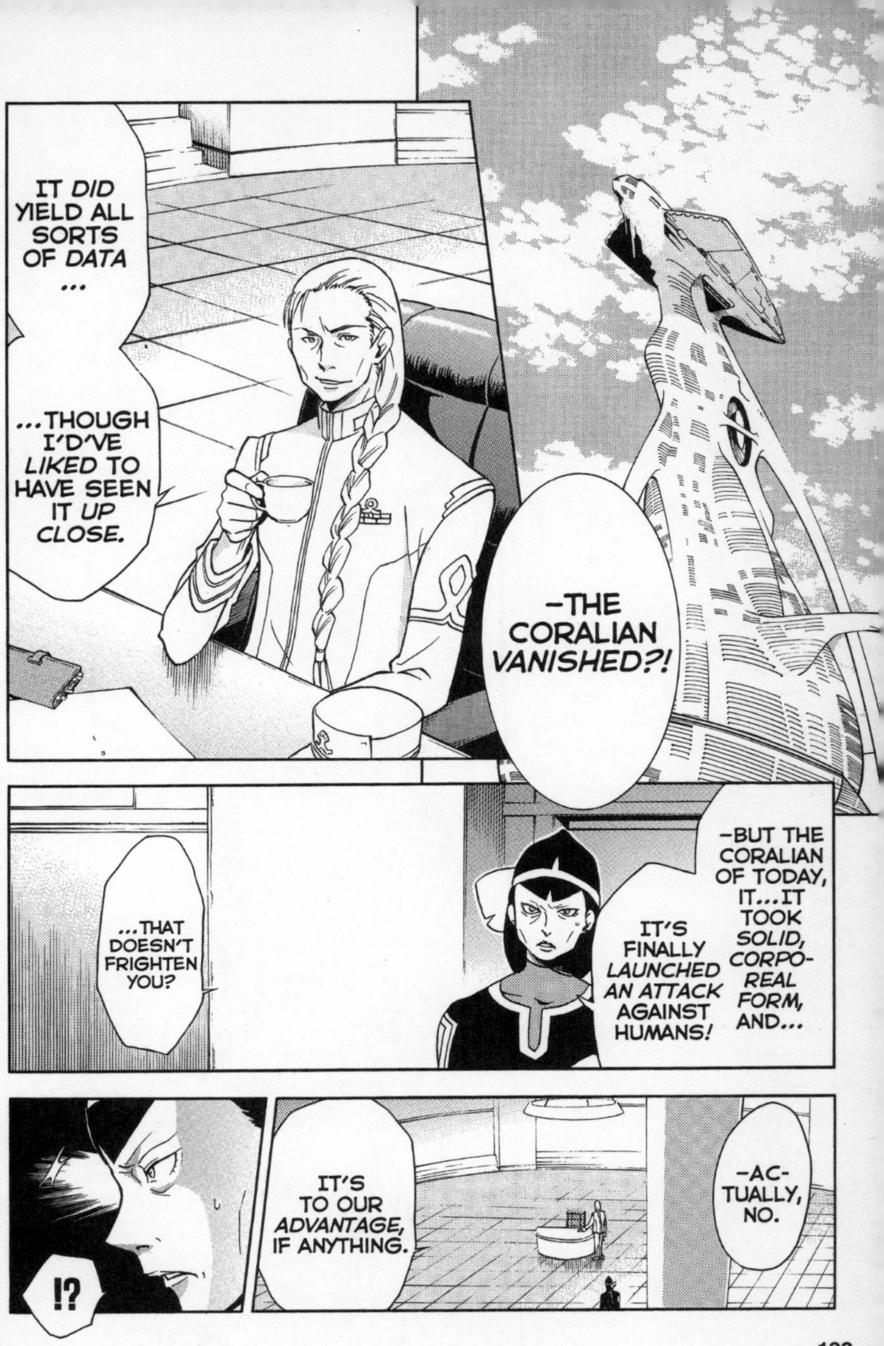
—THE CORALIAN VANISHED?!
IT DID YIELD ALL SORTS OF DATA...
...THOUGH I'D'VE LIKED TO HAVE SEEN IT UP CLOSE.
—BUT THE CORALIAN OF TODAY, IT...IT TOOK SOLID, CORPO-REAL FORM, AND...
IT'S FINALLY LAUNCHED AN ATTACK AGAINST HUMANS!
...THAT DOESN'T FRIGHTEN YOU?
—AC-TUALLY, NO.
IT'S TO OUR ADVANTAGE, IF ANYTHING.
!?

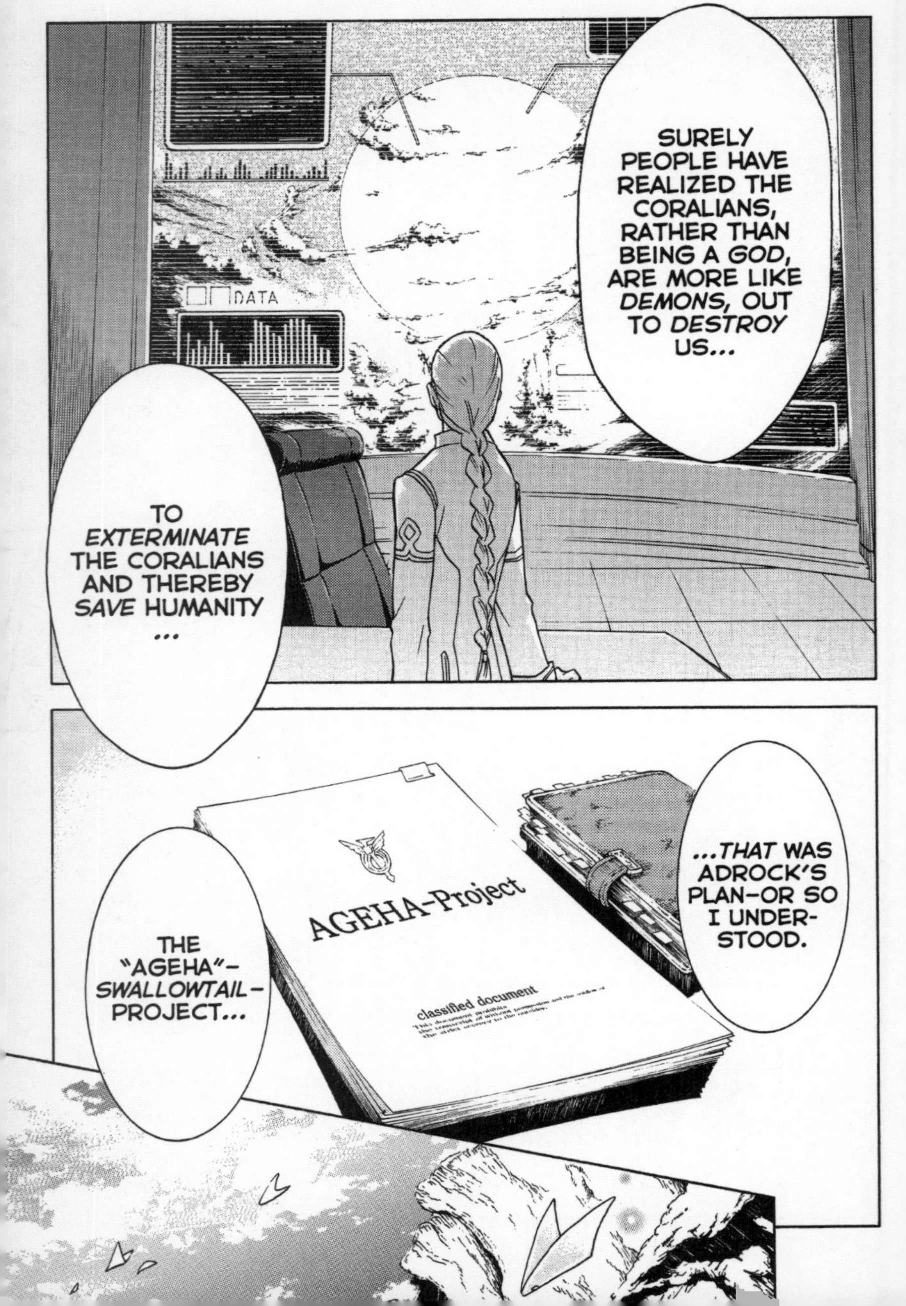

SURELY PEOPLE HAVE REALIZED THE CORALIANS, RATHER THAN BEING A *GOD*, ARE MORE LIKE *DEMONS*, OUT TO *DESTROY* US...
DATA
TO *EXTERMINATE* THE CORALIANS AND THEREBY *SAVE* HUMANITY ...
...*THAT* WAS ADROCK'S PLAN—OR SO I UNDER-STOOD.
AGEHA-Project
classified document
THE "AGEHA"—*SWALLOWTAIL*—PROJECT...

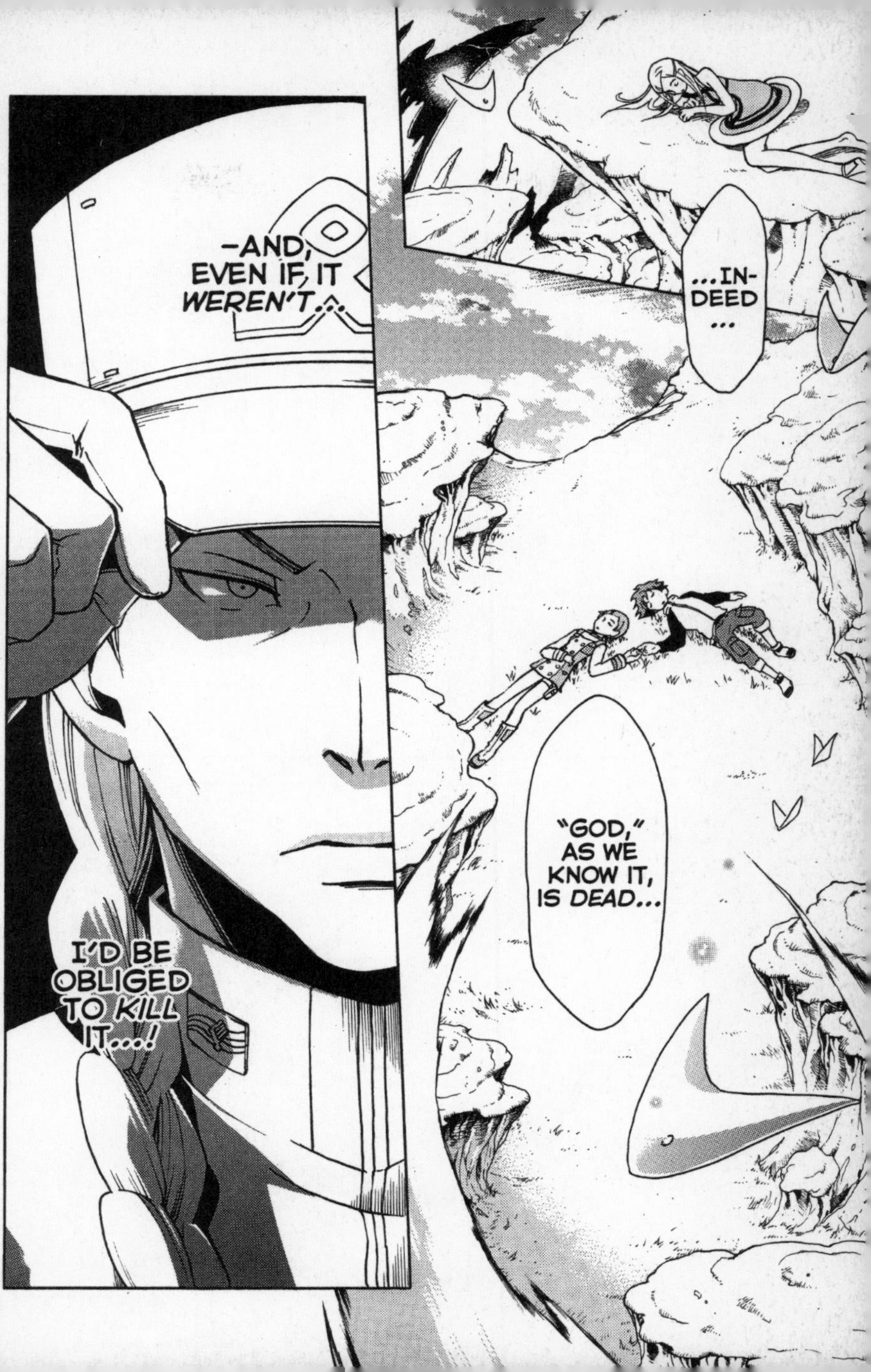
...IN-DEED...
"GOD," AS WE KNOW IT, IS *DEAD*...
-AND, EVEN IF IT *WEREN'T*...
I'D BE OBLIGED TO *KILL* IT...!

Psalms of
Planet
Eureka seveN

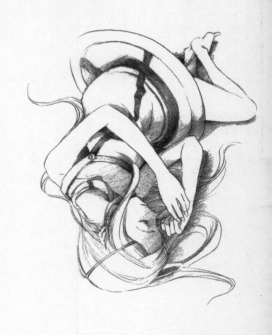

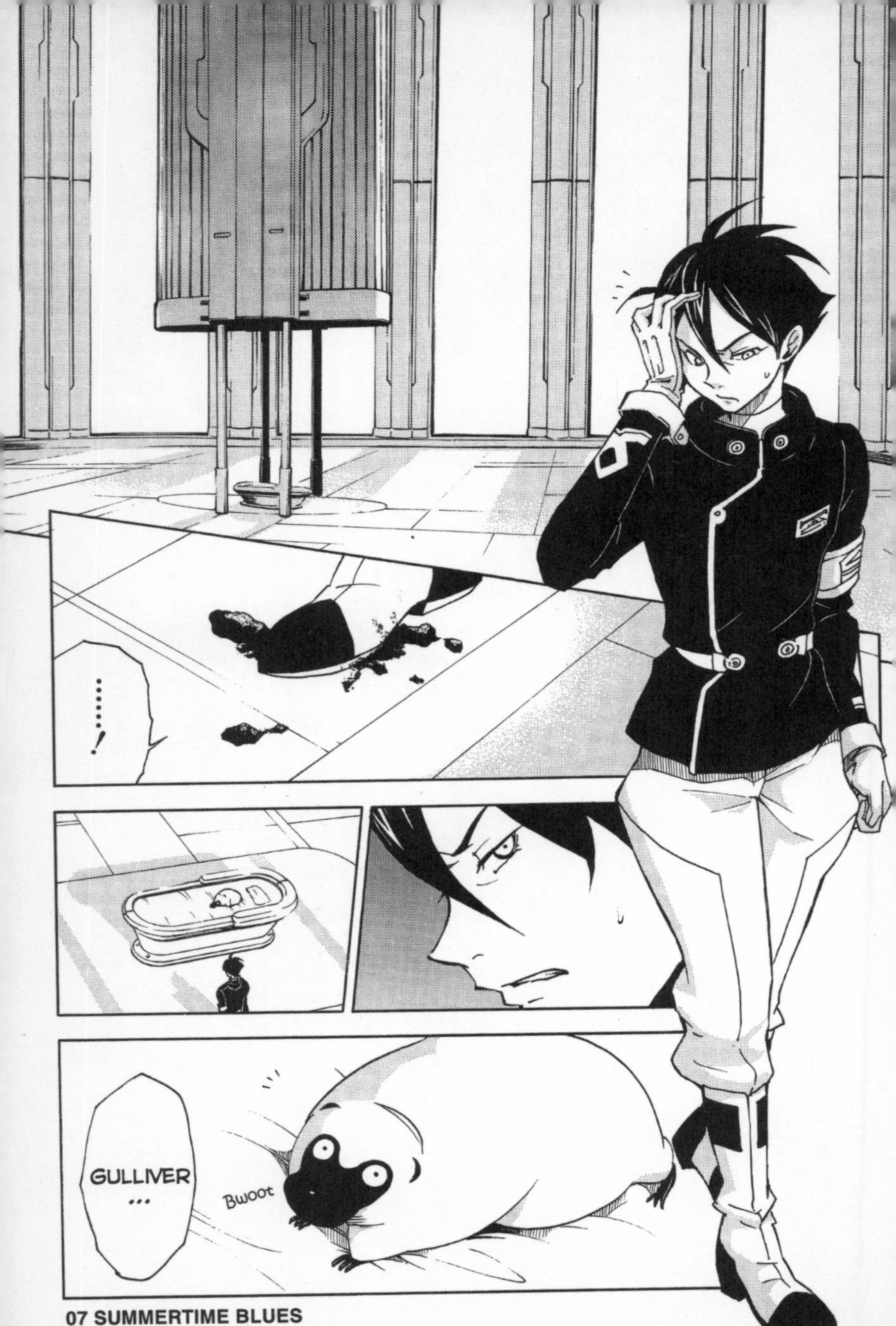
......!
Bwoot
GULLIVER
...

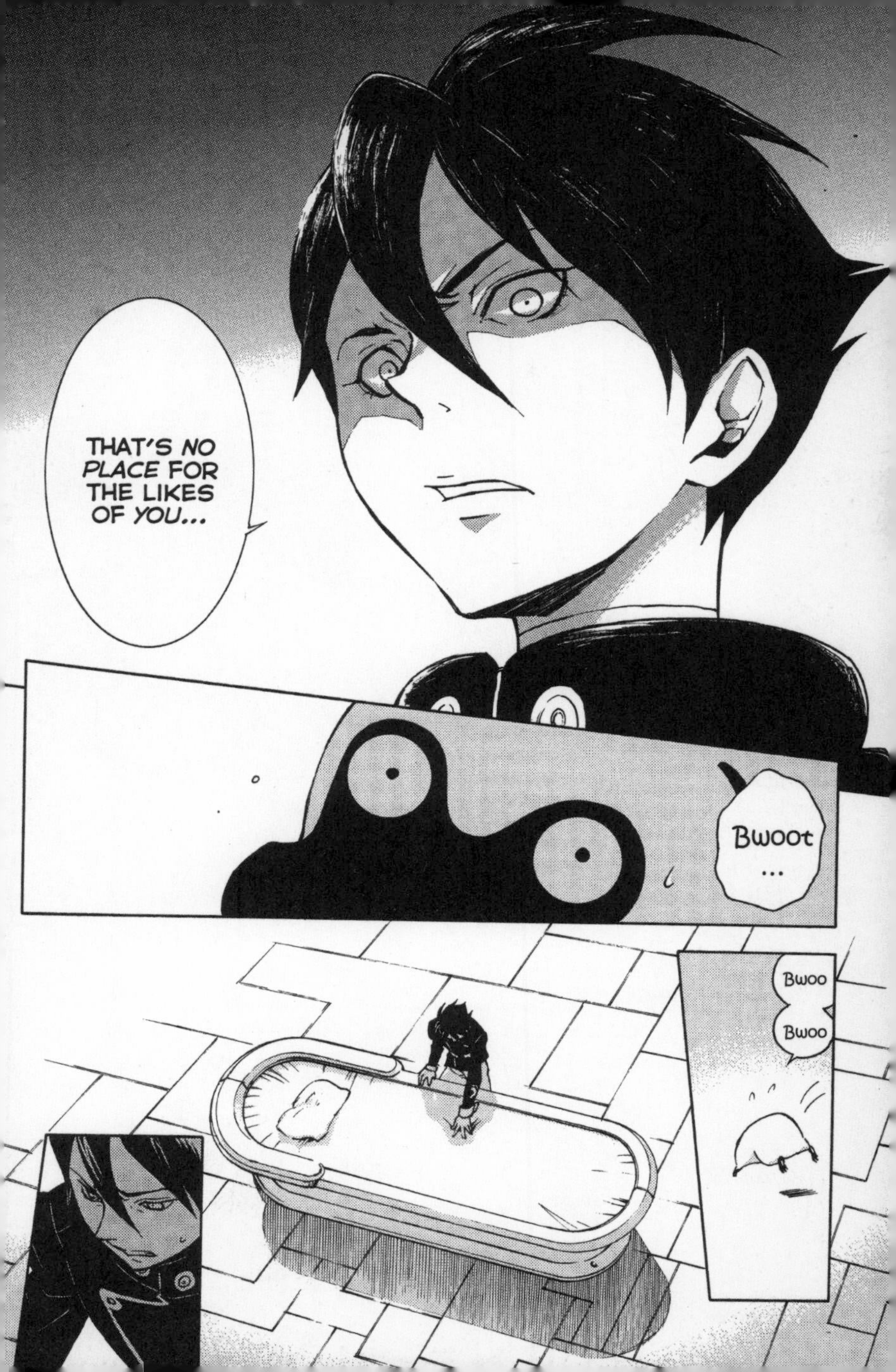
THAT'S NO *PLACE* FOR THE LIKES OF *YOU*...
Bwoot ...
Bwoo
Bwoo

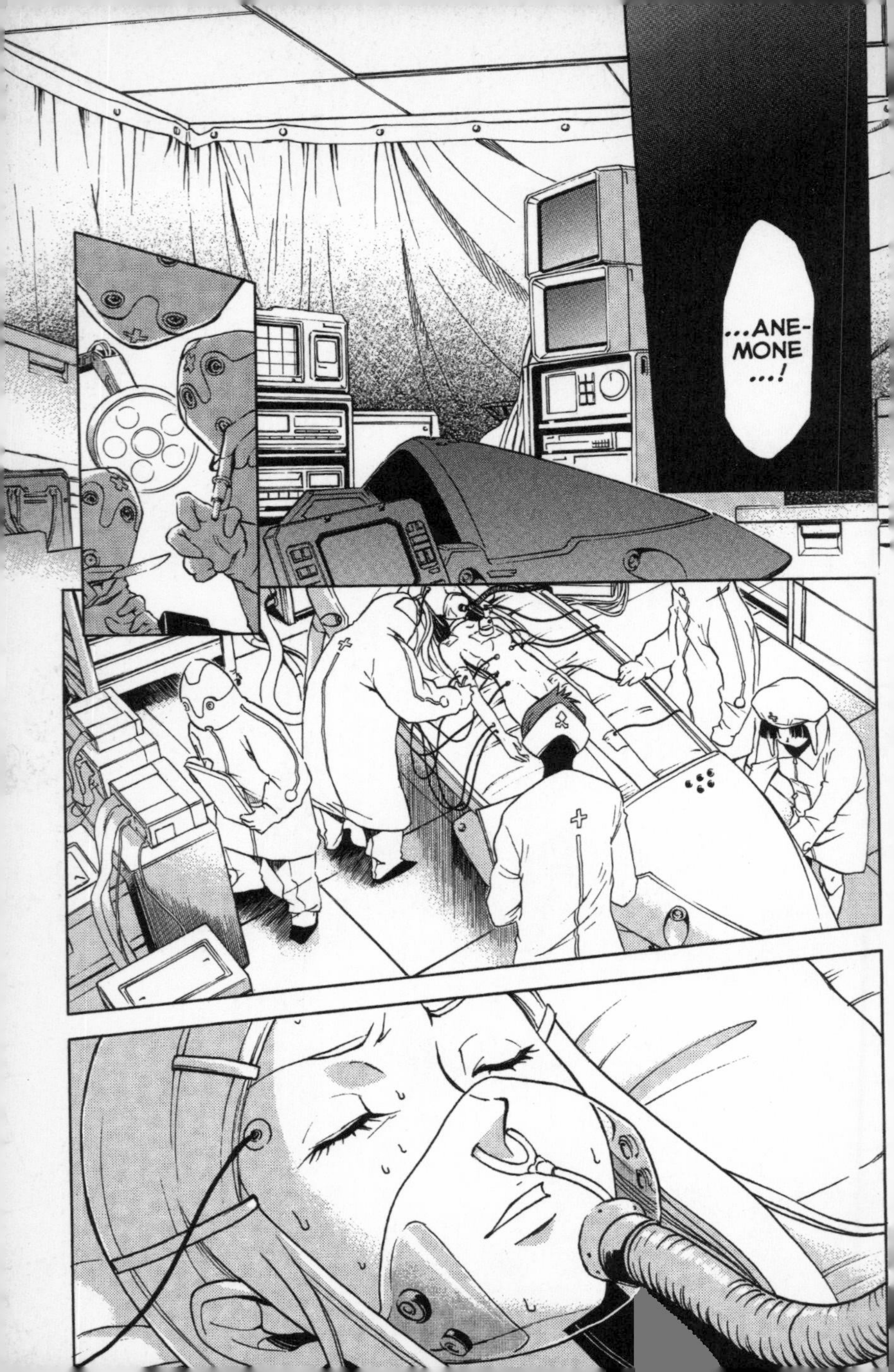
...ANE-
MONE
...!

07 SUMMERTIME BLUES

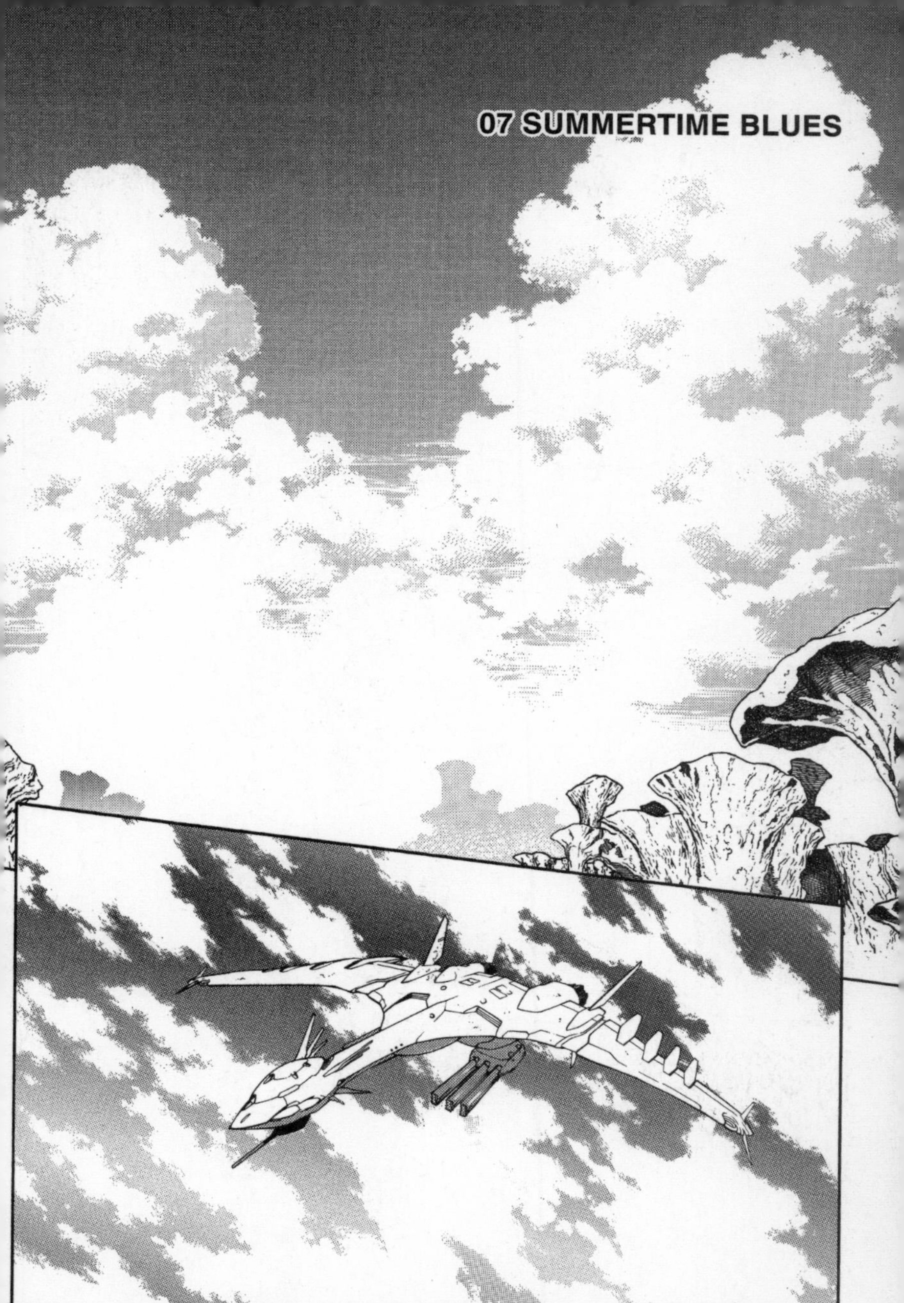

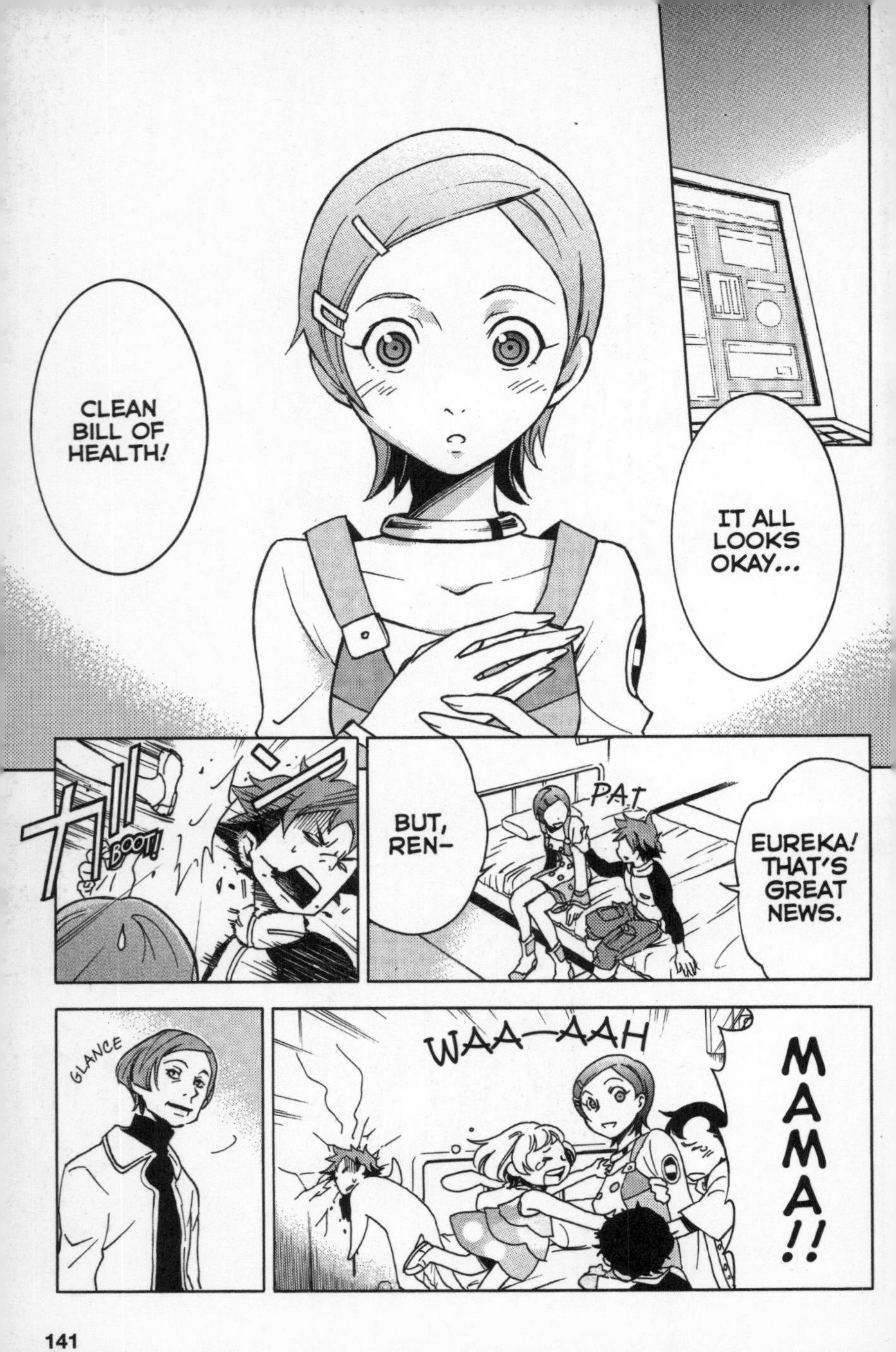
IT ALL LOOKS OKAY...
CLEAN BILL OF HEALTH!
EUREKA! THAT'S GREAT NEWS.
PAT
BUT, REN-
BOOT!
MAMA!!
WAA-AAH
GLANCE

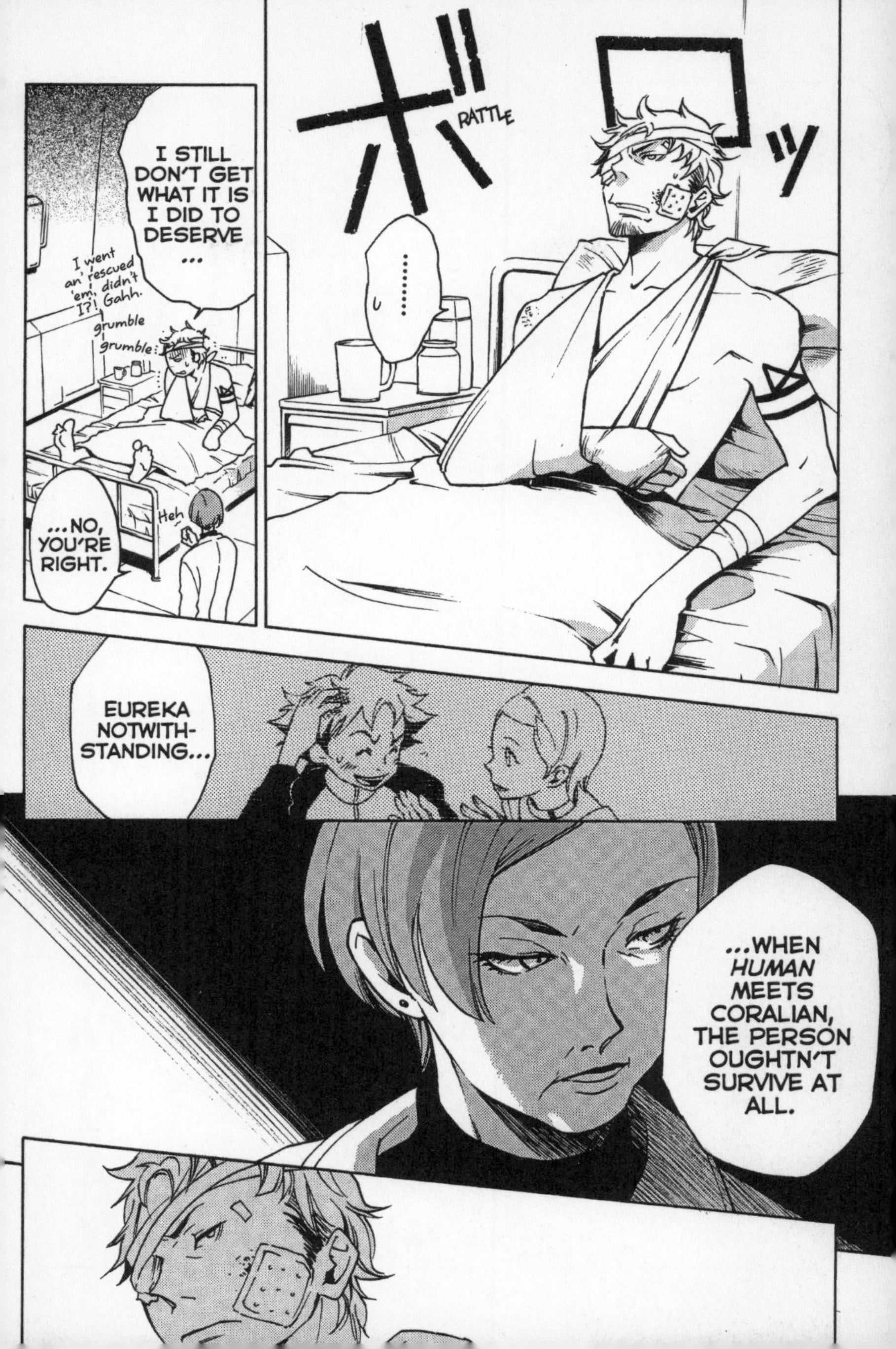
ボロッ
RATTLE
......
I STILL DON'T GET WHAT IT IS I DID TO DESERVE ...
I went an' rescued 'em, didn't I?! Gahh.
grumble grumble
Heh
...NO, YOU'RE RIGHT.
EUREKA NOTWITH-STANDING...
...WHEN *HUMAN* MEETS CORALIAN, THE PERSON OUGHTN'T SURVIVE AT ALL.

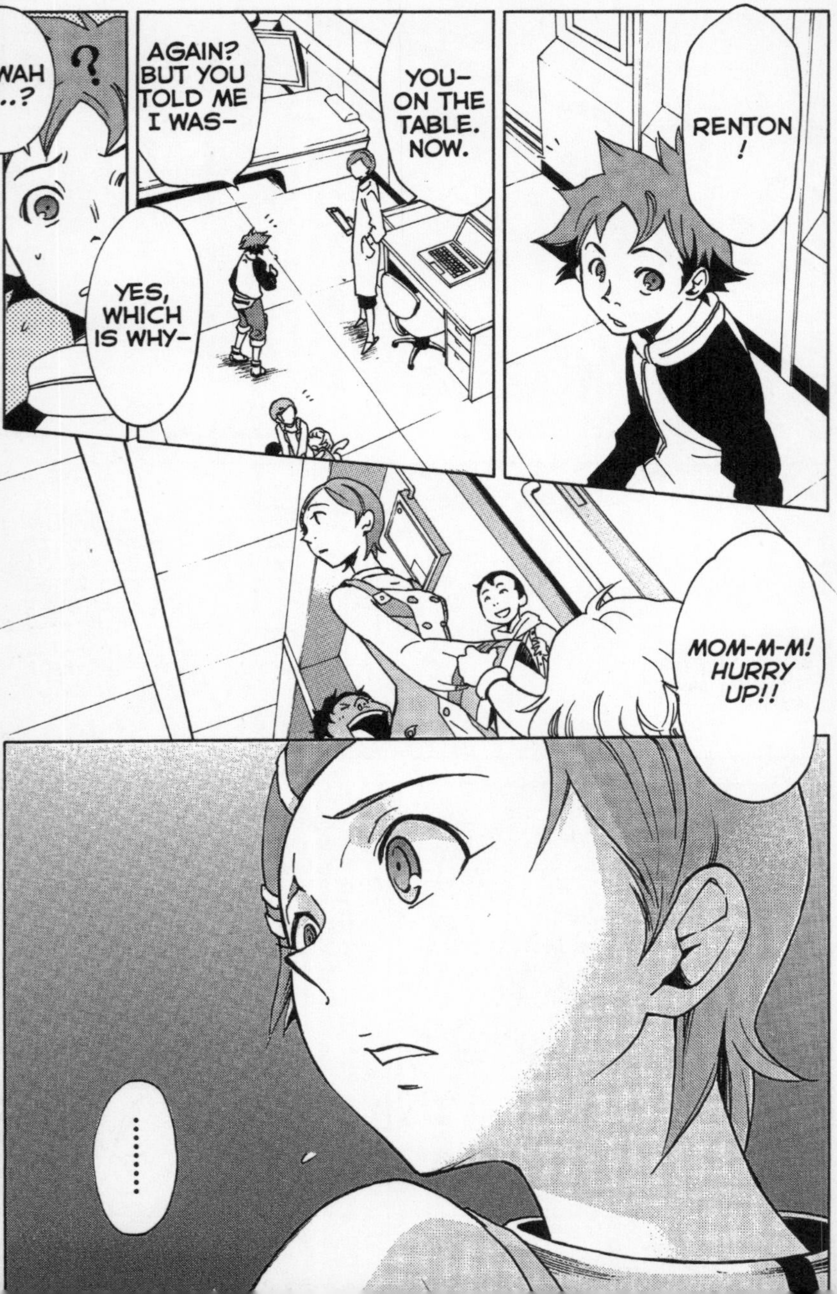
RENTON!
YOU– ON THE TABLE. NOW.
AGAIN? BUT YOU TOLD ME I WAS–
YES, WHICH IS WHY–
HWAH ...?
MOM-M-M! HURRY UP!!
....

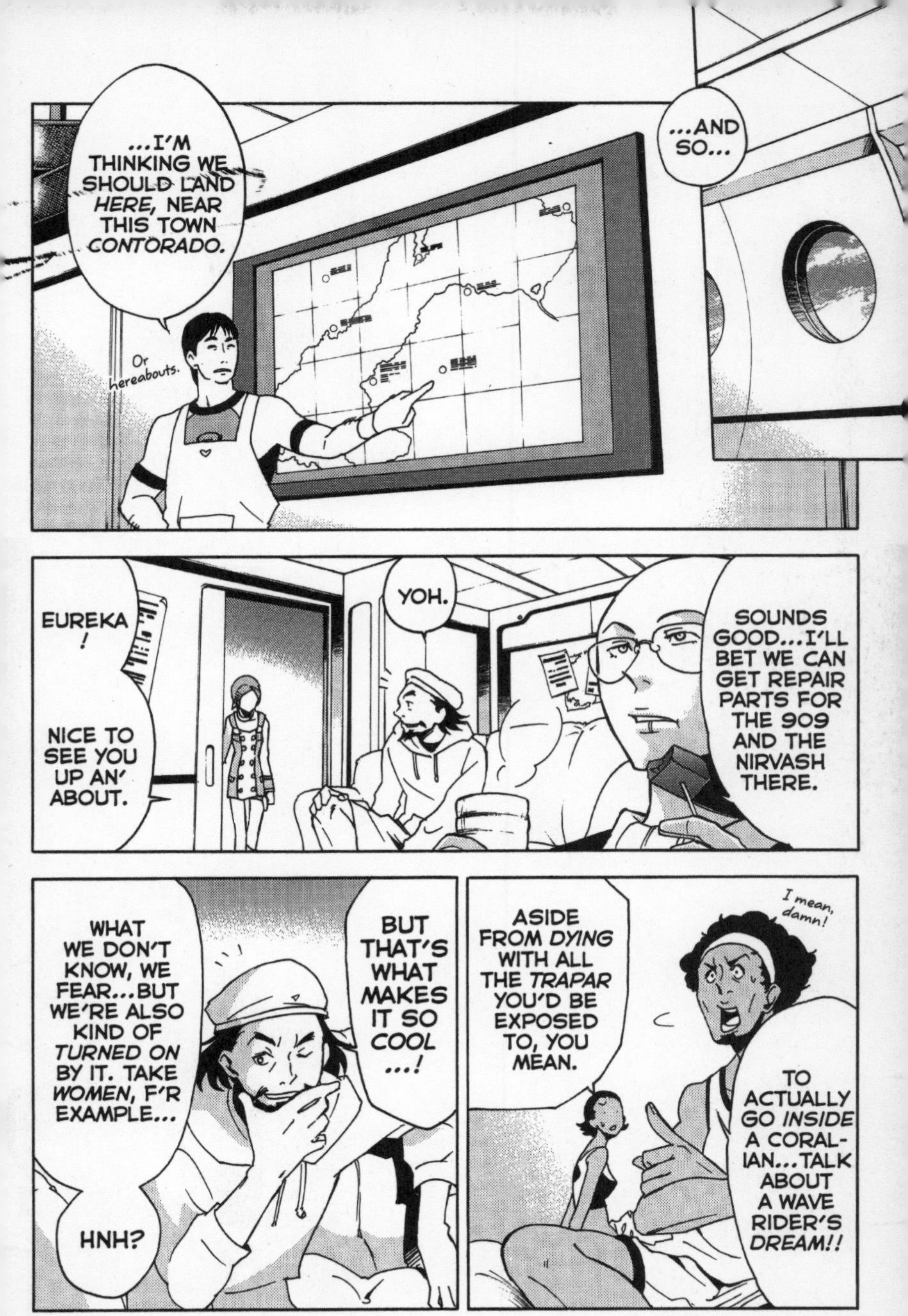
...AND SO...
...I'M THINKING WE SHOULD LAND *HERE*, NEAR THIS TOWN *CONTORADO*.
Or hereabouts.
SOUNDS GOOD...I'LL BET WE CAN GET REPAIR PARTS FOR THE 909 AND THE NIRVASH THERE.
YOH.
EUREKA!
NICE TO SEE YOU UP AN' ABOUT.
TO ACTUALLY GO *INSIDE* A CORAL-IAN...TALK ABOUT A WAVE RIDER'S *DREAM*!!
I mean, damn!
ASIDE FROM *DYING* WITH ALL THE *TRAPAR* YOU'D BE EXPOSED TO, YOU MEAN.
BUT THAT'S WHAT MAKES IT SO *COOL*...!
WHAT WE DON'T KNOW, WE FEAR...BUT WE'RE ALSO KIND OF *TURNED ON* BY IT. TAKE *WOMEN*, F'R EXAMPLE...
HNH?

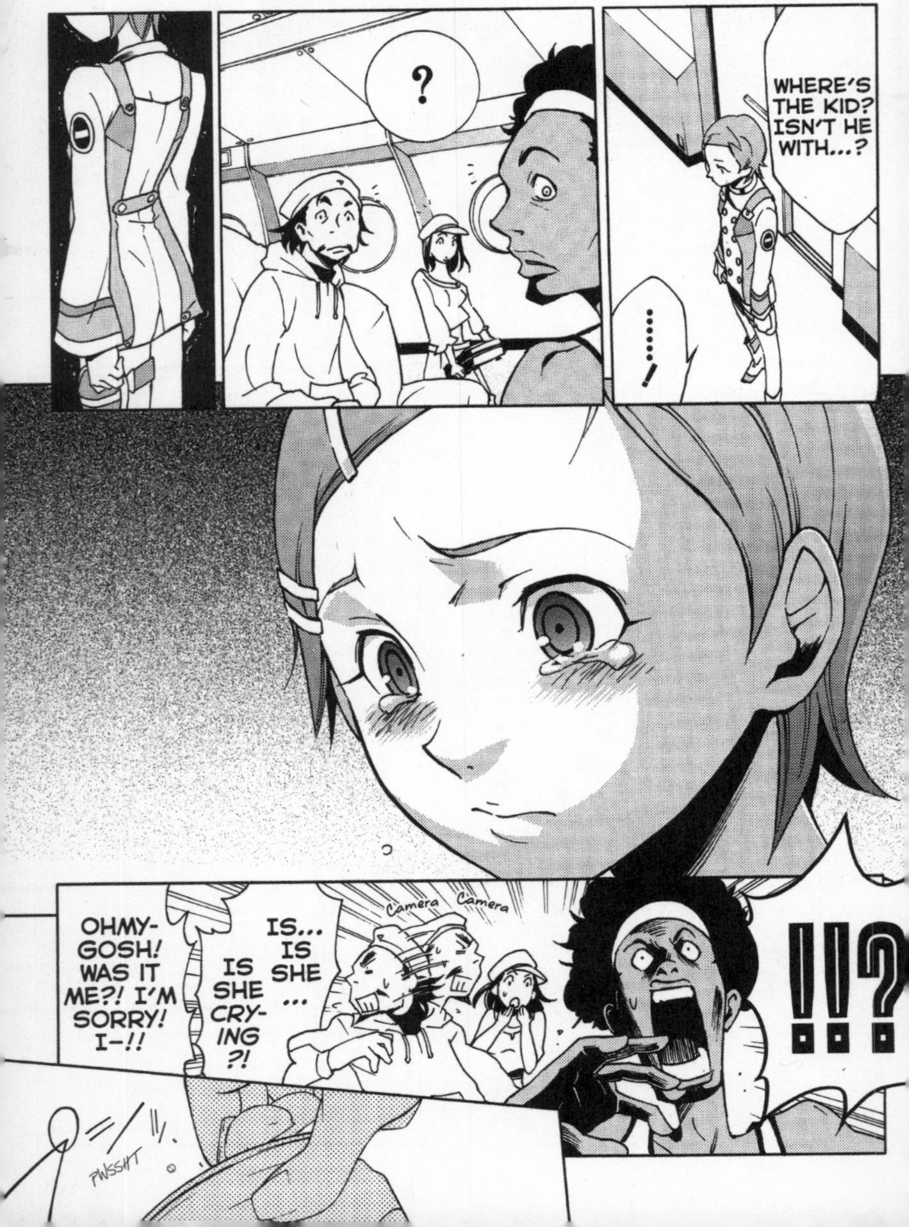
WHERE'S THE KID? ISN'T HE WITH...?
......!
?
!!?
Camera Camera
IS... IS SHE ...
IS SHE CRYING?!
OHMYGOSH! WAS IT ME?! I'M SORRY! I-!!
PWSSHT

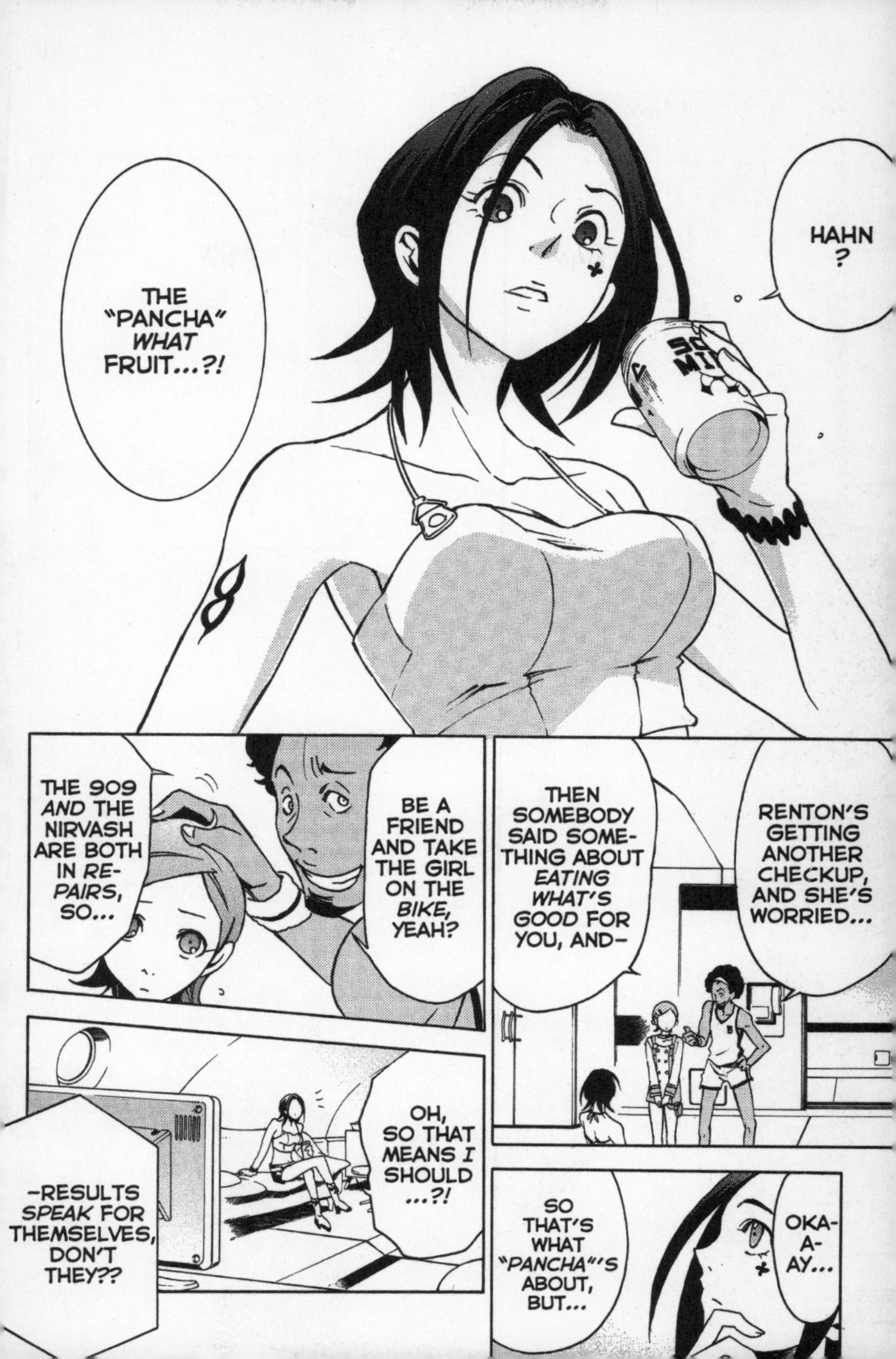
HAHN?
THE "PANCHA" WHAT FRUIT...?!
RENTON'S GETTING ANOTHER CHECKUP, AND SHE'S WORRIED...
THEN SOMEBODY SAID SOMETHING ABOUT EATING WHAT'S GOOD FOR YOU, AND–
BE A FRIEND AND TAKE THE GIRL ON THE BIKE, YEAH?
THE 909 AND THE NIRVASH ARE BOTH IN REPAIRS, SO...
OKA-A-AY...
SO THAT'S WHAT "PANCHA"'S ABOUT, BUT...
OH, SO THAT MEANS I SHOULD ...?!
–RESULTS SPEAK FOR THEMSELVES, DON'T THEY??

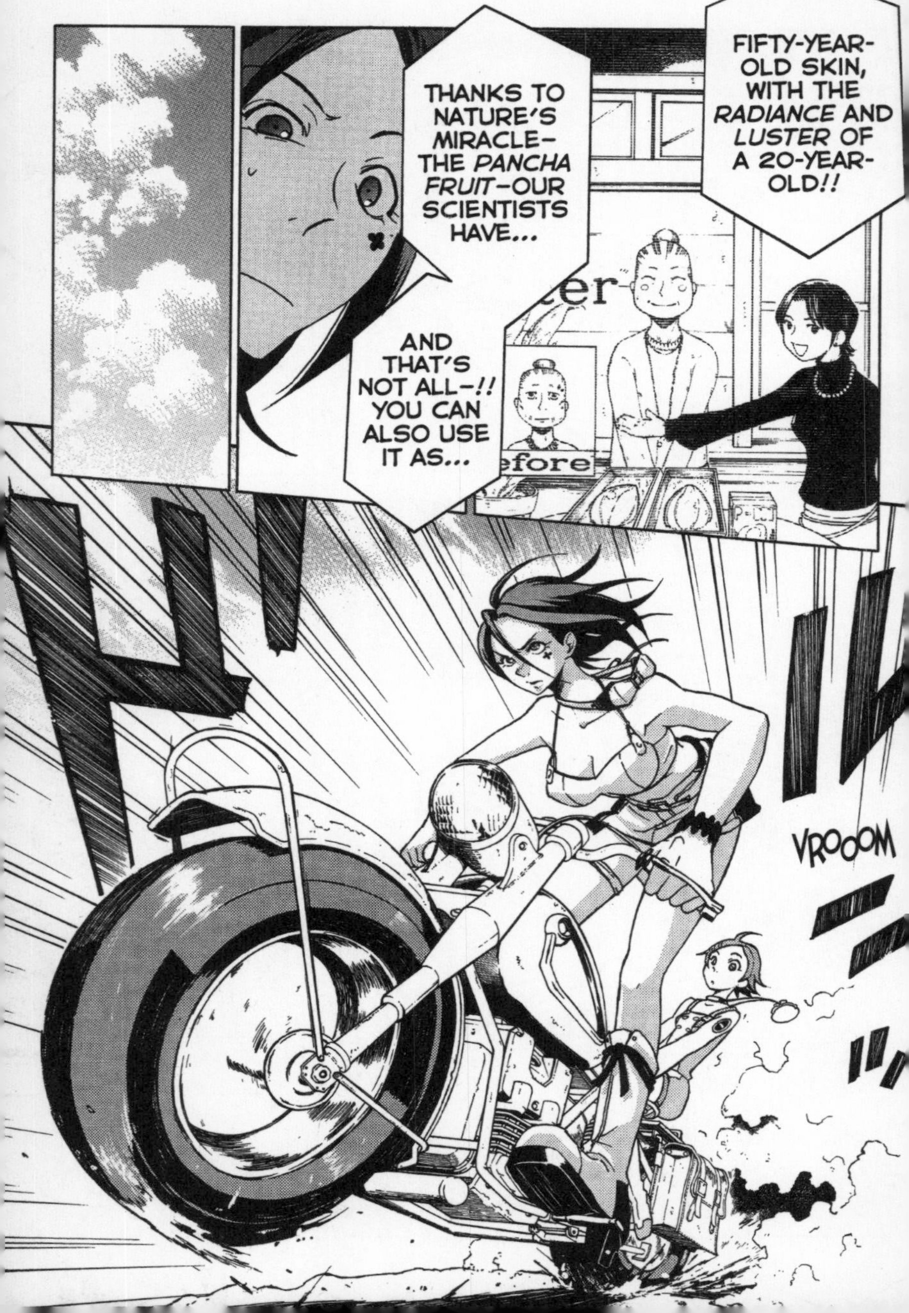
FIFTY-YEAR-OLD SKIN, WITH THE *RADIANCE* AND *LUSTER* OF A 20-YEAR-OLD!!
THANKS TO NATURE'S MIRACLE–THE *PANCHA FRUIT*–OUR SCIENTISTS HAVE...
AND THAT'S NOT ALL–!! YOU CAN ALSO USE IT AS...
VROOOM

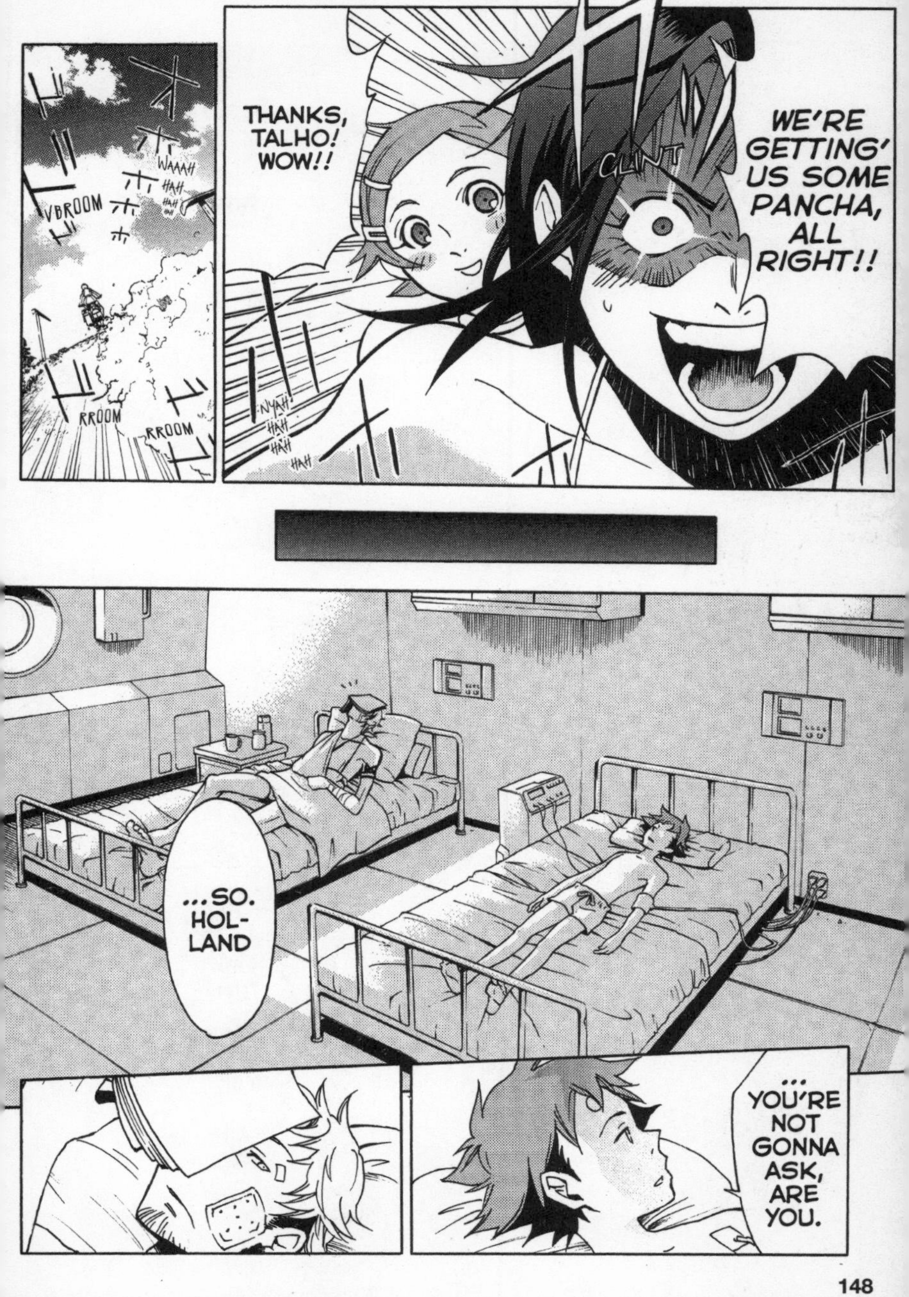
WE'RE GETTING' US SOME PANCHA, ALL RIGHT!!
GLINT
THANKS, TALHO! WOW!!
N'YAH HAH HAH HAH
WAAAH HAH HAH HAH
VBROOM
RROOM
RROOM
...SO. HOL-LAND
... YOU'RE NOT GONNA ASK, ARE YOU.

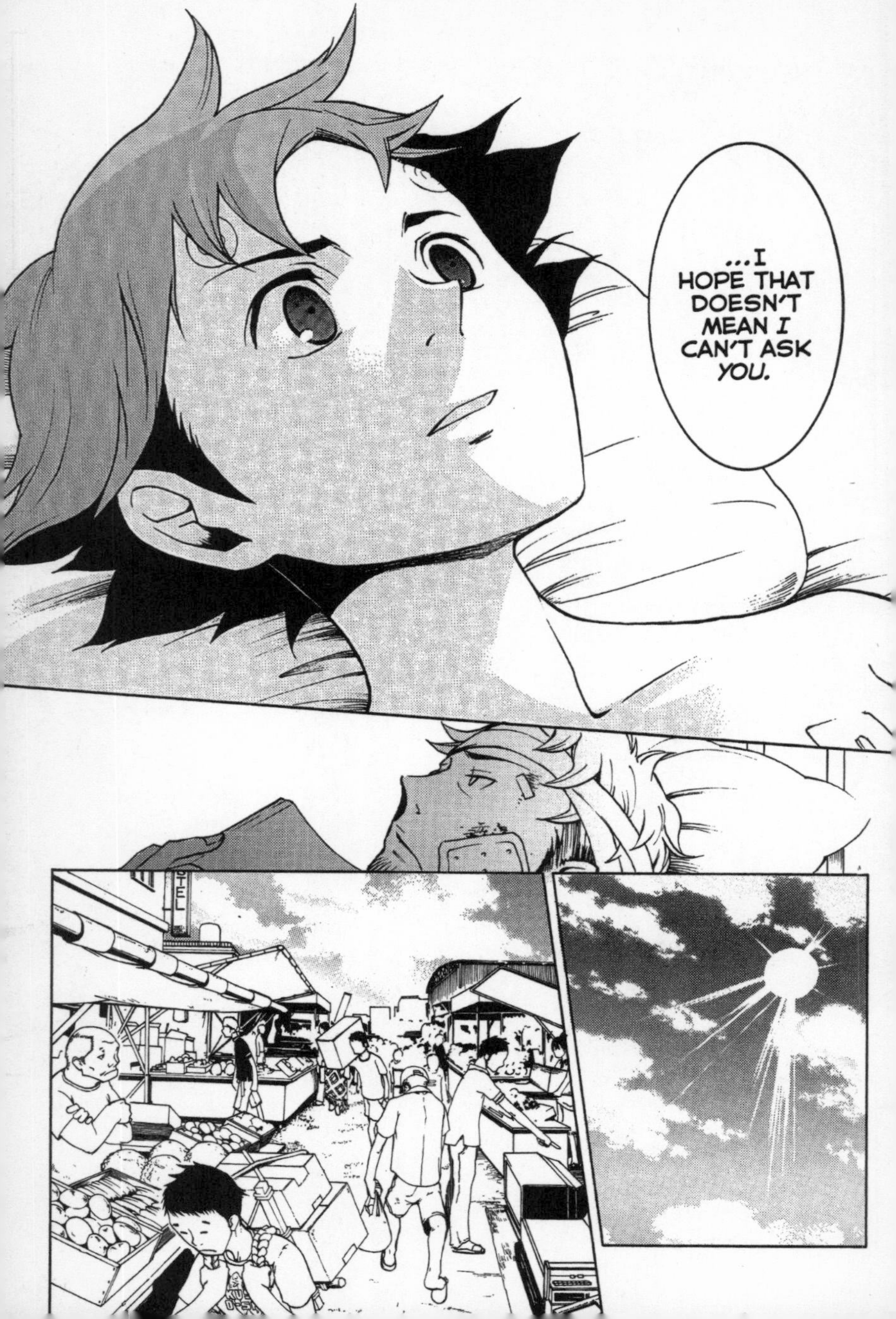
...I HOPE THAT DOESN'T MEAN *I* CAN'T ASK *YOU.*

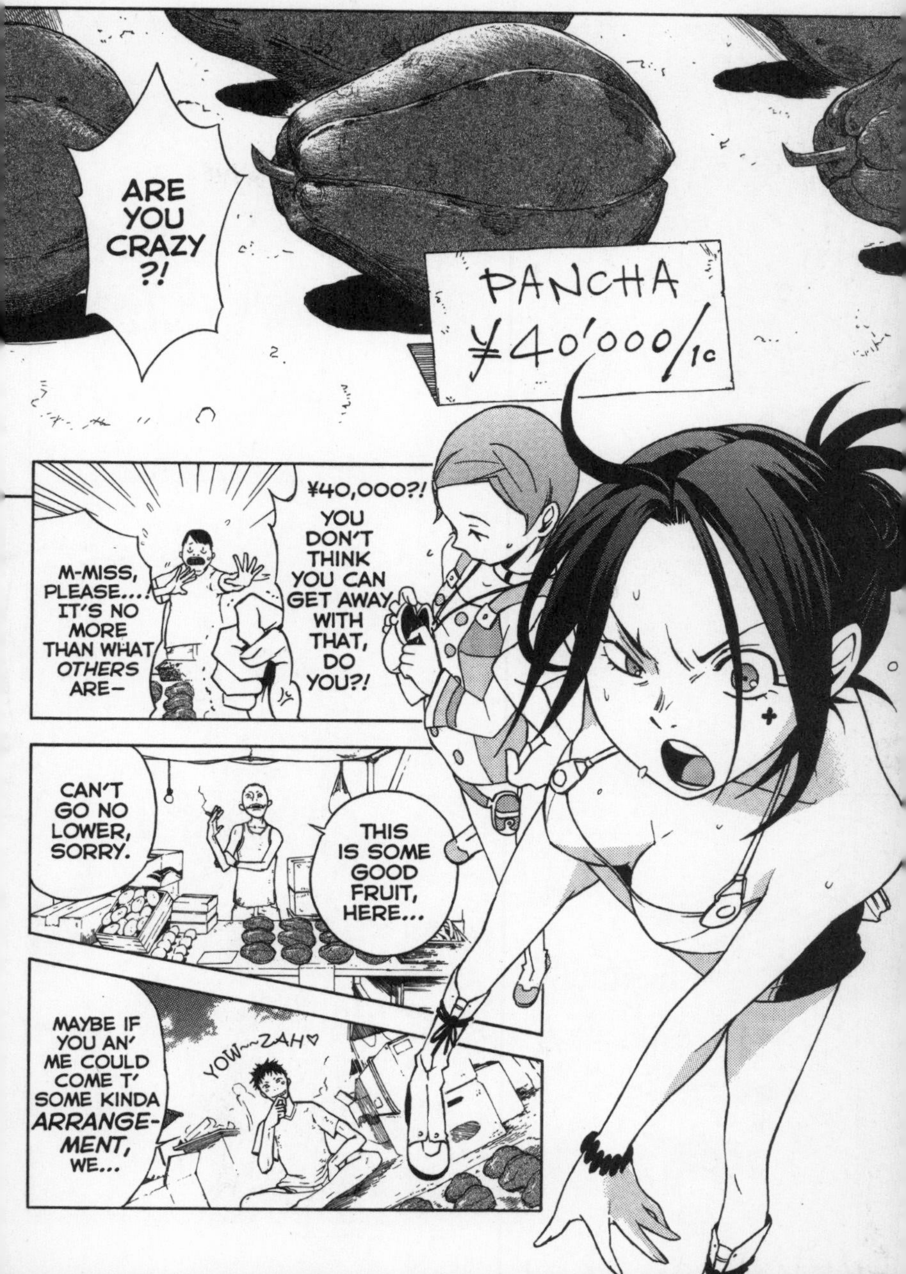
PANCHA ¥40'000/1c
ARE YOU CRAZY?!
¥40,000?! YOU DON'T THINK YOU CAN GET AWAY WITH THAT, DO YOU?!
M-MISS, PLEASE...! IT'S NO MORE THAN WHAT *OTHERS* ARE–
THIS IS SOME GOOD FRUIT, HERE...
CAN'T GO NO LOWER, SORRY.
YOW~~ZAH♡
MAYBE IF YOU AN' ME COULD COME T' SOME KINDA *ARRANGEMENT*, WE...

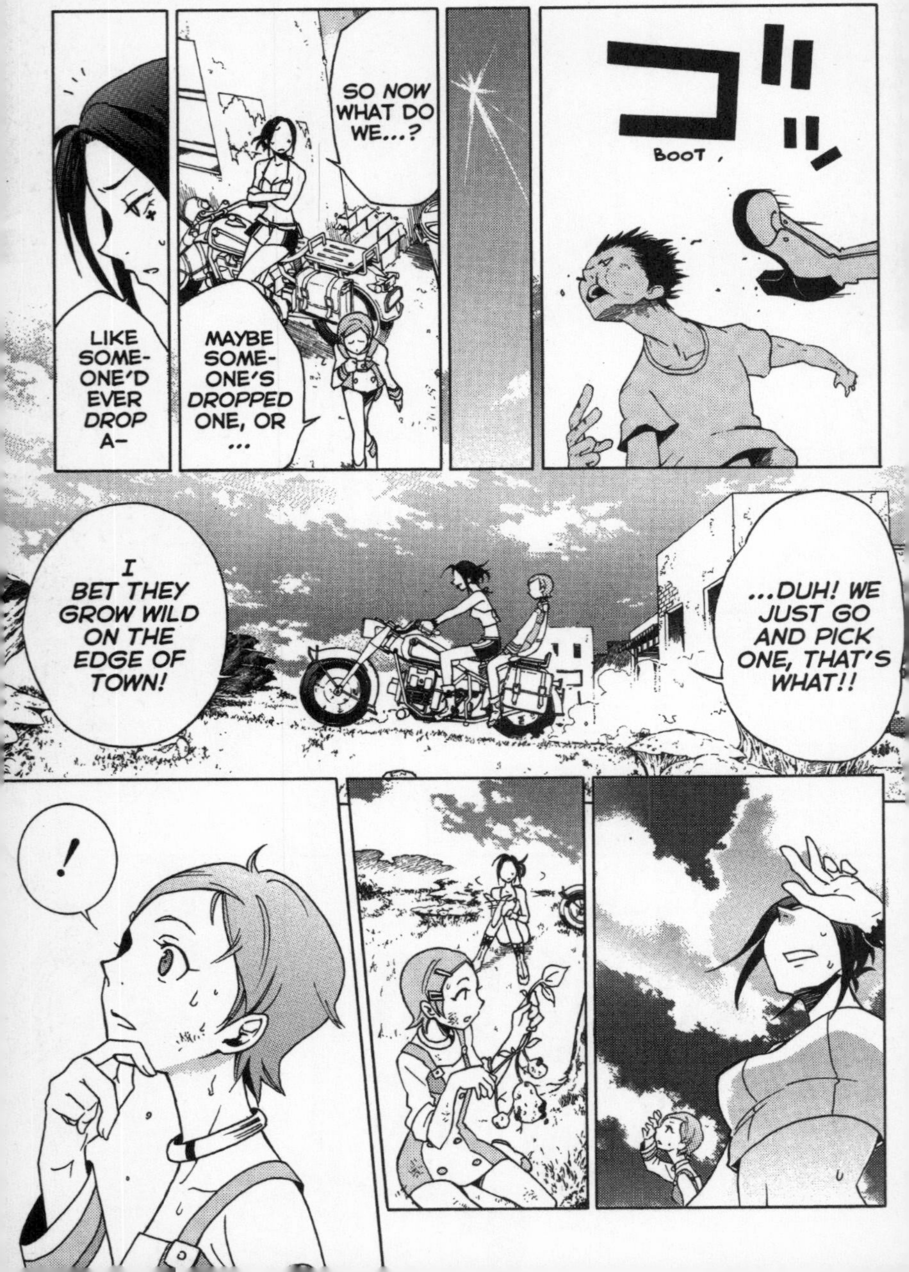
ゴッ
BOOT
SO NOW WHAT DO WE...?
MAYBE SOME-ONE'S DROPPED ONE, OR ...
LIKE SOME-ONE'D EVER DROP A-
...DUH! WE JUST GO AND PICK ONE, THAT'S WHAT!!
I BET THEY GROW WILD ON THE EDGE OF TOWN!
!

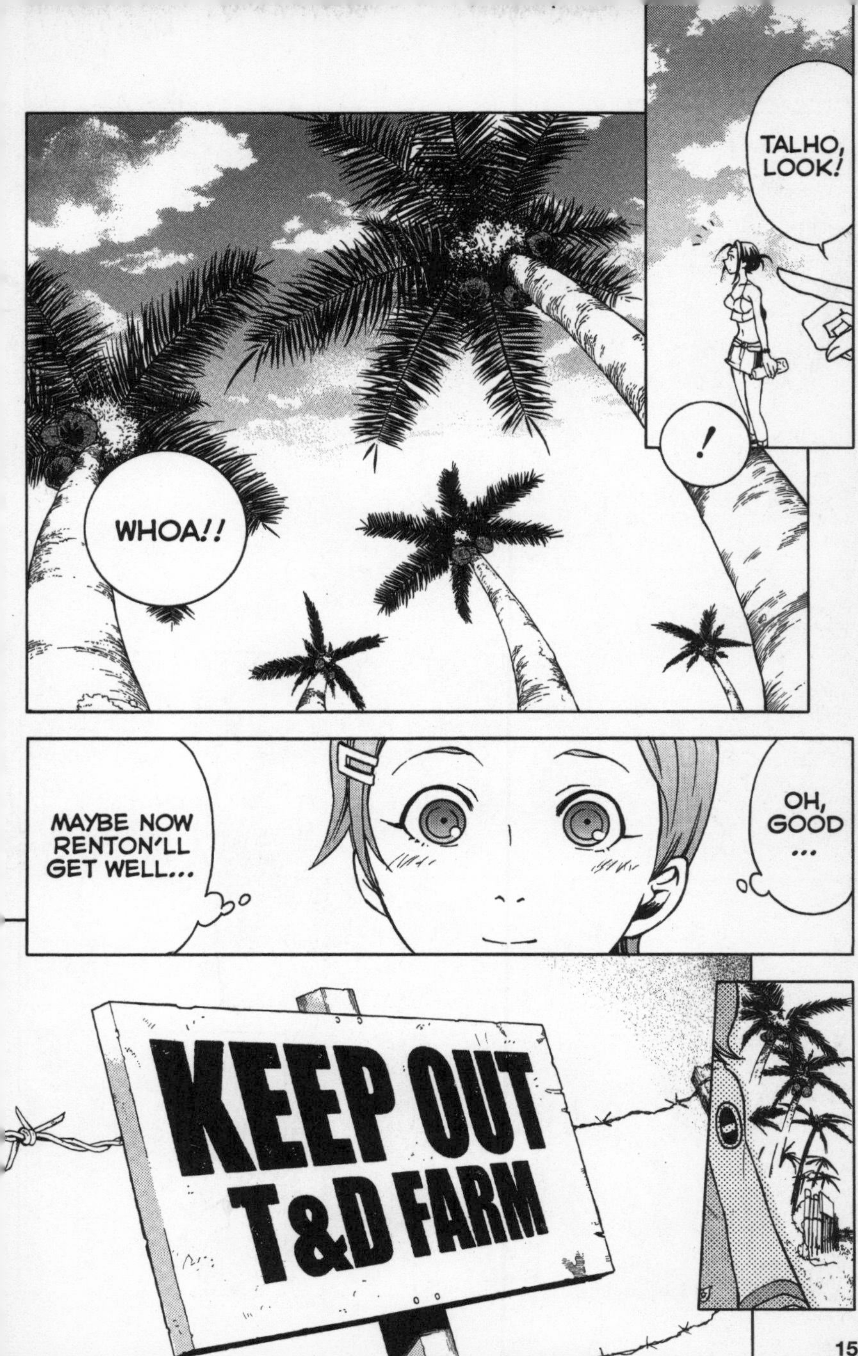
TALHO, LOOK!
!
WHOA!!
OH, GOOD ...
MAYBE NOW RENTON'LL GET WELL...
KEEP OUT
T&D FARM

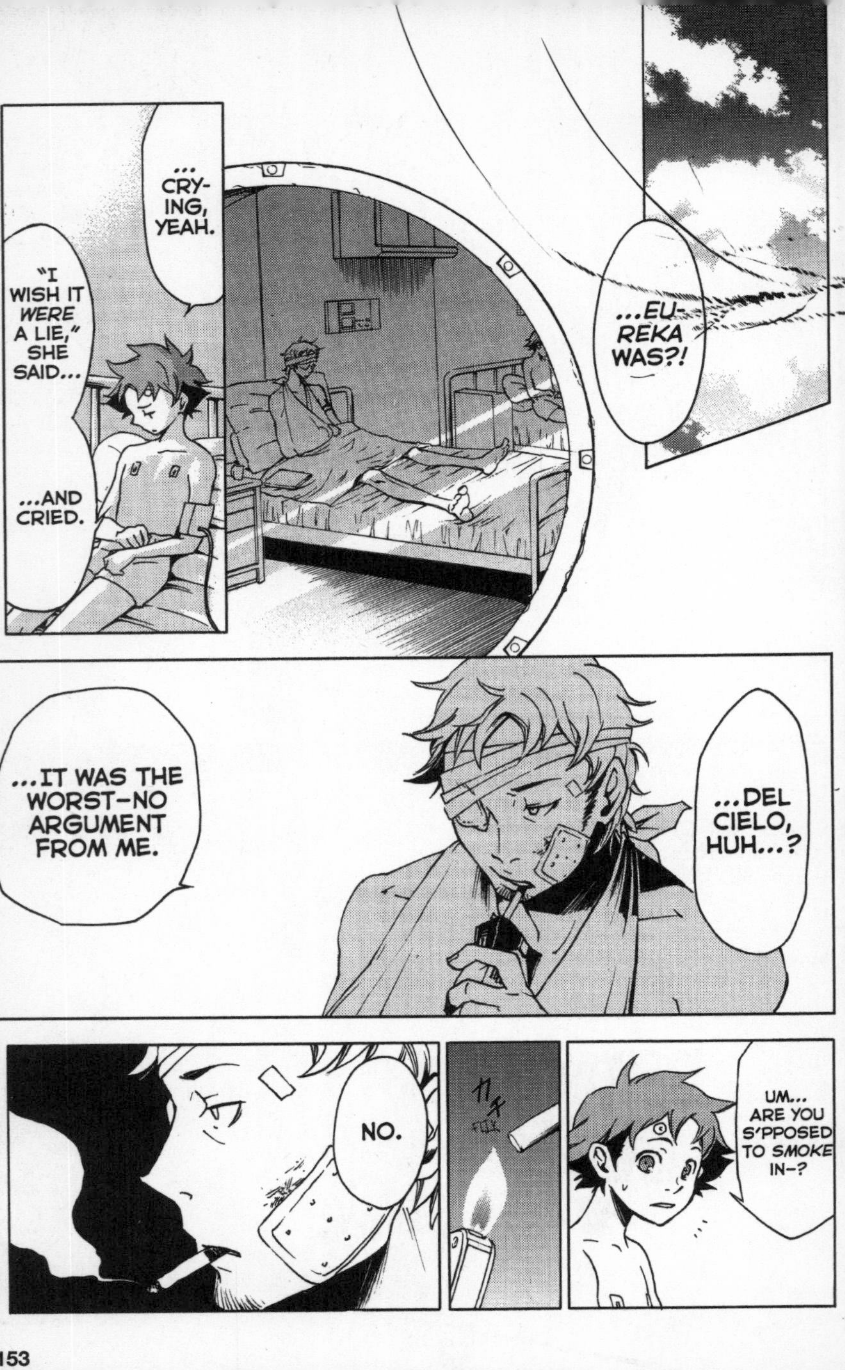
...EU-REKA WAS?!
...CRY-ING, YEAH.
"I WISH IT *WERE* A LIE," SHE SAID...
...AND CRIED.
...DEL CIELO, HUH...?
...IT WAS THE WORST—NO ARGUMENT FROM ME.
UM... ARE YOU S'PPOSED TO *SMOKE* IN—?
NO.

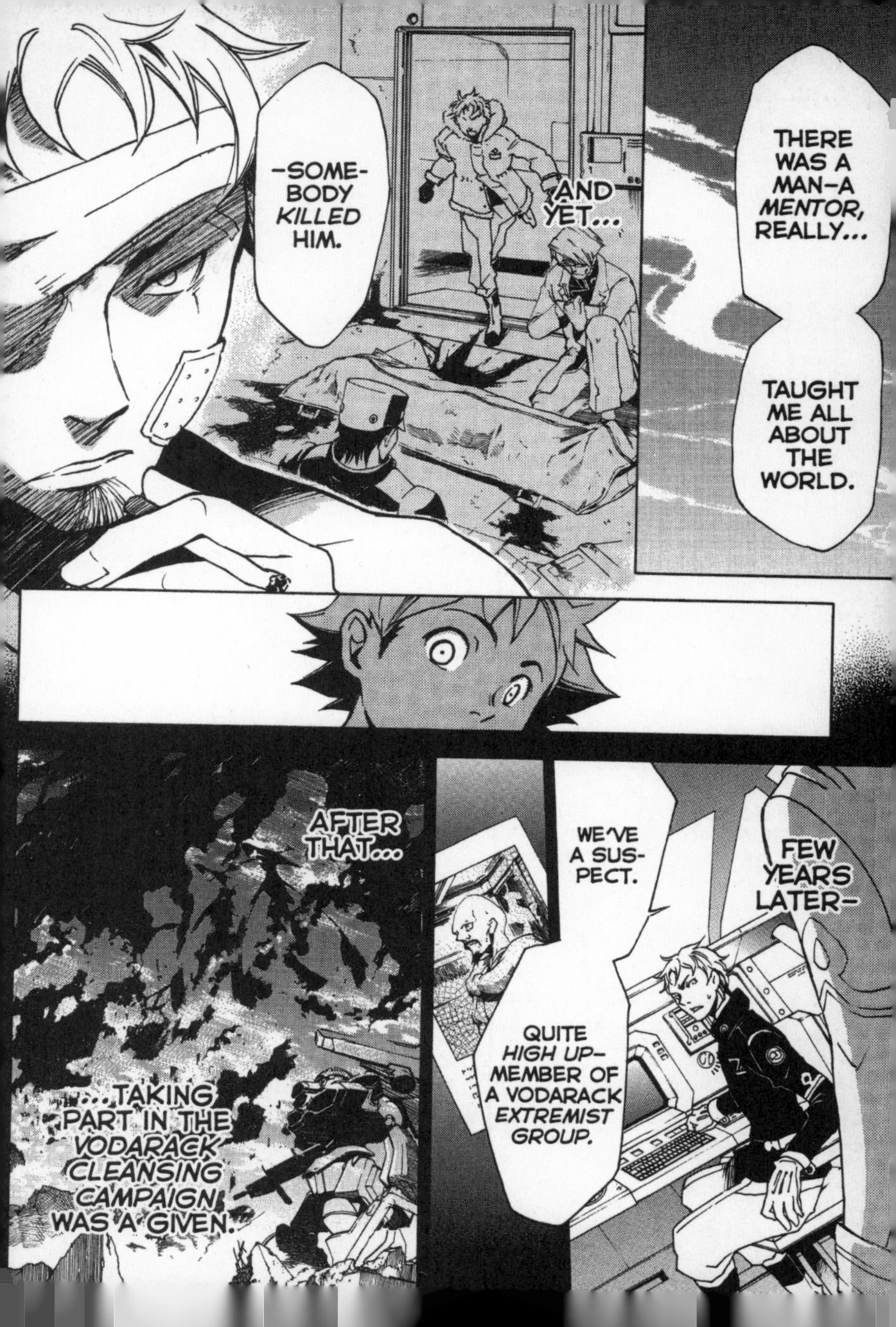
THERE WAS A MAN—A MENTOR, REALLY...
TAUGHT ME ALL ABOUT THE WORLD.
AND YET...
—SOME-BODY KILLED HIM.
FEW YEARS LATER—
WE'VE A SUS-PECT.
QUITE HIGH UP—MEMBER OF A VODARACK EXTREMIST GROUP.
AFTER THAT...
...TAKING PART IN THE VODARACK CLEANSING CAMPAIGN WAS A GIVEN.

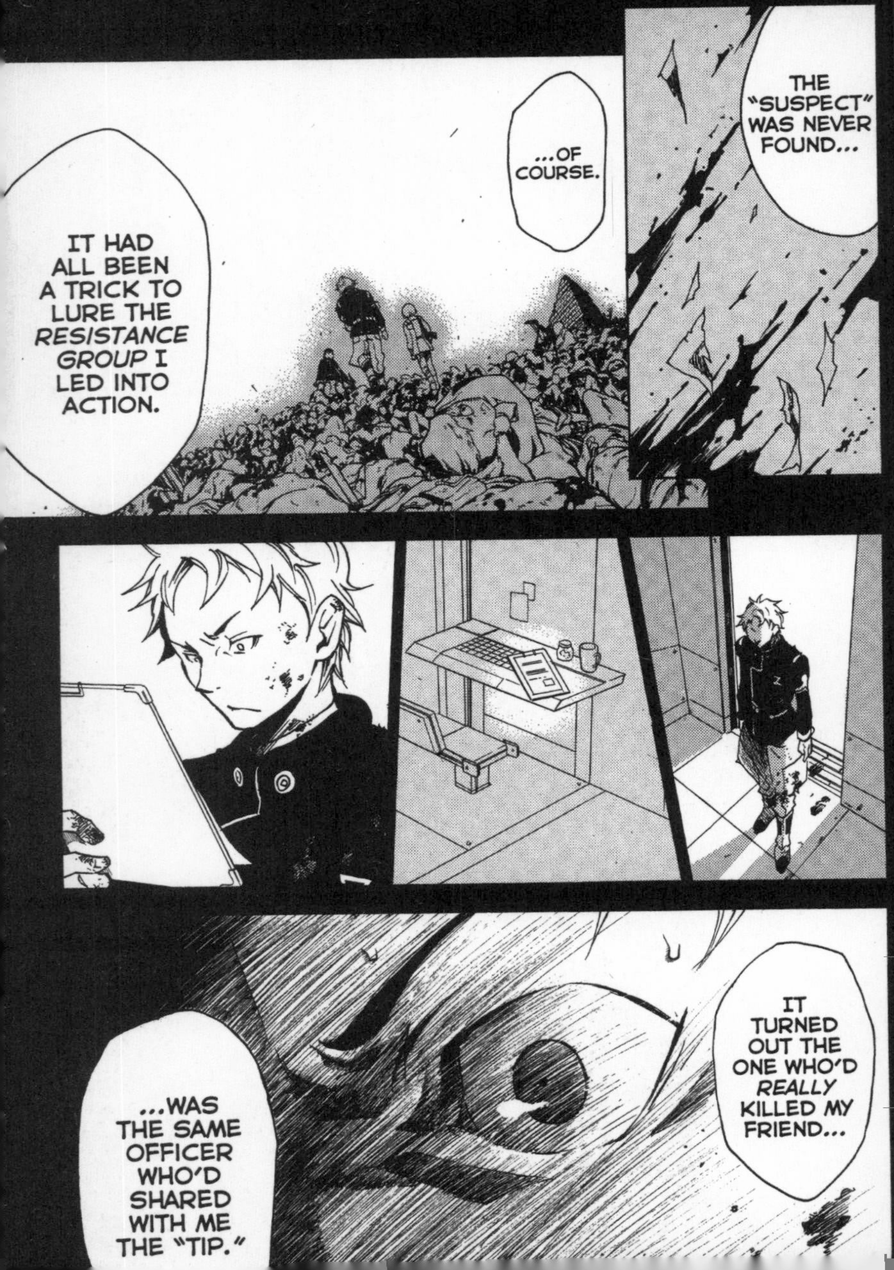
THE "SUSPECT" WAS NEVER FOUND...
...OF COURSE.
IT HAD ALL BEEN A TRICK TO LURE THE *RESISTANCE GROUP* I LED INTO ACTION.
IT TURNED OUT THE ONE WHO'D *REALLY* KILLED MY FRIEND...
...WAS THE SAME OFFICER WHO'D SHARED WITH ME THE "TIP."

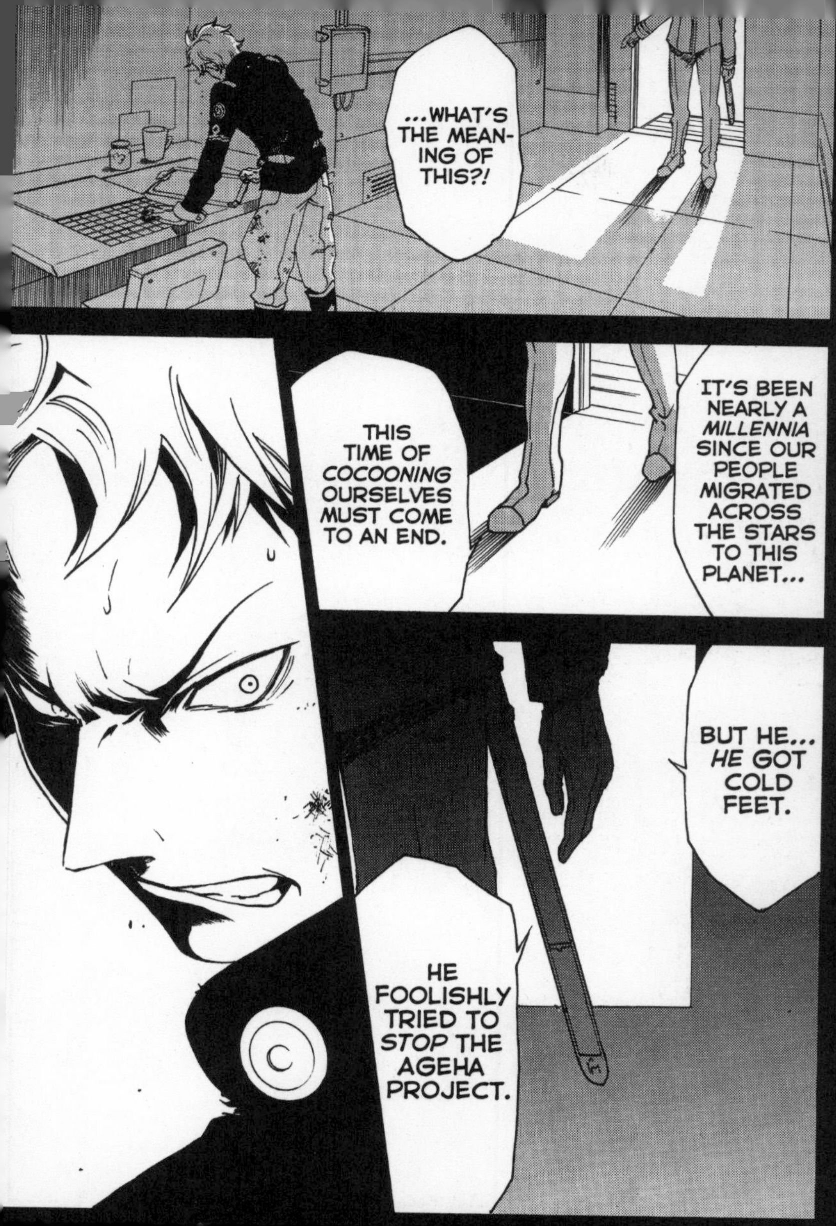

...WHAT'S THE MEAN-ING OF THIS?!
IT'S BEEN NEARLY A *MILLENNIA* SINCE OUR PEOPLE MIGRATED ACROSS THE STARS TO THIS PLANET...
THIS TIME OF *COCOONING* OURSELVES MUST COME TO AN END.
BUT HE... *HE* GOT COLD FEET.
HE FOOLISHLY TRIED TO *STOP* THE AGEHA PROJECT.

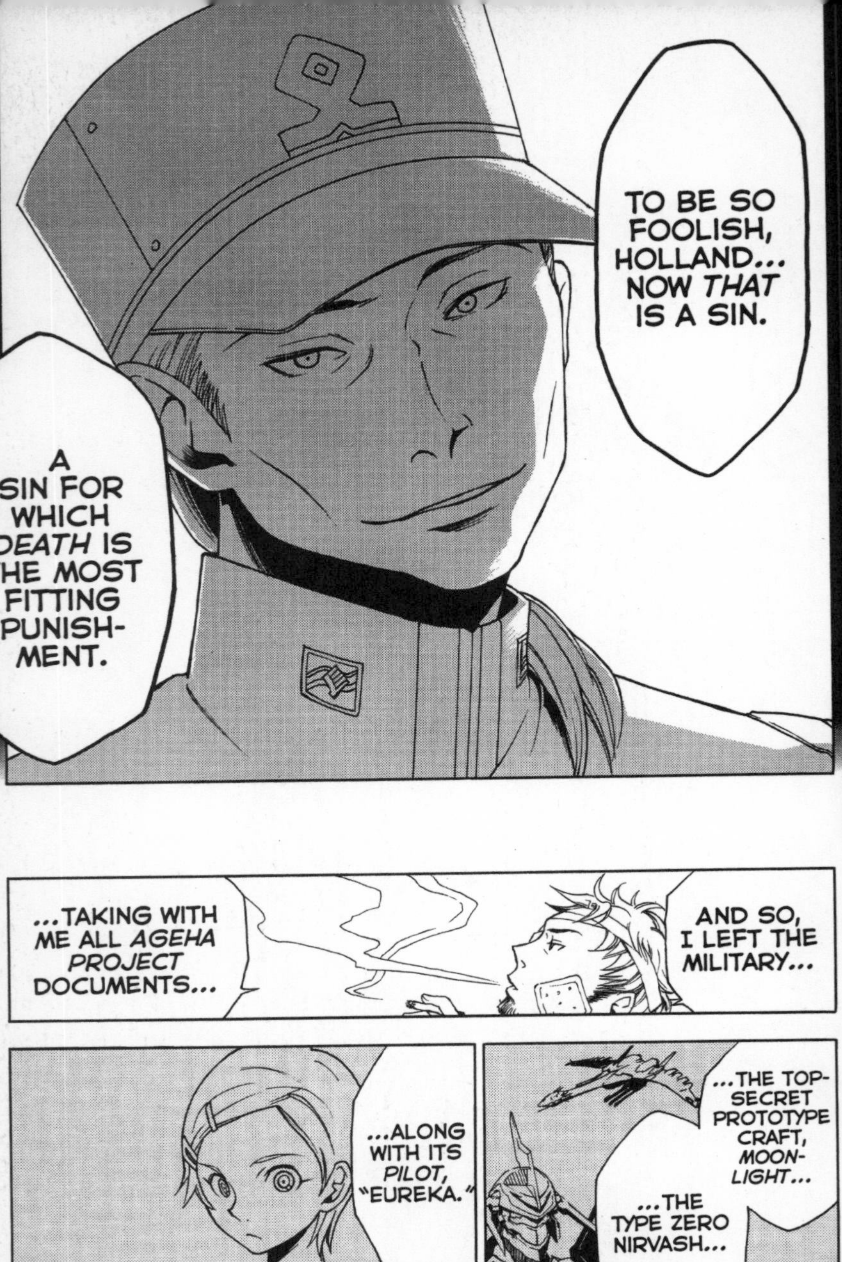
TO BE SO FOOLISH, HOLLAND... NOW *THAT* IS A SIN.
A SIN FOR WHICH *DEATH* IS THE MOST FITTING PUNISH-MENT.
AND SO, I LEFT THE MILITARY...
...TAKING WITH ME ALL *AGEHA PROJECT* DOCUMENTS...
...THE TOP-SECRET PROTOTYPE CRAFT, *MOON-LIGHT*...
...THE TYPE ZERO NIRVASH...
...ALONG WITH ITS *PILOT*, "EUREKA."

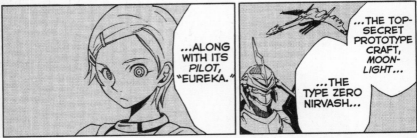

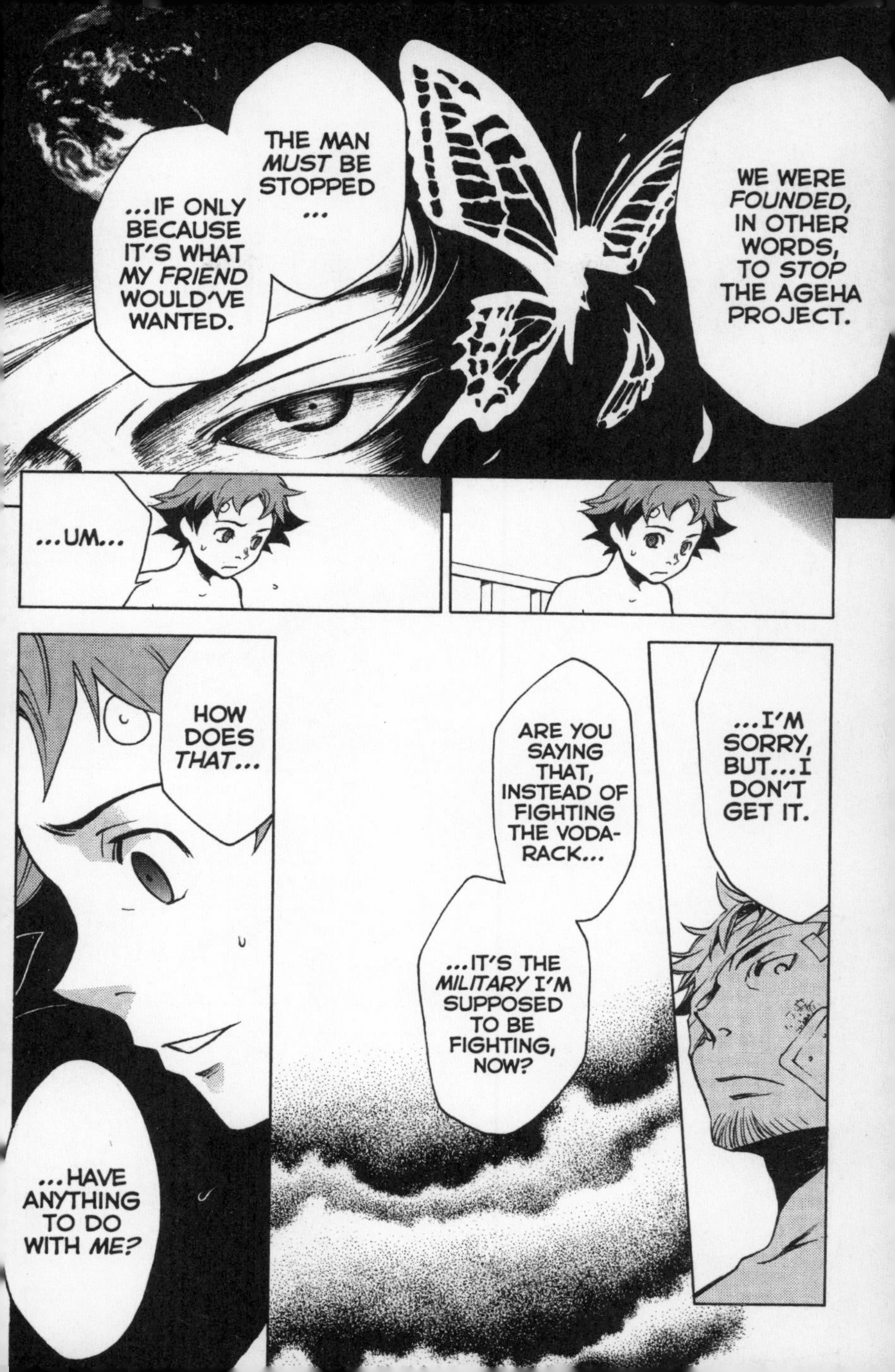
WE WERE *FOUNDED*, IN OTHER WORDS, TO *STOP* THE AGEHA PROJECT.
THE MAN *MUST* BE STOPPED ...
...IF ONLY BECAUSE IT'S WHAT *MY FRIEND* WOULD'VE WANTED.
...UM...
...I'M SORRY, BUT...I DON'T GET IT.
ARE YOU SAYING THAT, INSTEAD OF FIGHTING THE VODA-RACK...
...IT'S THE *MILITARY* I'M SUPPOSED TO BE FIGHTING, NOW?
HOW DOES *THAT*...
...HAVE ANYTHING TO DO WITH *ME*?

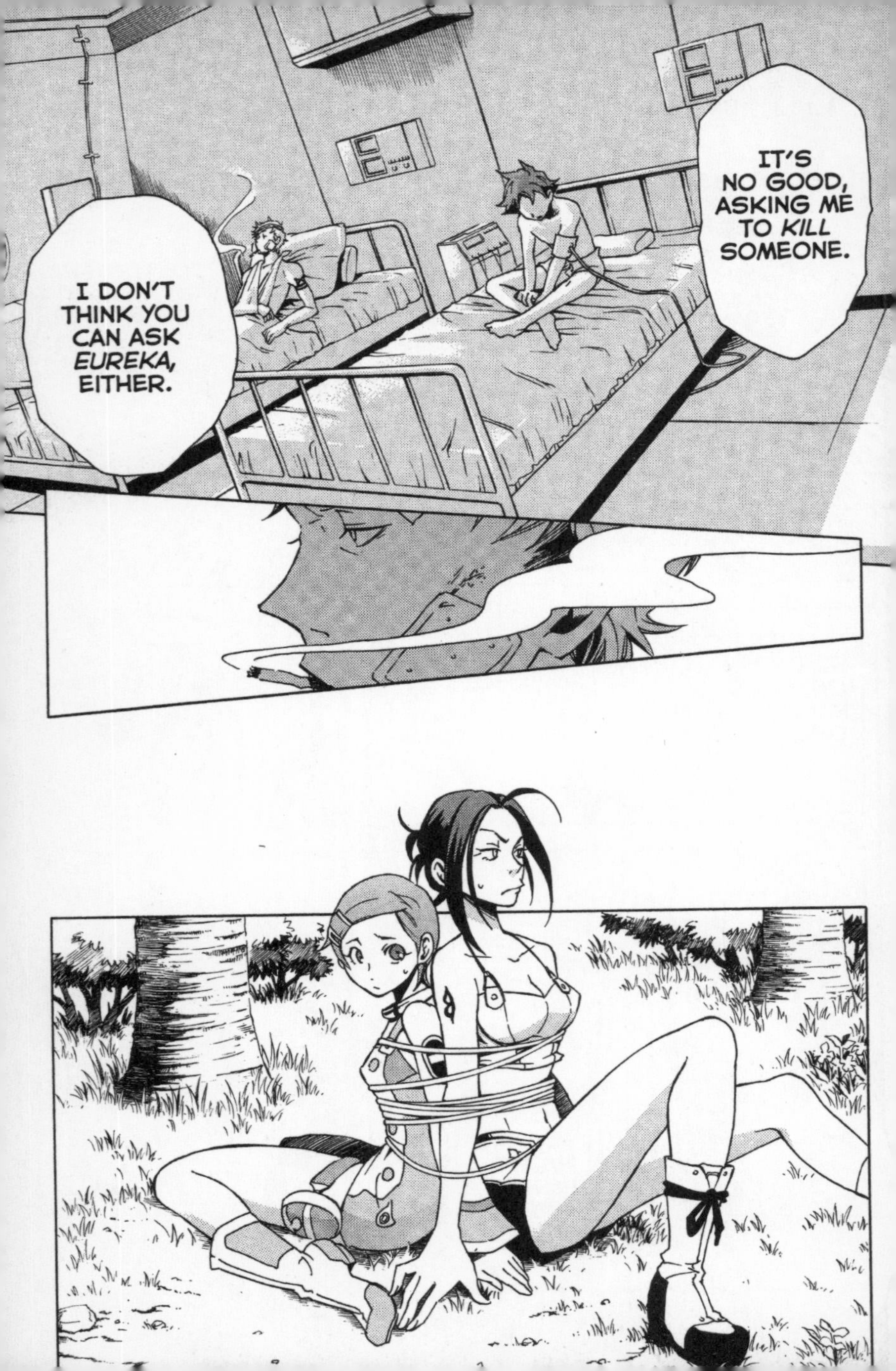
IT'S NO GOOD, ASKING ME TO *KILL* SOMEONE.
I DON'T THINK YOU CAN ASK *EUREKA*, EITHER.

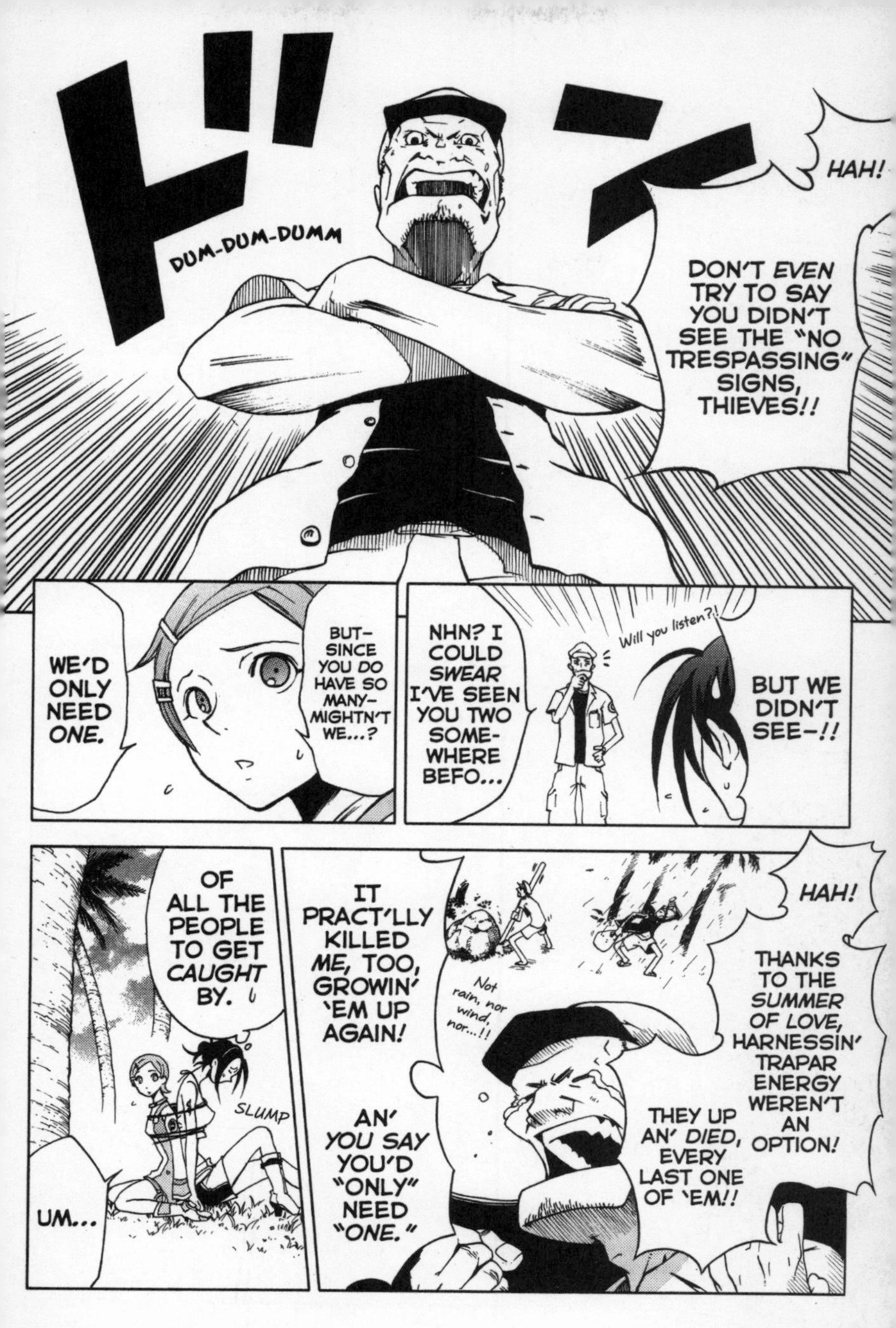
HAH!
DON'T EVEN TRY TO SAY YOU DIDN'T SEE THE "NO TRESPASSING" SIGNS, THIEVES!!
DUM-DUM-DUMM
BUT WE DIDN'T SEE–!!
Will you listen?!
NHN? I COULD SWEAR I'VE SEEN YOU TWO SOME-WHERE BEFO...
BUT– SINCE YOU DO HAVE SO MANY– MIGHTN'T WE...?
WE'D ONLY NEED ONE.
HAH!
THANKS TO THE SUMMER OF LOVE, HARNESSIN' TRAPAR ENERGY WEREN'T AN OPTION!
THEY UP AN' DIED, EVERY LAST ONE OF 'EM!!
IT PRACT'LLY KILLED ME, TOO, GROWIN' 'EM UP AGAIN!
Not rain, nor wind, nor...!!
AN' YOU SAY YOU'D "ONLY" NEED "ONE."
OF ALL THE PEOPLE TO GET CAUGHT BY.
SLUMP
UM...

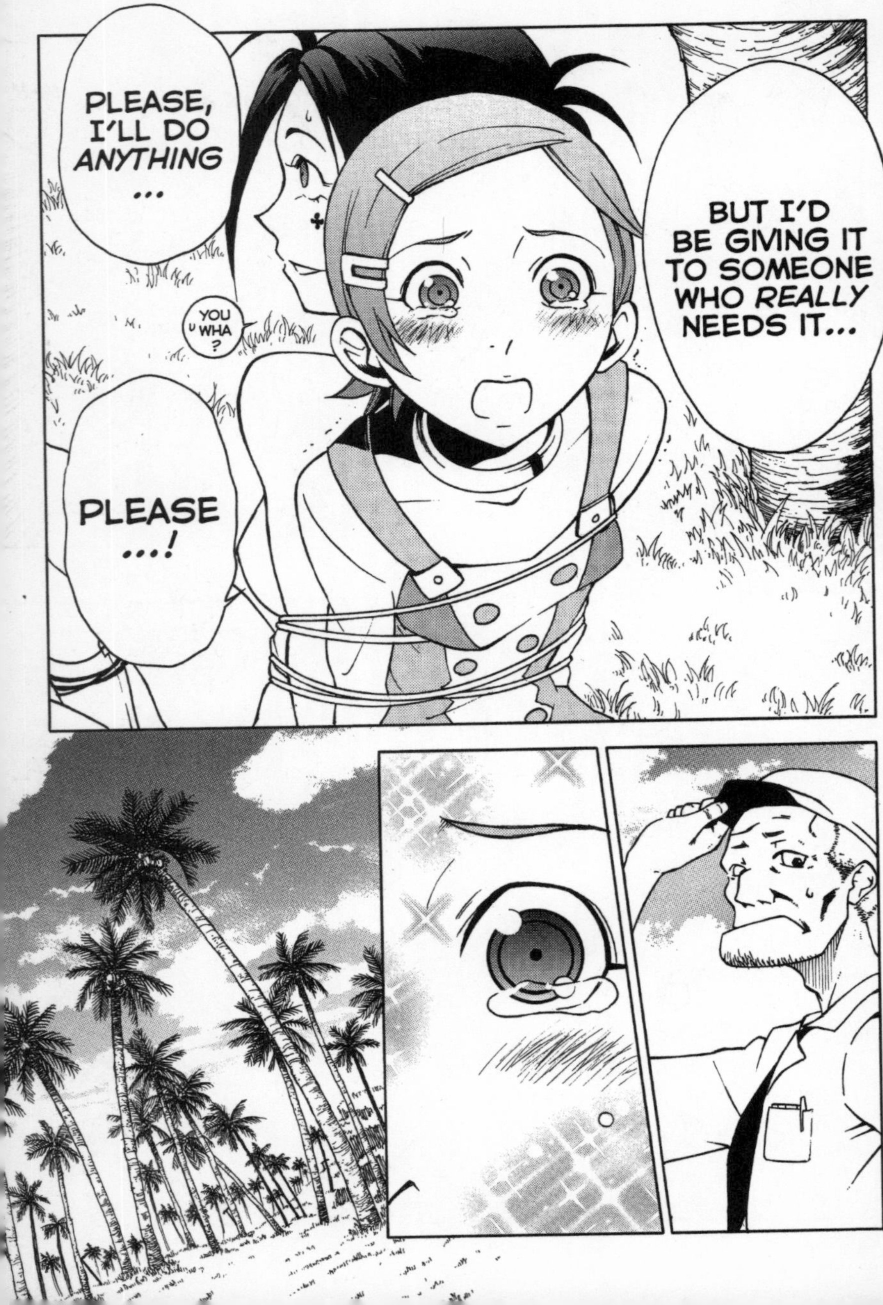
BUT I'D BE GIVING IT TO SOMEONE WHO REALLY NEEDS IT...
PLEASE, I'LL DO ANYTHING ...
YOU WHA?
PLEASE ...!

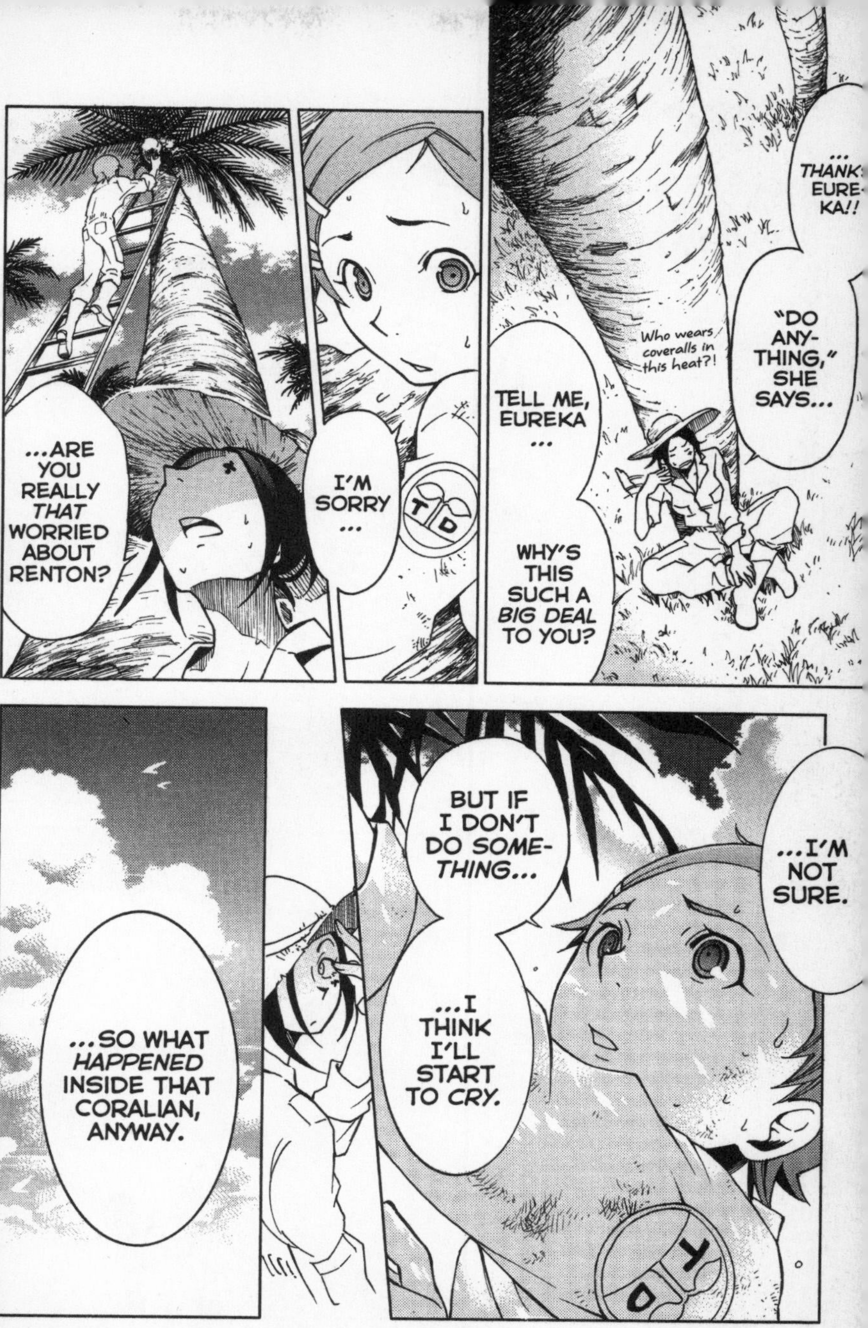
...THANK: EURE-KA!!
"DO ANY-THING," SHE SAYS...
Who wears coveralls in this heat?!
TELL ME, EUREKA ...
WHY'S THIS SUCH A *BIG DEAL* TO YOU?
I'M SORRY ...
...ARE YOU REALLY *THAT* WORRIED ABOUT RENTON?
...I'M NOT SURE.
BUT IF I DON'T DO *SOME-THING*...
...I THINK I'LL START TO *CRY.*
...SO WHAT *HAPPENED* INSIDE THAT CORALIAN, ANYWAY.

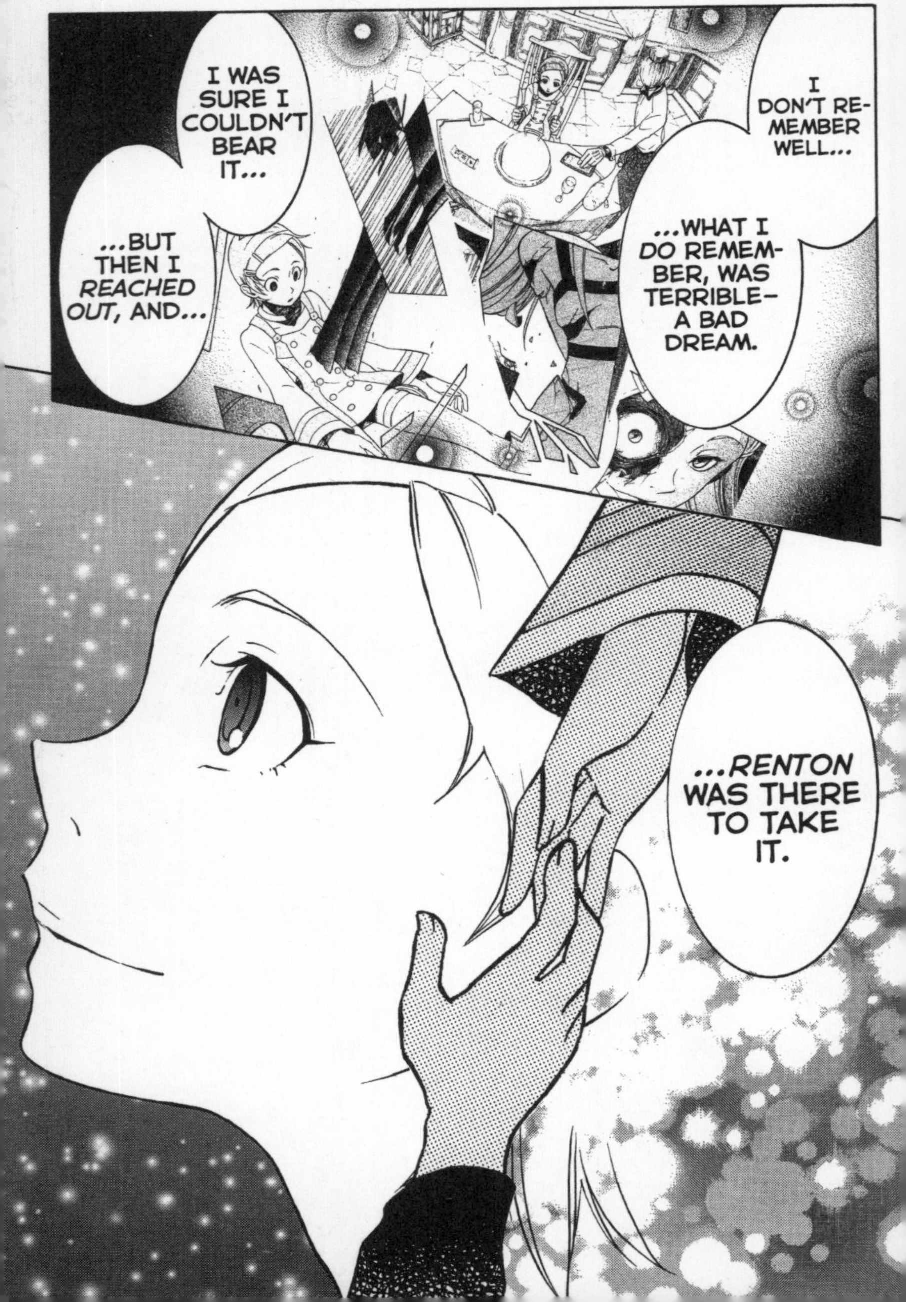
I DON'T RE-MEMBER WELL...
...WHAT I *DO* REMEMBER, WAS TERRIBLE–A BAD DREAM.
I WAS SURE I COULDN'T BEAR IT...
...BUT THEN I *REACHED* OUT, AND...
...*RENTON* WAS THERE TO TAKE IT.

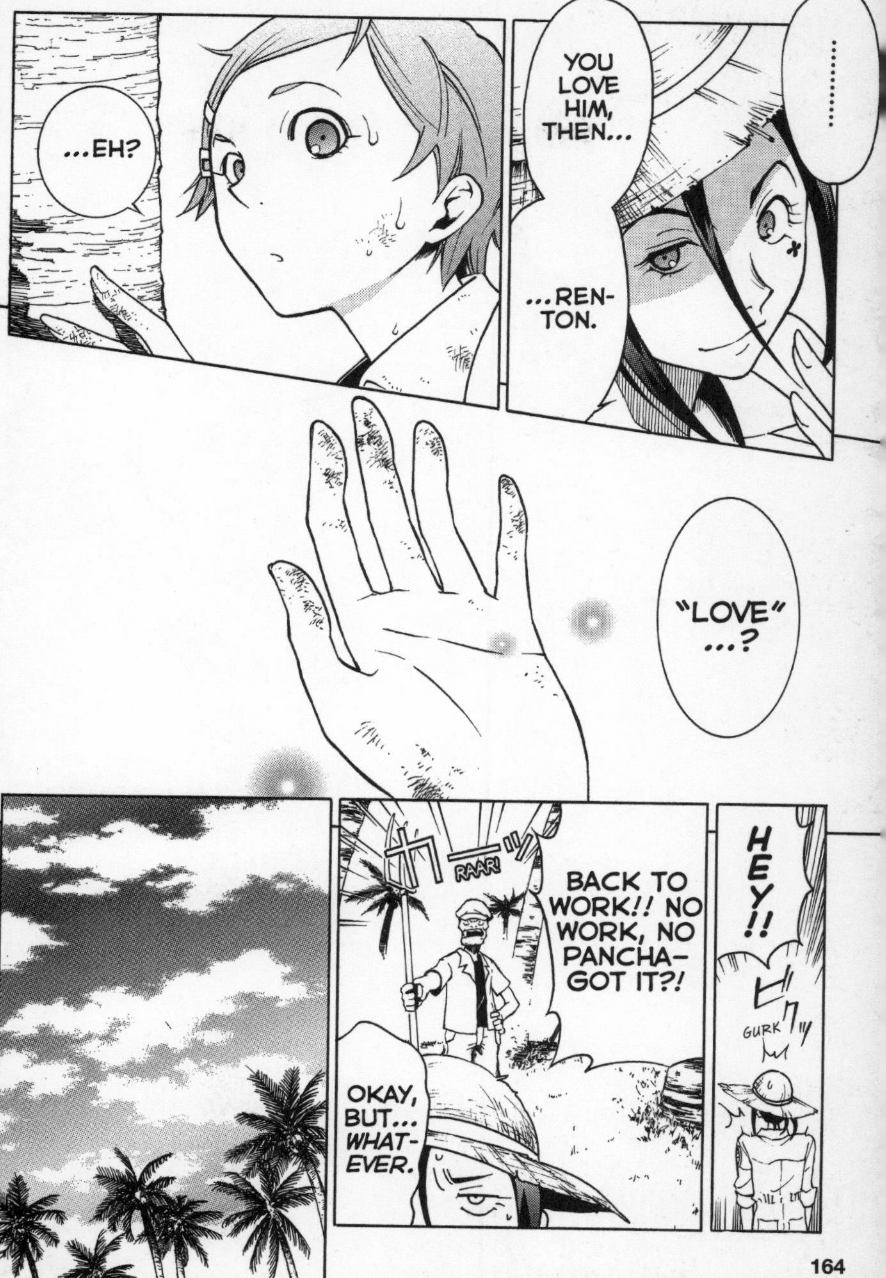
......
YOU LOVE HIM, THEN...
...REN-TON.
...EH?
"LOVE" ...?
HEY!!
GURK
RAAR!
BACK TO WORK!! NO WORK, NO PANCHA-GOT IT?!
OKAY, BUT... WHAT-EVER.

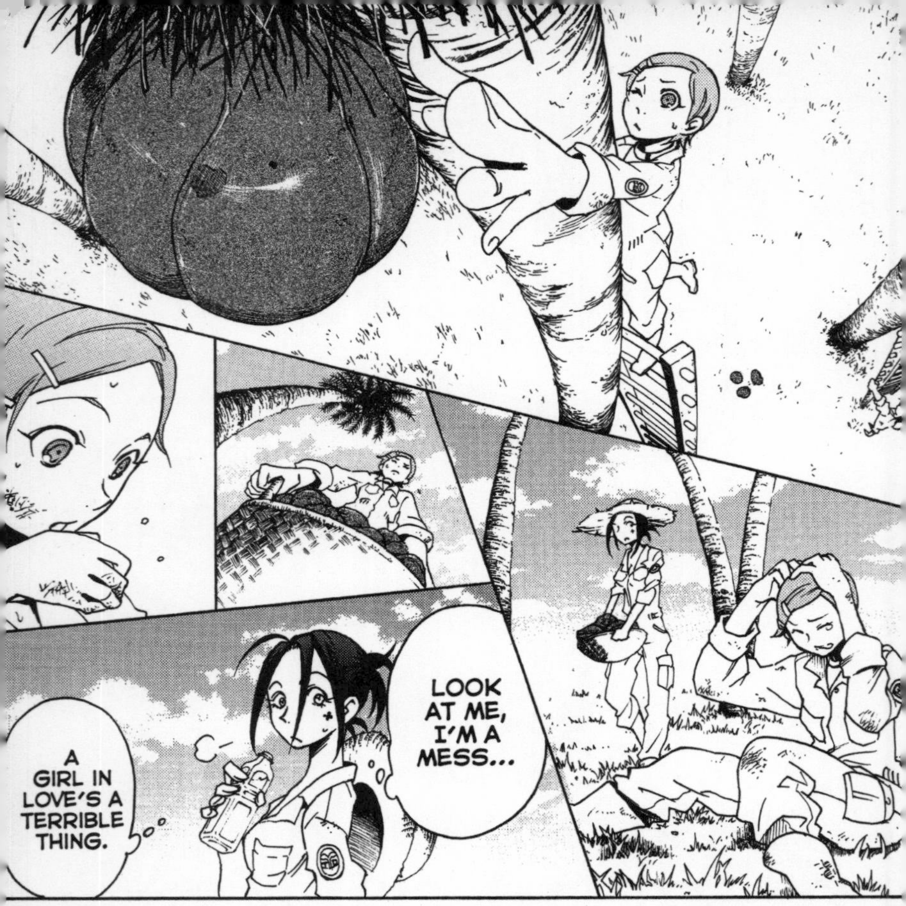
LOOK AT ME, I'M A MESS...
A GIRL IN LOVE'S A TERRIBLE THING.

[redacted]

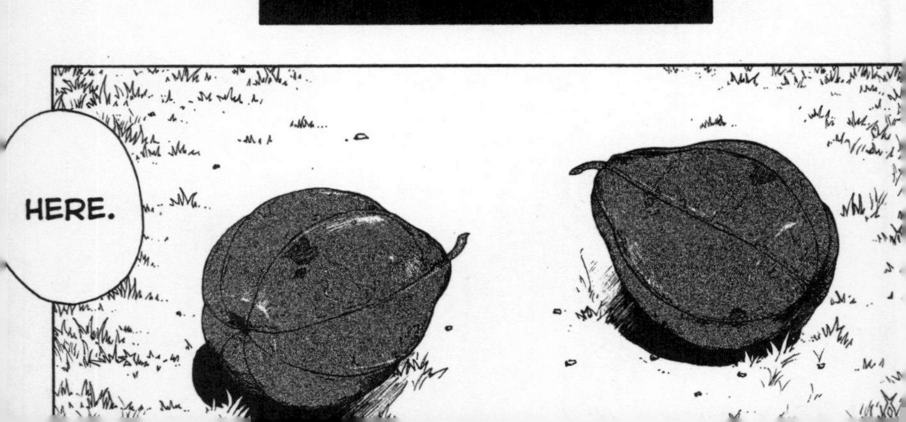
HERE.

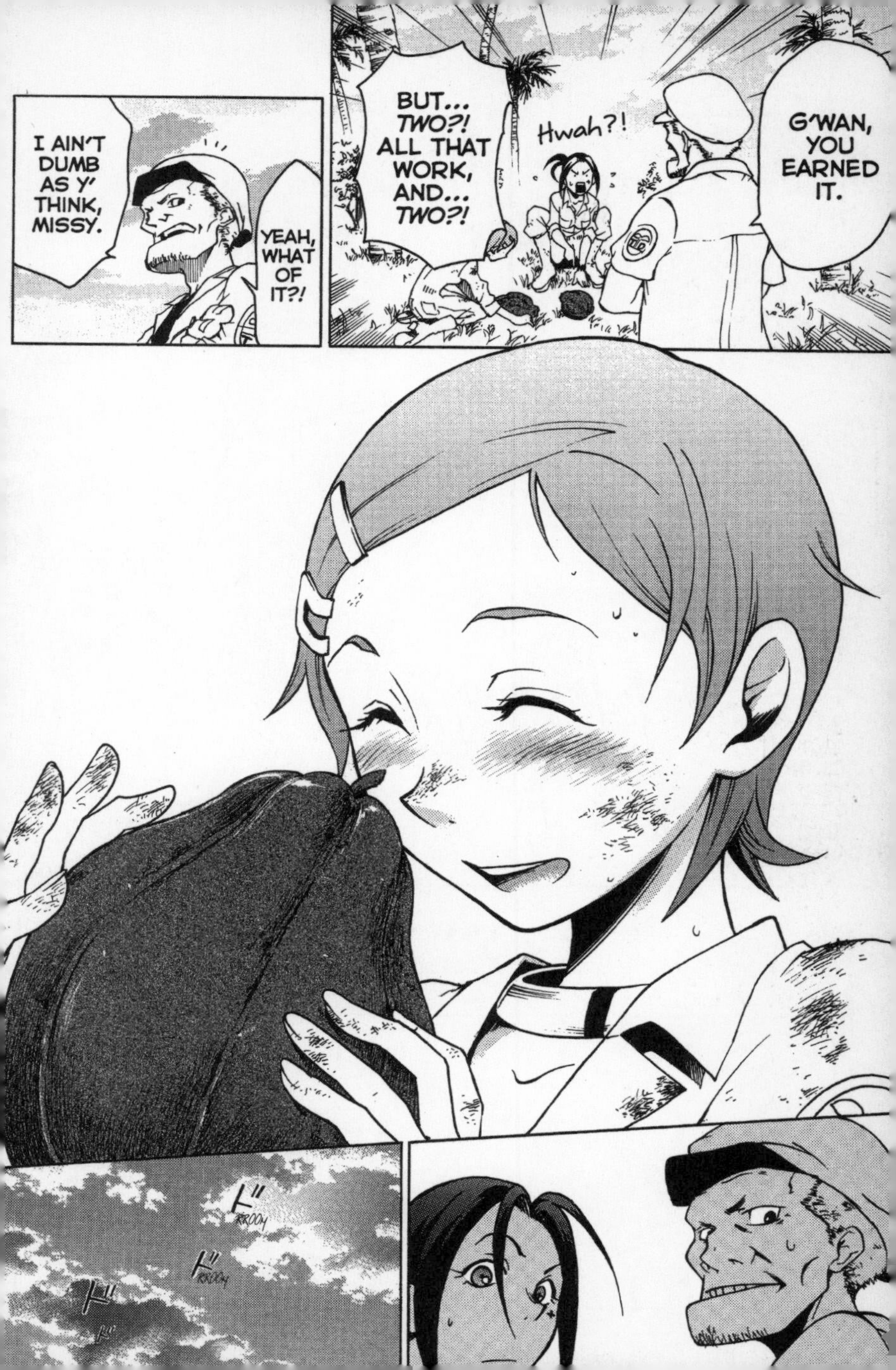
G'WAN, YOU EARNED IT.
Hwah?!
BUT... TWO?! ALL THAT WORK, AND... TWO?!
I AIN'T DUMB AS Y' THINK, MISSY.
YEAH, WHAT OF IT?!
ド" RROOM
ド" RROOM
ド"

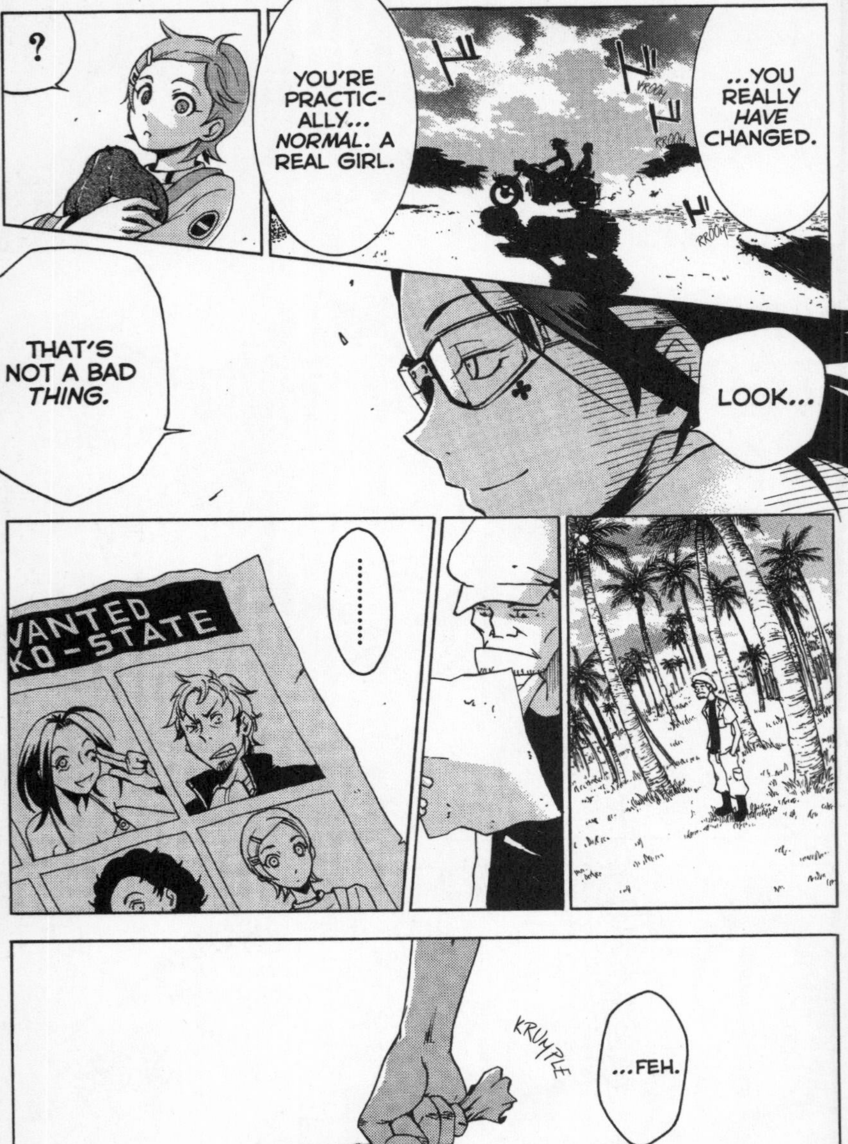
...YOU REALLY HAVE CHANGED.
VROOM
RROOM
RROOM
YOU'RE PRACTIC-ALLY... NORMAL. A REAL GIRL.
?
LOOK...
THAT'S NOT A BAD THING.
......
VANTED
KO-STATE
KRUMPLE
...FEH.

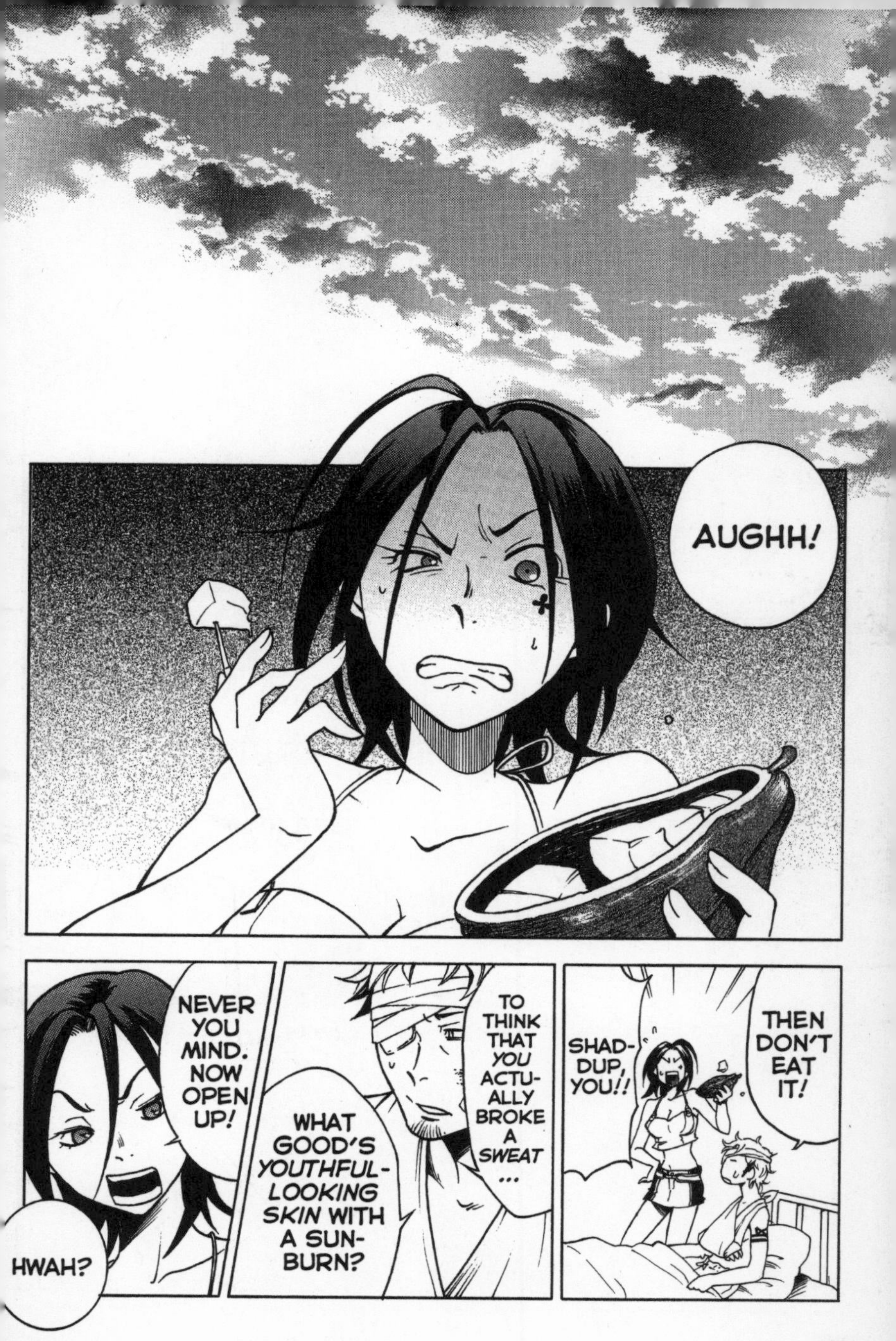
AUGHH!
THEN DON'T EAT IT!
SHAD-DUP, YOU!!
TO THINK THAT *YOU* ACTUALLY BROKE A *SWEAT*...
WHAT GOOD'S *YOUTHFUL*-LOOKING *SKIN* WITH A SUNBURN?
NEVER YOU MIND. NOW OPEN UP!
HWAH?

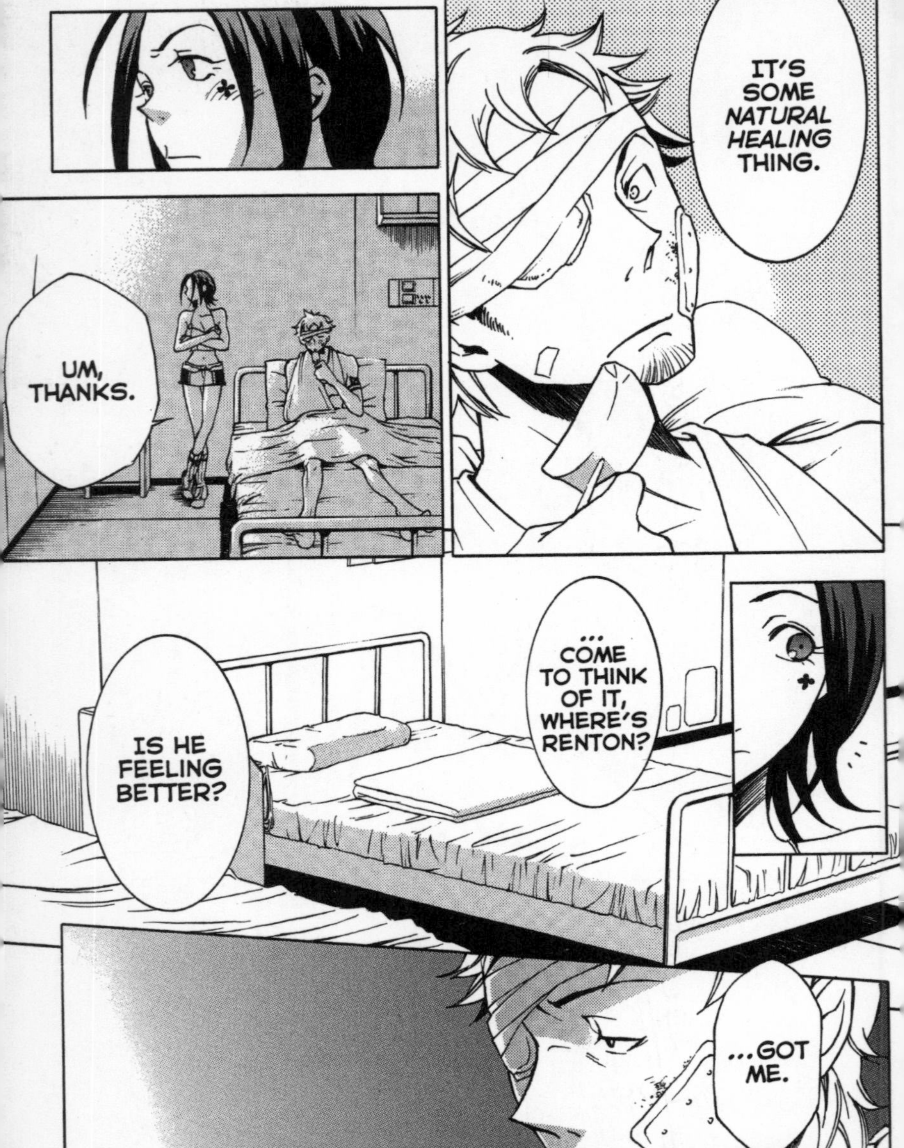
IT'S SOME NATURAL HEALING THING.
UM, THANKS.
...COME TO THINK OF IT, WHERE'S RENTON?
IS HE FEELING BETTER?
...GOT ME.
Chomp...

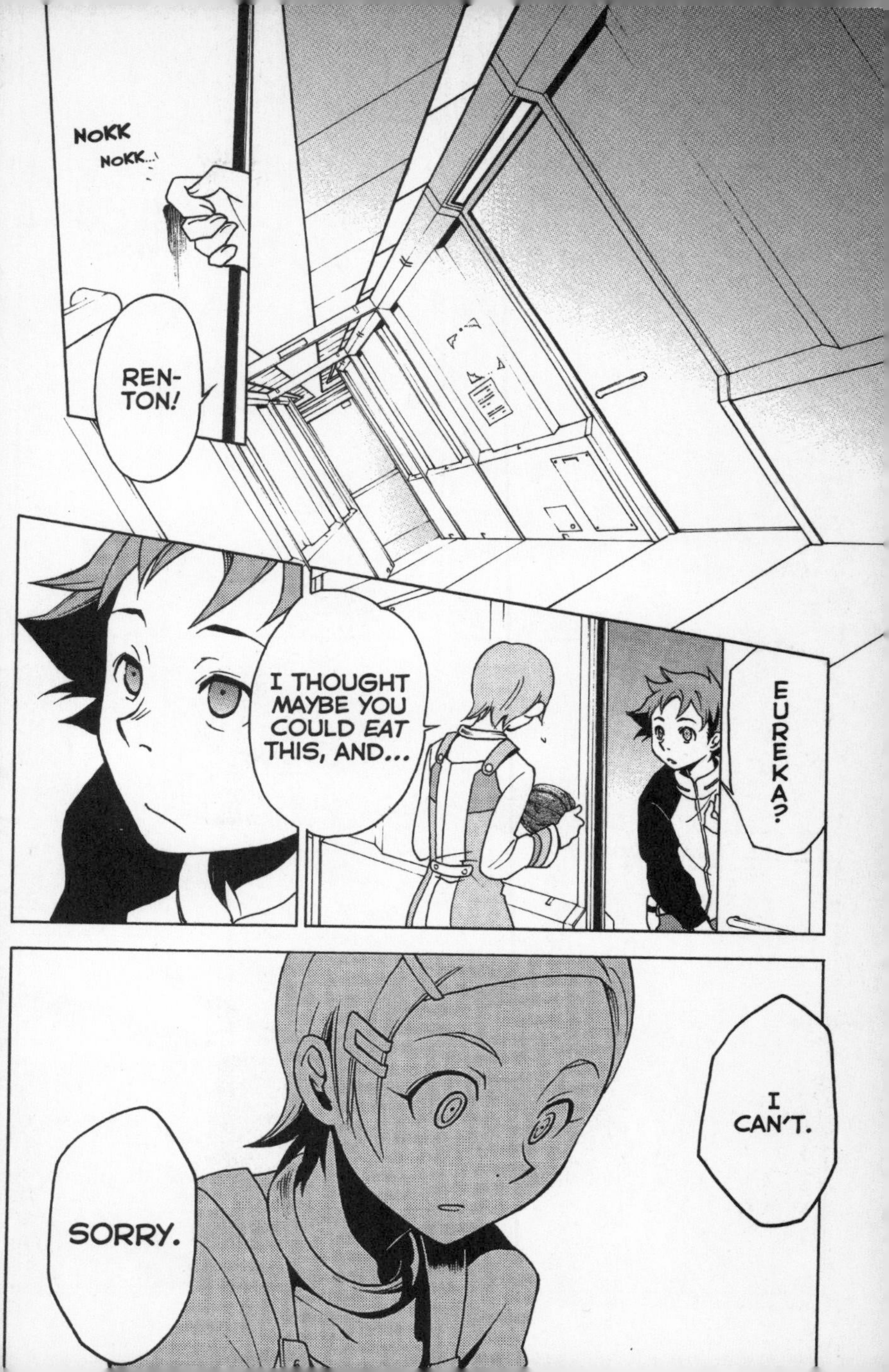
NOKK
NOKK...
REN-TON!
EUREKA?
I THOUGHT MAYBE YOU COULD *EAT* THIS, AND...
I CAN'T.
SORRY.

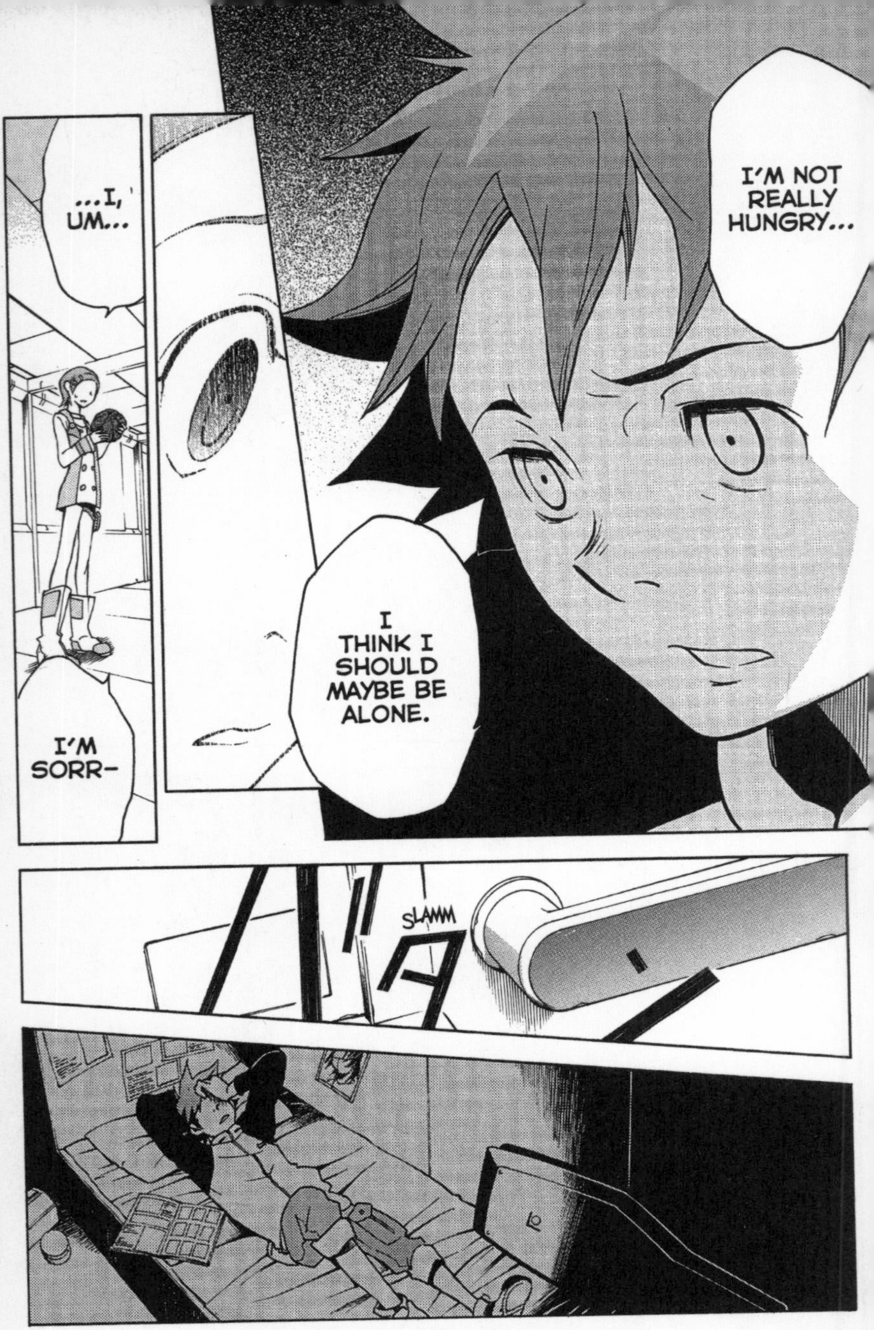
I'M NOT REALLY HUNGRY...
I THINK I SHOULD MAYBE BE ALONE.
...I, UM...
I'M SORR-
SLAMM

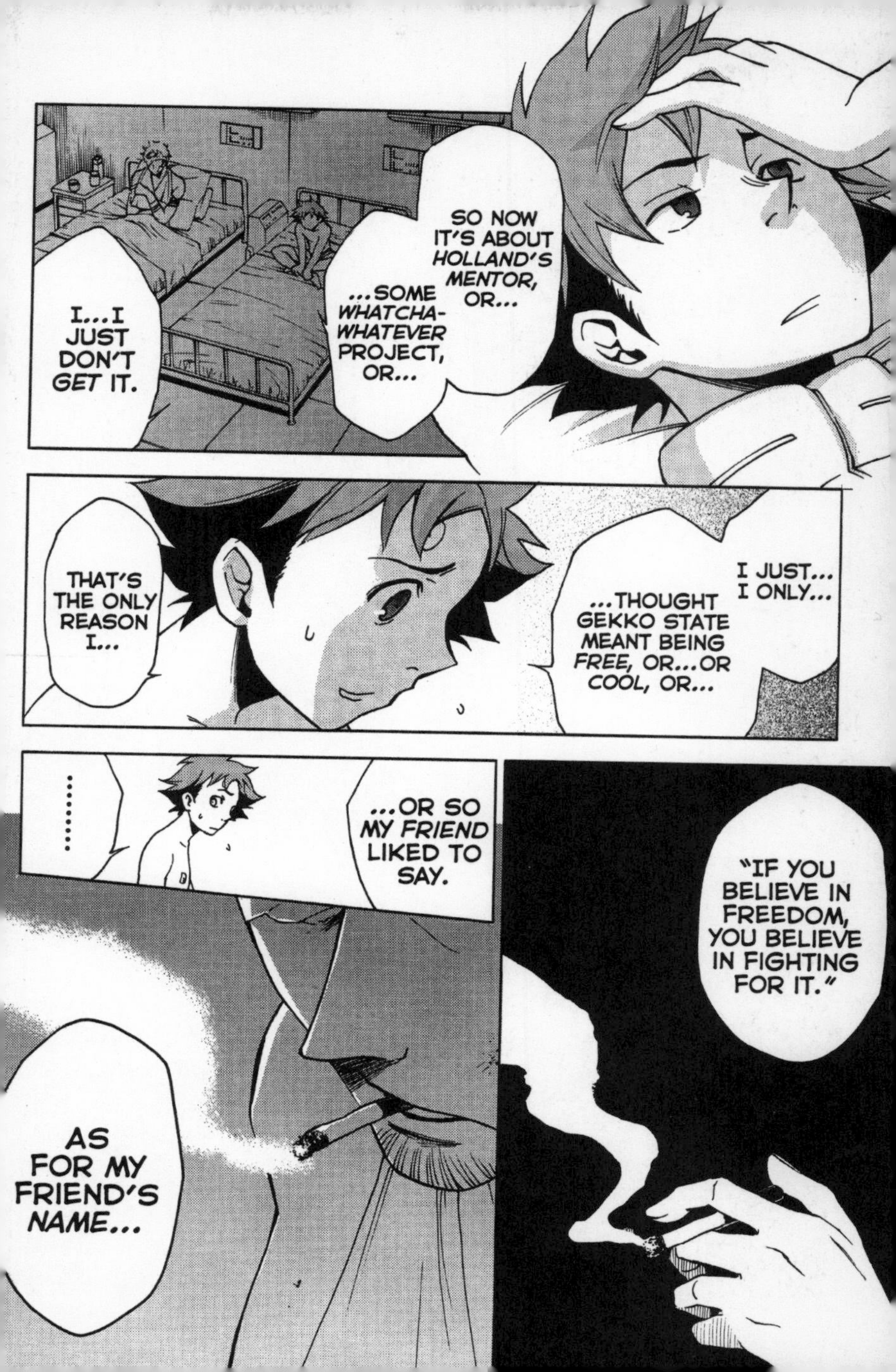
SO NOW IT'S ABOUT HOLLAND'S MENTOR, OR...
...SOME WHATCHA-WHATEVER PROJECT, OR...
I...I JUST DON'T GET IT.
I JUST... I ONLY...
...THOUGHT GEKKO STATE MEANT BEING FREE, OR...OR COOL, OR...
THAT'S THE ONLY REASON I...
"IF YOU BELIEVE IN FREEDOM, YOU BELIEVE IN FIGHTING FOR IT."
...OR SO MY FRIEND LIKED TO SAY.
....
AS FOR MY FRIEND'S NAME...

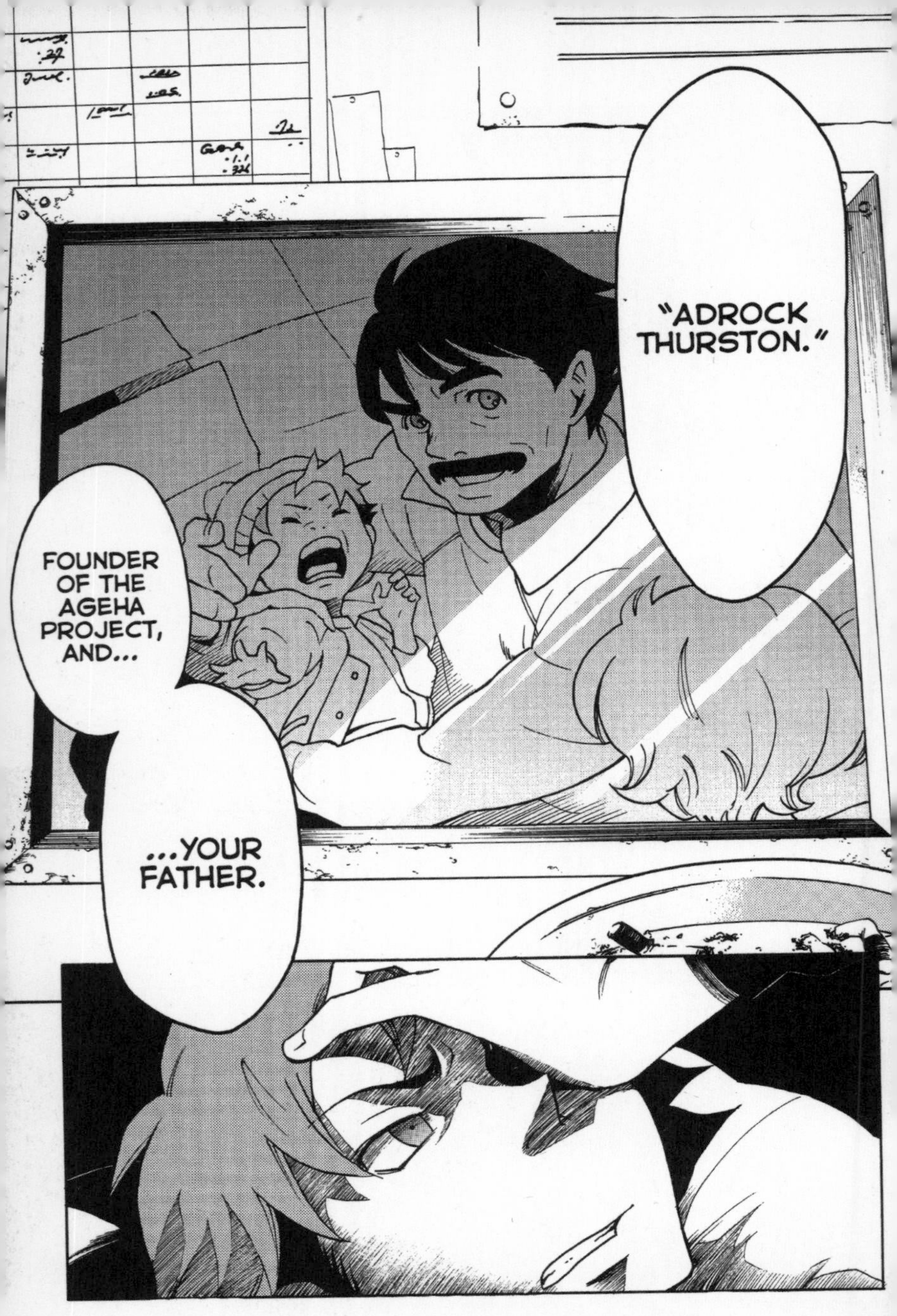
"ADROCK THURSTON."
FOUNDER OF THE AGEHA PROJECT, AND...
...YOUR FATHER.

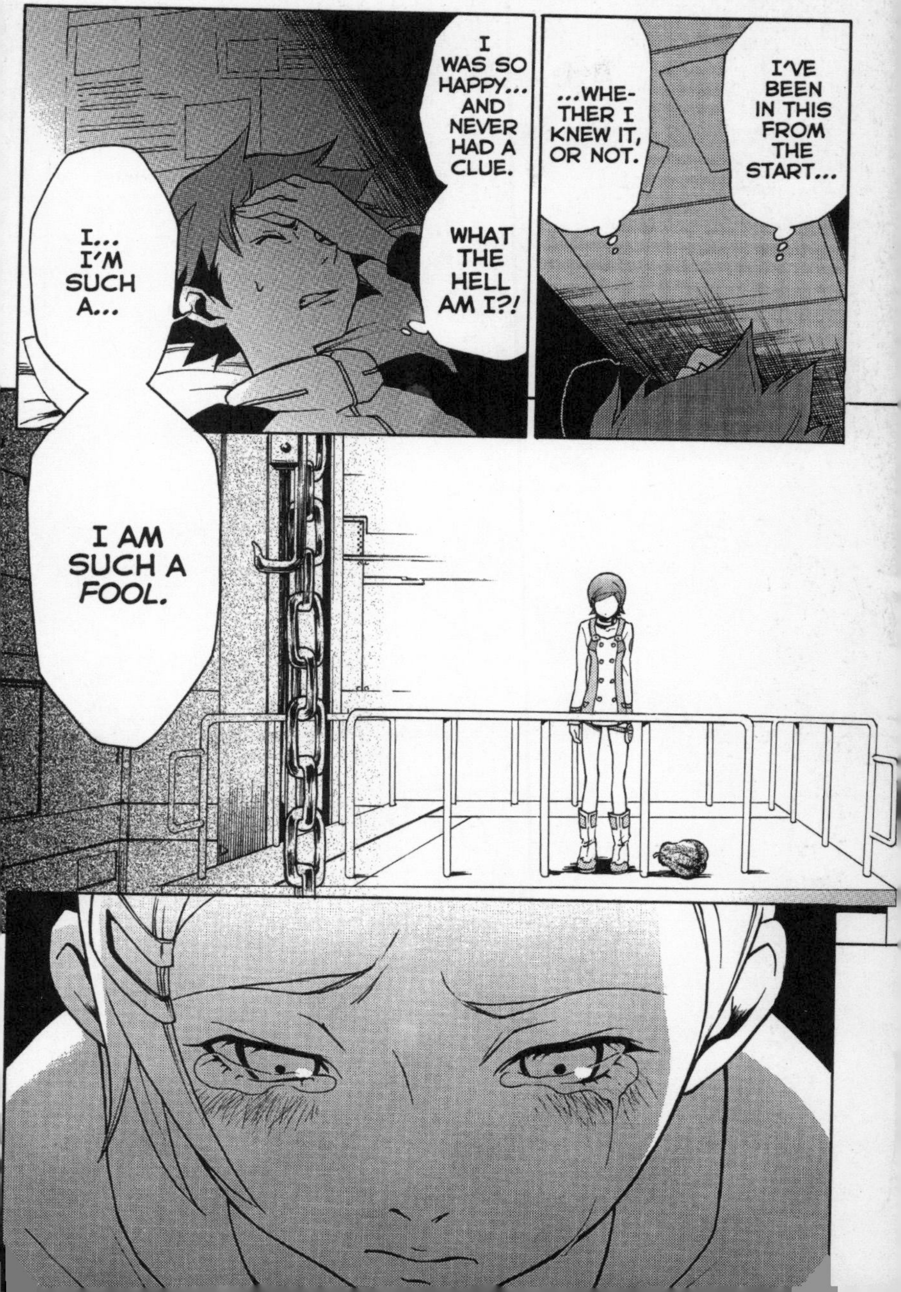
I'VE BEEN IN THIS FROM THE START...
...WHE-THER I KNEW IT, OR NOT.
I WAS SO HAPPY... AND NEVER HAD A CLUE.
WHAT THE HELL AM I?!
I... I'M SUCH A...
I AM SUCH A *FOOL*.

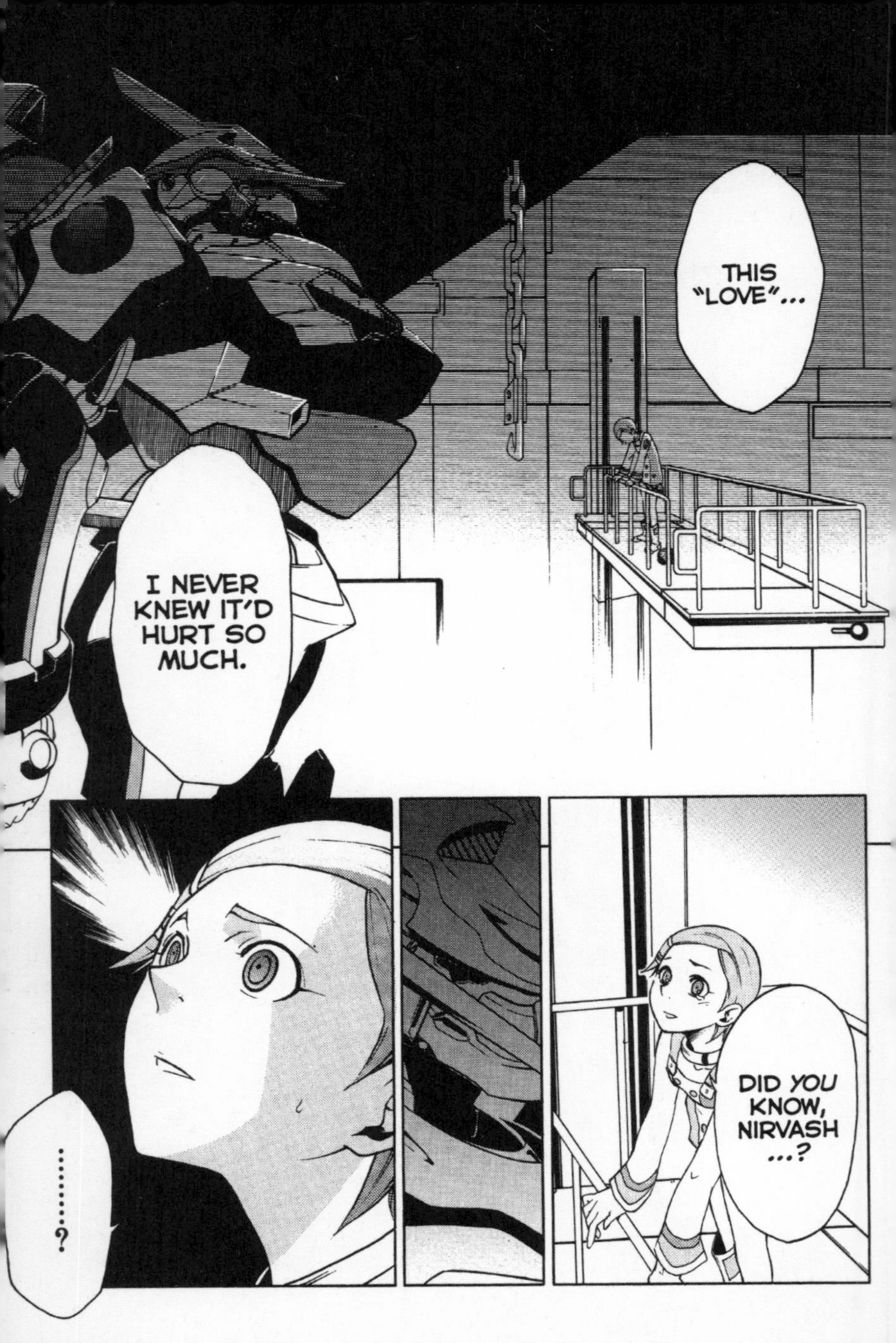
THIS "LOVE"...
I NEVER KNEW IT'D HURT SO MUCH.
DID *YOU* KNOW, NIRVASH ...?
......?

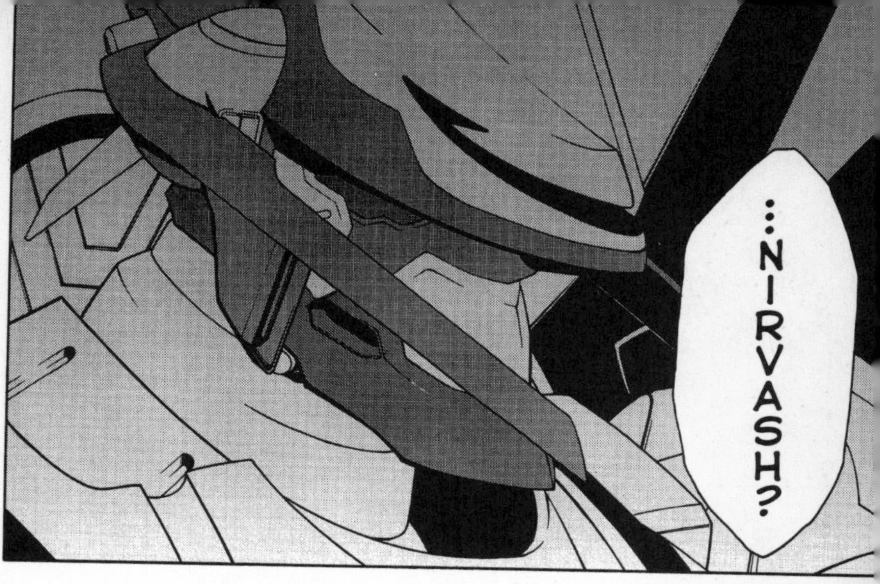
...NIRVASH?

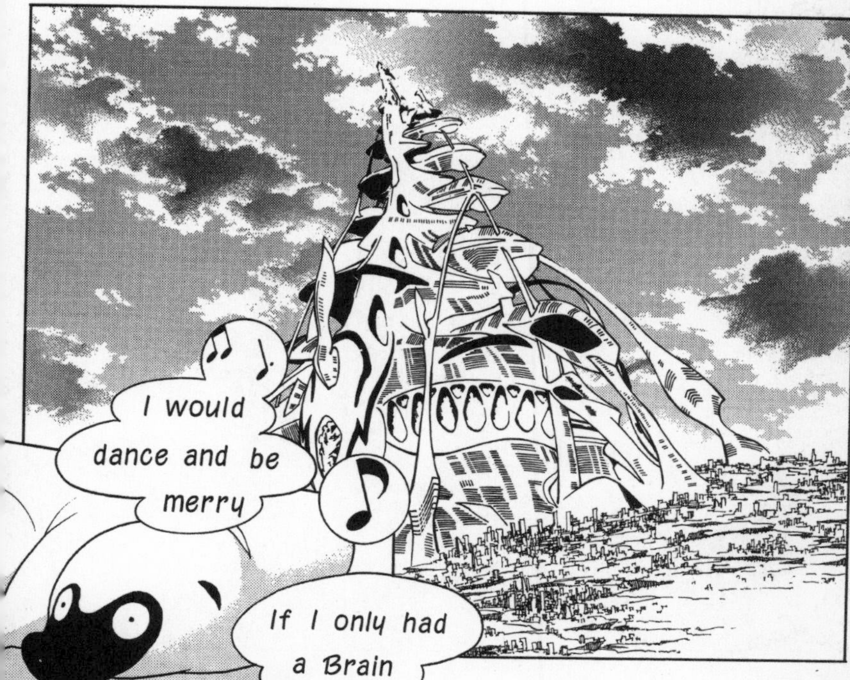
I would dance and be merry
If I only had a Brain

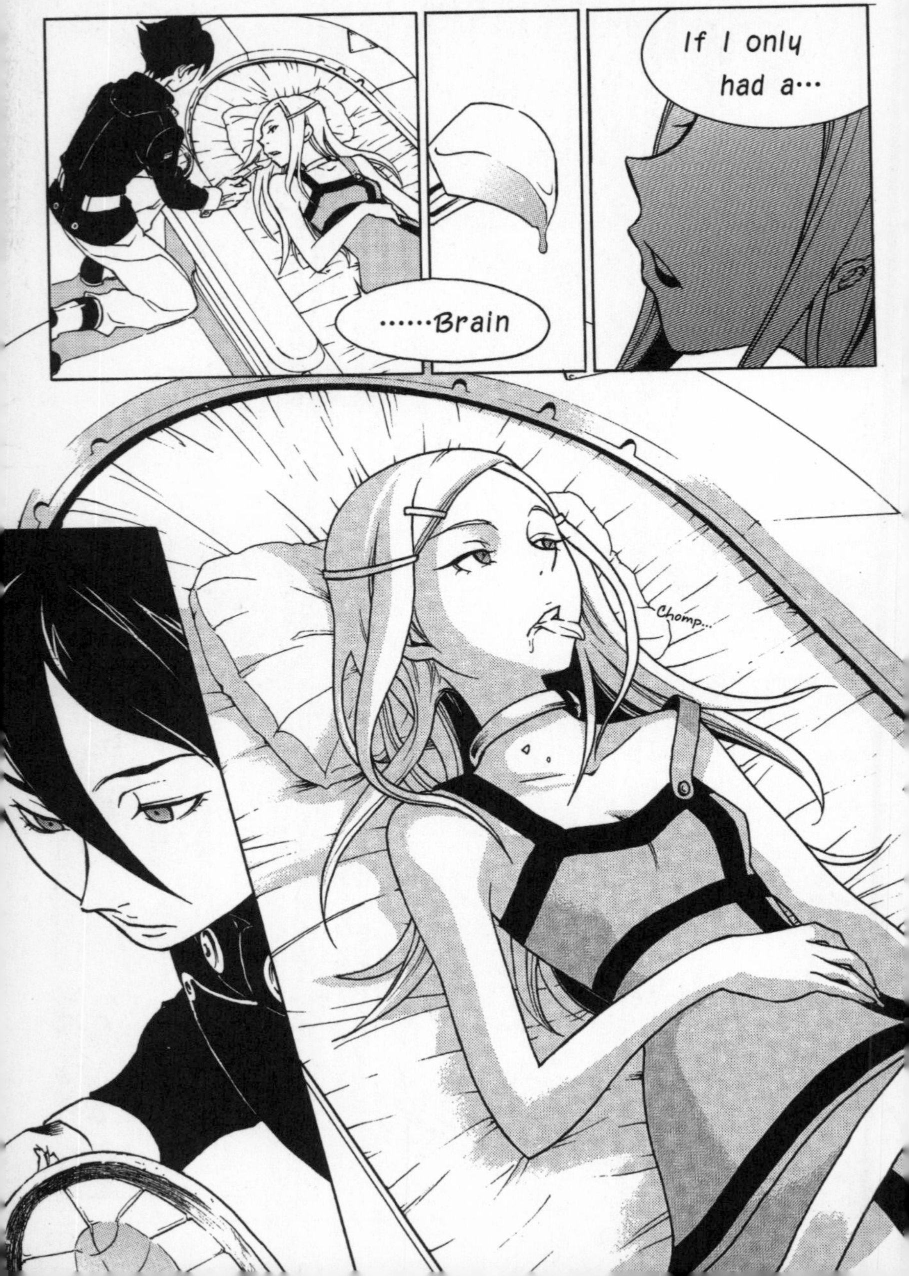
If I only had a···
······Brain
Chomp...

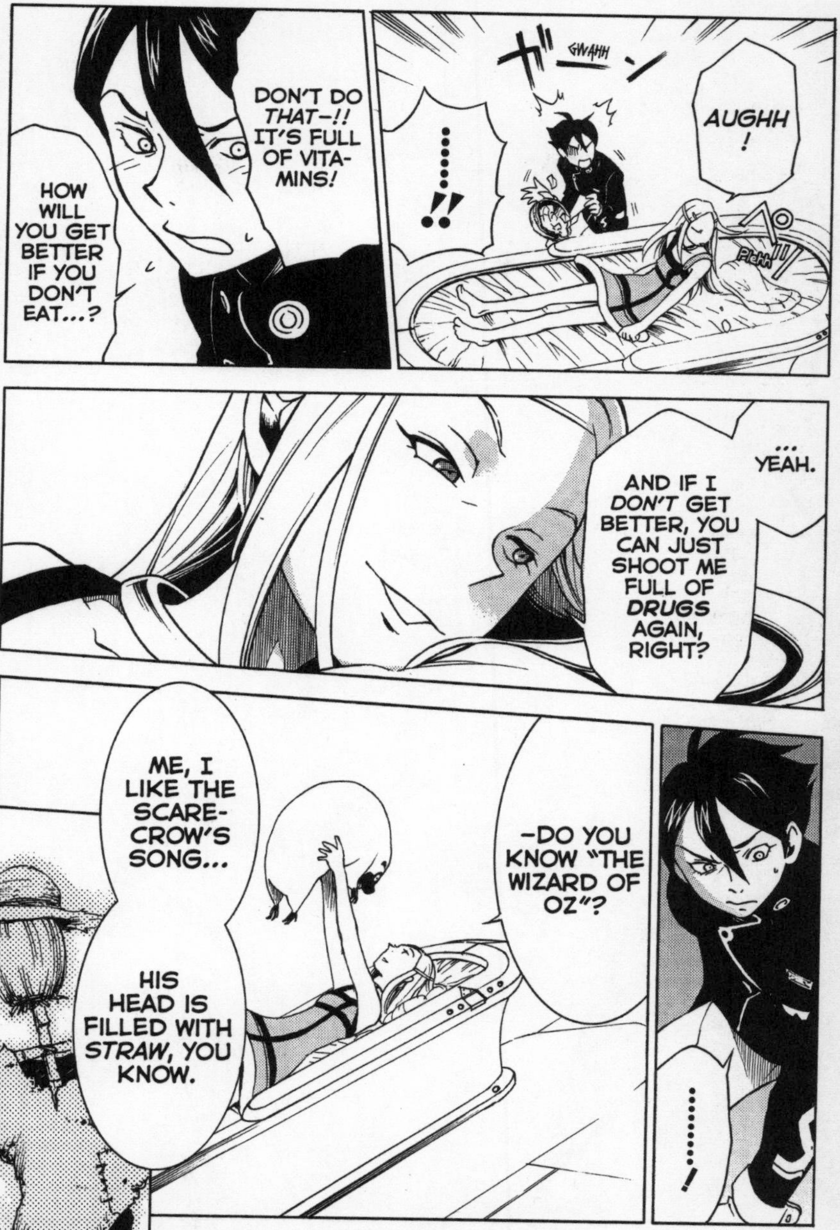
AUGHH!
GWAHH
......!!
Plehh
DON'T DO THAT-!! IT'S FULL OF VITA-MINS!
HOW WILL YOU GET BETTER IF YOU DON'T EAT...?
... YEAH.
AND IF I DON'T GET BETTER, YOU CAN JUST SHOOT ME FULL OF DRUGS AGAIN, RIGHT?
......!
-DO YOU KNOW "THE WIZARD OF OZ"?
ME, I LIKE THE SCARE-CROW'S SONG...
HIS HEAD IS FILLED WITH STRAW, YOU KNOW.

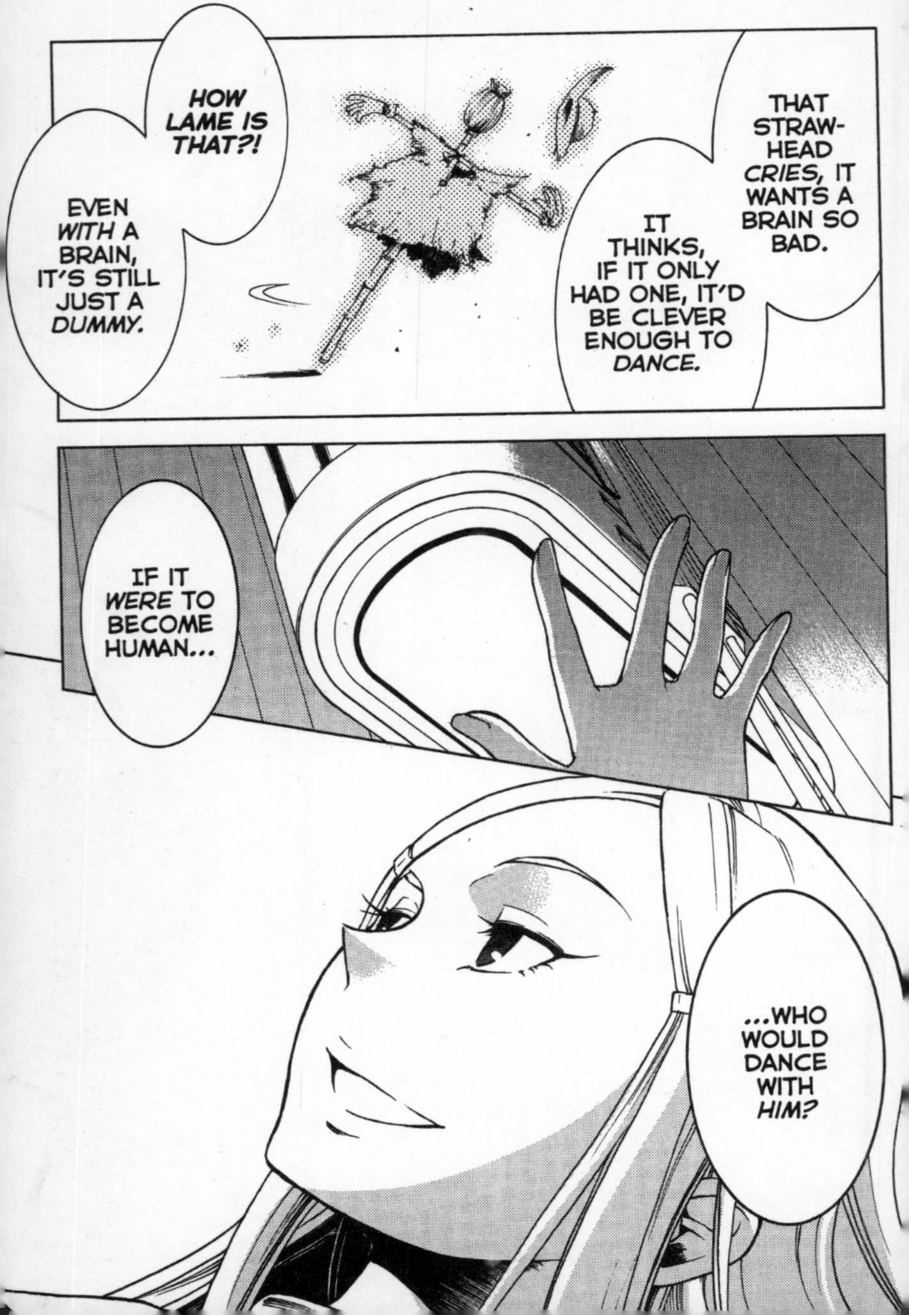
THAT STRAW-HEAD *CRIES,* IT WANTS A BRAIN SO BAD.
IT THINKS, IF IT ONLY HAD ONE, IT'D BE CLEVER ENOUGH TO *DANCE.*
HOW LAME IS THAT?!
EVEN *WITH* A BRAIN, IT'S STILL JUST A *DUMMY.*
IF IT *WERE* TO BECOME HUMAN...
...WHO WOULD DANCE WITH *HIM?*

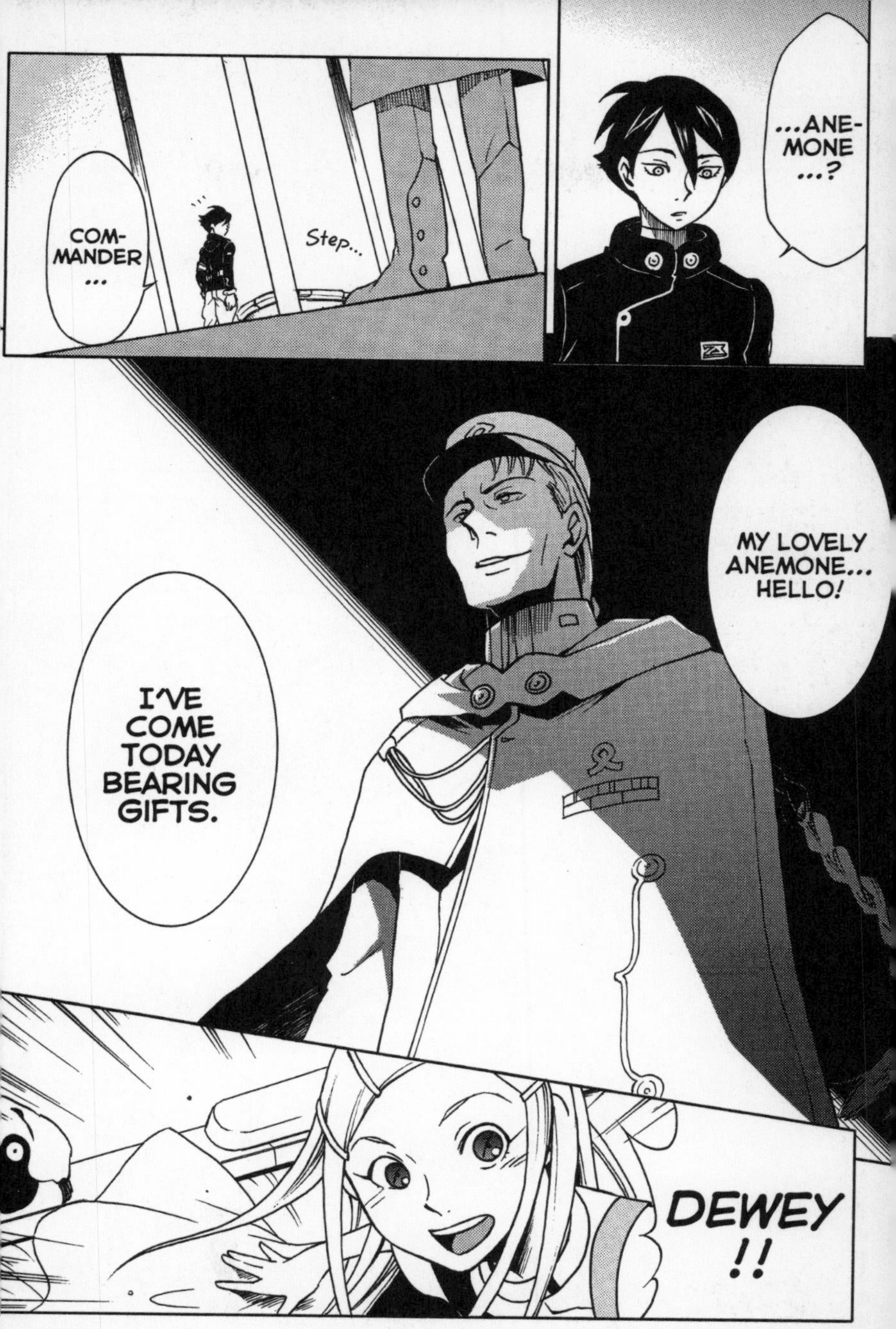
...ANE-MONE...?
Step...
COM-MANDER...
MY LOVELY ANEMONE... HELLO!
I'VE COME TODAY BEARING GIFTS.
DEWEY!!

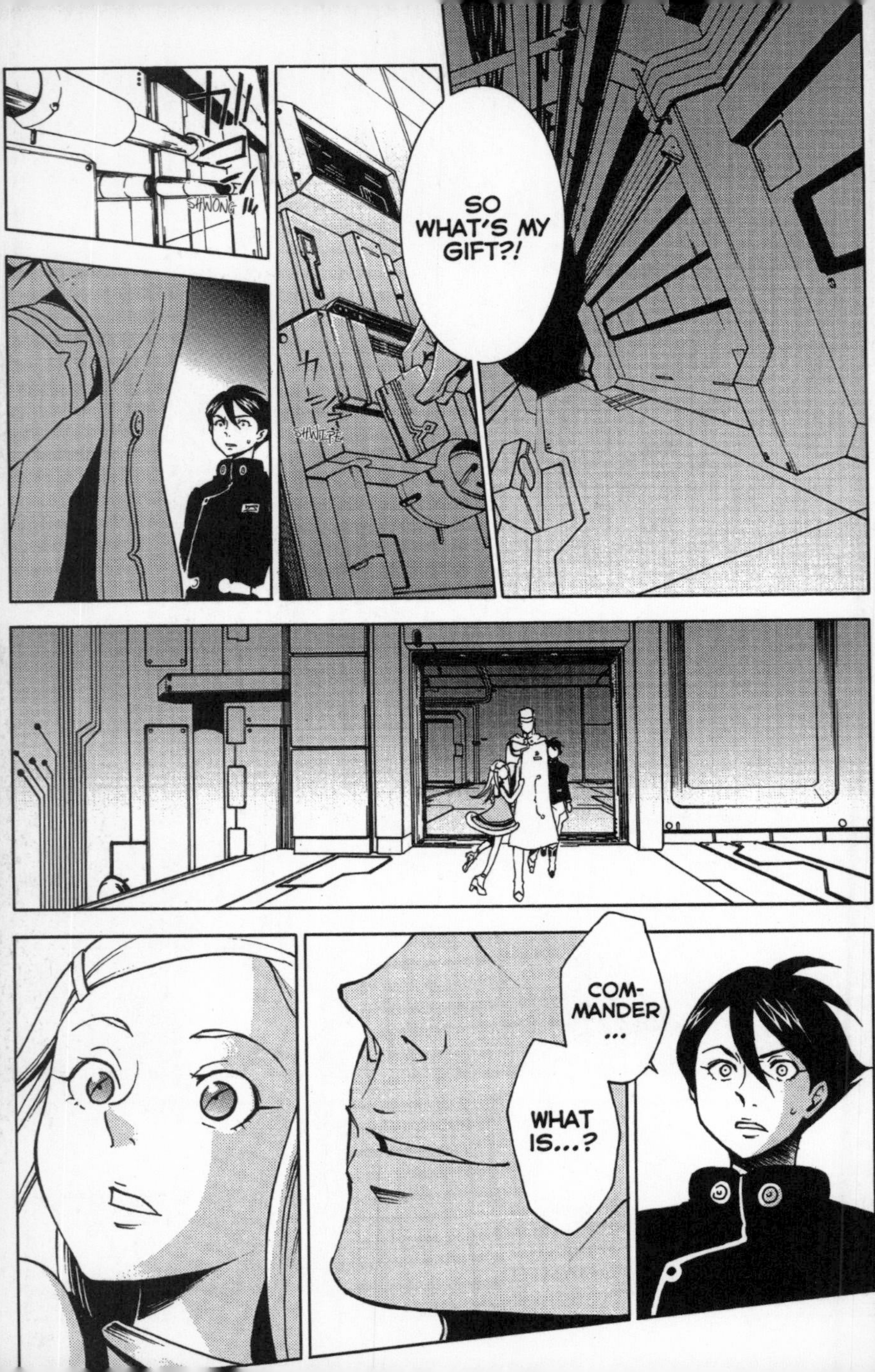
SO WHAT'S MY GIFT?!
SHWIPE
SHWONG
COM-MANDER ...
WHAT IS...?

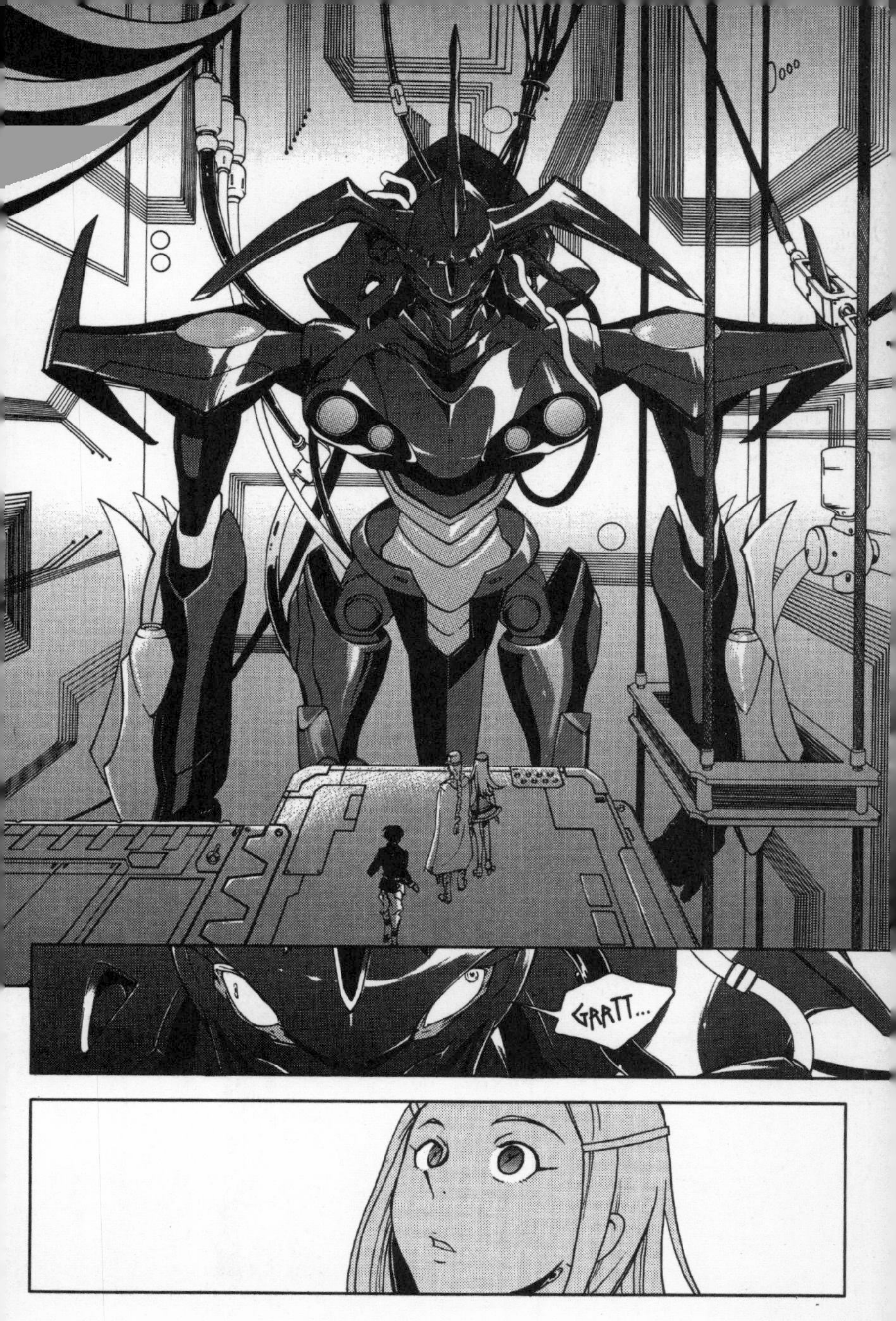
GRATT...

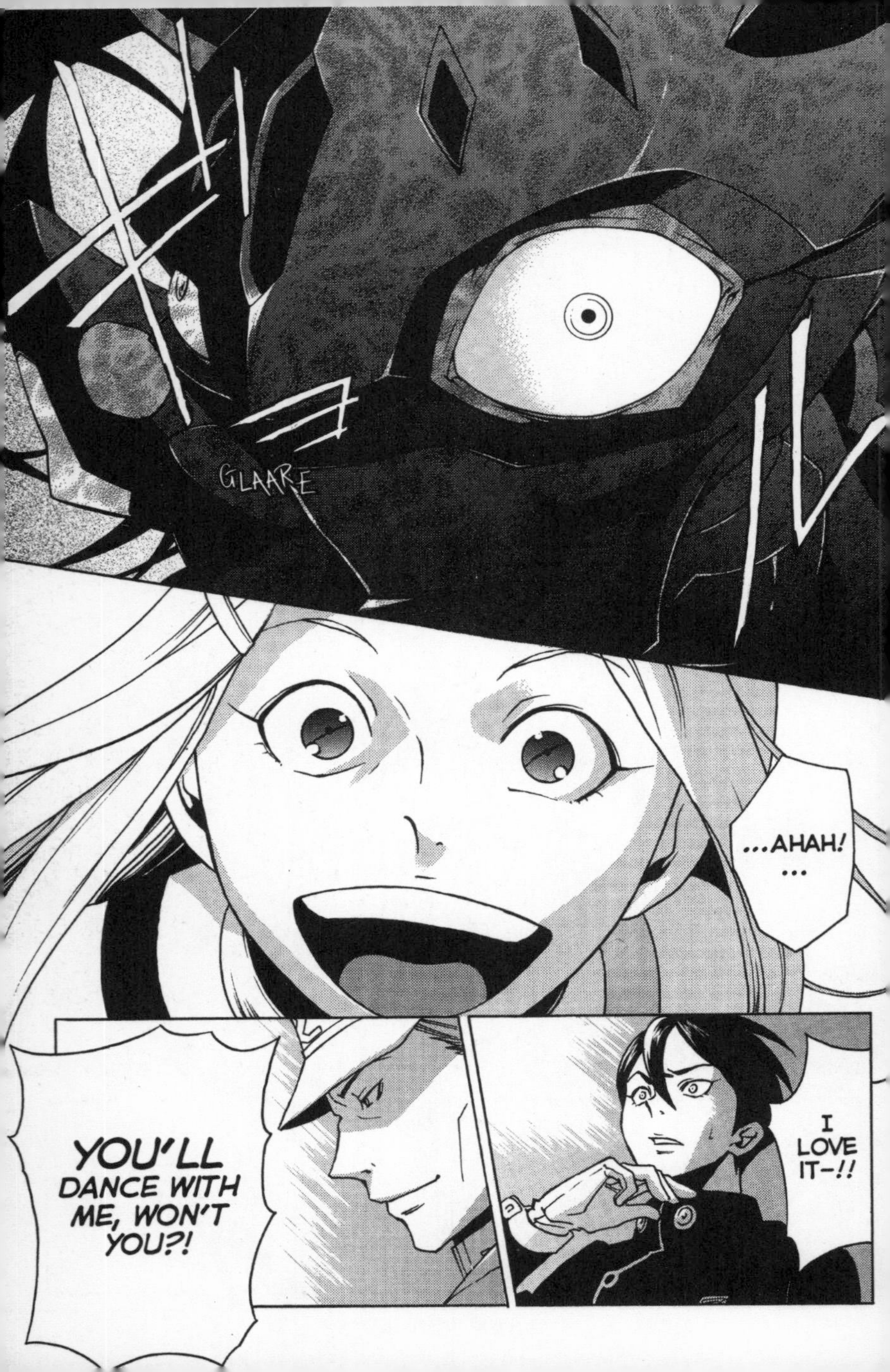
GLAARE
...AHAH! ...
I LOVE IT-!!
YOU'LL DANCE WITH ME, WON'T YOU?!

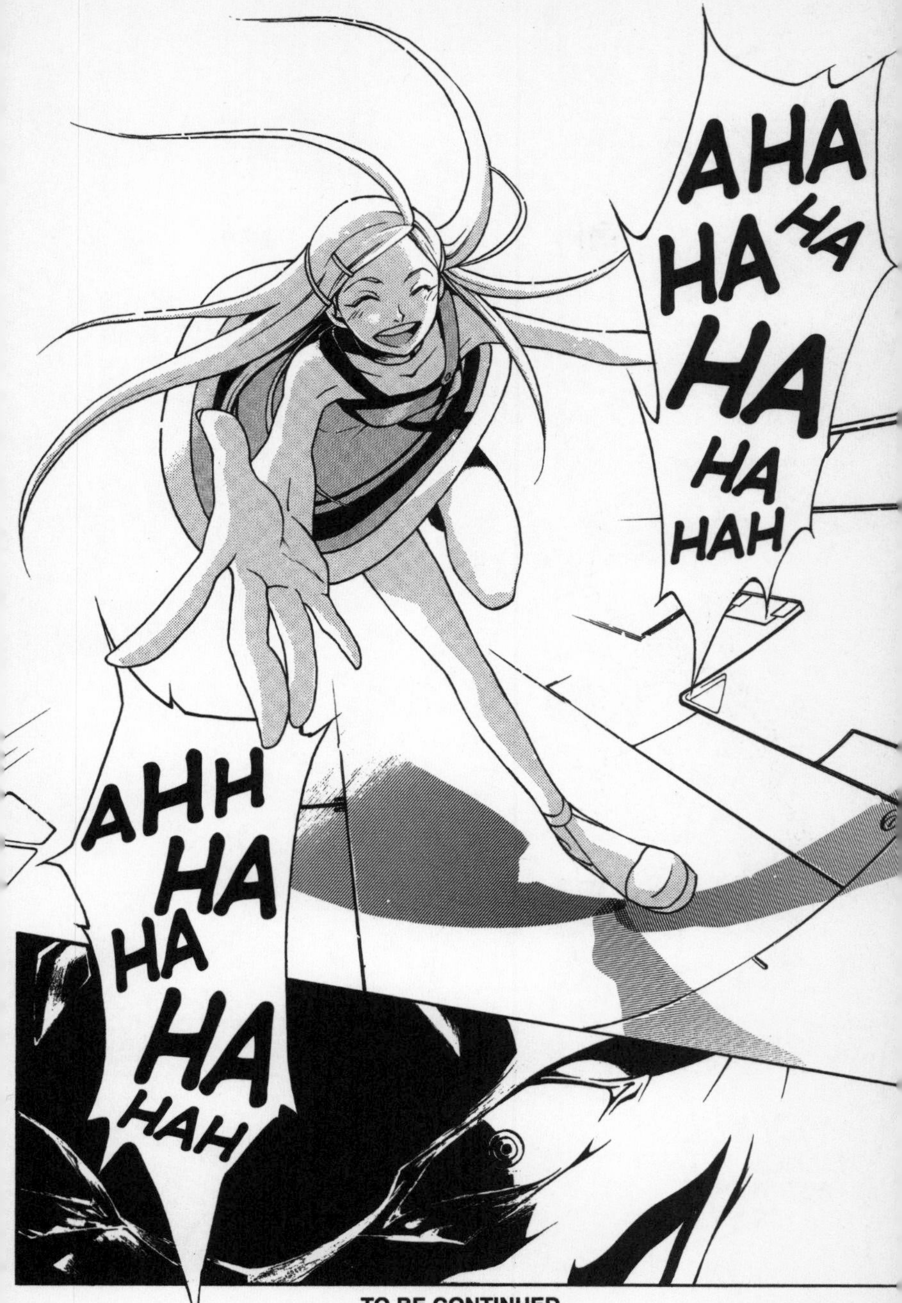
AHA HA HA HA HA HAH
AHH HA HA HA HAH

TO BE CONTINUED...

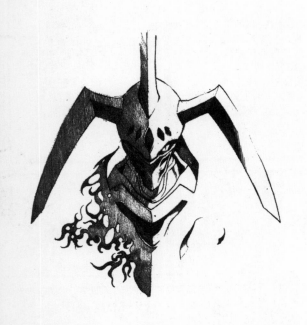

MY NAME IS DOMINIC SORRELL

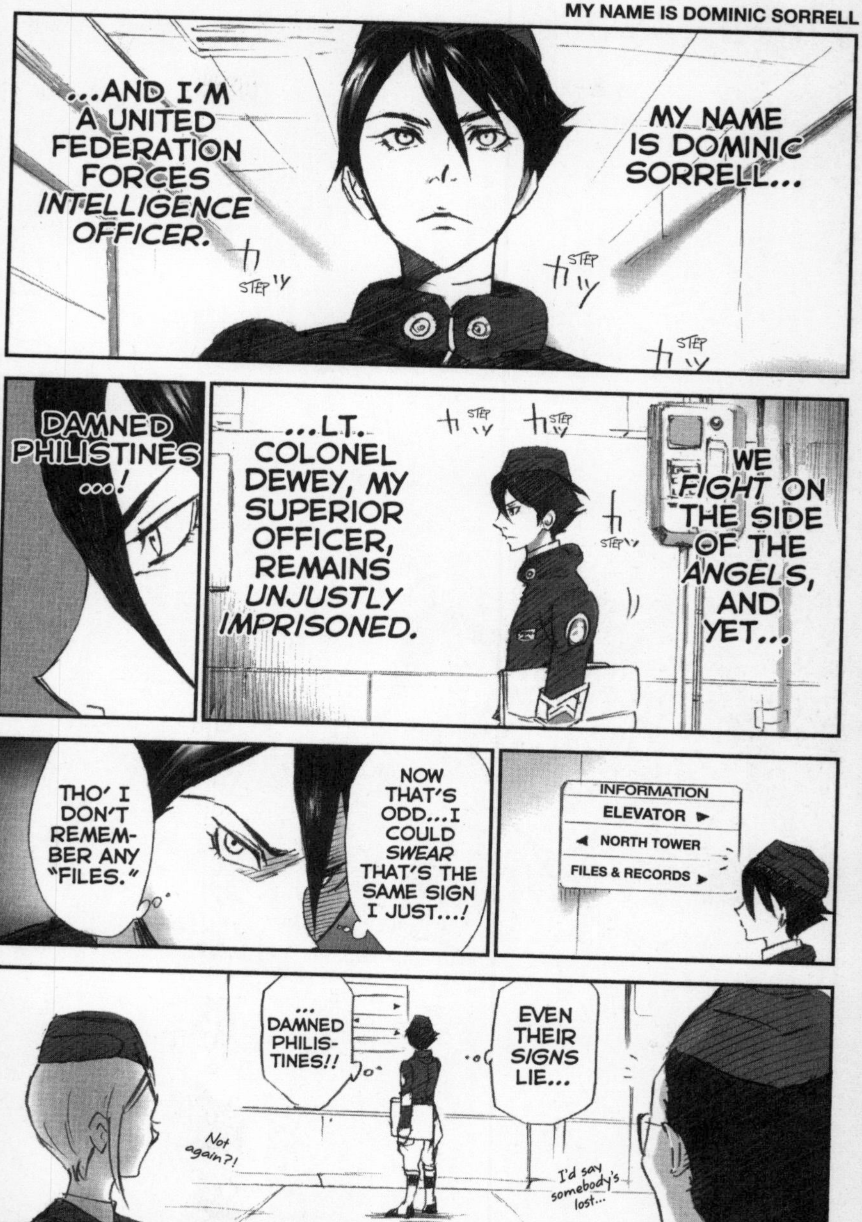
MY NAME IS DOMINIC SORRELL...
...AND I'M A UNITED FEDERATION FORCES INTELLIGENCE OFFICER.
STEP
STEP
STEP
WE FIGHT ON THE SIDE OF THE ANGELS, AND YET...
STEP
STEP
STEP
...LT. COLONEL DEWEY, MY SUPERIOR OFFICER, REMAINS UNJUSTLY IMPRISONED.
DAMNED PHILISTINES...!
INFORMATION
ELEVATOR
NORTH TOWER
FILES & RECORDS
NOW THAT'S ODD...I COULD SWEAR THAT'S THE SAME SIGN I JUST...!
THO' I DON'T REMEMBER ANY "FILES."
EVEN THEIR SIGNS LIE...
...DAMNED PHILISTINES!!
I'd say somebody's lost...
Not again?!

END-OF-VOLUME BONUS MANGA Kataoka Jinsei & Kondou Kazuma

ANEMONE'S SENSE OF STYLE

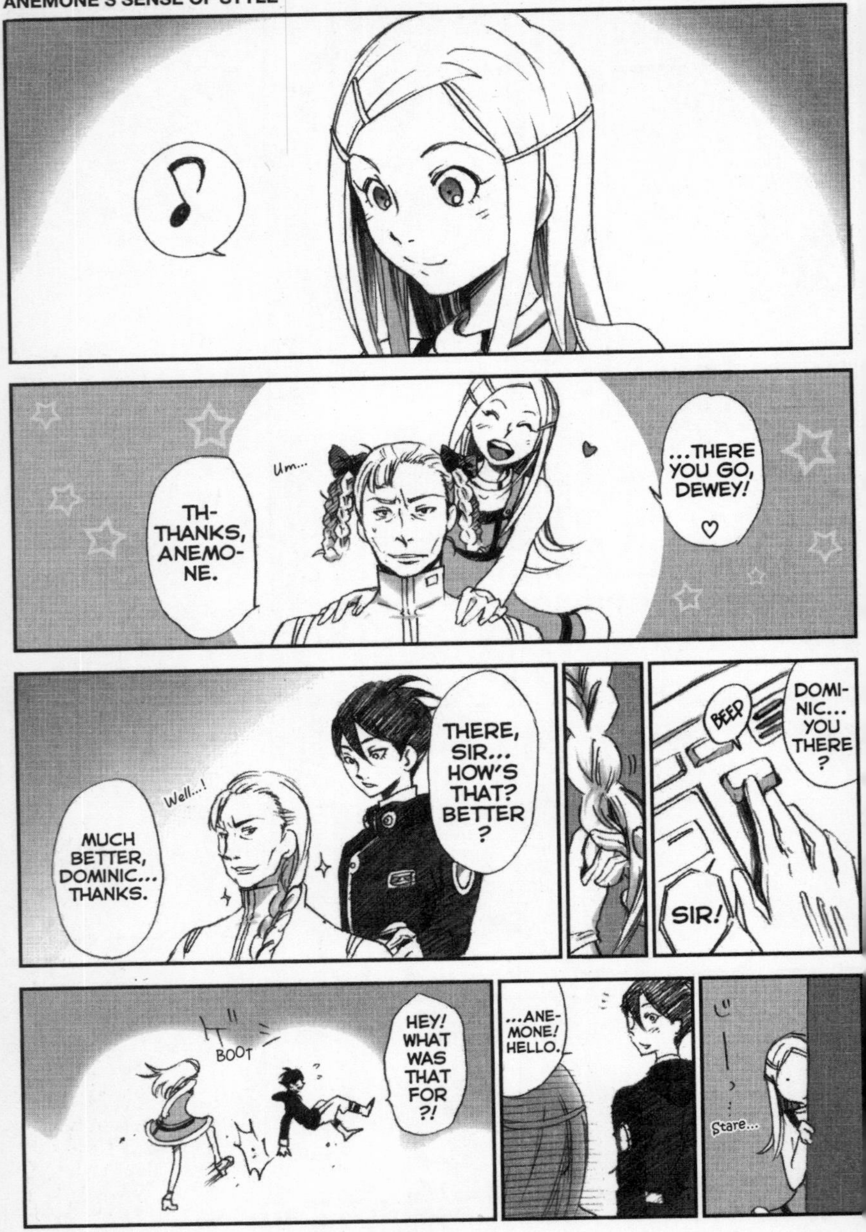
...THERE YOU GO, DEWEY! ♡
Um...
TH-THANKS, ANEMO-NE.
DOMI-NIC... YOU THERE ?
BEEP
SIR!
THERE, SIR... HOW'S THAT? BETTER ?
Well...!
MUCH BETTER, DOMINIC... THANKS.
Stare...
...ANE-MONE! HELLO.
HEY! WHAT WAS THAT FOR ?!
BOOT

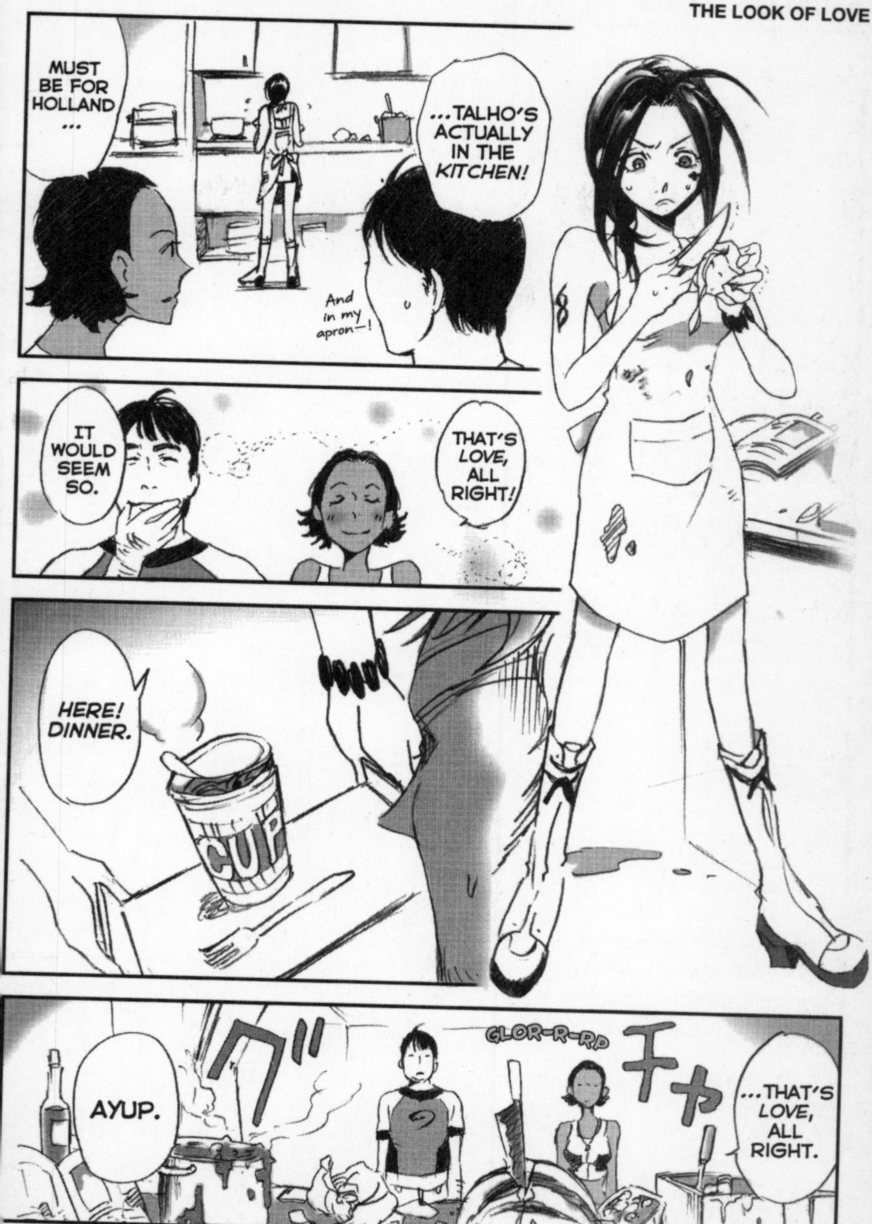
...TALHO'S ACTUALLY IN THE *KITCHEN!*
And in my apron—!
MUST BE FOR HOLLAND ...
THAT'S *LOVE,* ALL RIGHT!
IT WOULD SEEM SO.
HERE! DINNER.
CUP
...THAT'S *LOVE,* ALL RIGHT.
チャ
GLOR-R-RP
グ
AYUP.

TOMORROW'S FORECAST

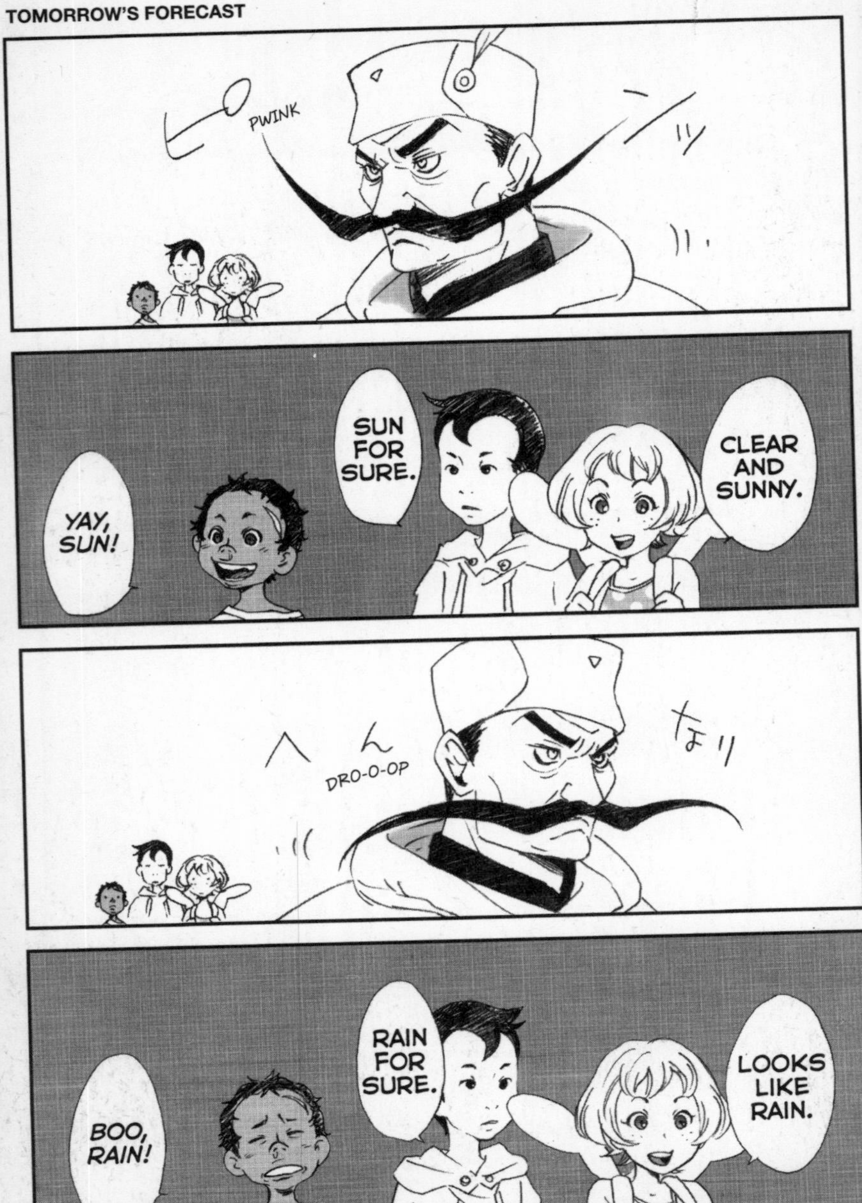
PWINK
CLEAR AND SUNNY.
SUN FOR SURE.
YAY, SUN!
DRO-O-OP
LOOKS LIKE RAIN.
RAIN FOR SURE.
BOO, RAIN!

TO BE CONTINUED...?

postscript

jinsei kataoka :character & story

When it comes to keeping up one's chin, the smog level today's been great.

I hope you're all doing well. Would that I might become as the wind, racing along the mountain roads...and yet, alas, having no driver's license, it is impossible, I think.

Instead, please accept my appreciation—which is like unto a typhoon—to those of you who've both helped me create the book, as well as read the finished product. Do not forsake me, I beg of you.

kazuma kondou :robots & color & more

And here's Volume 2, upon us already...! The time seems gone almost as I realize it. Being so new to it all, I've tended to race about with little idea where I'm going—I plan to continue the tradition. Thanks go out to all who've taken this manga in-hand to read...please know that I intend to do my best, from now on, to make sure you have something to read.

THANKS

Akihiko Higuchi
Uta Ekak
Shou Nakada
Ryou Fukuyama
Akihisa Takimoto

Takako Nobe
Ryouichi Saiyatani
Taku Nakamura

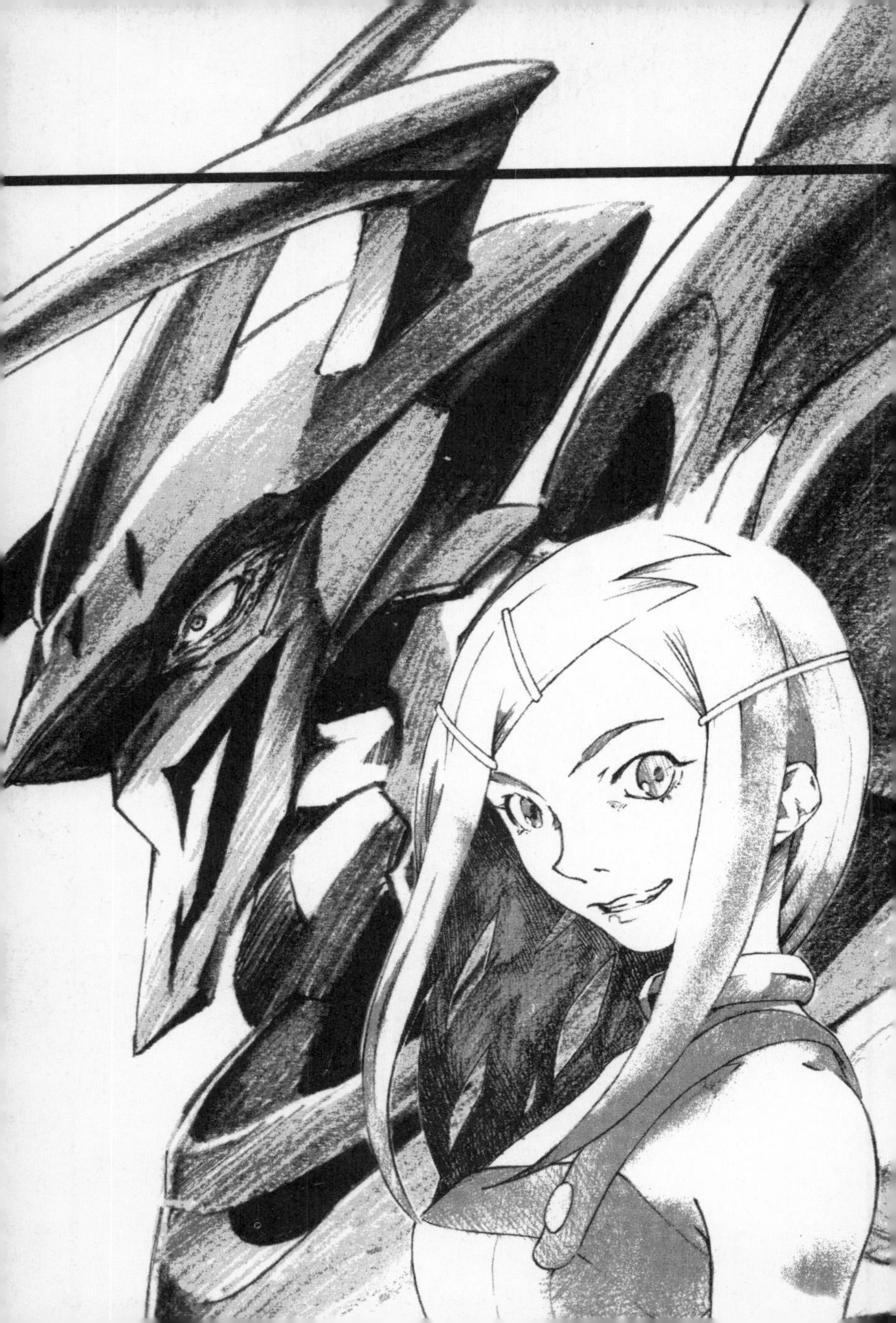

IF IT'S SO HARD TO BELIEVE THEN DON'T

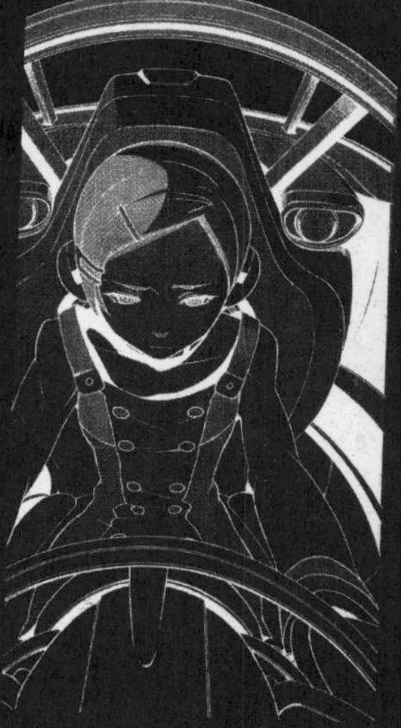

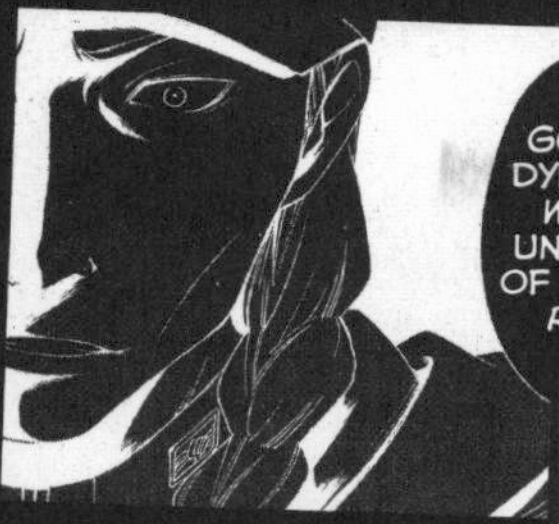
GO AND DYE THAT *WHITE* UNIFORM OF YOURS *RED.*

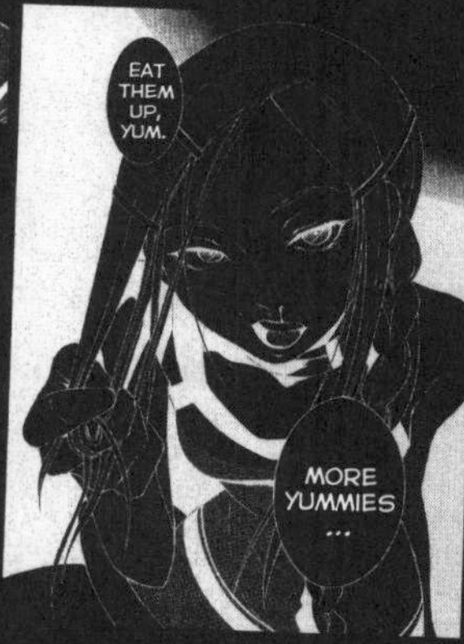
EAT THEM UP, YUM.
MORE YUMMIES ...

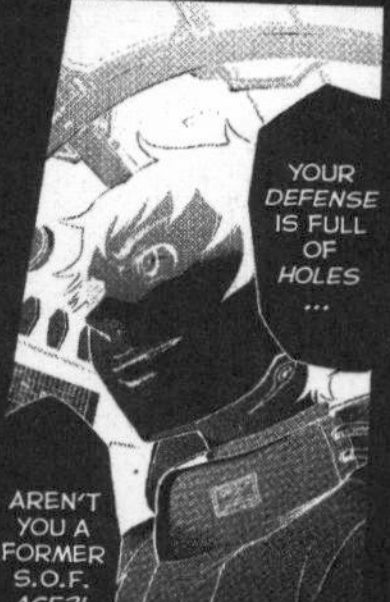
YOUR *DEFENSE* IS FULL OF *HOLES* ...
AREN'T YOU A FORMER S.O.F. *ACE?!*

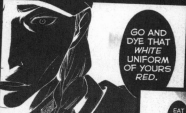

NEXT

Psalms of Planet Eureka seveN

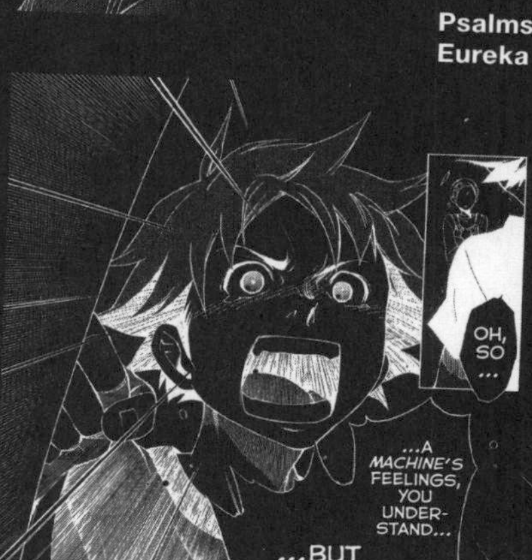
OH, SO ...
...A *MACHINE'S* FEELINGS, YOU UNDER-STAND...
...BUT MINE, YOU DON'T?!

Having learned that it was his father's death that made Holland leave the military, Renton struggles to come to grips with his own shock. Overwhelmed with concern for Renton, Eureka finds herself unable to understand her own feelings. Meanwhile, as the military launches an attack against *Moonlight*, Anemone sinks her claws into Eureka—is it "The End" at last?!

VOLUME 3

ON SALE, SPRING 2006

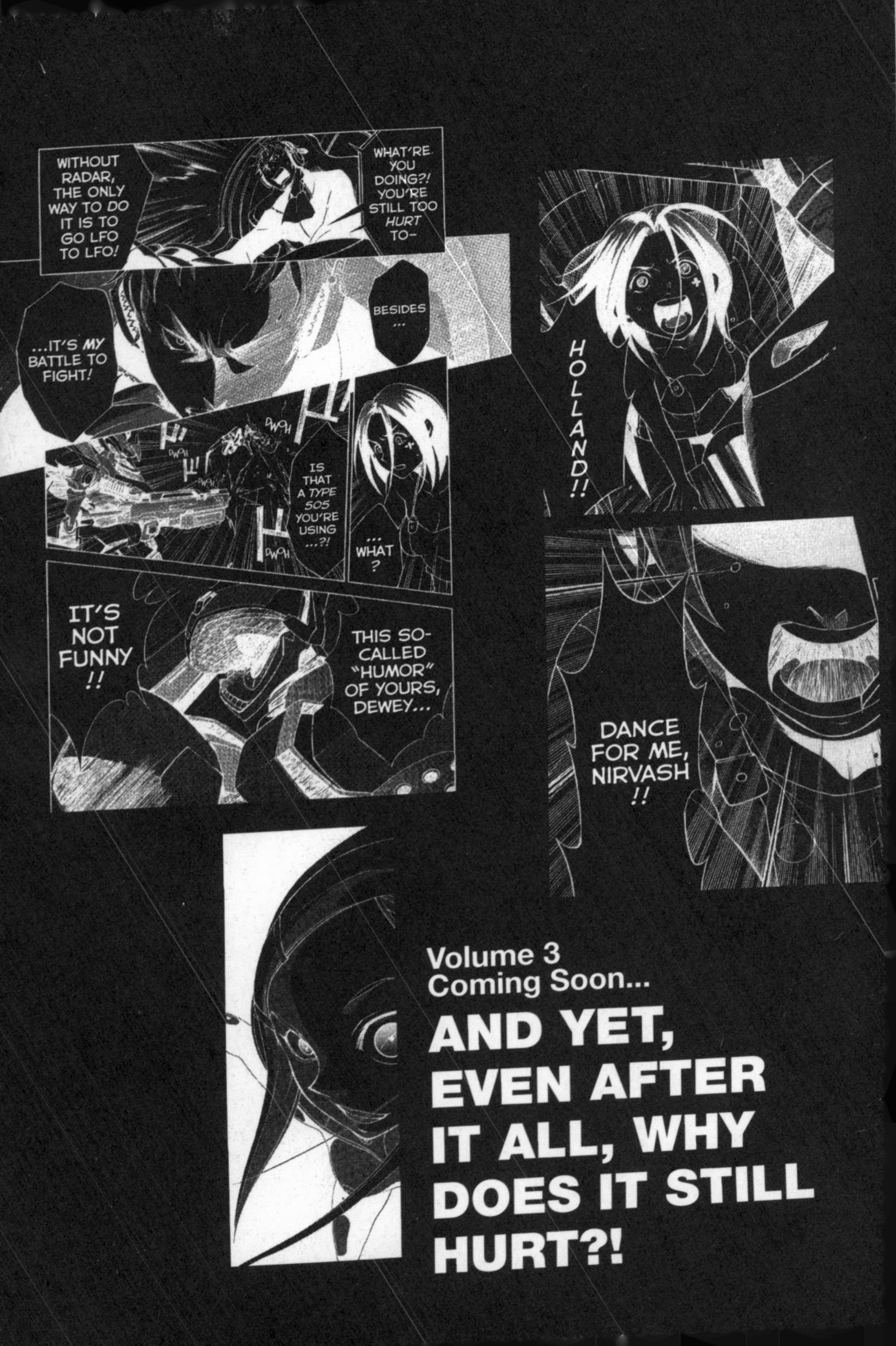
HOLLAND!!
DANCE FOR ME, NIRVASH!!
WHAT'RE YOU DOING?! YOU'RE STILL TOO *HURT* TO–
WITHOUT RADAR, THE ONLY WAY TO *DO* IT IS TO GO LFO TO LFO!
BESIDES...
...IT'S *MY* BATTLE TO FIGHT!
...WHAT?
IS THAT A *TYPE 505* YOU'RE USING...?!
DWOH
DWOH
DWOH
DWOH
THIS SO-CALLED "HUMOR" OF YOURS, DEWEY...
IT'S NOT FUNNY!!
Volume 3 Coming Soon...
AND YET, EVEN AFTER IT ALL, WHY DOES IT STILL HURT?!

TO BE CONTINUED IN
EUREKA SEVEN MANGA VOL. 3

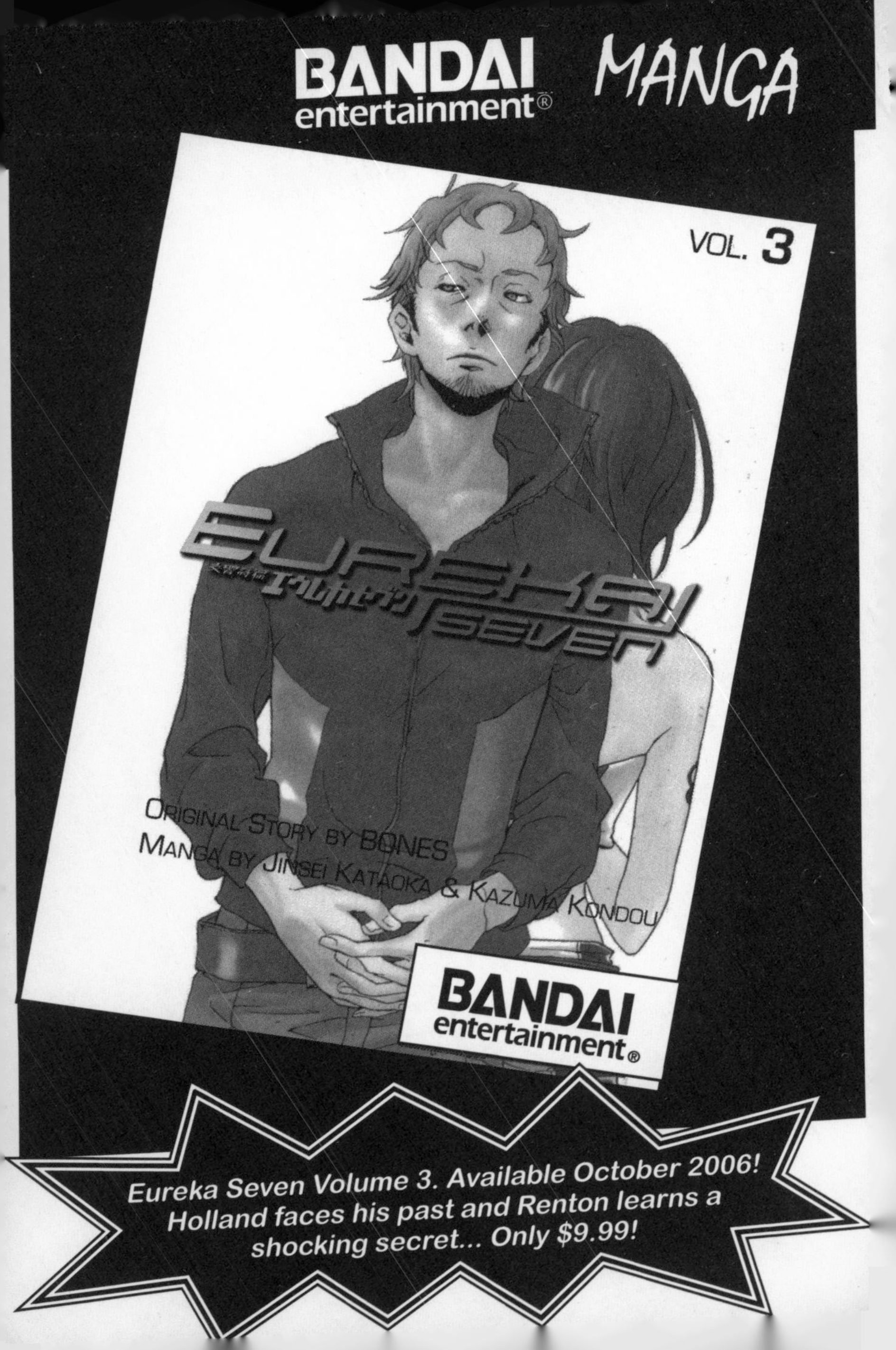
BANDAI entertainment® MANGA
VOL. 3
EUREKA SEVEN
ORIGINAL STORY BY BONES
MANGA BY JINSEI KATAOKA & KAZUMA KONDOU
BANDAI entertainment®
Eureka Seven Volume 3. Available October 2006!
Holland faces his past and Renton learns a shocking secret... Only $9.99!

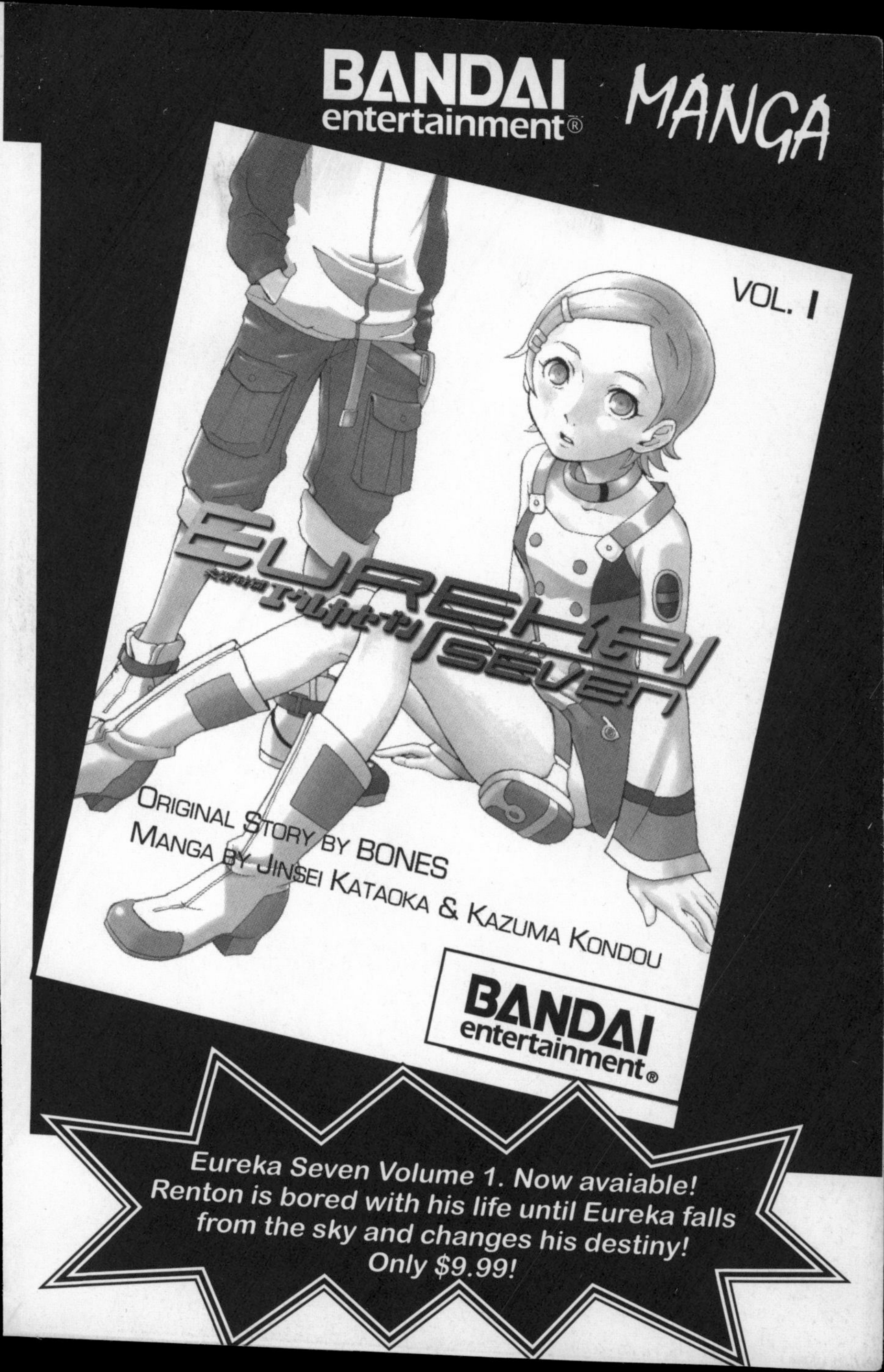
BANDAI entertainment®
MANGA
VOL. 1
EUREKA SEVEN
ORIGINAL STORY BY BONES
MANGA BY JINSEI KATAOKA & KAZUMA KONDOU
BANDAI entertainment®
Eureka Seven Volume 1. Now avaiable!
Renton is bored with his life until Eureka falls
from the sky and changes his destiny!
Only $9.99!

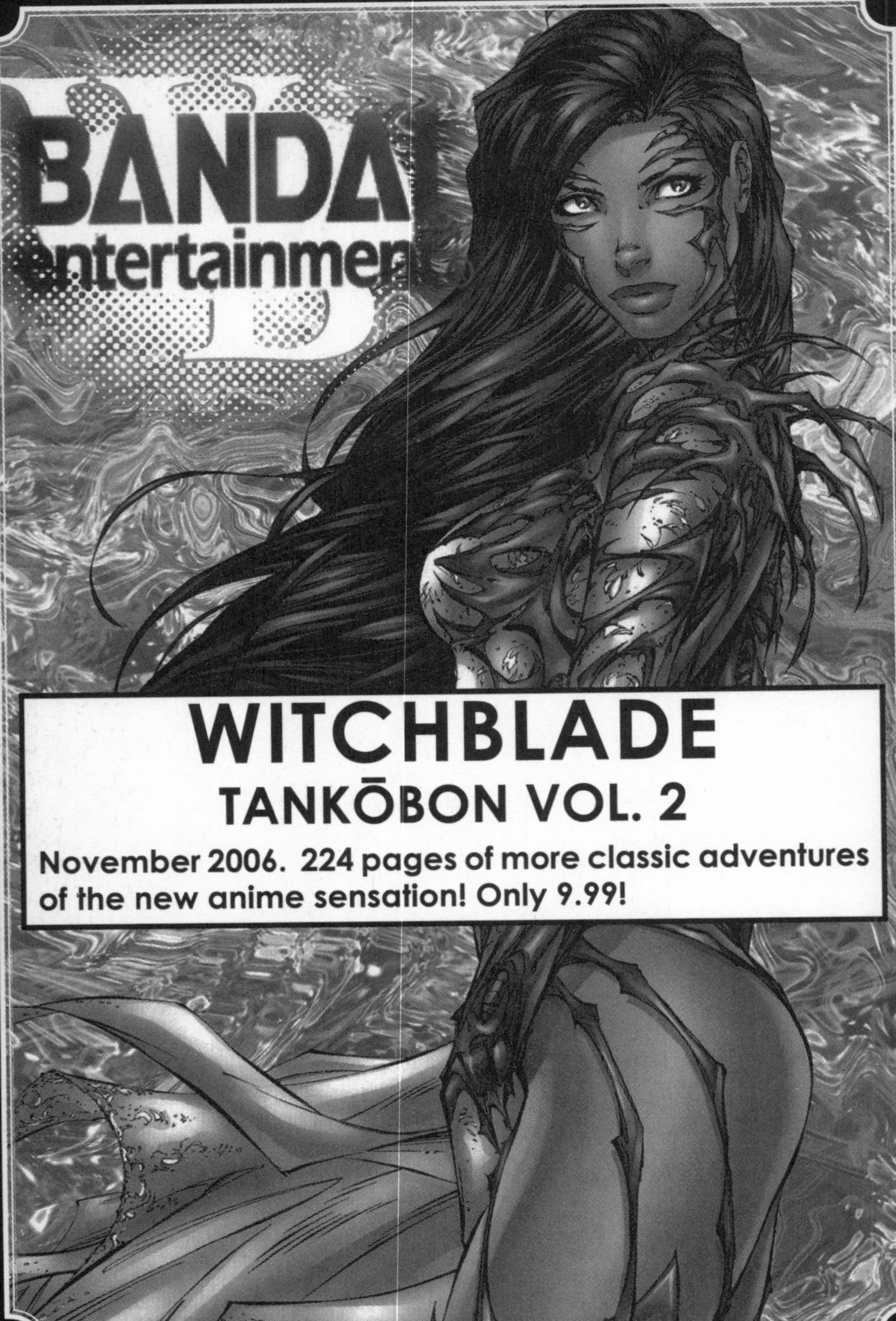
BANDAI
entertainment
WITCHBLADE
TANKŌBON VOL. 2
November 2006. 224 pages of more classic adventures of the new anime sensation! Only 9.99!

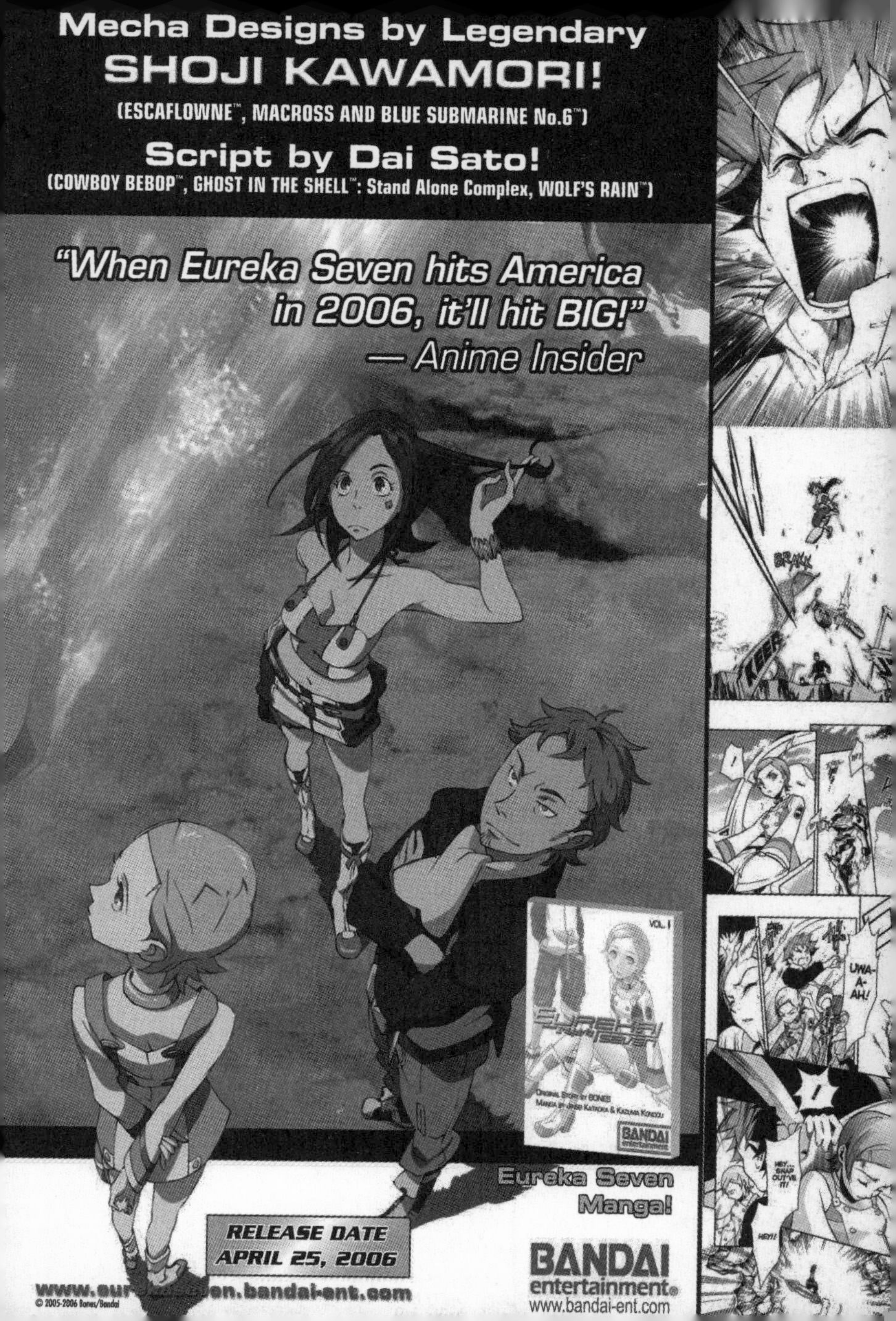

Mecha Designs by Legendary
SHOJI KAWAMORI!
(ESCAFLOWNE™, MACROSS AND BLUE SUBMARINE No.6™)
Script by Dai Sato!
(COWBOY BEBOP™, GHOST IN THE SHELL™: Stand Alone Complex, WOLF'S RAIN™)
"When Eureka Seven hits America in 2006, it'll hit BIG!"
— Anime Insider
VOL. 1
BANDAI entertainment
Eureka Seven Manga!
RELEASE DATE
APRIL 25, 2006
BANDAI
entertainment
www.bandai-ent.com
© 2005-2006 Bones/Bandai
BRAKK
UWA-A-AH!
HEY!!

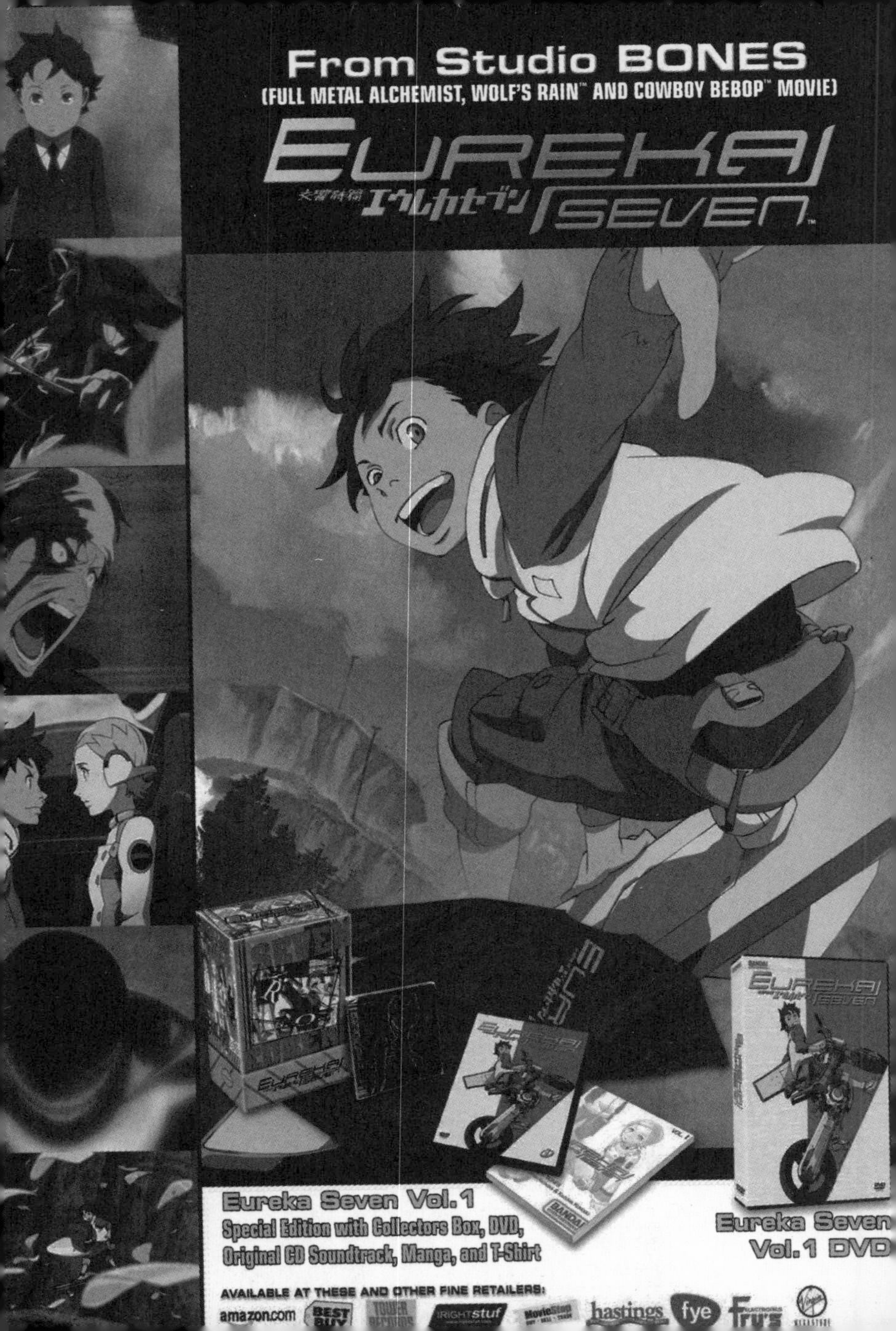

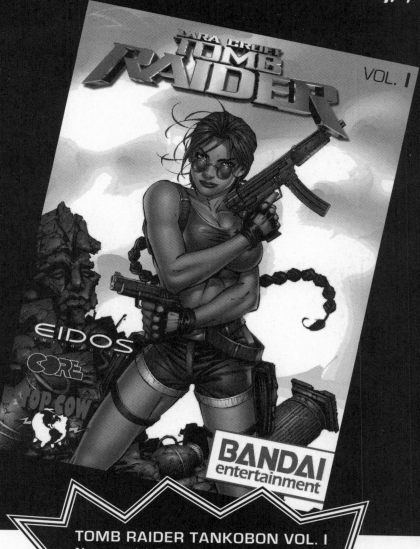

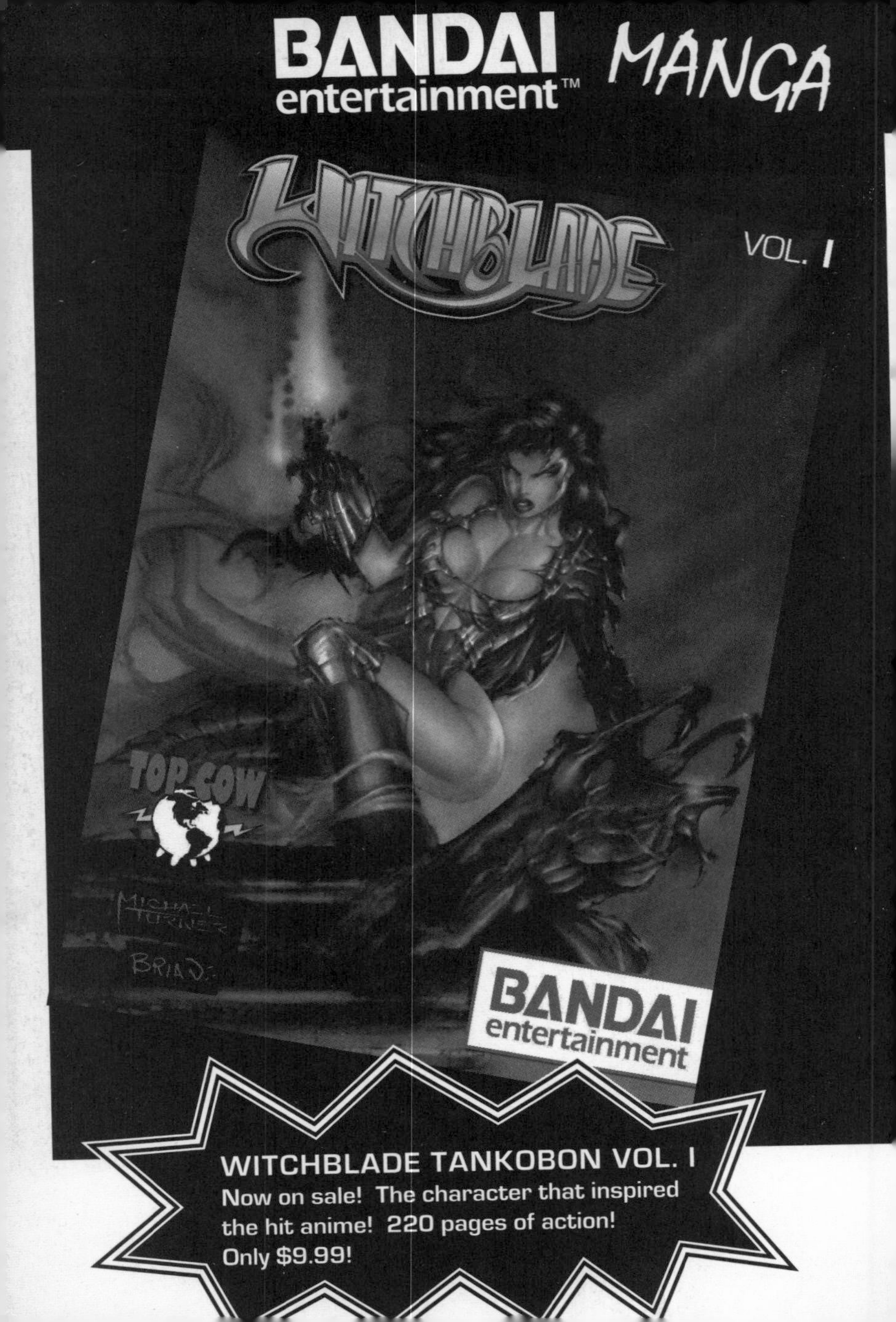
BANDAI entertainment™
MANGA
WITCHBLADE
VOL. I
TOP COW
BANDAI entertainment
WITCHBLADE TANKOBON VOL. I
Now on sale! The character that inspired the hit anime! 220 pages of action! Only $9.99!

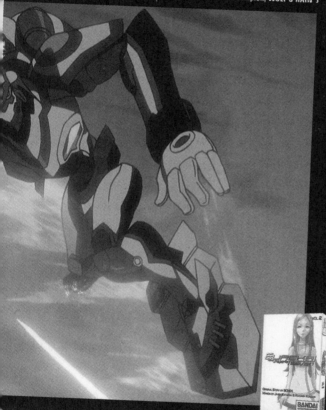
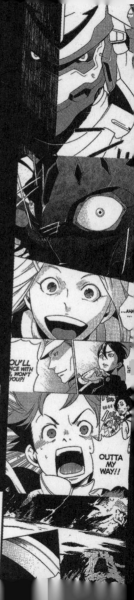

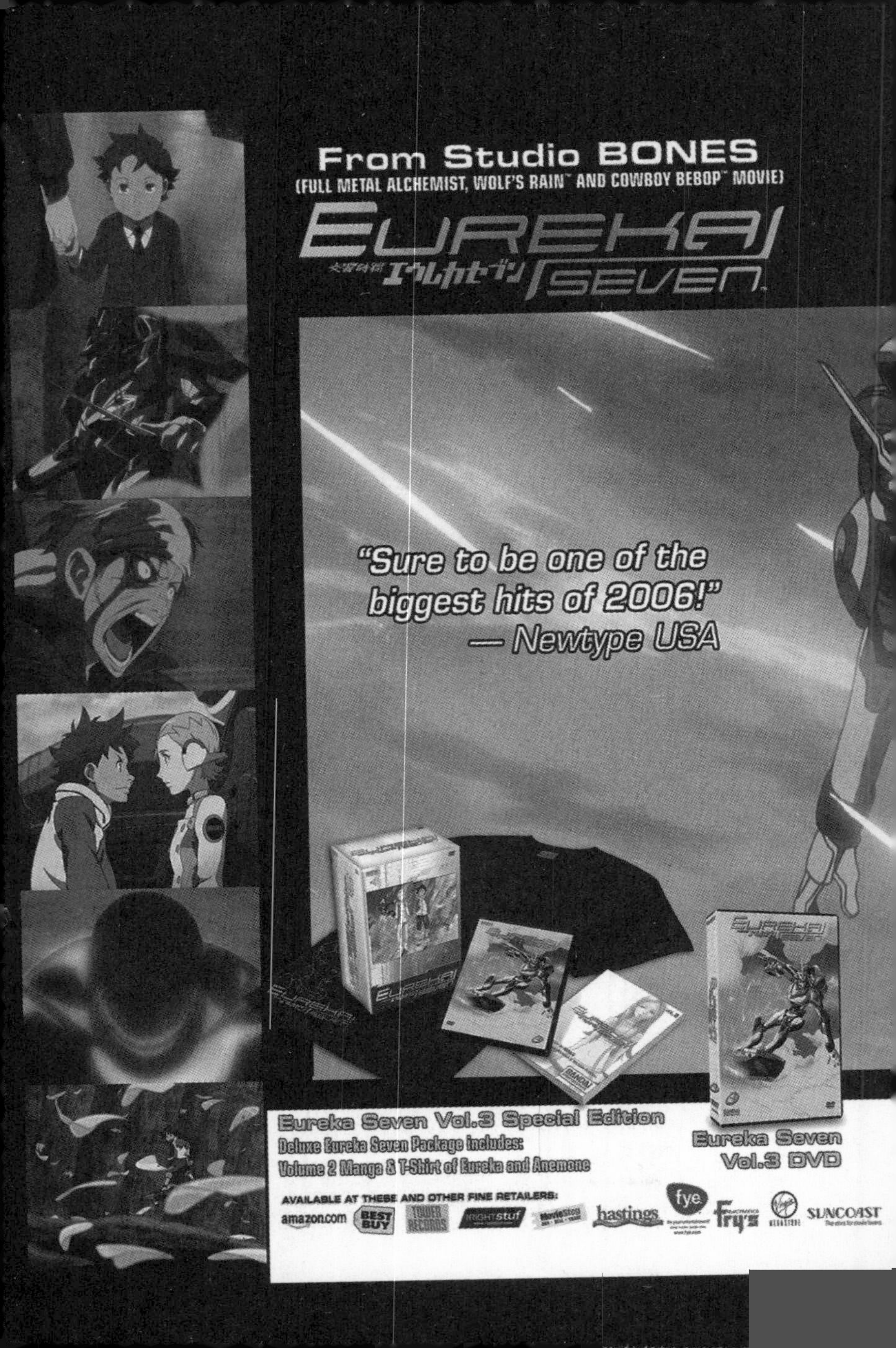
From Studio BONES
(FULL METAL ALCHEMIST, WOLF'S RAIN™ AND COWBOY BEBOP™ MOVIE)
EUREKA SEVEN
"Sure to be one of the biggest hits of 2006!"
— Newtype USA
Eureka Seven Vol.3 Special Edition
Deluxe Eureka Seven Package includes:
Volume 2 Manga & T-Shirt of Eureka and Anemone
Eureka Seven Vol.3 DVD
AVAILABLE AT THESE AND OTHER FINE RETAILERS:
amazon.com
BEST BUY
TOWER RECORDS
RIGHTSTUF
hastings
fye
Fry's
SUNCOAST

YOU ARE READING IN THE WRONG DIRECTION!

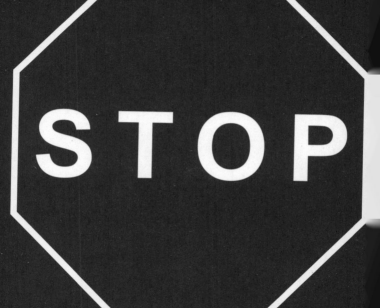

S T O P

MANGA READS RIGHT TO LEFT,
BACK TO FRONT, SO FLIP THIS
BOOK OVER AND ENJOY!